NUMBER TWO HUNDRED AND FOURTEEN

The Old Farmer's Almanac

CALCULATED ON A NEW AND IMPROVED PLAN FOR THE YEAR OF OUR LORD

2006

BEING 2ND AFTER LEAP YEAR AND (UNTIL JULY 4) 230TH YEAR OF AMERICAN INDEPENDENCE

Fitted for Boston and the New England states, with special corrections and calculations to answer for all the United States.

Containing, besides the large number of Astronomical Calculations and the Farmer's Calendar for every month in the year, a variety of

NEW, USEFUL, & ENTERTAINING MATTER.

Established in 1792 by Robert B. Thomas

In the end, it's not the years in your life that count. It's the life in your years.

–Abraham Lincoln, 16th U.S. president (1809–1865)

Cover T.M. registered in U.S. Patent Office

Copyright 2005 by Yankee Publishing Incorporated
ISSN 0078-4516

Library of Congress Card No. 56-29681

Original wood engraving by Randy Miller

Address all editorial correspondence to: THE OLD FARMER'S ALMANAC, DUBLIN, NH 03444

Contents

The Old Farmer's Almanac • 2006

(continued on page 4)

Smart Mower
for Small Lawns!

The **NEUTON**® **Cordless Electric Mower** uses no gas or oil, so it's quiet, clean, and starts instantly — *every* time! It is lightweight, so it's easy for *anyone* to use. So economical it costs just 10¢ to mow your lawn and *never* needs a tune-up. It's the *only* lawn mower that will also TRIM around trees and EDGE along your walk or driveway.

CONSUMERS
BEST BUY
DIGEST

So EASY to Start and Use...

...Just Grasp the handlebar and it starts!

Because the NEUTON® Mower is battery powered, pull starts, fumes, and noise are things of the past.

It has the power of a 5 HP gas mower, yet weighs half as much, so the NEUTON® Mower won't strain your arms, legs, or back.

The NEUTON® is lighter, easier to use, and smarter than other battery-electric mowers, too!

You can instantly add a fresh battery if you run out of charge.

Plus, this is the only mower in the world with an optional Trimmer/Edger attachment! No more 2nd and 3rd trips around your property to finish up trimming and edging after you mow!

TRIMS and EDGES, too! ▶

So why put up with the hard-starting, noise, and fumes of a gas mower?

Try a quiet, instant-starting NEUTON® Cordless Electric Mower today with our 6-Month RISK-FREE Trial. Just mail the coupon below, visit us online at **www.neutonmowers.com** or call the phone number below to receive a **FREE Catalog and Video** with complete details.

Call TOLL-FREE 1-800-736-1166

YES! Please rush my **FREE** Catalog and Video all about the quiet, easy-to-use, instant-starting **NEUTON® Cordless Electric Mower**, including prices, specifications, with Factory-Direct Savings and a **FREE BAGGER** now in effect!

Name _____

Address _____ OFA

City _____ State _____ ZIP _____

E-mail _____

NEUTON® Power Equipment, Dept. 51522X
127 Meigs Road, Vergennes, Vermont 05491

© 2005 CHP, Inc.

neuton®

Contents • continued from page 2

Better Sleep
Better Health
Better Bed

Furniture
components
not included

The Weightless Comfort™ of Tempur-Pedic!

In a recent survey, 92% of our enthusiastic owners report sleeping better and waking more refreshed!

Our sleep technology is recognized by NASA and raved about by the media. And ours is the _only_ mattress recommended worldwide by more than 25,000 medical professionals.

Yet this miracle has to be _felt_ to be believed.

While the thick, ornate pads that cover most mattresses are necessary to keep the hard steel springs inside, they create a hammock effect outside—and can actually *cause* pressure points. Inside *our* bed, billions of microscopic memory cells work in perfect harmony

to contour precisely to your every curve and angle.

Tempur-Pedic's Swedish scientists used NASA's early anti-G-force research to invent TEMPUR® pressure-relieving material—a remarkable new kind of visco-elastic bedding that *reacts* to body mass and temperature. It *automatically adjusts* to your exact shape and weight. And it's the reason why millions are falling in love with the first *really* new bed in 75 years: our high-tech Weightless Sleep™ marvel.

No wonder, 9 out of 10 enthusiastic Tempur-Pedic owners go out of their way to recommend our Swedish Sleep System® to friends and family. Please call us toll-free, without obligation, for your FREE DEMO KIT!

PRESSURE RELIEVING
SWEDISH MATTRESSES AND PILLOWS

Changing the way the world sleeps!™

FREE VIDEO/FREE SAMPLE/FREE INFO

888-702-8557

Call today or send fax 866-795-9367

Tastes & Trends

HOW WE LIVE

"The American residential landscape is shifting away from being an open space of lawn showing off the house structure. Even front lawns are being swept up in the ever-expanding living space, with seating areas and 'entry courts' to meet and greet visitors."

–Rosheen Styczinski, owner of New Eden Landscape Architecture in Milwaukee, Wisconsin

WHAT HOMEOWNERS WANT MOST

- Outdoor bedrooms, for sleeping under the stars
- Water features (to drown out traffic noise) and koi ponds
- Rooms specifically for dancing, reading, sewing, meditation, and makeup and grooming
- Pet suites, with shower and drinking fountain
- Separate living quarters for aging family members

COLOR MY WORLD

Makers of our accessories and amenities—from autos to napkins and home furnishings to stationery—are changing their palette:

IN	OUT
Warm, clean, bright colors	Grayish, muted colors
Reddened oranges	Coppery hues
Yellows	Slate or grayish blues

BIGGER ISN'T ALWAYS BETTER

Growing numbers of home buyers are trading four-car garages and vaulted ceilings for traditional conveniences such as walk-in pantries, breakfast nooks, and window seats. "People are realizing that the feeling of home has almost nothing to do with square footage," says Sarah Susanka, author of *The Not So Big House.* "You don't need more space— you need space that fits you better." Some owners of humongous homes who have buyer's remorse are finding

2006

creative ways to "repurpose" rarely used spaces such as formal dining rooms, turning them into libraries or homework stations.

compiled by
Anastasia Kusterbeck

BUILDERS ARE SEEING GREEN

▓ "2006 will be a breakout year for 'green' building," says Ray Tonjes, a builder from Austin, Texas, and the chairman of the National Association of Home Builders subcommittee on "green" building. The new trend will go beyond energy-efficient heating and cooling systems, with many builders using native materials such as limestone from local quarries to reduce pollution from transportation, and composite wood made from recycled sawdust and plastic bags. Even banks will get into the act, offering "green" mortgages that allow buyers to qualify for higher-price homes because of the savings on maintenance costs.

TOOLS ON LOAN

▓ More and more public libraries are letting folks borrow saws, staple guns, and wheelbarrows. The origin of the tool library dates back to World War II, when sons were charged with doing household repairs while their dads were overseas. Today's incarnations (in California, Oregon, and Michigan) are helping do-it-yourselfers.

FURNISHING FASHIONS

IN ▓ Timeworn, aged finishes

▓ Black accents on furniture

▓ Rugged natural materials such as bamboo, river stones, and raffia, which bring the outdoors inside

▓ Nostalgic, retro-inspired hues of turquoise, cherry red, and electric blue on appliances

OUT ▓ Incandescent light bulbs

▓ Sleek, hard-lined furniture

▓ Formal living and dining rooms

▓ Hard-to-clean, polished stainless steel appliances

Available now . . .

▓ Building materials and antimicrobial countertops equipped with germ-fighting properties

▓ Walls equipped with hidden microphones to "listen" at all times for commands such as "Watch TV!"

Coming soon . . .

▓ Robots that will perform more domestic duties, including window washing. Expect 4.1 million of them by 2007.

continued

7

ON THE FARM

CHICKENS FEATHER FARMERS' NESTS

■ The 5 billion pounds of feathers generated by America's poultry industry may soon be a financial boon to farmers. Quill-free chicken feathers can be used to make auto parts, building materials, medical devices, tires, and even dollar bills, according to the U.S. Department of Agriculture.

COME ON DOWN!

■ Mark November 17–23, 2006, on your calendar: It's National Farm-City Week. More than 18,000 U.S. and Canadian communities will celebrate cooperation between urban residents and farm families. Working farms will be open for visitors to see calf hutches, dairy barns, and milking parlors as well as demonstrations of everyday farm chores such as sheep shearing and cow milking.

MAKE MINE WHEAT

■ Environmentally unfriendly Styrofoam food holders are now being replaced by containers made of biodegradable wheat starch.

FRESH-PICKED FLAVOR

■ More growers are reaching trendy eateries with overnight shipments of gourmet veggies such as 'Peacock' kale, baby red brussels sprouts, 'Golden Ball' turnips, and 'Bull's Blood' beets.

AN END TO THE EXODUS?

■ To attract newcomers and preserve a way of life, an increasing number of midwestern towns are offering perks such as free land. North Dakota's "Prairie Opportunity" campaign asks, "Do you have what it takes to be a 21st-century pioneer?"

In Iowa and Minnesota, farmers are investing in systems to convert corn into ethanol and developing wind farms—among other initiatives. "We have an opportunity to create clean energy and put jobs back into the rural economy. This is our great challenge of the early 21st century," says Dave Miller, Iowa Farm Bureau's director of research.

IN THE GARDEN

COLORFUL FLOWERS AND VEGGIES

■ "The really keen vegetable judges are looking for colors we've never seen before," says Nona Wolfram-Koivula, executive director of All-America Selections. So are we. Watch for . . .

■ **Purple or creamy-white tomatoes and red and orange Swiss chard**

■ **Specially bred tomatoes, cucumbers, and peppers with increased multiple-disease resistance**

■ **More mildew-resistant zinnias and flowering vincas**

■ **More plants that naturally repel insects**

■ **New hybrids of tomatoes derived from heirlooms such as 'Brandywine'**

ORGANICS GO MAINSTREAM

■ One out of five homeowners with a yard or garden is planning to switch to organic gardening methods in the future, says Bruce Butterfield, research director for the National Gardening Association. Organic gardeners won't have to mix up their own concoctions using kitchen ingredients any longer; we'll be seeing a larger assortment of nontoxic pest- and disease-control products offered in stores.

A WRIGGLY WAY TO TEND YOUR GARDEN

■ Worm composting is all the rage for home gardeners in Vancouver, Canada—the city even established a telephone hot line to field calls for information, with workshops in high demand. "It's become pretty status quo to compost with a worm bin here," says Michael Levenston, director of City Farmer, which has distributed over 3,500 bins to date.

HOT COLLECTIBLES

"Don't assume that costume jewelry isn't worth anything. Little plastic pins can go for $1,000 if they're the right ones."

–Terry Kovel, coauthor of
Kovels' Antiques & Collectibles Price List 2005

RISING IN VALUE

■ Toys featuring television, radio, cartoon, or movie characters from before 1980— especially those currently making a comeback on cable TV

■ 1950s florist vases shaped like peasant ladies, teddy bears, or baby buggies

■ Mint-condition, pre–World War II, Japanese, battery-powered, celluloid robots

c o n t i n u e d

9

WEATHER VANE REPORT: BRING YOURS INDOORS!

■ If your home's roof sports a copper weather vane made before 1850, think twice before leaving it outside to brave the natural elements; it could be worth thousands. (Watch out for criminal elements, too. Booming auction prices have led to thefts of weather vanes from centenarian homes and barns in the Northeast.)

1950s FURNITURE FINDS

■ Nostalgic baby boomers are raising demand and prices for "mid-century modern" pieces dating from the 1950s. They're looking for *Sputnik*-inspired chandeliers; amoeba-shape wall clocks; chairs and tables with black, spindly, metal legs; and sofas with rows of marshmallow cushions.

THE WAY WE LOOK

"For 2006, women's fashion will take a dramatic turn toward a darker mood. Skirt and dress length will hover around the knee or below—don't look for a miniskirt trend unless the economy does a radical about-face."

–Jason Campbell, editor in chief of *JC Report*

REAL SIMPLE

■ The next fashion mantra might be "minimalize me." "People are getting tired of the time-consuming, personal approach to dressing that seems to require broaches, scarves, and far too many knickknacks and tchotchkes for anyone's closet,"

says Sally Singer, news fashion editor of *Vogue.* Simpler looks will include funnel-neck coats paired with flat boots, tailored jackets with pencil skirts, and tweed skirt suits with cashmere turtlenecks.

LUXURY, FOR A LIMITED TIME

■ Want the "must-have" handbag of the moment but can't afford the sticker price? New online programs allow members to "borrow" costly designer handbags for a limited time—and a fee. When you're ready for something new, simply return it and borrow (er ... rent) a different one. Jewelry rental services will be next.

WE'LL BE WEARING . . .

■ natural looks—but not really. High-tech yarns will mimic their natural counterparts but not be 100 percent pure themselves. The goal will be to *look* natural but not actually *be* natural.

■ more black, gray, brown, navy, and plum

■ colors that move in a "hetero-flexible" direction. Men's and women's clothing will feature the same hues.

■ the wide-leg trouser jean instead of the boot-cut jean

■ yoga styles that "don't look like gym clothes but are easy and stretchy," says Singer

GUY THINGS

■ Men who love gadgets are getting "two-in-one" personal care products, such as razors with built-in shaving cream dispensers and tube sticks with deodorant on one end and cologne at the other.

And, male-only spas with exotic offerings such as seaweed wraps and facials are cropping up in major cities. Men now make up over a third of all spa goers, up from a mere handful, says Spa Finder, a wellness services company.

THE PET WORLD

ON THE WING

■ Chickens may be the next big pet craze, if runaway sales of the compact, colorful Omlet Eglu coop in Britain are any indication. For about $600, buyers receive a coop complete with feed, egg boxes, and two chickens. "People give the chickens names, buy them treats such as strawberries, and get very upset if anything happens to them. But they also lay delicious eggs, so the owner gets a reward every day," says the coop's creator, Johannes Paul.

SMALL IS "BIG"

■ According to a recent survey of pet owners, there are more than 16.8 million hamsters, gerbils, mice, and other pint-size critters in American homes.

c o n t i n u e d

PAMPERED PETS

■ Parents with kids in college and young couples waiting to start families both have one thing in common: empty nests—and pets are the beneficiaries. We'll be seeing:

■ more hotels welcoming pets with amenities like massages, pet pillows, and dog sitters

■ animal education CDs to teach parrots to speak with accents, and videotapes to entertain pets while their owners are at work

■ dog toys recorded with the owner's voice to reduce separation anxiety

■ food dispensers with built-in cameras so that owners can observe pets eating or feed them remotely via the Internet

GOT YOU COVERED, PET

■ Pet insurance policies doubled to 2 million during 2004, with mainstream carriers getting into the act, and more than 1,000 companies offering employees pet care benefits. "I'm waiting for the first HMO for pets to come out," says Bob Vetere, COO of the American Pet Products Manufacturers Association, pointing to a national survey that showed that more than 45 percent of pet owners would spend $3,000 on their pet, if needed, and 20 percent would spend "whatever it took."

12

HOW WE WORK AND PLAY

"From parents who cut back their children's frantic schedules to cooks who promote 'slow' food to workers who have left highly paid, fast-track careers to be with their families—a rebellion against the speed and stress of American life is bubbling up at the grass roots."

–John de Graaf, national coordinator of Take Back Your Time, a U.S./Canadian initiative lobbying against overwork and overscheduling

VOLUNTARY CONTRIBUTIONS

■ Growing numbers of Americans are volunteering their time. For example, the National Park Service's volunteer program is reporting a record number of participants. In 2004, 140,000 people spent 5 million hours archiving photographs, maintaining trails, removing invasive plants, collecting garbage, and counting birds.

TONE IT DOWN

■ Stressed workers want peace and quiet: They're asking for special mesh doors for their cubicles that block colleagues from entering and new "white noise" machines to mask the office din.

TIE IT UP

■ The hobby of "fly tying" is going strong, especially with women and children. Tied flies are used not only for fly-fishing, but also for proud display in the home as art.

VERRRY LONG SHOTS

■ Gambling is on the rise in North America and gamblers are spending more these days, with Las Vegas visitors now budgeting $545 per trip to gamble—$54 more on average than in 2003.

If you're a very patient gambler and don't mind long odds, consider membership in Longbets.org, an online prediction site for scores that may not be settled for decades—if ever. Members post detailed arguments to predict the outcomes of weighty issues and challenge others to ante up cash bets, with all winnings donated to charity. Some current wagers:

■ By 2020, travel tickets to the Moon will be sold over the counter.

■ By 2020, it will be possible for urban houses to have a room designed for and dedicated to producing a household's entire water supply.

■ By 2050, we will receive intelligent signals from outside our solar system.

■ At least one human alive in the year 2000 will still be alive in 2150.

RETIREMENT = REHIREMENT

■ Increasingly, people will work at one career, retire for a while, and then return to school to prepare for another one. "Retirement will be replaced with a radical new life stage that is far more varied, exciting, and unpredictable than it was for prior generations," says David Baxter, vice president of research at Age Wave in San Francisco.

c o n t i n u e d

WHAT WORKING WOMEN WANT

▨ A team of researchers recently studied 909 working women, using the new "Day Reconstruction" approach to research, which focuses on daily activities rather than social status. Here's what they found:

▨ What women enjoy most: having lunch with coworkers, relaxing with friends, watching TV, shopping or cooking alone

▨ What women enjoy least: commuting, taking care of children, spending time with their bosses

Already here . . .

▨ Tourists using electric-powered, Segway "human transporters" instead of tour buses to explore cities

Coming soon . . .

▨ "Dual-mode transportation": private cars that you drive yourself on short trips but that run on automated guideways for long-distance travel

SIGNS OF THE TIMES

SAME COUNTRY, DIFFERENT CULTURE

▨ Residents of Quebec are sleeping more and working less than their counterparts in British Columbia, says a Leger marketing poll. That comes as no surprise to cultural observers: "We are a French society and quite different from the rest of Canada," says Claude Martin, professor of communications at the University of Montreal. "We take more time with cooking and eating, drink more wine, and argue more. Even our cars are different—they're smaller and more European."

GLOWING IN THE WIND

▨ With wind farms cropping up in the Pacific Northwest, Texas, Great Plains, mid-Atlantic region, and Northeast, more than 600,000 new households in the United States are expected to be powered by wind energy in the near future; that's in addition to the 1.6 million homes that used it in 2004. "Consumers . . . want clean power, and utilities see wind energy as insurance against the rising costs of electricity generated from natural gas," says Christine Real de Azua, for the American Wind Energy Association. It's expected that 6 percent of U.S. electricity will come from wind by 2020. (Less than 1 percent comes from wind currently.)

SQUIRREL TALE

■ Hunters are being paid up to 26 cents per squirrel tail by Antigo, Wisconsin–based Mepps, a fishing lure firm—but only if the tails are from squirrels harvested for food. "We do not advocate taking squirrels strictly for their tails," says a Mepps spokesman, who expects to receive 300,000 tails this year. Tail fur is used to dress the hooks of bass, trout, panfish, pike, and walleye lures.

THE GROWING GLOBAL VILLAGE

▨ The United Nations estimates that the world's population, currently at 6.4 billion, will rise to 9 billion in 300 years—

continued

down from earlier predictions of 12 billion. Other predictions:

- The average life expectancy will be 95 years by 2300. (Make that 106 years for people in Japan, who already live longer.)
- India will be the world's most populous country by 2050, followed by China and the United States.
- By 2050, there will be 1.8 billion people over 60 years of age (triple the current number) worldwide.

OUR HEALTH AND WELL-BEING

"If we get the funding, I think there is a 50 percent chance that we'll effectively cure aging by 2030. If not, it'll be delayed by at least ten years."

–Aubrey de Grey, geneticist,
Cambridge University

FROM FAT TO FIT WITH PETS

People share more than companionship with their pets. "We are facing a dual obesity epidemic in this country among people and their pets, and the idea came about to tackle both problems together," says Dr. Robert Kushner, medical director of the Wellness Institute at Northwestern Memorial Hospital in Chicago. "Our study showed that people and pets can buddy up and lose weight together." In a yearlong study, overweight owners took their dogs on daily walks and spent 30 minutes a day playing fetch, with both put on a reduced-calorie diet. Owners shed 11 pounds, on average, and the pets also became trimmer.

GREAT FUN, LESS FULFILLING

Fewer Canadians are seeking partners online than before, with revenue growth for Internet dating sites declining. "With online dating, you feel that you have infinite options for potential partners," says relationship expert Julia Sokol. "You don't feel special enough because there are so many other people that your date is meeting at the same time." Relationship experts predict that singles will seek companionship in traditional ways—in bookstores and coffee shops and at weddings and even funerals. A notable exception: Many in the over-50 crowd are just discovering Internet dating.

LOVE, AMERICAN-STYLE

Three million U.S. couples now live and work in different cities from one another, and the number of such couples over the age of 50 has tripled since 2001—due to Internet dating services, lengthier commutes, and worker relocations. "Society has finally started accepting long-distance relationships as a viable alternative," says Gregory Guldner, M.D., director of the California-based Center for the Study of Long-Distance Relationships.

GET FIT OR GET OUT

Some employee wellness programs are using a stick instead of a carrot by telling workers to quit smoking or lose their jobs,

16

c o n t i n u e d

in an effort to reduce insurance premiums. At Okemos, Michigan–based Weyco Inc., a health benefits administration company, tobacco use was banned, and eating coaches and eating disorder therapists were hired to help workers shed pounds. If these incentives don't work, smokers or obese workers will be fired—and legal experts expect other companies to follow suit.

THE DOCTOR IS . . . YOU
■ With patients expected to be more and more knowledgeable about their health, many are studying up. Waiting lists are the norm for lectures on microbiology, cancer, and heart disease offered at more than 80 hospitals and medical schools; some even grant "diplomas" for completion.

OUR MOOD

"We all have too much stuff in our lives that is meaningless. People will be looking for more meaning in the things they are purchasing."
–Ellen Sideri, CEO of forecasting service ESP Trendlab

REASON TO FROWN
■ Fed up with a growing tide of rudeness, Americans are turning to etiquette experts for help. "People are thinking a lot about this and really want to do something about it," reports Peggy Post, author and spokesperson for the Emily Post Institute in Burlington, Vermont. The top five complaints:

■ Loud cell phone conversations
■ Lack of response to an invitation
■ No thank-you notes sent for gifts
■ Rude kids in public
■ Road rage

REASON TO SMILE
■ We're as happy now as we've been at any time during the past 30 years, according to the General Social Survey from the National Opinion Research Center at the University of Chicago. Here are the latest findings:

■ Women are happier than men, although the gap is getting smaller.

■ Money can buy a little more happiness. "Happiness is greater among those with greater incomes, but the relationship is not as strong as many might think," says Tom Smith, the Center's director. "The poor are less happy, but the well-to-do are only a little happier than middle-income folks."

■ The happiness life curve is U-shape, meaning that people are happiest when they are very young and very old, and are least happy around age 40.

■ Marriage adds to happiness. □□

SO, WHAT ELSE IS NEW?
For more statistics, data, and other colorful details about our life and times, go to **Almanac.com/extras**.

Your Own Lip

There's no mistaking a good peach. It's one that makes you jut your chin forward as you bite it to keep the ambrosial juice from dripping all over your clothing. This peach is one that you pick from your backyard tree, a peach warmed by the sun and waiting to be plucked from its branch.

You can grow luscious peaches just about anywhere, as long as you're amenable to taking extra care in site selection and possibly choosing specially adapted varieties. Planting in containers is an option, too.

For a tree that will produce tasty fruit, yield a harvest the soonest, and have other desirable qualities such as pest resistance, plant a grafted tree that you purchase from a nursery. Most peach trees have flowers with both male and female parts that can pollinate each other, so you need to plant only one tree to get fruit.

ZONE IN

Peaches grow most successfully in Zones 6 through 9, where winter lows average from –10° to 30°F. The trees must be exposed to 700 to 1,000 hours of cool temperatures (less than 45°F) each winter before they can fully awaken to grow, flower, and then fruit.

An apple is an excellent thing— until you have tried a peach!

–George du Maurier, British writer (1834–1896)

PITY THE PIT

Peach pits are seeds, but a peach tree grown from a pit takes about five years to mature and produce fruit.

–Miki Duisterhof/Getty Images

by Lee Reich

smackin'-good
PEACHES

CONTINUED

If you have mild winters (Zones 8 and 9), in which the coldest temperature is still above 10°F, choose from among "low-chill" varieties such as 'Bonita', 'Desert Gold', and 'Ventura'. In colder regions, these trees would awaken too early in season and then be damaged or killed by subsequent freezing temperatures.

North of Zone 5 and where winters are especially cold (below −15°F), most peach varieties suffer damage, even if they are fully dormant. Good bets in such climates are 'Harbrite', 'Madison', and 'Reliance'.

WHITE OR YELLOW?

■ Most people grow peaches for flavor; deciding *which* flavor to go for is a delicious dilemma.

Supersweet white-flesh peaches taste as though they have been drenched in honey. Some good white varieties to grow if you live west of the Rockies

Yellow-flesh peach

include 'Babcock' and 'White Lady'. East of the Rockies, try 'Scarlet Pearl', 'LaWhite', and 'Morton'.

Yellow-flesh peaches have a richer flavor than white ones, but they are less sweet. (See varieties below.)

THE RIGHT SPOT

■ The best time to plant a peach tree is in the spring. Choose a location where it will receive at least six hours of summer sun daily. The best site is one that stays slightly cooler in late winter and early spring, such as on a

White-flesh peach

YELLOW-FLESH PEACHES

■ Yellow-flesh peaches are classed as either freestone or clingstone, depending on whether the pit adheres to the flesh. Freestone peaches have a rich flavor and buttery flesh.

Region	Recommended Varieties
Northeast	'Harrow Diamond', 'Redhaven'
Southeast	'Texstar', 'TexRoyal'
West	'Flavorcrest', 'Suncrest', 'Fairtime'
Anywhere (except in marginal peach-growing climates)	'Redhaven', 'Elberta', 'Rio-Oso-Gem'

■ Although less flavorful than freestone peaches, clingstones hold together better during cooking and are good for making cobblers and jams.

Region	Recommended Varieties
East	'Candor', 'Sunbrite'
West	'Indian Blood', 'Dixon'

−White-flesh peach photo above: Stark Bro's Nurseries & Orchards

north-facing slope or near the north side of a home or garage that is shaded from low winter sun but bathed in high summer sun.

Peach trees are not picky about soil. If your garden plants and/or lawn thrive in the soil you have now, peaches will, too. Make sure that the soil has moderate fertility and is near neutral in acidity (soil conditions are easily adjusted with compost, fertilizer, and lime). If the soil stays wet long after rains, plant the trees on a wide mound of soil that raises the tree roots two feet above ground level.

SETTING ROOTS

■ Peach trees are usually sold bare-root—that is, dormant and leafless, with the roots packed in wet leaves, sawdust, or shredded newspaper to keep them moist. Unpack your tree and plump up the roots by soaking them in water for about eight hours.

When you're ready to plant the tree, dig a hole twice as wide as the spread of the tree's roots and only deep enough to cover them. Hold the plant upright in the hole and backfill amongst the roots the soil you took out of it, jiggling the tree and pressing the soil with your fingers to make sure that no air pockets remain. Do not add fertilizer or organic materials to the backfill soil; the roots could burn or the soil level shift as the organic material decomposes.

Water thoroughly. Then, over the surface, spread a layer of organic material (compost, leaves, or straw) to help seal in moisture and combat weeds.

BRANCHING OUT

■ Peach trees need some light pruning after planting, preferably just when the tree begins to leaf out because that is when wounds heal quickly. The goal is to develop a vase shape, with three or four main branches directed up and

away from the trunk, each branch radiating out in a different direction and originating a few inches from its neighbor. If your tree already has well-placed branches, leave them alone unless they are spindly, in which case shorten them. During the growing season, new branches will grow off the trunk to make up any lack of well-placed branches.

Avoid overcrowding branches as your tree ages by ruthlessly removing all but the eventual three or four main branches. Secondary branches will grow off these. Remove any secondary branches that originate near the bases of these main branches.

After its first year and sometime between late fall and early spring when the ground is free of snow, spread a cup of 10-10-10 fertilizer on top of the

–illustration: Dolores Santoliquido/*The Pruning Book* by Lee Reich © The Taunton Press, Inc.

Peach trees need an annual spring pruning, and a severe one at that, as they will bear fruit only on branches that grew the previous season. Remove older branches and any that have died because of damage from winter snow and ice.

ground beneath its branches. Also, replenish the mulch beneath the tree whenever the soil starts to peek through, and spread ground limestone if the soil pH drops below 6.5. You'll know that your peach tree is happy if you see about 20 inches of new branch growth each year.

EASY PICKING

Expect to bite into your first homegrown peach a year or two after you plant the tree, and to begin annual harvest of two to three bushels per tree after about four years. Harvest at peak ripeness. Pluck off individual fruits when they have lost any tint of green and are slightly soft and part easily from the stem. Close your eyes, take a bite with your chin held forward, and savor your wealth.

TRY A PEACH IN A POT

A small, potted, peach tree is just right for a patio and can be easily moved indoors. Genetic dwarfs, also called patio peaches, are best for pots. With their closely spaced leaves and low, mounded form, these varieties—

—Stark Bro's Nurseries & Orchards

'Bonfire', 'Honey Babe', 'Garden Gold', and 'Bonanza'—are particularly decorative.

Use standard potting mix and a large pot with drainage holes. During the growing season, fertilize the tree regularly and keep the soil moist.

Like standard peaches, potted peaches must experience winter cold each year—but they can not tolerate temperatures much below freezing. The ideal winter home for a potted peach tree is a barely heated garage, an unheated basement, or a three-season "Florida" room. The leafless tree does not need light. If the tree begins to grow indoors at the end of winter, gradually acclimate it to the outdoors after risk of freezing has passed.

Every year or two, slide the tree out of its container, cut back some roots, and then repot it in the same pot with some new soil. Prune it every spring, not only to promote new, fruiting branches but also to keep the crown proportional to the size of the pot.

Left: 'Sensation' peach in a patio pot.

Gardening consultant and author **Lee Reich** lives in New Paltz, New York, and is the author of *The Pruning Book* (The Taunton Press, 1997).

(continued with a recipe)

Gardening

PEACH AND ALMOND STRUDEL

Save some of your peaches for this easy-to-make strudel.

8 sheets phyllo dough (wrap and reserve
  remaining for another use)
1/4 cup (1/2 stick) butter
1/2 cup almond paste, diced
2 cups thinly sliced fresh peaches*
1/2 cup sliced almonds
3 tablespoons sweetened condensed
  milk
2 tablespoons sugar

*Thawed frozen peaches will also work.

Preheat oven to 375°F. Brush the sheets of phyllo lightly with butter, stacking them up. Arrange the almond paste down the center of the dough, lengthwise. Lay peach slices on almond paste. Sprinkle with almonds, then drizzle with sweetened condensed milk. Roll up and place seam side down on a lightly greased cookie sheet. Brush top with any remaining butter, sprinkle with sugar. Bake for 25 to 30 minutes or until golden brown. Cut into slices to serve. If desired, serve with whipped cream or—better yet—cinnamon whipped cream. **Serves 6 to 10.**   □□

JUST PEACHY

For advice on pruning and protecting your peach tree, as well as nursery sources and more peach recipes, go to **Almanac.com/extras.**

MAKE IT METRIC. To convert this recipe to metric, see the Table of Measures.

A THING OR TWO ABOUT

ONIONS

Onions may be known as the stinking lilies,
but no good cook would be without them.

by Robin Sweetser

E ven though onions are cheap enough to buy by the bagful in the fall, for the greatest variety, you have to grow your own. When you do that, you have three choices: sets, seeds, or plants.

Onion sets are tiny onions that will become full-size onions in about 14 weeks. Look for small sets no bigger than three-quarters of an inch in diameter. Larger ones will not give you a greater head start; they often produce onions with thick necks that tend to go to seed.

There is a limited choice of varieties available as sets; 'Stuttgarter', a flavorful, semiflat, yellow onion that grows and stores well, is most often seen, along with 'Ebenezer'.

Onions grown from seed keep better than those

Layers of Lore

■

In the Middle Ages, it was believed that onion juice could cure baldness, snakebite, and rabies.

■

A generation or two ago, children were treated with a poultice of mashed onions applied as a paste to cover a wound.

■

A whole onion eaten at bedtime was prescribed to break a cold by morning, and sliced onions were placed on the soles of the feet to draw out fever.

■

Early settlers made a cough syrup by steeping raw onion slices in honey overnight.

■

A raw onion rubbed on a bee sting or insect bite will relieve the pain and itching.

–National Onion Association

Onion's skin very

thin,

Mild winter's

coming in.

Onion's skin thick

and tough,

Coming winter

cold and rough.

–weather proverb

grown from sets and are less likely to go to seed. Growing from seed also offers the widest range of varieties: red, yellow, or white; round, flat, or long; mild and sweet or pungent and tangy. Onion seeds should be started indoors, as they need soil temperatures above 50°F to germinate.

Onion plant choices are limited to whatever your local garden center sells. Several seed catalogs and mail-order companies offer plants for sale.

Onions like lots of sunshine and prefer sweet, fertile soil with near-neutral pH. (The sulfur that gives onions their bite comes from sulfur in the soil.) They grow best if planted where lettuce or squash grew the previous year, and fare poorly if they follow a cole crop, such as cabbage or broccoli. Since onions are shallow-rooted plants, keep them well weeded and mulch them to keep the soil moist and cool. To control onion root maggots, place floating row covers over the sets and plants immediately after planting.

Onions are sensitive to temperature and to the amount of daylight they receive. Cool weather encourages heavy leaf growth, so start your onions early. (Young onions will not be harmed by light frost, and April snow is sometimes referred to as "onion snow" because it can arrive after the onions have been planted.)

Leaf production stops and bulbs begin to form in the spring when there are about 12 hours or more of daylight. The more lush the top growth is at that point, the bigger the bulbs will be.

The Long and Short of ONION DAYS

A member of the lily family, the onion *(Allium cepa)* comes in many shapes, sizes, colors, flavors, and textures. Different varieties of onions have been bred for different areas of the country and length-of-day conditions. To figure out whether you should grow long-day or short-day onions, imagine a line running across the United States from the border between North and South Carolina to San Francisco (at roughly 36 degrees northern latitude). If you live

north of that line, plant long-day types; south of that line, plant short-day onions.

■ **In the North:** 'Walla Walla' (an heirloom originally brought to this country 100 years ago by a Corsican settler in Washington state's Walla Walla Valley) and 'Ailsa Craig' are good choices if you want huge onions. 'Southport Red Globe' and 'Red Florence' are good reds. Some reliable storage onions are 'Copra', 'Yellow Globe', and 'Sweet Sandwich', which gets sweeter the longer it is stored. 'Norstar' and 'Buffalo' are extra-early producers, but they need to be eaten by late December because they will not last.

■ **In the South:** If you want to grow sweet, Vidalia-type onions, look for the seeds of 'Hybrid Yellow Granex'. Other good choices are 'Texas 1015-Y Supersweet', a jumbo globe that stores well; 'Red Burgundy'; 'Southern Belle'; and the mild 'Crystal Wax White Bermuda'.

■ **Everywhere:** Day-neutral, or intermediate, onions don't care about the length of day and will produce an excellent crop anywhere. 'Super Star' is a mild, white onion that produces large, sweet bulbs weighing up to a pound each! 'Candy' is one of the golden onions. The flavor is sharp but sweet, and the thick-fleshed, jumbo-size bulbs store well. 'Red Stockton' forms a large, globe-shape onion with red-ringed, white flesh.

Harvest and Storage TIPS

W hen the onions' tops begin to dry out and fall over, push them all over and withhold water for about one week. Pull the onions and spread them out in the sun to allow the foliage to dry and the skin to toughen up, and they will keep better. If it is rainy, let them dry in a protected place such as a shed, garage, or barn.

Once cured, they can be hung in a mesh bag, spread no more than two deep in a box, or braided and hung in a cool (40° to 60°F), dry, well-ventilated area. Check periodically for sprouting or rotting onions and remove them. Don't store them in the refrigerator; it is too damp.

Sweet onions don't keep well because they have a high water content. To avoid bruising, store them so that they don't touch each other. One way to do this is to use old panty hose. Slip in the onions one at a time, tying a knot between each one. Hang them in a cool, dry place.

(continued with a recipe)

Three Onion POT PIE

1/4 cup butter or margarine
1 cup each, diced red, white, and yellow onions
1 cup sliced carrots
1 1/2 cups quartered mushrooms
1 cup sliced celery

3/4 cup diced red bell peppers
2 cups cubed chicken meat
1/2 cup all-purpose flour

SAUCE:
1/4 cup pale beer
3/4 cup cream

1 cup chicken broth
1 chicken bouillon
1 tablespoon fresh minced thyme
2 tablespoons minced Italian parsley
1/2 cup chopped fresh basil
1 teaspoon minced garlic
1/2 cup thinly sliced green onions
salt and pepper, to taste

pastry for 9-inch, double-crust pie

Preheat oven to 375°F. Combine the first set of ingredients, *except for flour*, in a large pot. Cook over medium-high heat for 10 minutes, stirring often. Add flour and the "sauce" ingredients; stir well. Bring to a simmer, and simmer for 10 minutes.

Place about ⅔ cup of filling in each of 12 small individual baking dishes. Divide the dough into 12 equal pieces and roll out each piece until it is just a little larger than the baking dish. Place rolled dough over the filling; crimp around the edges to seal. Cut a slit in the top to let steam escape while baking.

Bake pies for 45 minutes until the crust is brown. **Makes 12 servings.**

–adapted from the National Onion Association's CD, Bring on the Onions!

☐ ☐

Robin Sweetser, who lives in New Hampshire, grows the torpedo-shape 'Rouge de Florence', softball-size 'Candy', heirloom 'Siskiyou Sweet', and tangy, rock-hard, winter-keeping 'Copra', which she braids and hangs in the pantry.

–National Onion Association

FOR CRYING OUT LOUD

Get more information about growing onion sets from seeds, onion plant and seed sources, onion lore, and tasty onion recipes at **Almanac.com/extras.**

Frosts and Growing Seasons

■ Dates given are normal averages for a light freeze; local weather and topography may cause considerable variations. The possibility of frost occurring after the spring dates and before the fall dates is 50 percent. The classification of freeze temperatures is usually based on their effect on plants. **Light freeze:** 29° to 32°F—tender plants killed. **Moderate freeze:** 25° to 28°F—widely destructive effect on most vegetation. **Severe freeze:** 24°F and colder—heavy damage to most plants.

–courtesy of National Climatic Data Center

State	City	Growing Season (days)	Last Spring Frost	First Fall Frost	State	City	Growing Season (days)	Last Spring Frost	First Fall Frost
AK	Juneau	133	May 16	Sept. 26	ND	Bismarck	129	May 14	Sept. 20
AL	Mobile	272	Feb. 27	Nov. 26	NE	Blair	165	Apr. 27	Oct. 10
AR	Pine Bluff	234	Mar. 19	Nov. 8	NE	North Platte	136	May 11	Sept. 24
AZ	Phoenix	308	Feb. 5	Dec. 15	NH	Concord	121	May 23	Sept. 22
AZ	Tucson	273	Feb. 28	Nov. 29	NJ	Newark	219	Apr. 4	Nov. 10
CA	Eureka	324	Jan. 30	Dec. 15	NM	Carlsbad	223	Mar. 29	Nov. 7
CA	Sacramento	289	Feb. 14	Dec. 1	NM	Los Alamos	157	May 8	Oct. 13
CA	San Francisco	*	*	*	NV	Las Vegas	259	Mar. 7	Nov. 21
CO	Denver	157	May 3	Oct. 8	NY	Albany	144	May 7	Sept. 29
CT	Hartford	167	Apr. 25	Oct. 10	NY	Syracuse	170	Apr. 28	Oct. 16
DE	Wilmington	198	Apr. 13	Oct. 29	OH	Akron	168	May 3	Oct. 18
FL	Miami	*	*	*	OH	Cincinnati	195	Apr. 14	Oct. 27
FL	Tampa	338	Jan. 28	Jan. 3	OK	Lawton	217	Apr. 1	Nov. 5
GA	Athens	224	Mar. 28	Nov. 8	OK	Tulsa	218	Mar. 30	Nov. 4
GA	Savannah	250	Mar. 10	Nov. 15	OR	Pendleton	188	Apr. 15	Oct. 21
IA	Atlantic	141	May 9	Sept. 28	OR	Portland	217	Apr. 3	Nov. 7
IA	Cedar Rapids	161	Apr. 29	Oct. 7	PA	Carlisle	182	Apr. 20	Oct. 20
ID	Boise	153	May 8	Oct. 9	PA	Williamsport	168	Apr. 29	Oct. 15
IL	Chicago	187	Apr. 22	Oct. 26	RI	Kingston	144	May 8	Sept. 30
IL	Springfield	185	Apr. 17	Oct. 19	SC	Charleston	253	Mar. 11	Nov. 20
IN	Indianapolis	180	Apr. 22	Oct. 20	SC	Columbia	211	Apr. 4	Nov. 2
IN	South Bend	169	May 1	Oct. 18	SD	Rapid City	145	May 7	Sept. 29
KS	Topeka	175	Apr. 21	Oct. 14	TN	Memphis	228	Mar. 23	Nov. 7
KY	Lexington	190	Apr. 17	Oct. 25	TN	Nashville	207	Apr. 5	Oct. 29
LA	Monroe	242	Mar. 9	Nov. 7	TX	Amarillo	197	Apr. 14	Oct. 29
LA	New Orleans	288	Feb. 20	Dec. 5	TX	Denton	231	Mar. 25	Nov. 12
MA	Worcester	172	Apr. 27	Oct. 17	TX	San Antonio	265	Mar. 3	Nov. 24
MD	Baltimore	231	Mar. 26	Nov. 13	UT	Cedar City	134	May 20	Oct. 2
ME	Portland	143	May 10	Sept. 30	UT	Spanish Fork	156	May 8	Oct. 12
MI	Lansing	140	May 13	Sept. 30	VA	Norfolk	239	Mar. 23	Nov. 17
MI	Marquette	159	May 12	Oct. 19	VA	Richmond	198	Apr. 10	Oct. 26
MN	Duluth	122	May 21	Sept. 21	VT	Burlington	142	May 11	Oct. 1
MN	Willmar	152	May 4	Oct. 4	WA	Seattle	232	Mar. 24	Nov. 11
MO	Jefferson City	173	Apr. 26	Oct. 16	WA	Spokane	153	May 4	Oct. 5
MS	Columbus	215	Mar. 27	Oct. 29	WI	Green Bay	143	May 12	Oct. 2
MS	Vicksburg	250	Mar. 13	Nov. 18	WI	Janesville	164	Apr. 28	Oct. 10
MT	Fort Peck	146	May 5	Sept. 28	WV	Parkersburg	175	Apr. 25	Oct. 18
MT	Helena	122	May 18	Sept. 18	WY	Casper	123	May 22	Sept. 22
NC	Fayetteville	212	Apr. 2	Oct. 31		*Frosts do not occur every year.*			

Get growing at Almanac.com/garden.

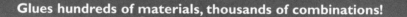

Put 'Em Up!

Preserve these favorite old-fashioned recipes while you can.

by Barbara Radcliffe Rogers

Before the freezer made preserving the bounty of the garden easy and reliable, pickling was the best way to keep many vegetables and fruits. Jams and jellies were made from vegetables as well. The results were delicious.

Here is a selection of recipes that have survived, carefully recorded and passed down in families and from friend to friend. We have brought them up to date with modern methods and, when possible, cut down on the amounts of sugar.

DILLED GREEN BEANS

If you wish to make these pickles in half-pint jars, use more beans and small hot peppers, small or half garlic cloves, and 4 small heads of dill.

2 heads fresh dill
2 long, hot peppers
2 cloves garlic, peeled
1/2 teaspoon cayenne pepper
1 pound small green beans, rinsed
1 1/2 cups water
1 cup cider vinegar
2 tablespoons salt

Place 1 head of dill in each of 2 sterilized pint canning jars, along with hot pepper, garlic clove, and ¼ teaspoon cayenne. Pack beans upright, dividing evenly between the jars and allowing the tops to extend out of the jars. When they are firmly packed, slice the tops off by running a sharp knife along the top of the jar. Put the remaining ingredients in a saucepan and bring to a boil. Pour the liquid over the beans, filling the jars to overflowing. Seal and process 15 minutes in boiling water. **Makes 2 pints.**

–illustration: Carol O'Malia

MELON PICKLES

Here's a good way to use a melon you cut open prematurely. Serve this delicately light pickle with chicken sandwiches.

1 hard, underripe, cantaloupe or honeydew
    melon
2 cups sugar
1/2 cup fresh lime juice
1/2 cup water
1 teaspoon whole peppercorns
1 teaspoon whole cloves
1 cinnamon stick
1 lime, thinly sliced

Cut the melon in half, remove the seeds, and, using a melon-baller, cut the entire melon into small balls (or peel the melon and cut it into 1-inch cubes). You should have about 1 quart of fruit. Combine the remaining ingredients, *except the lime slices,* in a large saucepan and boil gently for 5 minutes. Add the melon, turn the heat to medium, bring the contents back to a simmer, and then turn off the heat. (Don't cook the melon in the syrup.) Remove the cinnamon stick. Use a slotted spoon to transfer the melon to sterilized jars, dividing the pepper and cloves evenly among the jars. Divide the lime slices evenly, placing them flat along the sides of each jar. (Use a table knife to hold the melon away from the jar.) Fill with hot syrup. Seal and process 10 minutes in boiling water. **Makes about 3 pints.**

CARROT JAM

4 cups grated carrots (just under 2 pounds)
2 lemons, ground or thinly sliced, with juice
3 1/4 cups sugar

Simmer carrots in water for about 8 minutes, until just tender. Drain, but do not squeeze or crush. Return carrots to the pot and add lemons with juice and the sugar. Place over low heat and stir gently until the sugar has dissolved. Increase heat to medium and boil, stirring frequently, until the jam is thick. Pour into sterilized jars and seal. Process 10 minutes in boiling water. **Makes about 3 pints.**

> **KITCHEN TIP: To convert these recipes to metric, see the Table of Measures.**

(continued)

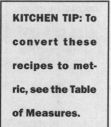

SWEET RED PEPPER JELLY

For extra bite, add one seeded hot red pepper.

1/2 cup cider vinegar
1 cup chopped, seeded, red bell peppers
1 cup water
2 cups apple juice or cider
1/4 teaspoon salt
1 package powdered pectin
3 1/2 cups sugar

Put the vinegar in a blender and add pepper pieces as you blend until the total measures 1½ cups. Combine water, juice or cider, salt, and pectin in a large pot and bring to a full boil. Add the pepper mixture and sugar all at once and return to a full boil. Boil 3 to 5 minutes and seal in sterilized jars. Process in boiling water 10 minutes. Place jars on a rack and turn them over every 5 minutes until the jelly thickens, to keep the tiny flecks of red pepper evenly distributed throughout the jelly. **Makes about 3 pints.**

> **KEEP A LID ON IT**
>
> To ensure a good seal on your jars, always wipe the rim clean after filling and just before putting the lid on.

ZUCCHINI BREAD AND BUTTER PICKLES

Even pickle devotees will be fooled into thinking that you've used cucumbers.

1 quart thinly sliced, unpeeled, small fresh zucchini
2 small to medium onions, thinly sliced
2 cloves garlic, sliced
1/4 cup salt
1 1/4 cups cider vinegar
1 1/4 cups sugar
1 teaspoon celery seed
2 teaspoons mustard seed
1/2 teaspoon turmeric

Sprinkle the zucchini, onions, and garlic with salt and cover with ice water. Let stand 2 hours. Drain, rinse in fresh cold water, and drain again. Combine the remaining ingredients in a large pot and boil 5 minutes. Add vegetables, remove the pot from the heat, and let stand 3 hours. Return the pot to a boil and cook 5 minutes. Pack pickles in sterilized jars. Seal and process 10 minutes in boiling water. **Makes about 3 pints.**

TOO SWEET?

Although sugar plays its role as a preservative, the vinegar in pickles does most of the work, so you can safely reduce the sugar in an old recipe if you find it too sweet. To adjust the sweetness of a pickle recipe, use these general proportions:

■ **Very tart: 2 parts vinegar to 1 part sugar**

■ **Moderately sweet: equal parts sugar and vinegar**

■ **Very sweet: 2 parts sugar to 1 part vinegar**

While you can not change the amounts of sugar used in jellies (both commercial pectin and the natural pectin in fruit need the correct proportion of sugar in order to jell properly), you can reduce sugar in old jam and marmalade recipes. The rule of thumb is that sugar should equal between one-half and two-thirds of the measurement of the fruit or vegetable. ☐☐

MORE JARRING IDEAS

Got a fat pumpkin? Had a heavy tomato harvest? Then pickle the pumpkin and turn the tomatoes into jam. For recipes and tips, go to **Almanac.com/extras.**

The Seedy Secrets of Your Garbage

Take the seeds and pits that you usually throw in the compost pile and turn them into fruitful houseplants.

GET YOUR VITAMIN C-EEDS

Citrus plants can be grown from seeds removed from oranges,

grapefruits, lemons, and tangerines. Soak the seeds overnight in water. Plant them ½ inch deep in moist potting soil. Cover the pot with a plastic bag or a piece of plastic wrap, and put it in a warm spot. Keep the soil moist. When the seeds start to grow (in a few weeks), remove the plastic. Keep the pot in a warm, sunny window.

A TASTE OF THE TROPICS

In the center of the mango, there is a large, hairy husk with a pit in it.

Scrape off the excess flesh from the husk, gently pry it open with a dull knife, and remove the pit. Fill a small plastic bag with dampened peat moss or sphagnum. Put the pit into the bag and surround it completely with moss. Seal the bag. Check every day to make sure that the pit is not too dry or too moist. When the roots are four inches long, transplant to a pot that is at least one inch wider than the pit.

ISLAND FLAVOR

The pineapple requires a serious time commitment—at least three and a half years from start to

bloom. To get one growing, hold the crown of leaves with one hand and the fruit with the other. Twist until the crown comes apart from the fruit, and then peel the bottom leaves away. The resulting stump holds the roots. Put the stump in a glass of water with activated charcoal, leaves up. Keep it in indirect light, and roots should appear in a few weeks. Then transplant it to a pot and put the pot in a window that gets a lot of sun. Keep the soil moist. Go on about your other business for three years. Then put the whole pot in a black plastic bag with a rotted apple cut in half, one half in the crown and one half in the soil. Seal, and open two weeks later. If you see growth in the crown, give it lots of sun. If not, seal for two more weeks. Flowers should appear six months after the first sign of growth. □□

–The Rare Pit & Plant Council and Meg Mitchell Moore

46

The Vermont Country Store®

Purveyors of the Practical & Hard-To Find

Tangee®

The Lipstick That Changes Color to Become Uniquely Your Own

The same lipstick.................on Judi.........................on Julie.....................on Michelle

Original Tangee Lipstick, Natural Beauty for 70 Years

Bring out your natural beauty with Tangee® The Original Formula Natural Lipstick, the orange lipstick that goes on clear and gradually transforms into the perfect shade for you. A secret of beautiful women for over 70 years, Tangee lipstick moisturizes lips to prevent drying and chapping and looks freshly applied for hours. Ideal for women who want to look beautiful without looking artificial. Buy one for your purse, vanity, and office drawer—you'll never want to be without Tangee. 0.13 oz. tube.

#40580 Tangee Lipstick **$12.95**

Tangee Rouge, Revived This Year

Tangee Rouge also changes color to complement each woman's unique complexion. We brought it back because we love the idea of rouge that transforms into the perfect shade for your skin. This pressed powder rouge, dusty rose in the container, can be applied with fingertips or makeup brush. 1 oz.

#45482 Tangee Rouge **$12.95**

Three Ways to Shop

Visit Our Stores

Come visit us at either of our stores in Vermont. Our original store in Weston is on Route 100, 20 miles from Manchester. Our Rockingham store is off I-91 on Route 103. For hours and directions, call the number at right or go to www.vermontcountrystore.com.

Visit Us Online
www.vermontcountrystore.com

For more hard-to-find products not in our catalogues, go online. At our website you will find Yankee Bargains, "web only" items, and more than 5,600 other great products.

Call to request a free catalogue
(Mention code 50339)

(802) 362-8364

chives

Yes, in the poor man's garden grow
Far more than herbs and flowers—
Kind thoughts, contentment, peace of mind,
And joy for many hours.
–Mary Howitt, poet (1799–1888)

A Kitchen Garden

A garden plan to bring fresh herbs from

your (back) doorstep into your kitchen.

by Nancy J. Ondra

sage

basil

(text begins on page 50)

–herb illustrations by Kristin Kest

48

A Most Unusual Gift of Love

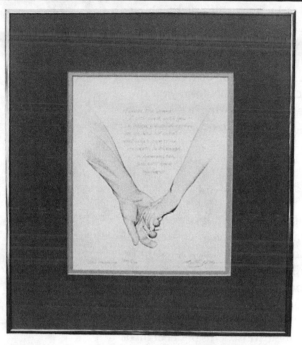

The poem reads: *"Across the years I will walk with you—*
in deep, green forests; on shores of sand:
and when our time on earth is through,
in heaven, too, you will have my hand."

Dear Reader,

The drawing you see above is called "The Promise." It is completely composed of dots of ink. After writing the poem, I worked with a quill pen and placed thousands of these dots, one at a time, to create this gift in honor of my youngest brother and his wife.

Now, I have decided to offer "The Promise" to those who share and value its sentiment. Each litho is numbered and signed by hand and precisely captures the detail of the drawing. As a wedding, anniversary or Christmas gift or simply as a standard for your own home, I believe you will find it most appropriate.

Measuring 14" by 16", it is available either fully framed in a subtle copper tone with hand-cut mats of pewter and rust at $95, or in the mats alone at $75. Please add $12.50 for insured shipping and packaging. Your satisfaction is completely guaranteed.

My best wishes are with you.

The Art of Robert Sexton, 491 Greenwich St. (at Grant), San Francisco, CA 94133

MasterCard and Visa orders welcome. Please send card name, card number, address and expiration date, or phone (415) 989-1630 between noon-8 P.M. EST. Checks are also accepted. *Please allow 3 weeks for delivery.*

"The Promise" *is featured with many other recent works in my book,* "Journeys of the Human Heart." *It, too, is available from the address above at $12.95 per copy postpaid. Please visit my Web site at*
www.robertsexton.com

■ **Fettuccine with garden-**
fresh pesto. Baby greens drizzled with tarragon vinaigrette. Creamy sherbet garnished
with lemon verbena and alpine strawberries.
Restaurant menu offerings? No—simply delicious dishes you can whip up right at home
with just-picked ingredients from your own
kitchen herb garden! Growing herbs to complement your cooking is far easier than you
might expect, and it takes very little space to
get an abundant harvest from spring to frost.

PLANT WHERE YOU CAN PICK

■ **Location is far more**
important than looks when it comes to creating a kitchen herb garden that's practical
and productive. Ideally, you want it to be
close to the house, so that it's convenient for
you to step out and harvest a handful of herbs
whenever you want them. However, you also
need to make sure that your plants will get
plenty of sunlight. Most herbs prefer eight or
more hours of sun per day; though they can
survive with less, they won't produce nearly
as much growth and may be less flavorful.
Generally, it's best to choose a location that
will provide adequate sunlight first and then
consider convenience.

Even though these versatile plants can
adapt to a wide range of soil conditions (including poor, dry sites),
most will grow even better if
you set them into improved soil.
Prepare the site just as you would
for a flower bed—remove any
existing grass and
weeds, loosen the
top 8 to 12 inches
of soil, and dig

parsley

Rosemary helpeth the brain,

strengtheneth the memorie,

and is very medicinable for

the head.

–Roger Hacket, doctor of divinity (c. 1607)

or till a 1- to 2-inch-deep layer of compost into the ground before planting. The resulting loose, enriched soil will support good growth from a wide variety of tasty herbs.

CHOOSE WHAT YOU'LL USE

■ **What's the number one** rule for a successful kitchen herb garden? Grow herbs you will cook with! Growing dozens of different herbs can be fun and educational, but it isn't very practical if you'll harvest only a few of them regularly. Of course, the more space you have available, the greater the variety of herbs with which you can experiment. Here are some pointers to help you decide what to plant.

■ **Fresh comes first.** If space is limited, concentrate on growing herbs that taste best when picked fresh. These include basil, chives, cilantro, dill, fennel, and French tarragon.

■ **Choose the classics.** The traditional quartet of parsley, sage, rosemary, and thyme—along with Greek oregano—deserves a place in every kitchen herb garden. These five herbs will complement just about any kind of savory dish.

■ **Don't forget the sweets.** If you have a little extra room, "sweet" herbs such as mints, lemon balm, and lemon verbena are a treat to grow and cook with. Besides complementing some savory dishes (as with mint for lamb and lemon herbs for fish), these fragrant and flavorful plants are a delight for desserts, punches, and hot and iced teas, too.

■ **Be adventurous.** If you have ample gardening space, consider trying different flavors of your favorite herbs (lemon and caraway thymes in addition to common thyme, for example), as well as less commonly used herbs, such as bay (grow it as a tender perennial in the garden or in a pot), borage, chervil, and summer savory. Other good candidates include arugula, mustard, and other salad greens, as well as garlic (grow it for its greens as well as the bulbs) and red and yellow alpine strawberries.

(continued)

The smell of basil is fit for a king's house.

–John Parkinson, apothecary
and herbalist (1567–1650)

*l e m o n
v e r b e n a*

Most culinary herbs grow quickly, and because you'll be picking only a few leaves or sprigs at a time, a single clump of each type is usually enough. Basil is one exception: If you plan to make lots of pesto during the summer, figure on growing five to ten plants per person. Basil is easy to start from seed (dill is, too), so pick up a pack in the spring and you can grow all you need. For other herbs, buying transplants is usually the most practical approach.

CARE AND SNIPPING

■ **Working compost into** the soil before planting and adding another 1-inch layer of compost as mulch after planting provides enough nutrients to keep most herbs happy and healthy without extra fertilizer. Mulching will also help prevent soil from splashing onto the plants from heavy rain or watering, so you'll spend less time washing them after harvest.

Why should a man die, when he can go to his garden for sage?

–10th-century saying

Give your herbs a week or so to settle in after transplanting, and then you can start picking them. Regular, light harvesting acts just like pruning and encourages bushy new growth, so don't hesitate to pick from your plants regularly. It's generally best to use scissors or garden shears to snip off the leaves and shoots you need, because pulling or tearing them off can damage the remaining stems or roots.

(Turn to page 56 for a kitchen garden planting plan.)

GROW YOUR OWN

Most garden centers carry a range of common culinary herb plants and seeds. If you can't find what you need there, or if you're seeking some of the more unusual herbs, go to **Almanac.com/extras** for a list of mail-order sources. For additional gardening resources, including the USDA Plant Hardiness Zone Map, visit **Almanac.com/garden/charts.**

dill

54

The Planting Plan

■ **Ready to try a kitchen herb garden?** Here's an 8-foot by 3-foot border garden that would fit perfectly along a sunny foundation by a back door for quick and easy harvesting. If you don't have enough sun next to your home, try it in an area that gets lots of light. Either way, make sure to leave a path at least 18 inches wide between the garden and any wall, deck, or fence behind it, so that you can easily reach all parts of the planting for harvesting. Keep in mind that even if you live in a cold climate, you can grow heat-loving perennial herbs as annual plants.

1. French tarragon
(Artemisia dracunculus)
1 plant; perennial
Zones 4 to 8.

2. Common sage
(Salvia officinalis)
1 plant; perennial
Zones 5 to 8.

3. Fennel
(Foeniculum vulgare)
1 plant; perennial
Zones 5 to 9.

4. Dill
(Anethum graveolens)
6 plants; hardy annual*

5. Sweet basil
(Ocimum basilicum)
6 plants; annual*

6. Lemon verbena
(Aloysia triphylla)
1 plant; tender perennial
Zones 8 to 11.

*Annuals are not zone specific.

7. Lemon grass
(Cymbopogon citratus)
1 plant; tender perennial
Zone 11.

8. Spearmint
(Mentha spicata)
1 plant grown in a pot
to discourage spreading;
perennial
Zones 4 to 8.

9. Lemon balm
(Melissa officinalis)
1 plant; perennial
Zones 3 to 8.

10. Lemon thyme
(Thymus x citriodorus)
3 plants; perennial
Zones 5 to 9.

11. Rosemary
(Rosmarinus officinalis)
1 plant; tender perennial
Zones 8 to 10.

12. Chives
(Allium schoenoprasum)
3 plants; perennial
Zones 3 to 9.

13. Greek oregano
(Origanum vulgare
subsp. *hirtum;* also sold
as *O. heracleoticum)*
1 plant; perennial
Zones 5 to 9.

14. Common thyme
(Thymus vulgaris)
3 plants; perennial
Zones 4 to 9.

15. Parsley
(Petroselinum crispum),
curly or Italian, 4 plants;
biennial grown as an
annual* □ □

Nancy J. Ondra is a freelance garden writer who lives in Bucks County, Pennsylvania. She is the author of nine gardening books, including *Perennial Design Solutions* (Storey Books, 2005), cowritten with Stephanie Cohen.

Symbolic Meanings of Herbs, Flowers, and Trees

Aloe .... Healing, protection, affection
Angelica .... Inspiration
Arborvitae ..... Unchanging friendship
Bachelor's button .. Single blessedness
Basil .... Good wishes, love
Bay .... Glory
Black-eyed Susan .... Justice
Carnation ...... Alas for my poor heart
Chamomile .... Patience
Chives .... Usefulness
Clover, white .... Think of me
Coriander .... Hidden worth
Cumin .... Fidelity
Fennel .... Flattery
Fern .... Sincerity
Geranium, oak-leaved .. True friendship
Goldenrod .... Encouragement
Heliotrope .... Eternal love
Holly .... Hope
Hollyhock .... Ambition
Honeysuckle .... Bonds of love
Horehound .... Health
Hyssop .... Sacrifice, cleanliness
Ivy .... Friendship, continuity
Lady's-mantle .... Comforting
Lavender .... Devotion, virtue
Lemon balm .... Sympathy
Marjoram .... Joy, happiness
Mint .... Eternal refreshment
Morning glory .... Affectation
Nasturtium .... Patriotism
Oak .... Strength
Oregano .... Substance
Pansy .... Thoughts
Parsley .... Festivity
Pine .... Humility

Poppy, red .... Consolation
Rose .... Love
Rosemary .... Remembrance
Rue .... Grace, clear vision
Sage .... Wisdom, immortality
Salvia, blue .... I think of you
Salvia, red .... Forever mine
Savory .... Spice, interest
Sorrel .... Affection
Southernwood .... Constancy, jest
Sweet pea .... Pleasures
Sweet woodruff .... Humility
Tansy .... Hostile thoughts
Tarragon .... Lasting interest
Thyme .... Courage, strength
Valerian .... Readiness
Violet .... Loyalty, devotion
Violet, blue .... Faithfulness
Violet, yellow .... Rural happiness
Willow .... Sadness
Zinnia ..... Thoughts of absent friends

Families Have Saved Up To 50% On Heating Costs
And never have to buy fuel — wood, oil, gas, kerosene — ever again!

Hydro-Sil is a unique room-by-room heating system that can **save you hundreds of dollars** in home heating costs by replacing old and inefficient heating. It can replace or supplement your electric heat, gas or oil furnace and woodstoves.

Hydro-Sil represents economy in heating: inside the heater case is a sealed copper tube filled with a harmless silicone fluid. **It's permanent. You'll never run out.** "**Hydro-Sil** Energy Star" thermostat controls a variable watt hydro element that is _only_ being supplied a _proportional_ amount of power on an as-needed basis. When Hydro-Sil is turned on, the silicone liquid is quickly heated, and with its heat retention qualities, continues to heat after the Hydro element shuts off. Hydro-Sil's room-by-room "Energy Star" digital control technology greatly increases energy savings and comfort.

MANY FAMILIES ARE BENEFITING – YOU CAN TOO!

- **F. Smalley** - _"A company that advertises the truth_ saved 50% compared to my gas heat. I found it hard to believe until my power bill came. Thanks a million!"

- **R. Hanson** - "I cannot begin to tell you how pleased I am with Hydro-Sil... the first time in 25 years our electric bill was reduced... **saved $635, over 40%!**"

Your Benefits with Hydro-Sil:

- Slash heating cost with Energy Star technology
- Lifetime warranty. No service contracts
- Safe, complete peace of mind
- Clean, no fumes, environmentally safe
- U.L. listed
- Preassembled — ready to use
- No furnaces, ducts, or chimneys
- Portable (110V) or permanent (220V)
- Whole house heating or single room

Proportional "Energy Star" thermostat!

220 VOLT PERMANENT	Approx. Area to Heat	Discount Price	Quantity
8' 2000 watts	250-300 s.f.	$279	
6' 1500 watts	180-250 s.f.	$249	
5' 1250 watts	130-180 s.f.	$229	
4' 1000 watts	100-130 s.f.	$209	
3' 750 watts	75-100 s.f.	$189	
2' 500 watts	50-75 s.f.	$169	
Thermostats	Call for options & exact heater needed		

110 VOLT PORTABLES (Thermostat Included)	Discount Price	Quantity
5' Hydro-Max 750-1500 watts	$219	
4' Convector – Dual watt	$179	
3' 750 watts – Silicone	$179	
$15.00 shipping per heater	$ _____	
Total Amount	$ _____	

Name _____

Address _____

City _____ St _____ Zip _____

Phone _____ _____

MasterCard or Visa Account Information:

Acct # _____

Expiration Date _____

Order today or contact us for more information
PHONE • WEB • MAIL
Check • MasterCard • Visa

1-800-627-9276
Visit our secure web site at

www.hydrosil.com
Hydro-Sil, P.O. Box, 662,
Fort Mill, SC 29715

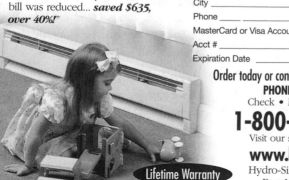

Lifetime Warranty

Beauty From Your Backyard

Garden-variety ways to give your skin a fresh, healthy glow—plus, a real eye-opener.
by Martha White

Fruit Smoother

■ Fight age lines and wrinkles with a facial masque made from any melon or a handful of strawberries. For a single application, combine the fruit with an equal amount of dairy cream, yogurt, or buttermilk in a blender (or food processor). Add one tablespoon of oats. Apply the concoction to your face, wait ten minutes, and then rinse with lukewarm water.

Tomato Tingler

■ For a scrub to treat blemished skin, combine a peeled and seeded tomato, one teaspoon of lemon juice, and one tablespoon of oats in a blender. Apply the mixture to the affected area, wait ten minutes, and then rinse with lukewarm water.

Carrot Cream

■ For relief from oily skin, treat it with a mashed-vegetable facial cream. Boil a peeled carrot (or sweet potato or an equivalent portion of fresh pumpkin) until it is soft. Make a paste by using a blender to combine the vegetable with a tablespoon of honey and a few drops of milk (or mash and mix by hand). Apply the paste to your skin, wait 20 minutes (it will harden, slightly), and then rinse with lukewarm water.

Cucumber Compress

■ Tired eyes? Refresh them with a ten-minute cucumber eye treatment. Place paper-thin rounds of cucumber (or potato) on your closed eyelids. If you prefer, grate the vegetable and apply it around your closed eyes.

In case of sensitive skin . . .

Before applying anything from your garden to your face, test the remedy on your inner arm. If, after ten minutes, the test area is red or itchy, don't use that preparation. ☐☐

Martha White, author of *Traditional Home Remedies,* has been a longtime contributor to The Old Farmer's Almanac publications.

Something's Cooking at
The Old Farmer's Almanac

Check out our collection of award-winning recipes from America's country fairs, food festivals, bake-offs, and national cooking competitions.

These cookbooks have something special for cooks of all levels. Spice up basic dishes or create culinary delights! You'll also find blue-ribbon tips and hints throughout the pages.

Best Home Baking

Our newest cookbook features 192 pages full of recipes for tasty baked goods. Recipes like:

* Apple-Toffee Cookies
* Onion Lovers' Bread
* Michigan Cherry Muffins

Bake something special for your family and friends today!
(Item 11200720)

Blue Ribbon Recipes

From appetizers to desserts, you can create a feast from 160 pages of award-winning recipes, such as:

* Creamy Crab Bisque
* Grecian Skillet Rib Eyes
* Idaho Potato Fajitas

You'll find wonderful recipes for every occasion!
(Item 11200710)

Each book offers:

* Wipe-clean laminated hard covers that resist kitchen spills.
* Cover illustrations by America's best-loved folk artist, Warren Kimble.
* Hidden wire bindings that stay flat while you're cooking.

To order, call **800-223-3166**
or visit **shop.almanac.com/2005COOK**

What's Good for the Garden

. . . is good for the gardener.

Garden chores—raking, hoeing, digging, mowing, weeding—produce not only a bountiful harvest but also a healthy and happy gardener. When working in your garden, consider these tips for a safe and fun garden workout.

■ **Plan three or more separate activities or motions (such as removing pests, planting, pruning, weeding, and digging) for each gardening session, each one ranging from five minutes to an hour.**

■ Switch your position and stance every 5 to 15 minutes. Crouch, then sit. Kneel on one knee, then on two knees; then stand and lunge.

■ **Exaggerate your motions. Rake or hoe with wide, sweeping strokes, keeping movement smooth and steady. Just as you think of repetitions with weight lifting, use good form, and work with a hoe or a shovel as if each exertion were a resistance-training repetition.**

■ Breathe in and out regularly.

■ **When lifting a potted plant, concrete block, or anything else in the garden, keep your back straight, bend from your knees, and use your legs instead of your back.**

■ Bend your knees as you dig, letting your legs, not your back or arms, do most of the work. Alternate between a right-handed and a left-handed stance.

■ **When hand weeding, spread your legs and bend at the knees, never at the waist. Or set one knee down behind you and put your other leg in front of you, knee bent, foot on the ground; weed for about 20 seconds, stand up, and alternate legs.** □ □

These tips are taken from the archives of *The Old Farmer's Almanac Gardener's Companion* and from *Fitness the Dynamic Gardening Way,* by Jeffrey Restuccio (Balance of Nature Publishing, 1992).

PSORIASIS?

Help Eliminate
- itching
- scaling
- flaking
- redness
- irritation

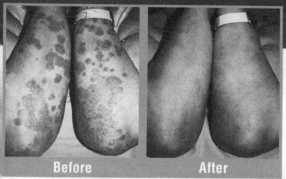

Before **After**

These results are not typical. Individual results will vary.

✓ No steroids
✓ No burning
✓ Non-prescription
✓ Contains Willowherb™
✓ Won't stain clothing
✓ Spray goes on like water
✓ Easy application - No oily mess

MEDICATED ACTIVE INGREDIENT

Restore your skin to a healthier, clearer state!

The Feeling of Brand New Skin
Thousands of customers agree!

"This product is so amazing...(my husband's condition) was completely cleared up using the Skin Zinc™ System...and the problem has not returned. It's like a dream come true."- Mary B.

"Now the symptoms of my seborrheic dermatitis are controlled and relieved." -Linda O.

"The Skin Zinc™ System has...changed my life for the better. I can now go out in public and not worry about someone cringing when they see my hands, thanks again." - Gene L.

A New "Steroid-Free" Broad Spectrum Relief™ Skin Treatment

The Advanced Skin Zinc™ Relief System is a powerful, double action medication. The medicated "mist" spray goes on like water to help eliminate painful, stubborn symptoms, including itching, scaling, flaking, and redness. Combined with the feathery-light, fast absorbing, specially medicated Skin Cylic™ cream, it helps stop the irritating symptoms of Psoriasis and Seborrheic Dermatitis. As your skin becomes smoother, the Skin Zinc™ Relief System promotes skin recovery and helps manage future irritations.

The Skin Zinc™ Satisfaction Guarantee

We are so confident that the Skin Zinc™ System will restore your skin to a healthier, clearer, more comfortable state, that you're backed by a 30-day money-back guarantee. If you aren't 100% satisfied, simply return the empty containers for a full refund of the product price when ordering by phone.

Call now for a 30-Day Risk-Free Trial of
Advanced Skin Zinc™ System

Mention Discount Code 12B and qualify for a FREE SUPPLY* and no extra S&H charge with your purchase!

1-800-507-5572

Free Supply With Your Purchase offer valid when you call this number only.

The Basic **Original** Skin Zinc™ System is available in the skin care aisle at **CVS/pharmacy**

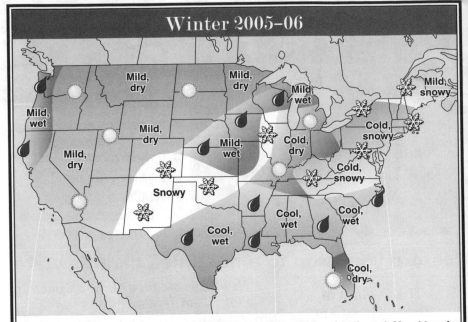

Winter 2005–06

These seasonal weather maps correspond to the winter (November through March) and summer (June through August) forecasts on page 196. A map of our 16 weather regions is on page 197; the detailed forecasts for those regions begin on page 198. For an explanation of our forecast methodology, see "How We Predict the Weather" on page 194.

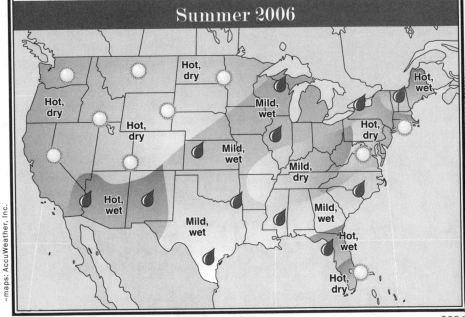

Summer 2006

–maps: AccuWeather, Inc.

"If I told you that I can end a lifetime of foot pain instantly, you probably wouldn't believe me..."

"Half a million other men and women didn't either... until they tried this revolutionary European discovery that positively killed their foot pain dead!

"Don't live with foot pain a moment longer! If you're ready to recapture the vitality and energy that healthy feet provide, I'll give you 60 days to try the remarkable foot support system I discovered in Europe. You will immediately experience relief and freedom from foot ailments. I GUARANTEE IT!

"How can I make such an unprecedented guarantee? Because I personally lived in constant, agonizing foot pain for years

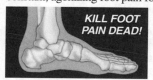

KILL FOOT PAIN DEAD!

before my exciting discovery. What started out as simple aching from corns and calluses grew into full-blown, incapacitating misery only a few other foot pain sufferers could understand.

"Believe me, I tried all the so-called remedies I could get my hands on (and feet into), but none of them really worked. It wasn't until my wife and I took a trip to Europe that I discovered a remarkable invention called Flexible Featherspring® Foot Supports. Invented in Germany, these custom-formed foot supports absorb shock as they cradle your feet as if on a cushion of air.

© FEATHERSPRING, 712 N. 34th Street, Seattle, WA 98103-8881

Harvey Rothschild,
Founder of Featherspring Int'l.

"Imagine my complete surprise as I slipped a pair of custom-formed Feathersprings into my shoes for the first time and began the road to no more pain. The tremendous pain and pressure I used to feel every time I took a step was gone! I could scarcely believe how great a relief I felt even after walking several hours. And after just a few days of use, my pain disappeared totally - *and has never returned.*

"Whatever your problem—corns, calluses, bunions, pain in the balls of your feet, toe cramps, fallen arches, burning nerve endings, painful ankles, back aches, or just generally sore, aching feet and legs – *my Feathersprings are guaranteed to end your foot pain or you don't pay a penny.*

"But don't just take my word for it: Experience for yourself the immediate relief and renewed energy that Feathersprings provide. Send for your FREE kit today on our no risk, 60-day trial offer!"

Visit our web site at: www.featherspring.com

Please send FREE INFORMATION KIT!

FEATHERSPRING INTERNATIONAL, INC.
712 N. 34th Street, Dept. OF016
Seattle, WA 98103-8881

Name _____

Address _____

City _____ State ____ Zip _____

Look for a **LARGE PINK ENVELOPE** containing all the details. No obligation. No salesperson will call.

The Old Farmer's Almanac

Established in 1792 and published every year thereafter

ROBERT B. THOMAS (1766–1846), *Founder*

YANKEE PUBLISHING INC.

EDITORIAL AND PUBLISHING OFFICES
P.O. Box 520, 1121 Main Street, Dublin, NH 03444
Phone: 603-563-8111 • Fax: 603-563-8252

EDITOR *(13th since 1792)*: Janice Stillman
ART DIRECTOR: Margo Letourneau
SENIOR EDITOR: Mare-Anne Jarvela
COPY EDITOR: Jack Burnett
SENIOR ASSOCIATE EDITOR: Heidi Stonehill
RESEARCH EDITOR: Martie Majoros
ASSISTANT EDITOR: Sarah Perreault
WEATHER GRAPHICS AND CONSULTATION:
AccuWeather, Inc.

PRODUCTION DIRECTOR: Susan Gross
PRODUCTION MANAGER: David Ziarnowski
SENIOR PRODUCTION ARTISTS: Lucille Rines,
Rachel Kipka, Nathaniel Stout

WEB SITE: ALMANAC.COM
CREATIVE DIRECTOR: Stephen O. Muskie
DESIGN COORDINATOR: Lisa Traffie
PROGRAMMER: Peter Rukavina

CONTACT US

We welcome your questions and comments about articles in and topics for this Almanac. Mail all editorial correspondence to Editor, The Old Farmer's Almanac, P.O. Box 520, Dublin, NH 03444-0520; fax us at 603-563-8252; or send e-mail to us at almanac@ yankeepub.com. *The Old Farmer's Almanac* can not accept responsibility for unsolicited manuscripts and will not acknowledge any hard-copy queries or manuscripts that do not include a stamped and addressed return envelope.

Thank you for buying this Almanac!
We hope you find it new, useful, and entertaining.
Thanks, too, to everyone who had a hand in it,
including advertisers, distributors, printers, and
sales and delivery people.

OUR CONTRIBUTORS

Bob Berman, our astronomy editor, is the director of Overlook Observatory in Woodstock and Storm King Observatory in Cornwall, both in New York. In 1976, he founded the Catskill Astronomical Society. Bob will go a long way for a good look at the sky: He has led many aurora and eclipse expeditions, venturing as far as the Arctic and Antarctic.

Castle Freeman Jr., who lives in southern Vermont, has been writing the Almanac's "Farmer's Calendar" essays for more than 20 years. The essays come out of his longtime interest in wildlife and the outdoors, gardening, history, and the life of rural New England. His most recent book is *My Life and Adventures* (St. Martin's Press, 2002).

George Greenstein, Ph.D., who has been the Almanac's astronomer for more than 25 years, is the Sidney Dillon Professor of Astronomy at Amherst College in Amherst, Massachusetts. His research has centered on cosmology, pulsars, and other areas of theoretical astrophysics, and on the mysteries of quantum mechanics. He has written three books and many magazine articles on science for the general public.

Celeste Longacre, our astrologer, often refers to astrology as "the world's second-oldest profession." A New Hampshire native, she has been a practicing astrologer for more than 25 years: "It is a study of timing, and timing is everything." Her book, *Love Signs* (Sweet Fern Publications, 1999), is available on her Web site, www.yourlovesigns.com.

Michael Steinberg, our meteorologist, has been forecasting weather for the Almanac since 1996. In addition to having college degrees in atmospheric science and meteorology, he brings a lifetime of experience to the task: He began making weather predictions when he attended the only high school in the world with weather Teletypes and radar.

THE 2006 EDITION OF

The Old Farmer's Almanac
Established in 1792 and published every year thereafter

ROBERT B. THOMAS (1766–1846), *Founder*

YANKEE PUBLISHING INC.
P.O. Box 520, 1121 Main Street, Dublin, NH 03444
Phone: 603-563-8111 • Fax: 603-563-8252

GROUP PUBLISHER: John Pierce
PUBLISHER *(23rd since 1792):* Sherin Wight
EDITOR IN CHIEF: Judson D. Hale Sr.
DIRECT RETAIL SALES MANAGER: Cindy Schlosser
DIRECT RETAIL SALES ASSISTANT: Stacey Korpi

ADVERTISING
33 Union St., Boston, MA 02108

FOR ADVERTISING RATES AND INFORMATION
800-736-1100 • Almanac.com/advertising

ACCOUNT MANAGERS: John Ewald, Ryan Garvey
Direct Response: Steve Hall, Judy Glock
ADVERTISING SERVICES MANAGER:
Santina Tarasi-Marquiis
PRODUCTION ARTIST: Janet Calhoun

ADDITIONAL ADVERTISING REPRESENTATION
CLASSIFIED: Gallagher Group • 203-263-7171
Robert Bernbach • 914-769-0051

FOR RETAIL SALES
Contact Cindy Schlosser, 800-729-9265, ext. 126,
or Stacey Korpi, ext. 160.

The Old Farmer's Almanac publications are available at special discounts for bulk purchases for sales promotions or premiums. Contact MeadWestvaco, 800-333-1125.

SUBSCRIBE TO THIS ALMANAC
Subscription: 3 years, $15 (plus $4.95 s/h)
Call 800-288-4284 to subscribe.

Jamie Trowbridge, *President;* Judson D. Hale Sr., John Pierce, *Senior Vice Presidents;* Jody Bugbee, Judson D. Hale Jr., Sherin Wight, *Vice Presidents.*

To Patrons

An Almanac for the Next Generation

Dear Readers,

We have such big news that we would like to invite you all to gather together with us under a big tent for an all-expenses-paid, days-long celebration befitting the historic "first" announcement that follows. Circumstances of time and distance prohibit us from doing that, but we *would* if we *could*—and that's the spirit in which we share this:

The Old Farmer's Almanac, the oldest continuously published periodical in North America, just got younger! Please join us in welcoming the newest member of our family of publications, *The Old Farmer's Almanac for Kids.*

Over the years, many of you, now parents and grandparents, have told us that you "grew up with" *The Old Farmer's Almanac.* Thinking back on those days and sharing those memories bring a smile to your face

(and ours)—and are what inspired us to bring this new publication to life.

The Old Farmer's Almanac for Kids was developed with children ages 8 and up in mind, but it is guaranteed to satisfy the young at heart of any age. Its 192 full-color, ad-free, undated pages are chock full of amaz-

ing stories, fun activities, wacky tales, and fascinating facts relating to many of the topics in the "adult" edition—weather, nature, astronomy, history, farming, gardening, sports, health, and a whole lot more. The softcover book, just slightly larger than the traditional Almanac, is available in bookstores and larger retail stores, as well as on our Web site, Almanac.com. **(continued)**

Members of the staff of The Old Farmer's Almanac

Match these faces with their names at Almanac.com/staff.   **2006**

Why wait ten months?

Now you can have rich, dark compost _in just 14 days!_

With the amazing ComposTumbler, you'll have bushels of crumbly, ready-to-use compost — _in just 14 days!_ (And, in the ten months it takes to make compost the old way, your ComposTumbler can produce _hundreds of pounds_ of rich food for your garden!)

Say good-bye to that messy, open compost pile (and to the flies, pests, and odors that come along with it!) Bid a happy farewell to the strain of trying to turn over heavy, wet piles with a pitchfork.

Compost the Better Way

Compost-making with the ComposTumbler is neat, quick and easy!

Gather up leaves, old weeds, kitchen scraps, lawn clippings, etc. and toss them into the roomy 18-bushel drum. Then, once each day, give the ComposTumbler's _gear-driven_ handle a few easy spins.

The ComposTumbler's Magic

Inside the ComposTumbler, carefully positioned mixing fins blend materials, pushing fresh mixture to the core where the temperatures are the hottest (up to 160°) and the composting bacteria most active.

After just 14 days, open the door, and you'll find an abundance of dark, sweet-smelling "garden gold" — ready to enrich and feed your garden!

NEW SMALLER SIZE!

Now there are 2 sizes. The 18-bushel original ComposTumbler and the NEW 9.5-bushel Compact ComposTumbler. Try either size risk-free for 30 days!

See for yourself! Try the ComposTumbler risk-free with our 30-Day Home Trial!

Call Toll-Free 1-800-880-2345

NOW ON SALE— SAVE UP TO $115!

ComposTumbler®

The choice of more than 250,000 gardeners

☐ YES! Please rush FREE information on the ComposTumbler, including special savings and 30-Day Home Trial.

Name _____

Address _____

City _____

State _____ ZIP _____

MAIL TO:
ComposTumbler
30 Wright Ave., **Dept. 42016C**
Lititz (Lancaster Co.), PA 17543

© 2005 PBM Group

Speaking of Web sites, to complement and expand on the contents of the Almanac for Kids, we have created a companion site, Almanac4kids.com. It is loaded with special features, daily fun facts, and activities, as well as a *free* ten-chapter Activity Guide, which has dozens of ideas designed to help your kids and you—individually, with friends, and as a family—make the most of the Almanac for Kids. (Teachers, you'll love the Web site and activity guide, too.) Take a look, try it out, and tell us what you think at Almanac.com/feedback.

Of course, that's not all that's new. *The 2006 Old Farmer's Almanac* is the 214th consecutive edition. Back by popular demand (and near the front!) are the November and December calendar pages from the prior year. Also, we report on the accuracy of last year's winter weather forecasts and identify a few of the factors that influenced the prevailing conditions (see page 196).

By the way, you *are* invited to drop in and say hello any time you're in the neighborhood. We'll be here, celebrating the first and latest Almanacs (and preparing the next ones), 'til the cows come home.   J. S., June 2005

However, it is by our works and not our words that we would be judged. These, we hope, will sustain us in the humble though proud station we have so long held in the name of

Your obedient servant,

Astronomical Glossary

Aphelion (Aph.): The point in a planet's orbit that is farthest from the Sun.

Apogee (Apo.): The point in the Moon's orbit that is farthest from Earth.

Celestial Equator (Eq.): The imaginary circle around the celestial sphere that can be thought of as the plane of Earth's equator projected out onto the sphere.

Celestial Sphere: An imaginary sphere projected into space that represents the entire sky, with an observer on Earth at its center. All celestial bodies other than Earth are imagined as being on its inside surface.

Conjunction: The time at which two or more celestial bodies appear closest in the sky. (Actual dates for conjunctions are given in the **Right-Hand Calendar Pages, 97–123;** the best times to view closely aligned bodies are given in the **SKY WATCH** section of the **Left-Hand Calendar Pages, 96–122.**) **Inferior (Inf.):** Mercury or Venus is between the Sun and Earth. **Superior (Sup.):** The Sun is between a planet and Earth.

Declination: The celestial latitude of an object in the sky, measured in degrees north or south of the celestial equator; analogous to latitude on Earth. The Almanac gives the Sun's declination at noon.

Dominical Letter: A letter from A to G, denoting Sundays in the ecclesiastical calendar for a given year, determined by the date on which the first Sunday falls. If it falls on January 1, the letter (for the year) is A; if it falls on January 2, the letter is B; and so on.

Eclipse, Lunar: The full Moon enters the shadow of Earth, which cuts off all or part of the sunlight reflected off the Moon. **Total:** The Moon passes completely through the **umbra** (central dark part) of Earth's shadow. **Partial:** Only part of the Moon passes through the umbra. **Penumbral:** The Moon passes through only the **penumbra** (area of partial darkness surrounding the umbra). **(See page 78 for more eclipse information.)**

Eclipse, Solar: Earth enters the shadow of the new Moon, which cuts off all or part of the Sun's light. **Total:** Earth passes through the umbra (central dark part) of the Moon's shadow, resulting in totality for observers within a narrow band on Earth. **Annular:** The Moon appears silhouetted against the Sun, with a ring of sunlight showing around it. **Partial:** The Moon blocks only part of the Sun.

Ecliptic: The apparent annual path of the Sun around the celestial sphere. The plane of the ecliptic is tipped $23\frac{1}{2}°$ from the celestial equator.

Elongation: The difference in degrees between the celestial longitudes of a planet and the Sun. **Greatest Elongation (Gr. Elong.):** The greatest apparent distance of a planet from the Sun, as seen from Earth.

Epact: A number from 1 to 30 that indicates the Moon's age on January 1 at Greenwich, England; used for determining the date of Easter.

Equinox: When the Sun crosses the celestial equator. This occurs two times each year: **Vernal** around March 21 and **Autumnal** around September 23.

Evening Star: A planet that is above the western horizon at sunset and less than 180° east of the Sun in right ascension.

Golden Number: A number in the 19-year cycle of the Moon, used for determining the date of Easter. (Approximately every 19 years, the Moon's phases occur on the same dates.) Add 1 to any given year and divide by 19; the remainder is the Golden Number. If there is no remainder, the Golden Number is 19.

Julian Period: A period of 7,980 years beginning January 1, 4713 B.C. Devised in 1583 by Joseph Scaliger, it provides a chronological basis for the study of ancient history. To find the Julian year, add 4,713 to any year.

Midnight: Astronomical midnight is the time when the Sun is opposite its highest point in the sky (noon). Midnight is neither A.M. nor P.M., although 12-hour digital clocks typically display midnight as 12:00 A.M. On a 24-hour time cycle, 00:00, rather than 24:00, usually indicates midnight.

Moon on Equator: The Moon is on the celestial equator.

Moon Rides High/Runs Low: The Moon is highest above or farthest below the celestial equator.

Moonrise/Moonset: When the Moon rises above/sets below the horizon.

Moon's Phases: The changing appearance of the Moon, caused by the different angles at which it is illuminated by the Sun. **First Quarter:** Right half (in Northern Hemisphere) of the Moon is illuminated. **Full:** The Sun and the Moon are in opposition; the entire disk of the Moon is illuminated. **Last Quarter:** Left half (in Northern Hemisphere) of the Moon is illuminated. **New:** The Sun and the Moon are in conjunction; the entire disk of the Moon is darkened.

Moon's Place, Astronomical: The actual position of the Moon within the constellations on the celestial sphere. **Astrological:** The astrological position of the Moon within the zodiac according to calculations made more than 2,000 years ago. Because of precession of the equinoxes and other factors, this is not the Moon's actual position in the sky.

Morning Star: A planet that is above the eastern horizon at sunrise and less than 180° west of the Sun in right ascension.

Node: Either of the two points where a celestial body's orbit intersects the ecliptic. **Ascending:** When the body is moving from south to north of the ecliptic. **Descending:** When the body is moving from north to south of the ecliptic.

Occultation (Occn.): When the Moon or a planet eclipses a star or planet.

Opposition: The Moon or a planet appears on the opposite side of the sky from the Sun (elongation 180°).

Perigee (Perig.): The point in the Moon's orbit that is closest to Earth.

Perihelion (Perih.): The point in a planet's orbit that is closest to the Sun.

Precession: The slowly changing position of the stars and equinoxes in the sky resulting from variations in the orientation of Earth's axis.

Right Ascension (R.A.): The celestial longitude of an object in the sky, measured eastward along the celestial equator in hours of time from the vernal equinox; analogous to longitude on Earth.

Roman Indiction: A number within a 15-year cycle, established January 1, A.D. 313, as a fiscal term. Add 3 to any given year in the Christian era and divide by 15; the remainder is the Roman Indiction. If there is no remainder, it is 15.

Solar Cycle: In the Julian calendar, a period of 28 years, at the end of which the days of the month return to the same days of the week.

Solstice, Summer: The Sun reaches its greatest declination (23½°) north of the celestial equator, around June 21. **Winter:** The Sun reaches its greatest declination (23½°) south of the celestial equator, around December 21.

Stationary (Stat.): The apparent halted movement of a planet against the background of the stars shortly before it appears to move backward/westward (retrograde motion) or forward/eastward (direct motion).

Sun Fast/Slow: When a sundial reading is ahead of (fast) or behind (slow) clock time.

Sunrise/Sunset: The visible rising and setting of the upper edge of the Sun's disk across the unobstructed horizon of an observer whose eyes are 15 feet above ground level. □ □

We're looking for people to—

Write Children's Books

By Kristi Holl

I f you've ever dreamed of writing for children, here's your chance to test that dream. . . and find out if you have the aptitude to make it a reality. If you do, we'll teach you how to crack one of today's most rewarding markets for new writers.

The $2 billion children's market

The tremendous recent success of children's books has made the general public aware of what we've known for years: There's a huge market out there. And there's a growing need for new writers trained to create the nearly $2 billion of children's books purchased every year. . . plus the stories and articles needed by more than 600 publishers of magazines for and about children and teenagers.

Who are these needed writers? They're ordinary people like you and me.

"But am I good enough?"

I was once where you may be now. My occasional thoughts of writing had been pushed down by self-doubt, and I didn't know where to turn for help. Then, on an impulse, I sent for the Institute's free writing aptitude test and it turned out to be the spark I needed. I took their course and my wonderful author-instructor helped me to discover, step-by-step, that my everyday life—probably not much different from yours—was an endless creative resource for my writing!

The promise that paid off

The Institute made the same promise to me that they'll make to you, if you demonstrate basic writing aptitude: *You will complete at least one manuscript suitable to submit to editors by the time you finish the course.*

I really didn't expect to be pub-lished before I finished the course, but I was. I sold three stories. And I soon discovered that that was not unusual at the Institute. Now, as a graduate and a nationally published author of 24 children's books, and more than 180 stories and articles, I'm teaching: I'm passing along what I've learned to would-be writers like you.

One-on-one training with your own instructor

My fellow instructors—all of them pro-fessional writers or editors—work with their students the same way I work

Kristi Holl, a graduate of our course, has published 24 books and more than 180 stories and articles. She is now an instructor at the Institute.

...th mine: When you've completed an ssignment on your own schedule, at your own pace, you send it to me. I read it and reread it to make sure I get everything out of it that you've put into it. Then I edit it line-by-line and send you a detailed letter explaining my edits. I point out your strengths and show you how to shore up your weaknesses. Between your pushing and my pulling, you learn how to write—and how to market what you write.

I am the living proof

What I got from my instructor at the Institute changed me from a "wannabe" into a nationally published writer. While there's no guarantee that every student will have the same success, we're showered with letters like these from current and former students.

"Since graduating from your course," says Heather Klassen, Edmonds, WA, "I've sold 125 stories to magazines for children and teenagers."

"Before this, I didn't know if my work was typical or bland, or if there was even a spark of life in it," writes Kate Spanks, Maple Ridge, BC. "I now have over 30 articles published. . . .."

". . .a little bird. . .has just been given freedom"

This course has helped me more than I can say," says Jody Drueding, Boston, MA. "It's as if a little bird that was locked up inside of me has just been given the freedom of the garden."

". . .I was attracted by the fact that you require an aptitude test," says Nikki Arko, Raton, NM. "Other schools sign you up as long as you have the money to pay, regardless of talent or potential."

"I'd take the course again in a heartbeat!"

"My most recent success has been the publication of the novel I started for my last Institute assignment," writes Jennifer Jones, Homer, NY. "Thank you for giv-

ing me the life I longed for."

"I'd take the course again in a heartbeat!", says Tonya Tingey, Woodruff, UT. "It made my dream a reality,"

Don't let your dream die— send for your free test today!

If life as a successful writer is your dream, here's your chance to test that dream. We've developed a revealing aptitude test based on our 36 years of experience. Just fill out and mail the coupon below to receive your free test and a 32-page introduction to our course, *Writing for Children and Teenagers,* and 80 of our instructors. *There is no oblig- ation.*

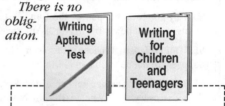

Get both free

Institute of Children's Literature
93 Long Ridge Road
West Redding, CT 06896-0812

Yes, please send me your free Writing Aptitude Test and illustrated brochure. I understand I'm under no obligation, and no salesperson will visit me.

Please circle one and print name clearly:
Mr.   Mrs.   Ms.   Miss   F5150

_____
Name

_____
Street

_____
City

_____
State   Zip

Recommended for college credits by the Connecticut Board for State Academic Awards and approved by the Connecticut Commissioner of Higher Education.

COPYRIGHT © ICL 2005, A DIVISION OF THE INSTITUTE, INC.

Eclipses

■ There will be four eclipses in 2006, two of the Sun and two of the Moon. Solar eclipses are visible only in certain areas and require eye protection to be viewed safely. Lunar eclipses are technically visible from the entire night side of Earth, but during a penumbral eclipse, the dimming of the Moon's illumination is slight.

MARCH 14: penumbral eclipse of the Moon. The eclipse will be under way as the Moon rises. The end of the eclipse will be visible throughout North America, except in Alaska and the extreme western parts of Canada and the United States. The Moon will enter the penumbra at 4:21 P.M. EST (1:21 P.M. PST) and will leave the penumbra at 9:13 P.M. EST (6:13 P.M. PST).

MARCH 29: total eclipse of the Sun. This eclipse will not be visible in North America.

SEPTEMBER 7: partial eclipse of the Moon. This eclipse will not be visible in North America.

SEPTEMBER 22: annular eclipse of the Sun. This eclipse will not be visible in North America.

Full-Moon Dates (Eastern Time)				
	2006	2007	2008	2009	2010
Jan.	14	3	22	10	30
Feb.	12	2	20	9	28
Mar.	14	3	21	10	29
Apr.	13	2	20	9	28
May	13	2 & 31	19	9	27
June	11	30	18	7	26
July	10	29	18	7	25
Aug.	9	28	16	5	24
Sept.	7	26	15	4	23
Oct.	6	26	14	4	22
Nov.	5	24	13	2	21
Dec.	4	23	12	2 & 31	21

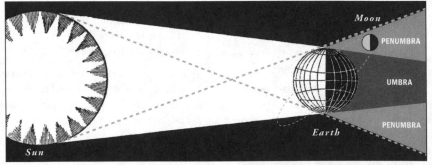

In a lunar eclipse *(above)*, the Earth is between the Sun and the Moon. The umbra is the central dark part of the shadow created during an eclipse. The penumbra is the area of partial darkness surrounding the umbra. During a penumbral lunar eclipse, the Moon passes through only the penumbra.

Total Solar Eclipse Dates, 2006–2010	
DATE	REGIONS WITH VISIBLE TOTALITY
2006 March 29	Africa, Turkey, Russia, Brazil
2008 August 1	Northern Canada, Greenland, Siberia, China
2009 July 22	India, China, central Pacific Ocean
2010 July 11	South Pacific Ocean, southern South America

Bright Stars

Transit Times

■ This table shows the time (EST or EDT) and altitude of a star as it transits the meridian (i.e., reaches its highest elevation while passing over the horizon's south point) at Boston on the dates shown. The transit time on any other date differs from that of the nearest date listed by approximately four minutes per day. To find the time of a star's transit for your location, convert its time at Boston using Key Letter C.*

| Star | Constellation | Magnitude | Time of Transit (EST/EDT) Boldface–P.M. Lightface–A.M. | | | | | | Altitude (degrees) |
			Jan. 1	Mar. 1	May 1	July 1	Sept. 1	Nov. 1	
Altair	Aquila	0.8	**12:49**	8:57	5:57	1:58	**9:50**	**4:50**	56.3
Deneb	Cygnus	1.3	**1:40**	9:48	6:48	2:48	**10:41**	**5:41**	92.8
Fomalhaut	Psc. Aus.	1.2	**3:55**	**12:03**	9:03	5:03	12:55	**7:56**	17.8
Algol	Perseus	2.2	**8:05**	**4:13**	**1:14**	9:14	5:10	12:10	88.5
Aldebaran	Taurus	0.9	**9:33**	**5:41**	**2:41**	10:41	6:37	1:38	64.1
Rigel	Orion	0.1	**10:11**	**6:19**	**3:19**	11:19	7:16	2:16	39.4
Capella	Auriga	0.1	**10:13**	**6:21**	**3:21**	11:21	7:17	2:18	93.6
Bellatrix	Orion	1.6	**10:22**	**6:30**	**3:30**	11:30	7:26	2:27	54.0
Betelgeuse	Orion	var. 0.4	**10:52**	**7:00**	**4:00**	**12:00**	7:56	2:57	55.0
Sirius	Can. Maj.	−1.4	**11:41**	**7:49**	**4:50**	**12:50**	8:46	3:46	31.0
Procyon	Can. Min.	0.4	12:39	**8:43**	**5:44**	**1:44**	9:40	4:40	52.9
Pollux	Gemini	1.2	12:45	**8:49**	**5:49**	**1:50**	9:46	4:46	75.7
Regulus	Leo	1.4	3:08	**11:12**	**8:13**	**4:13**	**12:09**	7:09	59.7
Spica	Virgo	var. 1.0	6:25	2:33	**11:29**	**7:29**	**3:25**	10:25	36.6
Arcturus	Boötes	−0.1	7:15	3:23	12:20	**8:20**	**4:16**	11:16	66.9
Antares	Scorpius	var. 0.9	9:28	5:36	2:36	**10:33**	**6:29**	**1:29**	21.3
Vega	Lyra	0	11:36	7:44	4:44	12:40	**8:36**	**3:36**	86.4

Rise and Set Times

■ To find the time of a star's rising at Boston on any date, subtract the interval shown at right from the star's transit time on that date; add the interval to find the star's setting time. To find the rising and setting times for your city, convert the Boston transit times above using the Key Letter* shown at right before applying the interval. The directions in which the stars rise and set, shown for Boston, are generally useful throughout the United States.

Deneb, Algol, Capella, and Vega are circumpolar stars—they never set but appear to circle the celestial north pole.

Star	Interval (h. m.)	Rising Key	Dir.	Setting Key	Dir.
Altair	6 36	B	EbN	E	WbN
Fomalhaut	3 59	E	SE	D	SW
Aldebaran	7 06	B	ENE	D	WNW
Rigel	5 33	D	EbS	B	WbS
Bellatrix	6 27	B	EbN	D	WbN
Betelgeuse	6 31	B	EbN	D	WbN
Sirius	5 00	D	ESE	B	WSW
Procyon	6 23	B	EbN	D	WbN
Pollux	8 01	A	NE	E	NW
Regulus	6 49	B	EbN	D	WbN
Spica	5 23	D	EbS	B	WbS
Arcturus	7 19	A	ENE	E	WNW
Antares	4 17	E	SEbE	A	SWbW

*The values of Key Letters are given in the Time Corrections table (page 237).

–Beth Krommes

The Visible Planets

■ Listed here for Boston are the times (EST/EDT) of the visible rising and setting of the planets Venus, Mars, Jupiter, and Saturn on the 1st, 11th, and 21st of each month and December 31. The approximate times of their visible rising and setting on other days can be found by interpolation. The capital letters that appear beside the times are Key Letters and are used to convert the times for other localities **(see pages 92 and 237)**. For all planet rise and set times, visit Almanac.com/astronomy.

Venus

♀ **This is a mediocre year for the cloud-covered planet.** It begins with a brief, brilliant, evening-star appearance lasting a single week, until January 7. After a January 13 inferior conjunction north of the Sun, it emerges as a low morning star of great splendor in February and March, at magnitude −4.6. It then slowly fades and never regains its early-year dazzle. Following its superior conjunction on October 27, Venus slowly emerges back into the evening sky after sunset, remaining low. Although it is visible throughout nearly all of 2006, except in autumn, it is never very high.

Jan. 1 ....**set**	**6:00** A	Apr. 1 ......rise	3:36 D	Jul. 1 ....rise	3:13 A	Oct. 1 ......rise	6:05 C
Jan. 11 ......**set**	**5:05** B	Apr. 11 ...rise	4:27 D	Jul. 11 .....rise	3:17 A	Oct. 11 ....rise	6:29 C
Jan. 21 ...rise	5:56 D	Apr. 21 ...rise	4:17 C	Jul. 21 .....rise	3:26 A	Oct. 21 ....rise	6:54 D
Feb. 1 .....rise	4:59 D	May 1 .....rise	4:05 C	Aug. 1 .....rise	3:42 A	Nov. 1 ......**set**	**4:43** B
Feb. 11 ....rise	4:27 D	May 11 ...rise	3:53 C	Aug. 11 ...rise	4:02 A	Nov. 11 .....**set**	**4:38** A
Feb. 21 ...rise	4:08 D	May 21 ...rise	3:41 B	Aug. 21 ...rise	4:24 A	Nov. 21 ....**set**	**4:37** A
Mar. 1 .....rise	3:59 D	Jun. 1 ......rise	3:30 B	Sept. 1 ....rise	4:51 B	Dec. 1 ......**set**	**4:42** A
Mar. 11 ...rise	3:51 D	Jun. 11 ...rise	3:21 B	Sept. 11 ...rise	5:16 B	Dec. 11 .....**set**	**4:53** A
Mar. 21 ...rise	3:44 D	Jun. 21 ...rise	3:15 A	Sept. 21 ...rise	5:40 B	Dec. 21 .....**set**	**5:10** A
						Dec. 31 .....**set**	**5:32** A

Mars

♂ **Things start out brilliantly for Mars, which opens the** year in Aries at magnitude −0.8. But it is fading rapidly from its great opposition of November 2005, and it continues to decline throughout 2006. It is very near the Moon on January 8 and February 5. The "red planet" is no longer impressive after April, although it does have an outstanding close conjunction with Saturn in Cancer from June 14–17. Chugging through another four constellations until arriving at its October 23 solar conjunction in Virgo, it invisibly enters the morning sky, where it stands in Ophiuchus at year's end.

Jan. 1 ....set	2:40 D	Apr. 1 ......set 12:18 E		Jul. 1 ....**set**	**10:32** D	Oct. 1 ......set	**6:42** B
Jan. 11 ......set	2:16 D	Apr. 11 .....set	1:05 E	Jul. 11 ......**set**	**10:08** D	Oct. 11 .....set	**6:18** B
Jan. 21......set	1:56 E	Apr. 21 .....set 12:49 E		Jul. 21 ......**set**	**9:44** D	Oct. 21 .....set	**5:54** B
Feb. 1 ....set	1:37 E	May 1 ......set 12:33 E		Aug. 1 ......**set**	**9:17** D	Nov. 1 .....rise	6:03 D
Feb. 11 .....set	1:22 E	May 11 ....set 12:16 E		Aug. 11 ...**set**	**8:52** D	Nov. 11 ...rise	5:59 D
Feb. 21.....set	1:08 E	May 21 .....**set 11:58** E		Aug. 21 ...**set**	**8:26** C	Nov. 21...rise	5:55 D
Mar. 1 ......set 12:57 E		Jun. 1 ......**set 11:37** E		Sept. 1 ......**set**	**7:58** C	Dec. 1 .....rise	5:52 E
Mar. 11 .....set 12:45 E		Jun. 11......**set 11:16** E		Sept. 11 ...**set**	**7:33** C	Dec. 11 ...rise	5:49 E
Mar. 21 ....set 12:32 E		Jun. 21......**set 10:54** E		Sept. 21 ....**set**	**7:07** C	Dec. 21 ...rise	5:45 E
						Dec. 31...rise	5:41 E

Boldface—P.M.; Lightface—A.M.

Find more heavenly details at Almanac.com/astronomy.

2006

Jupiter

The largest planet is best seen from April through August, when it is out at nightfall and remains up for much or all of the night. It can be viewed during its opposition on May 4 in Libra, and from the beginning of the year, when it rises a few hours before dawn, through October, when it appears as a low evening twilight object. After its conjunction with the Sun on November 21, it appears in late December as a bright star in the morning twilight.

Jan. 1	.....rise	2:38	D	Apr. 1	......**rise**	**9:02**	D	Jul. 1	........set	1:48	B
Jan. 11	....rise	2:06	D	Apr. 11	....**rise**	**9:17**	D	Jul. 11	.....set	1:09	B
Jan. 21	....rise	1:34	D	Apr. 21	...**rise**	**8:32**	D	Jul. 21	......set	12:26	B
Feb. 1	....rise	12:56	D	May 1	......**rise**	**7:47**	D	Aug. 1	......set	11:45	B
Feb. 11	....rise	12:21	D	May 11	....set	5:21	B	Aug. 11	...**set**	**11:07**	B
Feb. 21	....**rise**	**11:41**	D	May 21	....set	4:38	B	Aug. 21	....**set**	**10:31**	B
Mar. 1	......**rise**	**11:10**	D	Jun. 1	.......set	3:52	B	Sept. 1	......**set**	**9:52**	B
Mar. 11	....**rise**	**10:30**	D	Jun. 11	....set	3:10	B	Sept. 11	....**set**	**9:17**	B
Mar. 21	....**rise**	**9:49**	D	Jun. 21	....set	2:29	B	Sept. 21	....**set**	**8:42**	B

Oct. 1	.......**set**	**8:08**	B
Oct. 11	.....**set**	**7:34**	A
Oct. 21	.....**set**	**7:01**	A
Nov. 1	.......**set**	**5:24**	A
Nov. 11	....**set**	**4:52**	A
Nov. 21	.. .**set**	**4:20**	A
Dec. 1	.....rise	6:15	E
Dec. 11	...rise	5:47	E
Dec. 21	...rise	5:18	E
Dec. 31	...rise	4:49	E

Saturn

The most beautiful planet is at its best early in the year, with an opposition, in Cancer, on January 27. Its rings are well presented, and it is visible for North American observers through spring. Saturn becomes an increasingly low, early-night object by June and vanishes behind the Sun in a conjunction on August 7. In September, it reappears before dawn as a morning star, rising two hours earlier per month; by mid-December, it's up after 9:30 P.M. Saturn meets Mars on June 14–17, Venus on August 26, and the Moon on December 10.

Jan. 1	......**rise**	**6:34**	A	Apr. 1	.......set	2:54	E	Jul. 1	........**set**	**10:10**	D
Jan. 11	.....**rise**	**5:51**	A	Apr. 11	....set	3:15	E	Jul. 11	.....**set**	**9:34**	D
Jan. 21	.....**rise**	**5:07**	A	Apr. 21	....set	2:36	E	Jul. 21	.....**set**	**8:58**	D
Feb. 1	......set	6:55	E	May 1	.......set	1:58	E	Aug. 1	......**set**	**8:19**	D
Feb. 11	....set	6:13	E	May 11	....set	1:20	E	Aug. 11	...rise	5:29	A
Feb. 21	....set	5:32	E	May 21	....set	12:39	E	Aug. 21	...rise	4:57	A
Mar. 1	......set	4:59	E	Jun. 1	........**set**	**11:59**	E	Sept. 1	....rise	4:20	A
Mar. 11	....set	4:18	E	Jun. 11	......**set**	**11:22**	E	Sept. 11	....rise	3:47	B
Mar. 21	...set	3:38	E	Jun. 21	......**set**	**10:46**	E	Sept. 21	...rise	3:14	B

Oct. 1	......rise	2:40	B
Oct. 11	....rise	2:06	B
Oct. 21	....rise	1:31	B
Nov. 1	.....**rise**	**11:48**	B
Nov. 11	....**rise**	**11:11**	B
Nov. 21	...**rise**	**10:33**	B
Dec. 1	......**rise**	**9:55**	B
Dec. 11	....**rise**	**9:15**	B
Dec. 21	....**rise**	**8:35**	B
Dec. 31	....**rise**	**7:54**	B

Mercury

The best month to view Mercury is February. As an evening star in the west, it is at its brightest from the 6th to the 20th. On the 14th, it is in conjunction with Uranus. Mercury also makes a showing in June, especially during the month's first half, and when it appears with the Moon, Mars, and Saturn on the 27th. The planet's best predawn sightings are in early August and late November. It will make headlines on November 8 when it transits the Sun, and it will be very close to Jupiter on December 10.

DO NOT CONFUSE ■ *Mars and Saturn, June 14 to 17: Mars is reddish and much less bright.* ■ *Predawn Mercury and Venus, August 1 to 18: Venus is higher and much brighter.* ■ *Mercury with a sunspot, November 8: Only Mercury changes position.* ■ *Mercury, Mars, and Jupiter, December 9: Jupiter is the brightest, while Mars is the dimmest.* ■ *Jupiter and Mercury, December 10: Jupiter is brighter and whiter.*

The Twilight Zone

How to determine the length of twilight and the times of dawn and dark.

■ Twilight is the time preceding sunrise and again following sunset, when the sky is partially illuminated. The three ranges of twilight are defined according to the Sun's position below the horizon. Civil twilight occurs when the Sun is between the horizon and 6 degrees below the horizon (visually, the horizon is clearly defined). Nautical twilight occurs when the Sun is between 6 and 12 degrees below the horizon (the horizon is indistinct). Astronomical twilight occurs when the Sun is between 12 and 18 degrees below the horizon (sky illumination is imperceptible). When the Sun is at 18 degrees (dawn or dark) or below, there is no illumination.

LENGTH OF TWILIGHT (hours and minutes)

LATITUDE	Jan. 1 to Apr. 10	Apr. 11 to May 2	May 3 to May 14	May 15 to May 25	May 26 to July 22	July 23 to Aug. 3	Aug. 4 to Aug. 14	Aug. 15 to Sept. 5	Sept. 6 to Dec. 31
25°N to 30°N	1 20	1 23	1 26	1 29	1 32	1 29	1 26	1 23	1 20
31°N to 36°N	1 26	1 28	1 34	1 38	1 43	1 38	1 34	1 28	1 26
37°N to 42°N	1 33	1 39	1 47	1 52	1 59	1 52	1 47	1 39	1 33
43°N to 47°N	1 42	1 51	2 02	2 13	2 27	2 13	2 02	1 51	1 42
48°N to 49°N	1 50	2 04	2 22	2 42	—	2 42	2 22	2 04	1 50

TO DETERMINE THE LENGTH OF TWILIGHT: The length of twilight changes with latitude and the time of year and is independent of time zones. Use the **Time Corrections** table, **page 237,** to find the latitude of your city or the city nearest you. Use that figure in the chart above with the appropriate date to calculate the length of twilight in your area.

TO DETERMINE WHEN DAWN OR DARK WILL OCCUR: Calculate the sunrise/sunset times for your locality, using the instructions in **How to Use This Almanac, page 92.** Subtract the length of twilight from the time of sunrise to determine when dawn breaks. Add the length of twilight to the time of sunset to determine when dark descends.

E X A M P L E :

Boston, Mass. (latitude 42°22')

Sunrise, August 1	5:37 A.M. EDT
Length of twilight	−1 52
Dawn breaks	3:45 A.M.
Sunset, August 1	8:04 P.M. EDT
Length of twilight	+1 52
Dark descends	9:56 P.M.

Principal Meteor Showers

SHOWER	BEST VIEWING	POINT OF ORIGIN	DATE OF MAXIMUM*	PEAK RATE (/HR.)**	ASSOCIATED COMET
Quadrantid	Predawn	N	Jan. 4	80	—
Lyrid	Predawn	S	Apr. 22	12	Thatcher
Eta Aquarid	Predawn	SE	May 4	20	Halley
Delta Aquarid	Predawn	S	July 30	10	—
Perseid	Predawn	NE	Aug. 11–13	75	Swift-Tuttle
Draconid	Late evening	NW	Oct. 9	6	Giacobini-Zinner
Orionid	Predawn	S	Oct. 21–22	25	Halley
Taurid	Late evening	S	Nov. 9	6	Encke
Leonid	Predawn	S	Nov. 18	20	Tempel-Tuttle
Andromedid	Late evening	S	Nov. 25–27	5	Biela
Geminid	All night	NE	Dec. 13–14	65	—
Ursid	Predawn	N	Dec. 22	12	Tuttle

*May vary by one or two days in either direction.   **Approximate.

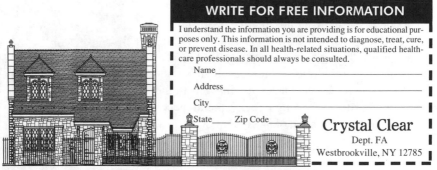

It sounds like science fiction: Scientists launch a spacecraft on a path to meet a comet, gather samples of it, and return them to Earth. If the mission is successful, the scientists will solve more of the mysteries of our universe. • by Bob Berman

Above: Halley's comet, due to return to view in 2061. Below: An artist's depiction of Comet Wild-2 as would have been seen from *Stardust* during a flyby on January 2, 2004.

That's exactly what will happen if all goes according to plan. The Stardust Mission blasted off from the Cape Canaveral Air Station on February 7, 1999, and on January 2, 2004, it successfully swiped dust from Comet Wild-2 (pronounced "vilt"). On January 15, 2006, the *Stardust* spacecraft is scheduled to return to

COMET WATCH!

Earth, parachuting its precious cargo into Utah to eager researchers who will finally get to see what our neighborhood's primordial matter was like before the Sun and planets formed from it. Wild, indeed.

But hold on. Why bother going millions of miles? Why not just examine meteorites?

METEORS VS. METEORITES

■ A meteor is an object in the act of traveling.

■ A meteorite is a stone that has already landed.

Here's why. Most meteors are just bits of comets, or comet debris (fragile stones and ices), so skimpy that they burn to dust or vapor before reaching Earth. They rain down through our atmosphere all the time: Meteors are as common as lightning; ten strike our atmosphere every second. Those that make it to the ground—meteorites—are tough, rocky, metal pieces of asteroids, moons, or even planets, but not comets.

Unlike meteors, comets rarely strike Earth. So there's only one way to obtain comet samples: Make the long trip and meet one in space.

THE VIEW FROM HERE

For amateur astronomers, comets offer a wide range of visual experiences: faint telescope targets; binocular objects; faint to medium-faint naked-eye objects with or without tails; and great comets with bright tails. Most years, not even one comet appears to the naked eye. Nonetheless, when one does appear, you'll want to know what you're looking at.

Comets are chunks of dusty ice of varying size: A big comet might be 20 miles across, while the smallest ones are so tiny—beach ball–size—that they go totally undetected. When a comet comes close enough

LOOK, UP IN THE SKY . . .

■ It's a comet! No, it's a meteor!

Wait a minute. Which is it?

A meteor streaks and vanishes. A comet hovers, seemingly motionless, against the background stars, when in fact it is zooming along at several miles per second. Every night, a comet is in a slightly different spot.

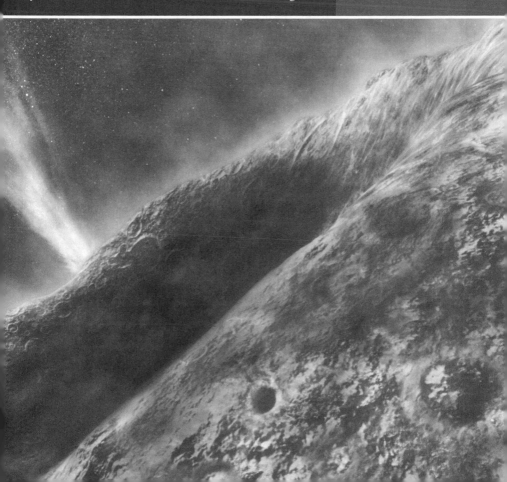

Comets are like cats. They have tails, and they do precisely what they want.

–David H. Levy, codiscoverer of Comet Shoemaker-Levy 9 (b. 1948)

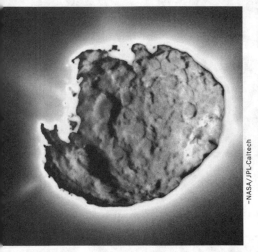

In this composite image taken by *Stardust*, Wild-2 displays an intensely active surface.

—NASA/JPL-Caltech

to the Sun (closer than the orbit of Mars or so), its outer ice turns to vapor and any trapped dust is released. The water vapor and the released dust spread out to form a long tail that always points away from the Sun (because the Sun's "wind" of fast-moving subatomic particles is pushing against it). This tail is a comet's most spectacular feature.

There are two kinds of comets. Short-period comets are predictable. They have relatively short orbits, which they complete in less than a century. Long-period comets have longer orbits around the Sun, so they typically come near Earth only every 20,000 to 30,000 years. Long-period comets are detected a few months to a year or so before their orbit brings them close enough to the Sun to develop a tail. They're composed of pris-

tine materials, so once they fire up, they tend to be much brighter and more spectacular than short-period ones.

The most predictable aspect of comets is their unpredictability. Once a comet is detected, astronomers can precisely calculate where in the sky it will be visible from night to night, but not how its ices will sublimate and therefore how bright it will be. Comets are renowned for fooling astronomers. One of the most famous misjudgments occurred in late 1973, when the editors of *TIME* announced Comet Kohoutek as "the comet of the century" on the cover. Kohoutek turned out to be a dud. Later, in January 2004, there were high hopes for Comet Machholz, but it neither developed a striking tail nor attained eye-catching brightness. On the other hand, West, in 1976, turned out to be nothing short of spectacular, much to even many experts' surprise. Some long-period comets, such as Neat and Linear, which appeared in 2004, were faintly visible to the naked eye, but only for observers under dark, rural skies.

Despite comets' capriciousness, each year usually brings a faint, smudgy, often tailless one (many comets have scant or visibly absent tails; Machholz is a good example of this) within view of backyard telescopes, and every other year, on average, brings one or two that can be observed through binoculars.

About a dozen new comets are discovered every year, but few are impressive. You can expect to see only one truly

ON, COMET!
ON, STARDUST!
Keep an eye on the sky for comets and on the ground for the return of the Stardust Mission. Go to **Almanac.com/extras.**

spectacular, or "great," comet about every 15 years, on average, and such an apparition is almost always unpredicted. ("Great" is the term used to describe any comet brilliant enough to be easily visible to the naked eye, even in light-polluted cities.) Surveys show that people rate a great comet as one of the top three celestial spectacles, behind only total solar eclipses and grand auroral displays. The best comets of the last 30 years that everyone could potentially see with the naked eye were Hale-Bopp in 1997, Hyakutake in 1996 (which had an easily seen body but faint tail), and West in 1976 (cloudy conditions made for poor visibility).

All of the great comets are long-period, except for Halley, which is the brightest and most famous short-period one. Its approximately 76-year orbit brought it here for a wonderful visit in 1910 and a mediocre return in the fall of 1985 and spring of 1986 (Earth was in the wrong part of its orbit). Halley's next opportunities for viewing will be in 2061, when it will be very large and perfectly placed for us in the Northern Hemisphere. In 2137, it will—amazingly—span half the sky, making the best appearance in two millennia!

Too soon to plan for 2061? Simply wait for the next major long-period comet. These provide the greatest spectacles anyway. In 1910, Halley was actually upstaged by a much brighter long-period comet, the so-called great January comet (which is not due to return for tens of thousands of years).

A comet is the only celestial object that bears the name of its discoverer (usually an extremely patient amateur). The presence or absence of a tail—and how bright the tail appears—determine whether the lucky astronomer gains worldwide fame. Depending on what happens in January 2006, the same may be said of the researchers involved in the Stardust Mission.

THE CRASH FACTOR

■ Approaching comets often inspire rumors of a collision with Earth. Such popular misconceptions are a reliable feature of bright comets, but nobody seems to remember that none of the doomsday predictions occurred the last time one came around. A comet is a low-mass object that can not affect a planet unless it actually collides with it. (How much damage could a comet do? A very tiny one, such as the object that struck Tunguska, Siberia, in 1908, could flatten everything for 50 miles in all directions. A big one could wipe out 99 percent of the life forms on Earth and change the course of our planet's history.) Tiny, unseen comets hit our atmosphere so often—each releasing its water into our atmosphere—that an inch of depth is added to Earth's oceans every 20,000 years. Some scientists believe that this explains how our planet got its water in the first place, and that the comets' organic materials may have even delivered the building blocks of life. □ □

Bob Berman is the Almanac's astronomy editor. His most recent book is *Strange Universe* (Henry Holt, 2003).

New lure's catch rate may be too high for some tournaments.

Out-fishes other bait 19 to 4 in one contest.

Uses aerospace technology to mimic a real fish.

Swims with its tail.

ORLANDO, FL— A small company in Connecticut has developed a new lure that mimics the motion of a real fish so realistically eight professionals couldn't tell the difference between it and a live shad when it "swam" toward them on retrieval. The design eliminates wobbling, angled swimming and other unnatural motions that problem other hard bait lures. It swims upright and appears to propel itself with its tail.

New lure swims like a real fish--nearly triples catch in Florida contest.

Curiously, the company may have designed it too well. Tournament fishermen who have used it said it's possible officials will not allow it in contests where live bait is prohibited. They claim it swims more realistically than anything they have ever seen. If so, that would hurt the company's promotional efforts. Winning tournaments is an important part of marketing a new lure.

Fish would probably prefer to see it restricted. I watched eight veteran fishermen test the new lure (called The KickTail®) on a lake outside Orlando FL for about four hours. Four used the KickTail and four used a combination of their favorite lures and shiners (live bait). The four using the KickTail caught 41 fish versus 14 for the other four. In one boat the KickTail won 19 to 4. The KickTail also caught bigger fish, which suggests it triggers larger, less aggressive fish to strike.

The KickTail's magic comes from a patented technology that breaks the tail into five segments. As water rushes by on retrieval, a little-known principle called aeronautical flutter causes the tail to wag left and right, as if the lure were propelling itself with its tail. Unlike other hard baits, the head remains stationary—only the tail wags. A company spokesman told me this.

"Marine biologists will tell you that the more a lure swims like a real fish, the more fish it will catch. Well, the only live thing the KickTail doesn't do is breathe. It's always swimming wild and free. Fish can't stand it. We've seen fish that have just eaten go for the KickTail. It's like having another potato chip."

Whether you fish for fun or profit, if you want a nearly 3 to 1 advantage, I would order now before the KickTail becomes known. The company even guarantees a refund, if you don't catch more fish and return the lures within 30 days. There are three versions: a floater, a diver and a "dying shad" with a weed guard. Each lure costs $9.95 and you must order at least two. There is also a "Super 10-Pack" with additional colors for only $79.95, a savings of almost $20.00. S/h is only $6.00 no matter how many you order.

To order call **1-800-873-4415** or click **www.ngcsports.com** anytime of any day or send a check or M.O. (or cc number and exp. date) to NGC Sports **(Dept. KT-940)**, 60 Church Street, Yalesville, CT 06492. CT orders add sales tax. The KickTail is four inches long and works in salt and fresh water.

KTS-5   © NGC Worldwide, Inc. 2006   **Dept. KT-940**

"Grape Juice Can Heal WHAT?"

(By Frank K. Wood)

If you'd like to prevent — and even help defeat — many common ailments, including heart disease, type 2 diabetes, and arthritis with delicious foods you already love to eat, you need *Unleash the Inner Healing Power of Foods,* an informative new book just released to the public by FC&A Medical Publishing in Peachtree City, Georgia.

Find out which foods are loaded with the vitamins, minerals, and nutrients that scientists say prevent aging and disease — foods like olive oil (helps prevent wrinkles and lowers blood pressure), green tea (eases ulcer pain and strengthens bones) ... even garlic (enhances memory and helps prevent strokes). Get this book and start eating your way to better health today!

The authors provide many health tips with full explanations.

► Amazing but true! Just 2 servings a week fight depression, heart attack, stroke, diabetes, and cancer!

► Need to shed fat? No sweat — drink this all-natural, nutrient-loaded beverage from your supermarket 3 times a day! From a study by a Yale University researcher.

► Everybody knows what parsley is, but you need to know what wonders it can do for your health.

► This one substance fights type 2 diabetes, heart disease, stroke, impotence, and cancer.

► A French study has found that eating these two fruits can help prevent and reverse hardening of the arteries.

► Is this the last diet plan you'll ever need? In less than one month, women and men on this delicious and nutritious plan lost weight without dieting, reduced their cholesterol 21%, improved their sense of well-being, felt less anxiety, fear, and depression, reduced chest pain by 91%, felt renewed energy, and required much less sleep!

► An amazing amount of artery-cleaning power is found in just one handful of this little fruit. And they're delicious, too!

► Ten best healthy eating tips for losing weight permanently and lowering blood pressure quickly, naturally.

► Wow! This inexpensive, ultra low-calorie vegetable has ultra high cancer-fighting nutrients. Researchers say it prevents cancer of the colon, brain, breast, stomach, bladder, and lung!

► Save your eyesight, no matter your age. These foods reduce your risk of blindness in old age by nearly half.

► How many nuts does it take to improve eyesight? Less than you think! It's no joke.

► Increase circulation, boost energy, and improve your concentration — five herbs you can grow yourself to boost your brain's performance.

► You may not have to worry about being overweight again! The "Nothing Forbidden" diet plan anybody can follow!

► Painful joints? You may find real pain relief naturally just by balancing these two nutrients found in eggs, meat, milk, and fish.

Learn all these amazing secrets and more. To order a copy, just return this notice with your name and address and a check for $9.99 plus $3.00 shipping and handling to: **FC&A, Dept. 8OF06, 103 Clover Green,** Peachtree City, GA 30269. We will send you a copy of *Unleash the Inner Healing Power of Foods.*

You get a no-time-limit guarantee of satisfaction or your money back.

You must cut out and return this notice with your order. Copies will not be accepted!
IMPORTANT — FREE GIFT
OFFER EXPIRES IN 30 DAYS

All orders mailed within 30 days will receive a free gift, *Simple Solutions to Common Health Problems*, guaranteed. **Order right away!**   ©FC&A 2005

How to Use This Almanac

The calendar pages (96–123) are the heart of *The Old Farmer's Almanac*. They present sky sightings and astronomical data for the entire year and are what make this book a true almanac, a "calendar of the heavens." In essence, these pages are unchanged since 1792, when Robert B. Thomas published his first edition. The long columns of numbers and symbols reveal all of nature's precision, rhythm, and glory—providing an astronomical look at the year 2006.

The Seasons of the Year

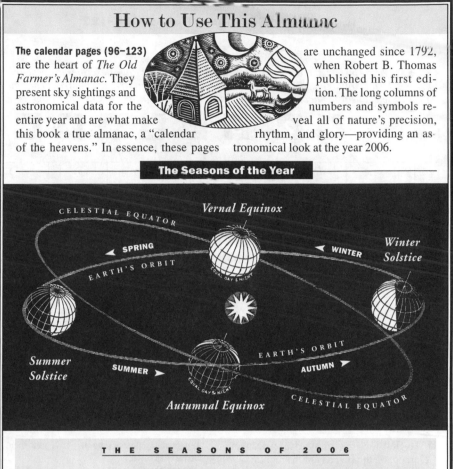

THE SEASONS OF 2006

Spring . . . . March 20, 1:26 P.M. EST	Fall . . . . September 23, 12:03 A.M. EDT
Summer . . . . June 21, 8:26 A.M. EDT	Winter . . . . December 21, 7:22 P.M. EST

■ The seasons occur because as the Earth revolves around the Sun, its axis remains tilted at 23.5 degrees from the perpendicular. This tilt causes different latitudes on Earth to receive varying amounts of sunlight throughout the year.

In the Northern Hemisphere, the summer solstice (around June 21) marks the beginning of summer and occurs when the North Pole is tilted toward the Sun. The winter solstice (around December 21) marks the beginning of winter and occurs when the North Pole is tilted away from the Sun.

The equinoxes occur when the hemispheres equally face the Sun and receive equal amounts (12 hours each) of daylight and darkness. The vernal equinox (around March 21) marks the beginning of spring; the autumnal equinox (around September 23) marks the beginning of autumn. In the Southern Hemisphere, the seasons are the reverse of those in the Northern Hemisphere.

continued

C
A
L
E
N
D
A
R

The Left-Hand Calendar Pages • 96–122

S A M P L E   M O N T H

SKY WATCH ☆ *The box at the top of each Left-Hand Calendar Page describes the best times to view celestial highlights, including conjunctions, meteor showers, and planets. (The dates on which select astronomical events occur appear on the Right-Hand Calendar Pages.)*

All times are given in Eastern Standard Time. ☞ **Bold** = P.M. ☞ Light = A.M.

Day of Year	Day of Month	Day of Week	☼ Rises h. m.	Key	☼ Sets h. m.	Key	Length of Day h. m.	Sun Fast m.	Declina- tion of Sun ° ′	High Tide Times Boston	☽ Rises h. m.	Key	☽ Sets h. m.	Key	☽ Place	☽ Age
1	1	A	7 14	E	**4 23**	A	9 09	12	22 s.58	11¾ —	8 56	E	**6 09**	B	SAG	2
2	2	M.	7 14	E	**4 24**	A	9 10	12	22 53	12½ **12½**	9 33	E	**7 31**	C	CAP	3
3	3	Tu.	7 14	E	**4 24**	A	9 10	11	22 47	1¼ **1½**	10 03	D	**8 51**	C	AQU	4

The Left-Hand Calendar Pages (detail above) contain daily Sun and Moon rise and set times, the length of day, high tide times, the Moon's place and age, and more for Boston. Examples of how to calculate astronomical times are shown below.

1 To calculate the sunrise/sunset times for your locale: Each sunrise/sunset time is assigned a Key Letter whose value is given in minutes in the **Time Corrections** table on **page 237**. Find your city in the table, or the city nearest you, and add or subtract those minutes to/from Boston's sunrise or sunset time given.

E X A M P L E :

■ To find the time of sunrise in Denver, Colorado, on the first day of the month:

Sunrise, Boston, with Key Letter E (above)	7:14 A.M. EST
Value of Key Letter E for Denver (p. 237)	+ 7 minutes
Sunrise, Denver	7:21 A.M. MST

2 To determine your city's length of day, find the sunrise/sunset Key Let-

ATTENTION, READERS: *All times given in this edition of the Almanac are for Boston, Massachusetts, and are in Eastern Standard Time (EST), except from 2:00 A.M., April 2, until 2:00 A.M., October 29, when Eastern Daylight Time (EDT) is given. Key Letters (A–E) are provided so that you can calculate times for other localities.*

ter values for your city on **page 237**. Add or subtract the sunset value to/from Boston's length of day. Then simply *reverse* the sunrise sign (from minus to plus, or plus to minus) and add or subtract this value to/from the result of the first step.

E X A M P L E :

■ To find the length of day in Richmond, Virginia:

Length of day, Boston (above)	9h. 09m.
Sunset Key Letter A for Richmond (p. 241)	+ 41m.
	9h. 50m.
Reverse sunrise Key Letter E for Richmond (p. 241, +11 to −11)	− 11m.
Length of day, Richmond	9h. 39m.

3 Use the Sun Fast column to change sundial time to clock time in Boston. A sundial reads natural time, or Sun time, which is neither Standard nor Daylight time except by coincidence. *Subtract* the minutes given in the Sun Fast column (except where the number is preceded by an asterisk [*], in which case *add* the minutes) to get Boston clock time, and use Key Letter C in the table on **page 237** to convert the time to your city.

E X A M P L E :

■ To change sundial time to clock time in Boston, or Salem, Oregon:

Sundial reading (Boston or Salem)	12:00 noon
Subtract Sun Fast (p. 92)	– 12 minutes
Clock time, Boston	11:48 A.M. EST
Use Key Letter C for Salem (p. 240)	+ 27 minutes
Clock time, Salem	12:15 P.M. PST

4 This column gives the degrees and minutes of the Sun from the celestial equator at noon EST or EDT.

5 This column gives the times of high tides in Boston. For example, the first high tide occurs at 11:45 A.M. and the second occurs at 12:30 A.M. the next day. (A dash indicates that high tide occurs on or after midnight and so is recorded on the next day.) Figures for calculating high tide times and heights for localities other than Boston are given in the Tide Corrections table on **page 234.**

–Beth Krommes

6 To calculate the moonrise/moonset times for localities other than Boston, follow the example in the next column, making a correction for longitude (see table, above right). For the longitude of your city, see **page 237.** (Note: A dash in the moonrise/moonset columns indicates that rise or set times occur on or after midnight and are recorded on the next day.)

Longitude of city	Correction minutes
58°–76°	0
77°–89°	+1
90°–102°	+2
103°–115°	+3
116°–127°	+4
128°–141°	+5
142°–155°	+6

E X A M P L E :

■ To determine the time of moonrise in Lansing, Michigan:

Moonrise, Boston, with Key Letter E (p. 92)	8:56 A.M. EST
Value of Key Letter E for Lansing (p. 239)	+ 54 minutes
Correction for Lansing longitude, 84°33'	+ 1 minute
Moonrise, Lansing	9:51 A.M. EST

Use the same procedure to determine the time of moonset.

7 The Moon's Place is its *astronomical* placement in the heavens. (This should not be confused with the Moon's *astrological* place in the zodiac, as explained on **page 230.**) All calculations in this Almanac are based on astronomy, not astrology, except for the information on **pages 229–231.**

In addition to the 12 constellations of the zodiac, this column may indicate others: Auriga **(AUR),** a northern constellation between Perseus and Gemini; Cetus **(CET),** which lies south of the zodiac, just south of Pisces and Aries; Ophiuchus **(OPH),** a constellation primarily north of the zodiac but with a small corner between Scorpius and Sagittarius; Orion **(ORI),** a constellation whose northern limit first reaches the zodiac between Taurus and Gemini; and Sextans **(SEX),** which lies south of the zodiac except for a corner that just touches it near Leo.

8 The last column gives the Moon's Age, which is the number of days since the previous new Moon. (The average length of the lunar month is 29.53 days.)

continued

The Right-Hand Calendar Pages • 97–123

SAMPLE MONTH

- Weather prediction rhyme.
- Day of the month.
- Day of the week.
- The bold letter in this column is the Dominical Letter, a traditional ecclesiastical designation for Sunday. For 2006, the Dominical Letter is **A**, because the first Sunday of the year falls on the first day of January.
- Notable celestial events appear in this typeface with these symbols. (See opposite page for an explanation of symbols.)
- Sundays and special holy days generally appear in this typeface.
- Proverbs, poems, and adages appear in this typeface.
- Religious feasts generally appear in this typeface.
- Civil holidays generally appear in this typeface.
- Noteworthy historical events, folklore, and legends appear in this typeface.
- First high tide at Boston on this sample day is 8.9 feet; second high tide is 8.1 feet.

Ring out the old, ring in the new,
Ring, happy bells, across the snow. –Alfred, Lord Tennyson

Day of Month	Day of Week	Dates, Feasts, Fasts, Aspects, Tide Heights	Weather
1	**A**	Holy Name • ☾ at perig. • ☌♀☾ • Tides {11.6 / —	*Pitter,*
2	M.	☌♆☾ • A moon of Jupiter, Elara, discovered, 1905 • Tides {9.9 / 11.6 •	*patter,*
3	Tu.	☌♅☾ • Construction for Brooklyn Bridge, N.Y.C., began, 1870 • Tides {10.1 / 11.5	*slush*
4	W.	St. Elizabeth Ann Seton • ⊕ at perihelion • {10.2 / 11.0	*and*
5	Th.	Twelfth Night • ☾ on Eq. • *The heart is never neutral.* • Tides {10.2 / 10.5	*splatter,*
6	Fr.	Epiphany • ☾ at ☊ • Indianapolis designated as the name for capital of Ind., 1821	*snow-*
7	Sa.	Distaff Day • George Washington elected first U.S. President, 1789 • Tides {10.2 / 9.3	*men*
8	**A**	1st S. af. Ep. • ☌♂☾ • N.Y.C. stayed below 0°F all day, 1859	*shrink*
9	M.	Plough Monday • Writer C. Parr Traill born, 1802 • Tides {10.1 / 8.6	*and then*
10	Tu.	*A favorable January brings us a good year.* • {10.1 / 8.5	*grow*
11	W.	Alabama seceded from the Union, 1861 • Tides {10.1 / 8.6	*fatter.*
12	Th.	☾ rides high • Forward pass made legal in football, 1906 • Tides {10.1 / 8.6 •	*Varied—*
13	Fr.	St. Hilary • ♀ in inf. ☌ • Opera was heard live for first time on radio, 1910 •	*Now*
14	Sa.	Full Wolf ○ • First successful cesarean operation in U.S., 1794 • {10.2 / 8.7	*we're*
15	**A**	2nd S. af. Ep. • ☌♄☾ • Tides {10.1 / —	*buried!*
16	M.	**Martin Luther King Jr.'s Birthday (observed)** • {8.8 / 10.0 •	*It's*
17	Tu.	☾ at apo. • Ben Franklin born, 1706 • Pres. Rutherford B. Hayes died, 1893 • {8.8 / 9.8	*cold*
18	W.	*Love, cough, and smoke can't well be hid.* • Tides {8.9 / 9.6	*as a*
19	Th.	☾ on Eq. • First Brown vs. Harvard ice hockey game (Brown won, 6–0), 1898 • {8.9 / 9.2	*witch's*
20	Fr.	☾ at ☋ • Astronaut Edwin "Buzz" Aldrin born, 1930 •	*. . . well,*
21	Sa.	Smoking in public places in N.Y.C. became illegal for women, 1908 • Tides {8.9 / 8.5	*you*
22	**A**	3rd S. af. Ep. • Britain's Queen Victoria died, 1901 • {8.9 / 8.1	*know.*

☞ *For explanations of Almanac terms, see the glossaries on pages 74, 124, and 236.*

Predicting Earthquakes

–Beth Krommes

■ Note the dates in the **Right-Hand Calendar Pages** when the Moon rides high or runs low. The date of the high begins the most likely five-day period of earthquakes in the Northern Hemisphere; the date of the low indicates a similar five-day period in the Southern Hemisphere. Also noted are the two days each month when the Moon is on the celestial equator, indicating the most likely time for earthquakes in either hemisphere.

■ Throughout the **Right-Hand Calendar Pages** are groups of symbols that represent notable celestial events. The symbols and names of the principal planets and aspects are:

☉	Sun	♆	Neptune
○●☾	Moon	♇	Pluto
☿	Mercury	♂	Conjunction (on the
♀	Venus		same celestial
⊕	Earth		longitude)
♂	Mars	☊	Ascending node
♃	Jupiter	☋	Descending node
♄	Saturn	☍	Opposition (180 degrees
♁	Uranus		from Sun)

E X A M P L E :

♂♁☾ next to the third day of the month (see opposite page) means that on that date a conjunction (♂) of Uranus (♁) and the Moon (☾) occurs: They are aligned along the same celestial longitude and appear to be closest together in the sky.

Earth at Perihelion and Aphelion

■ The Earth will be at *perihelion,* or 91,405,956 miles from the Sun, on January 4, 2006. The Earth will be at *aphelion,* or 94,507,891 miles from the Sun, on July 3, 2006.

2006 Calendar Highlights

Movable Religious Observances

Septuagesima Sunday	**February 12**
Shrove Tuesday	**February 28**
Ash Wednesday	**March 1**
Palm Sunday	**April 9**
First day of Passover	**April 13**
Good Friday	**April 14**
Easter	**April 16**
Orthodox Easter	**April 23**
Rogation Sunday	**May 21**
Ascension Day	**May 25**
Whitsunday–Pentecost	**June 4**
Trinity Sunday	**June 11**
Corpus Christi	**June 18**
Rosh Hashanah	**September 23**
First day of Ramadan	**September 24**
Yom Kippur	**October 2**
First Sunday of Advent	**December 3**
First day of Chanukah	**December 16**

Chronological Cycles

Dominical Letter	A
Epact	30
Golden Number (Lunar Cycle)	12
Roman Indiction	14
Solar Cycle	27
Year of Julian Period	6719

–Beth Krommes

Eras

ERA	YEAR	BEGINS
Byzantine	7515	September 14
Jewish (A.M.)*	5767	September 23
Chinese (Lunar) [Year of the Dog]	4704	January 29
Roman (A.U.C.)	2759	January 14
Nabonassar	2755	April 22
Japanese	2666	January 1
Grecian (Seleucidae)	2318	September 14 (or October 14)
Indian (Saka)	1928	March 22
Diocletian	1723	September 11
Islamic (Hegira)*	1427	January 31

Year begins at sunset the evening before.

THE ELEVENTH MONTH • 2005

SKY WATCH ☆ *Mars comes to opposition on the 7th. At a brilliant magnitude –2.3, it rises at sunset, is out all night, and is quite high at midnight in Aries. The nearly full Moon joins Mars on the 14th. Venus achieves greatest elongation on the 3rd, but its 47-degree solar separation is wasted, since it's south of the ecliptic and not very high. Still, watch it closely when it meets the Moon on the 5th. Saturn rises before 11:00 P.M. at midmonth; it floats alongside the Moon on the 21st. Jupiter, above the crescent Moon on the 29th, returns as a predawn planet low in the east. November's Leonid meteor showers will definitely be "off" this year; even if they do appear, they'll be ruined by an almost-full Moon.*

●	New Moon	1st day	20th hour	25th minute
☽	First Quarter	8th day	20th hour	57th minute
○	Full Moon	15th day	19th hour	57th minute
☾	Last Quarter	23rd day	17th hour	11th minute

To use this page, see p. 92; for Key Letters, see p. 237; for Tide Corrections, see p. 234.
All times are given in Eastern Standard Time. ☞ **Bold** = P.M. ☞ Light = A.M.

Day of Year	Day of Month	Day of Week	☀ Rises h. m.	Key	☀ Sets h. m.	Key	Length of Day h. m.	Sun Fast m.	Declination of Sun ° '	High Tide Times Boston		☽ Rises h. m.	Key	☽ Sets h. m.	Key	☽ Place	☽ Age
305	1	Tu.	6 18	D	**4 37**	B	10 19	32	14 s. 37	10¼	**10¾**	5 49	E	**4 15**	B	VIR	0
306	2	W.	6 19	D	**4 36**	B	10 17	32	14 56	11	**11½**	7 00	E	**4 43**	A	LIB	1
307	3	Th.	6 20	D	**4 35**	B	10 15	32	15 14	11½	—	8 14	E	**5 17**	A	LIB	2
308	4	Fr.	6 21	D	**4 34**	B	10 13	32	15 33	12¼	**12¼**	9 28	E	**6 01**	A	SCO	3
309	5	Sa.	6 23	D	**4 32**	B	10 09	32	15 52	1	**1**	10 37	E	**6 58**	A	OPH	4
310	6	**B**	6 24	D	**4 31**	B	10 07	32	16 10	1¾	**2**	11 36	E	**8 06**	A	SAG	5
311	7	M.	6 25	D	**4 30**	B	10 05	32	16 27	2¾	**2¾**	**12 24**	E	**9 22**	B	SAG	6
312	8	Tu.	6 27	D	**4 29**	A	10 02	32	16 44	3¾	**3¾**	**1 01**	E	**10 40**	B	CAP	7
313	9	W.	6 28	D	**4 28**	A	10 00	32	17 02	4¾	**5**	**1 31**	E	**11 58**	B	CAP	8
314	10	Th.	6 29	D	**4 27**	A	9 58	32	17 18	5¾	**6**	**1 56**	D	—	–	AQU	9
315	11	Fr.	6 30	D	**4 26**	A	9 56	32	17 35	6¾	**7**	**2 18**	D	1 14	C	AQU	10
316	12	Sa.	6 32	D	**4 25**	A	9 53	31	17 51	7¾	**8**	**2 40**	C	2 28	D	PSC	11
317	13	**B**	6 33	D	**4 24**	A	9 51	31	18 07	8½	**9**	**3 02**	B	3 42	D	PSC	12
318	14	M.	6 34	D	**4 23**	A	9 49	31	18 23	9½	**10**	**3 26**	B	4 56	E	ARI	13
319	15	Tu.	6 35	D	**4 22**	A	9 47	31	18 38	10¼	**10¾**	**3 55**	A	6 10	E	ARI	14
320	16	W.	6 36	D	**4 21**	A	9 45	31	18 53	11	**11½**	**4 29**	A	7 24	E	TAU	15
321	17	Th.	6 38	D	**4 20**	A	9 42	31	19 08	11¾	—	**5 11**	A	8 35	E	TAU	16
322	18	Fr.	6 39	D	**4 20**	A	9 41	31	19 22	12¼	**12¼**	**6 02**	A	9 38	E	TAU	17
323	19	Sa.	6 40	D	**4 19**	A	9 39	30	19 36	1	**1**	**7 00**	A	10 32	E	AUR	18
324	20	**B**	6 41	D	**4 18**	A	9 37	30	19 49	1¾	**1¾**	**8 03**	B	11 15	E	GEM	19
325	21	M.	6 43	D	**4 17**	A	9 34	30	20 02	2½	**2¾**	**9 08**	B	11 50	E	CAN	20
326	22	Tu.	6 44	D	**4 17**	A	9 33	30	20 15	3½	**3½**	**10 12**	B	**12 17**	E	CAN	21
327	23	W.	6 45	D	**4 16**	A	9 31	29	20 28	4¼	**4½**	**11 15**	B	**12 40**	D	LEO	22
328	24	Th.	6 46	D	**4 16**	A	9 30	29	20 39	5¼	**5¼**	—	–	**1 00**	D	LEO	23
329	25	Fr.	6 47	D	**4 15**	A	9 28	29	20 52	6	**6¼**	12 18	C	**1 19**	D	LEO	24
330	26	Sa.	6 48	D	**4 14**	A	9 26	28	21 03	6¾	**7¼**	1 20	D	**1 37**	C	VIR	25
331	27	**B**	6 50	E	**4 14**	A	9 24	28	21 14	7½	**8**	2 24	D	**1 55**	B	VIR	26
332	28	M.	6 51	E	**4 14**	A	9 23	28	21 24	8¼	**8¾**	3 30	E	**2 16**	B	VIR	27
333	29	Tu.	6 52	E	**4 13**	A	9 21	27	21 34	9	**9½**	4 40	E	**2 42**	A	VIR	28
334	30	W.	6 53	E	**4 13**	A	9 20	27	21 s. 44	9¾	**10¼**	5 54	E	**3 13**	A	LIB	29

NOVEMBER HATH 30 DAYS • 2005

There comes the sound of childish feet
And childish laughter loud and sweet,
And little hands stretch eager palms
To beg the firelight's golden alms. –James Berry Bensel

Day of Month	Day of Week	Dates, Feasts, Fasts, Aspects, Tide Heights	Weather ↓
1	Tu.	All Saints' • New ● • First national weather service in U.S. began operation, 1870	*Teeth-*
2	W.	All Souls' • *To the brave man every land is a native country.* • { 10.6 / 9.6	*chattering,*
3	Th.	☌☿☾ • ☿ Gr. Elong. (24° E.) • ♀ Gr. Elong. (47° E.) • { 10.8 / — •	*then*
4	Fr.	Sunspot 486 produced record-breaking X28-class solar flare, 2003 • Tides { 9.6 / 10.9 •	*a*
5	Sa.	☌♀☾ • Susan B. Anthony cast her ballot, earning a fine, 1872 •	*spattering.*
6	**B**	25th S. af. P. • ☾ runs low • Tides { 9.2 / 10.7 •	*Too*
7	M.	♂ at ☍ • Former U.S. First Lady Eleanor Roosevelt died, 1962 • { 9.0 / 10.5	*good*
8	Tu.	Election Day • ☌♆☾ • Abraham Lincoln reelected as U.S. president, 1864 •	*to*
9	W.	☾ at perig. • Al Capp's Sadie Hawkins Day first celebrated, 1938 • { 9.0 / 10.1 •	*be*
10	Th.	☌⛢☾ • U.S. Marine Corps established, 1775 • Tides { 9.3 / 10.0 •	*true;*
11	Fr.	St. Martin of Tours • Veterans Day • Tides { 9.7 / 10.0 •	*skies*
12	Sa.	Sadie Hawkins Day • Indian Summer • ☾ on Eq. • ☾ at ☊ • { 10.2 / 10.1	*of*
13	**B**	26th S. af. P. • Thousands of meteors fell per hour, 1833 •	*cobalt*
14	M.	☿ stat. • *You can not make a crab walk straight.* • Tides { 11.1 / 10.1 •	*blue,*
15	Tu.	Full Beaver ○ • ☌♂☾ • Astronomer Sir William Herschel born, 1738 •	*and*
16	W.	⛢ stat. • President Nixon approved construction of an Alaskan pipeline, 1973 •	*warmer,*
17	Th.	St. Hugh of Lincoln • Sculptor Auguste Rodin died, 1917 • Tides { 11.1 / —	*too!*
18	Fr.	U.S. railroads adopted four standard time zones, 1883 • *Necessity sharpens industry.* •	*Make*
19	Sa.	☾ rides high • Hudson Bay Co. ceded territory to Canada, 1869 • Tides { 9.2 / 10.4 •	*the*
20	**B**	27th S. af. P. • Yo-yo patented, 1866 • { 8.9 / 10.0 •	*best*
21	M.	☌♄☾ • *Wonder is the seed of science.* • Tides { 8.6 / 9.5 •	*of*
22	Tu.	♄ at stat. • National Hockey League formed, 1917 • Tides { 8.4 / 9.2 •	*it—*
23	W.	St. Clement • ☾ apo. • Horseshoe-manufacturing machine patented, 1835	*you're*
24	Th.	Thanksgiving • ☿ in inf. ☌ • Tides { 8.3 / 8.7 •	*likely*
25	Fr.	First sword-swallower performance in U.S., 1817 • *After feasting, fasting.* • { 8.5 / 8.6 •	*not*
26	Sa.	☾ on Eq. • Public streetcar service began in N.Y.C., 1832 • Tides { 8.8 / 8.7 •	*to*
27	**B**	1st S. of Advent • ☾ at ☋ • Tides { 9.2 / 8.8 •	*like*
28	M.	*Who throws a stone at the sky may have it fall on his head.* • Tides { 9.7 / 9.0 •	*the*
29	Tu.	☌♃☾ • Committee of Secret Correspondence organized by 2nd Continental Congress, 1775	*rest*
30	W.	St. Andrew • Meteorite hit woman in her home, Sylacauga, Ala., 1954 • { 10.5 / 9.3	*of it!*

Food is our common ground, a universal experience.
–James Beard, American chef

Farmer's Calendar

■ "The pleasure that is in sorrow," a poet has written, "is sweeter than the pleasure of pleasure itself." Hence the beauty of the fall of the year, and hence our particular delight in the spectacle it presents to our senses. It's a spectacle of decline, deterioration, and bereavement—a melancholy spectacle. We respond to it for that very reason. We love the fall because of its melancholy, not in spite of it.

The sweet sadness of the year's end doesn't set in until most of the autumn leaves are gone from the trees. The autumn colors are too bright and too busy to have the effect, though they point to it. It's when the leaves are brown, and few, and the branches and trunks of the trees are gray that they begin to produce the emotional tone of this season, the tone of loss. The low skies of November, the dun ponds and frozen brooks, are a dark setting.

But although the season has a sorrowful character, it isn't a depressing time. On the contrary: The atmosphere of these last weeks before winter comes is the antithesis of depression. The senses—the feelings—become more receptive, educated by the stripped-down, impoverished look of the land. Maybe the last leaves, long dead, that hang on the trees are few in number, but you consider each one of them. Maybe the subdued little salt-and-pepper birds of November don't know many songs, but they have a companionable presence the brighter summer birds lack. In a part of the year that withholds the occasions for high spirits, the pleasure that we take is the pleasure of reflection, and it's keen, because it goes down deep.

SKY WATCH ☆ *Venus reaches greatest brilliancy on the 9th at magnitude –4.6, after hovering near the crescent Moon on the 4th. It moves from Sagittarius to Capricornus, then retrogrades and falls toward the Sun. Mars, out nearly all night, is magnificent. Mercury has a nice predawn apparition. Nearby Jupiter enters Libra, its home for the next year. Saturn rises at around 8:00 P.M. at midmonth and brightens beyond the zero-magnitude threshold in advance of its opposition next month. The midmonth Geminid meteors are spoiled by a bright Moon. Winter begins with the solstice on the 21st, at 1:35 P.M. EST.*

●	New Moon	1st day	10th hour	1st minute
☽	First Quarter	8th day	4th hour	36th minute
○	Full Moon	15th day	11th hour	15th minute
☾	Last Quarter	23rd day	14th hour	36th minute
●	New Moon	30th day	22nd hour	12th minute

To use this page, see p. 92; for Key Letters, see p. 237; for Tide Corrections, see p. 234.
All times are given in Eastern Standard Time. ☞ **Bold** = P.M. ☞ Light = A.M.

Day of Year	Day of Month	Day of Week	☼ Rises h. m.	Key	☼ Sets h. m.	Key	Length of Day h. m.	Sun Fast m.	Declination of Sun ° '	High Tide Times Boston	☽ Rises h. m.	Key	☽ Sets h. m.	Key	☽ Place	☽ Age
335	1	Th.	6 54	E	**4 13**	A	9 19	27	21 s.53	10½ 11	7 09	E	**3 54**	A	SCO	0
336	2	Fr.	6 55	E	**4 12**	A	9 17	26	22 02	11¼ **11¾**	8 22	E	**4 47**	A	OPH	1
337	3	Sa.	6 56	E	**4 12**	A	9 16	26	22 11	**12** —	9 27	E	**5 54**	A	SAG	2
338	4	**B**	6 57	E	**4 12**	A	9 15	26	22 19	12¾ **12¾**	10 20	E	**7 10**	B	SAG	3
339	5	M.	6 58	E	**4 12**	A	9 14	25	22 27	1½ **1¾**	11 02	E	**8 29**	B	CAP	4
340	6	Tu.	6 59	E	**4 12**	A	9 13	25	22 34	2½ **2½**	11 34	E	**9 48**	C	CAP	5
341	7	W.	7 00	E	**4 12**	A	9 12	24	22 40	3¼ **3½**	**12 01**	D	**11 04**	C	AQU	6
342	8	Th.	7 00	E	**4 11**	A	9 11	24	22 46	4¼ **4¾**	**12 23**	D	—	–	AQU	7
343	9	Fr.	7 02	E	**4 12**	A	9 10	23	22 52	5¼ **5¾**	**12 45**	C	12 18	D	PSC	8
344	10	Sa.	7 03	E	**4 12**	A	9 09	23	22 58	6¼ **6¾**	**1 06**	B	1 30	E	PSC	9
345	11	**B**	7 03	E	**4 12**	A	9 09	23	23 03	7¼ **7¾**	**1 29**	B	2 42	E	PSC	10
346	12	M.	7 04	E	**4 12**	A	9 08	22	23 07	8¼ **8¾**	**1 55**	B	3 55	E	ARI	11
347	13	Tu.	7 05	E	**4 12**	A	9 07	22	23 11	9 **9¾**	**2 26**	A	5 08	E	ARI	12
348	14	W.	7 06	E	**4 12**	A	9 06	21	23 15	9¾ **10½**	**3 05**	A	6 19	E	TAU	13
349	15	Th.	7 07	E	**4 12**	A	9 05	21	23 18	10½ **11¼**	**3 52**	A	7 25	E	TAU	14
350	16	Fr.	7 08	E	**4 13**	A	9 05	20	23 20	11¼ —	**4 48**	A	8 22	E	AUR	15
351	17	Sa.	7 08	E	**4 13**	A	9 05	20	23 22	12 **12**	**5 50**	A	9 10	E	GEM	16
352	18	**B**	7 09	E	**4 13**	A	9 04	19	23 24	12¾ **12¾**	**6 54**	B	9 48	E	CAN	17
353	19	M.	7 10	E	**4 14**	A	9 04	19	23 26	1½ **1½**	**7 59**	B	10 18	E	CAN	18
354	20	Tu.	7 10	E	**4 14**	A	9 04	18	23 26	2 **2¼**	**9 03**	C	10 42	E	LEO	19
355	21	W.	7 11	E	**4 15**	A	9 04	18	23 26	2¾ **3**	**10 05**	C	11 03	D	LEO	20
356	22	Th.	7 11	E	**4 15**	A	9 04	17	23 26	3½ **3¾**	**11 06**	D	11 22	D	LEO	21
357	23	Fr.	7 11	E	**4 16**	A	9 05	17	23 25	4¼ **4½**	—	–	11 40	C	VIR	22
358	24	Sa.	7 11	E	**4 16**	A	9 05	16	23 24	5¼ **5½**	12 08	D	11 58	C	VIR	23
359	25	**B**	7 12	E	**4 17**	A	9 05	16	23 23	6 **6¼**	1 12	E	**12 17**	B	VIR	24
360	26	M.	7 12	E	**4 18**	A	9 06	15	23 21	6¾ **7¼**	2 19	E	**12 40**	B	VIR	25
361	27	Tu.	7 12	E	**4 18**	A	9 06	15	23 18	7½ **8¼**	3 29	E	**1 08**	A	LIB	26
362	28	W.	7 13	E	**4 19**	A	9 06	14	23 15	8½ **9**	4 44	E	**1 44**	A	LIB	27
363	29	Th.	7 13	E	**4 20**	A	9 07	14	23 12	9¼ **10**	5 59	E	**2 31**	A	SCO	28
364	30	Fr.	7 13	E	**4 21**	A	9 08	13	23 07	10 **10¾**	7 09	E	**3 33**	A	SAG	0
365	31	Sa.	7 13	E	**4 21**	A	9 08	13	23 s.03	10¾ **11½**	8 09	E	**4 47**	A	SAG	1

DECEMBER HATH 31 DAYS • 2005

Life is mostly froth and bubble;
Two things stand like stone:
Kindness in another's trouble,
Courage in your own. –Adam Lindsay Gordon

Day of Month	Day of Week	Dates, Feasts, Fasts, Aspects, Tide Heights	Weather ↓
1	Th.	New ● • Scrabble trademark registered, 1948 • Tides { 10.9 / 9.4 •	*Cold*
2	Fr.	St. Viviana • "In God We Trust" promoter Charles E. Bennett born, 1910 • { 11.1 / 9.5 •	*and*
3	Sa.	☾ runs low • ☿ stat. • Discovery of "Pumpkin Papers" secret documents announced, 1948	*snowy!*
4	B	2nd S. of Advent • ☌♀☾ • { 9.5 / 11.3 •	*Colder*
5	M.	☾ at perig. • ☌♆☾ • U.S. president Martin Van Buren born, 1782 •	*and*
6	Tu.	St. Nicholas • *No sweet without sweat.* • Tides { 9.4 / 10.8 •	*snowier!*
7	W.	St. Ambrose • **National Pearl Harbor Remembrance Day** • ☌♅☾ •	*Not*
8	Th.	"In Flanders Fields" poem published, 1915 • Tides { 9.6 / 10.0 •	*quite*
9	Fr.	☾ on Eq. • ☾ at ☊ • ♀ Gr. Bril. • Canada's first coin club formed, 1862 •	*as*
10	Sa.	St. Eulalia • ♂ stat. • Mississippi became the 20th state, 1817 • { 10.0 / 9.5 •	*cold,*
11	B	3rd S. of Advent • UNICEF established, 1946 • { 10.3 / 9.4	*but*
12	M.	☌♂☾ • ☿ Gr. Elong. (21° W.) • Tides { 10.6 / 9.3 •	*probably*
13	Tu.	St. Lucia • *One today is worth two tomorrows.* • Tides { 10.7 / 9.3 •	*blowier!*
14	W.	Halcyon Days • Ember Day • *National Velvet* premiered, 1944 • { 10.8 / 9.3 •	*Guess:*
15	Th.	**Full Cold** ○ • ☌♇☉ • Philadelphia streets first cleaned by machine, 1854 •	*a*
16	Fr.	Ember Day • ☾ rides high • Current Cape Hatteras, N.C., lighthouse began operation, 1870	*mess!*
17	Sa.	Ember Day • *The wise understand half a word.* • Tides { 9.1 / 10.4 •	*Had*
18	B	4th S. of Advent • National Anti-Saloon League founded, 1895	*enough?*
19	M.	☌♄☾ • Mark Twain received a patent for suspenders, 1871 • { 8.8 / 9.9 •	*That's*
20	Tu.	☾ at apo. • Louisiana Purchase finalized, 1803 • Tides { 8.7 / 9.6 •	*tough!*
21	W.	St. Thomas • **Winter Solstice** • Crossword puzzle debuted, 1913 • { 8.6 / 9.3 •	*Same*
22	Th.	Beware the Pogonip. • First string of Christmas tree lights created, 1882 • Tides { 8.5 / 8.9	*stuff,*
23	Fr.	☾ on Eq. • ♀ stat. • *Daylight now lengthens to the extent of a gnat's yawn.* •	*only*
24	Sa.	☾ at ☋ • Treaty of Ghent, agreement to end War of 1812, signed, 1814 • { 8.7 / 8.4	*harder!*
25	B	Christmas Day • Explorer Samuel de Champlain died, 1635 •	*2006*
26	M.	First day of Chanukah • **Boxing Day (Canada)** • ☌♃☾ •	*could*
27	Tu.	St. John • *The Howdy Doody Show* debuted, 1947 • Tides { 9.6 / 8.5 •	*be*
28	W.	Holy Innocents • "A Neglected Anniversary" bathtub hoax published, 1917 •	*worse—*
29	Th.	☌☿☾ • Gaslights first used at the White House, 1848 • Tides { 10.6 / 9.0 •	*better*
30	Fr.	New ● • ☾ runs low • –48°F, Mazama and Winthrop, Wash., 1968 •	*fill your*
31	Sa.	St. Sylvester • *With bounteous cheer, conclude the year.* • { 11.4 / 9.6 •	*larder!*

Farmer's Calendar

■ The coming around each year of winter is the chief seasonal fact of life in this part of the country. The necessity for responding to prolonged cold, ice, and snow is the condition of man's existence in the north, and our responses are deeply ingrained in us. The onset of winter may overtake or otherwise confound our preparations, but it doesn't surprise us. Others react differently.

The first real snow of the year always seems to take the two dogs on this place by surprise. They're little, low-built creatures; to them, a couple of inches of snow are no joke. Leaving the house early on the first snowy morning, they stop short. They apparently have no memory of snow from past years. Soon, they sally forth, but where yesterday morning they dashed out into the yard at full tilt, now they move slowly, tentatively, through the new snow. Soon, being dogs, they figure out that you can eat snow. This is a revelation, because, unlike the other things they like to eat—that is, practically everything—the snow is available in unlimited and unrestricted quantities. The pair of them plow along through the stuff, happily rooting, tossing, and chomping.

The family cats also make the annual rediscovery of snow, but their reaction is more human. They are disenchanted. The boldest cat leaves the house, steps into the snow. She pauses. She raises one foot, then another, and shakes it. Then she stalks resignedly on. She doesn't try to eat the snow. She doesn't pretend to like it. Perhaps she understands that in five or six months, it will be gone.

SKY WATCH ☆ *The first evening of the year finds the crescent Moon to the left of brilliant, retrograding Venus. Look fast—Venus is visible in the evening sky for just one week. After a conjunction with the Sun on the 13th, it quickly becomes a predawn morning star visible after the 20th. Mars, in the southeast at nightfall, is at its greatest brilliancy of the year. Jupiter, in Libra, rises by 3:00 A.M. Saturn, in Cancer, is at its brightest this month and reaches opposition on the 27th. It rises by 7:00 P.M. and is out the rest of the night. The Moon is close to Mars on the 8th, somewhat near Saturn on the 14th and 15th, and close to Jupiter on the 23rd. Earth reaches perihelion, its closest point to the Sun, on the 4th.*

☽	First Quarter	6th day	13th hour	56th minute
○	Full Moon	14th day	4th hour	48th minute
☾	Last Quarter	22nd day	10th hour	14th minute
●	New Moon	29th day	9th hour	15th minute

To use this page, see p. 92; for Key Letters, see p. 237; for Tide Corrections, see p. 234.
All times are given in Eastern Standard Time. ☞ **Bold = P.M.** ☞ Light = A.M.

Day of Year	Day of Month	Day of Week	☼ Rises h. m.	Key	☼ Sets h. m.	Key	Length of Day h. m.	Sun Fast m.	Declination of Sun ° '	High Tide Times Boston	☾ Rises h. m.	Key	☾ Sets h. m.	Key	Place	Age
1	1	**A**	7 14	E	**4 23**	A	9 09	12	22 s.58	11¾ —	8 56	E	**6 09**	B	SAG	2
2	2	M.	7 14	E	**4 24**	A	9 10	12	22 53	12½ 12½	9 33	E	**7 31**	C	CAP	3
3	3	Tu.	7 14	E	**4 24**	A	9 10	11	22 47	1¼ 1½	10 03	D	**8 51**	C	AQU	4
4	4	W.	7 14	E	**4 25**	A	9 11	11	22 41	2 2¼	10 27	D	**10 08**	D	AQU	5
5	5	Th.	7 14	E	**4 26**	A	9 12	10	22 34	3 3¼	10 50	C	**11 22**	D	PSC	6
6	6	Fr.	7 13	E	**4 27**	A	9 14	10	22 27	4 4¼	11 11	C	—	–	PSC	7
7	7	Sa.	7 13	E	**4 28**	A	9 15	10	22 19	4¾ 5¼	11 33	B	12 34	E	PSC	8
8	8	**A**	7 13	E	**4 29**	A	9 16	9	22 11	5¾ 6½	11 58	B	1 46	E	ARI	9
9	9	M.	7 13	E	**4 30**	A	9 17	9	22 03	6¾ 7½	12 28	A	2 58	E	ARI	10
10	10	Tu.	7 13	E	**4 31**	A	9 18	8	21 55	7¾ 8½	1 03	A	4 09	E	TAU	11
11	11	W.	7 12	E	**4 33**	A	9 21	8	21 45	8¾ 9½	1 47	A	5 16	E	TAU	12
12	12	Th.	7 12	E	**4 34**	A	9 22	7	21 35	9½ 10¼	2 39	A	6 15	E	AUR	13
13	13	Fr.	7 12	E	**4 35**	A	9 23	7	21 25	10¼ 11	3 39	A	7 06	E	GEM	14
14	14	Sa.	7 11	E	**4 36**	A	9 25	7	21 14	11 11¾	4 43	A	7 46	E	GEM	15
15	15	**A**	7 11	E	**4 37**	A	9 26	6	21 03	11¾ —	5 48	B	8 19	E	CAN	16
16	16	M.	7 10	E	**4 38**	A	9 28	6	20 52	12¼ 12¼	6 52	B	8 45	E	LEO	17
17	17	Tu.	7 10	E	**4 40**	A	9 30	6	20 41	1 1	7 55	C	9 07	D	LEO	18
18	18	W.	7 09	E	**4 41**	A	9 32	5	20 29	1½ 1¾	8 56	D	9 26	D	LEO	19
19	19	Th.	7 09	E	**4 42**	A	9 33	5	20 16	2¼ 2¼	9 57	D	9 44	D	LEO	20
20	20	Fr.	7 08	E	**4 43**	A	9 35	5	20 03	2¾ 3	10 59	D	10 02	C	VIR	21
21	21	Sa.	7 07	E	**4 44**	A	9 37	4	19 49	3½ 3¾	—	–	10 20	B	VIR	22
22	22	**A**	7 07	E	**4 46**	A	9 39	4	19 36	4¼ 4¾	12 03	E	10 41	B	VIR	23
23	23	M.	7 06	D	**4 47**	A	9 41	4	19 22	5 5¾	1 10	E	11 05	B	LIB	24
24	24	Tu.	7 05	D	**4 48**	A	9 43	4	19 07	6 6½	2 21	E	11 36	A	LIB	25
25	25	W.	7 04	D	**4 49**	A	9 45	3	18 52	7 7½	3 34	E	**12 16**	A	SCO	26
26	26	Th.	7 04	D	**4 51**	A	9 47	3	18 37	7¾ 8½	4 46	E	**1 10**	A	OPH	27
27	27	Fr.	7 03	D	**4 52**	A	9 49	3	18 22	8¾ 9½	5 50	E	**2 17**	A	SAG	28
28	28	Sa.	7 02	D	**4 53**	A	9 51	3	18 06	9¾ 10½	6 44	E	**3 37**	B	SAG	29
29	29	**A**	7 01	D	**4 55**	A	9 54	3	17 50	10½ 11¼	7 27	E	**5 01**	B	CAP	0
30	30	M.	7 00	D	**4 56**	A	9 56	2	17 34	11½ —	8 00	E	**6 25**	C	CAP	1
31	31	Tu.	6 59	D	**4 57**	A	9 58	2	17 s.17	12 12¼	8 28	D	**7 47**	D	AQU	2

JANUARY HATH 31 DAYS • 2006

Ring out the old, ring in the new,
Ring, happy bells, across the snow. –Alfred, Lord Tennyson

Day of Month	Day of Week	Dates, Feasts, Fasts, Aspects, Tide Heights	Weather
1	A	**Holy Name** • ☾ AT PERIG. • ☌♀☾ • Tides {11.6 —	*Pitter,*
2	M.	☌♆☾ • A moon of Jupiter, Elara, discovered, 1905 • Tides {9.9 11.6	*patter,*
3	Tu.	☌♅☾ • Construction of Brooklyn Bridge, N.Y.C., began, 1870 • Tides {10.1 11.5	*slush*
4	W.	**St. Elizabeth Ann Seton** • ⊕ AT PERIHELION • {10.2 11.0	*and*
5	Th.	Twelfth Night • ☾ ON EQ. • *The heart is never neutral.* • Tides {10.2 10.5	*splatter,*
6	Fr.	**Epiphany** • ☾ AT ☊ • Indianapolis designated as the name for capital of Ind., 1821	*snow-*
7	Sa.	Distaff Day • George Washington elected first U.S. president, 1789 • Tides {10.2 9.3	*men*
8	A	**1st S. af. Ep.** • ☌♂☾ • N.Y.C. stayed below 0°F all day, 1859	*shrink*
9	M.	Plough Monday • Writer C. Parr Traill born, 1802 • Tides {10.1 8.6	*and then*
10	Tu.	*A favorable January brings us a good year.* • {10.1 8.5	*grow*
11	W.	Alabama seceded from the Union, 1861 • Tides {10.1 8.6	*fatter.*
12	Th.	☾ RIDES HIGH • Forward pass made legal in football, 1906 • Tides {10.1 8.6	*Varied—*
13	Fr.	**St. Hilary** • ♀ IN INF. ☌ • Opera was heard live for first time on radio, 1910	*Now*
14	Sa.	**Full Wolf** ○ • First successful cesarean operation in U.S., 1794 • {10.2 8.7	*we're*
15	A	**2nd S. af. Ep.** • ☌♄☾ • Tides {10.1 —	*buried!*
16	M.	**Martin Luther King Jr.'s Birthday (observed)** • {8.8 10.0	*It's*
17	Tu.	☾ AT APO. • Ben Franklin born, 1706 • Pres. Rutherford B. Hayes died, 1893 • {8.8 9.8	*cold*
18	W.	*Love, cough, and smoke can't well be hid.* • Tides {8.9 9.6	*as a*
19	Th.	☾ ON EQ. • First Brown vs. Harvard ice hockey game (Brown won, 6–0), 1898 • {8.9 9.2	*witch's*
20	Fr.	☾ AT ☋ • Astronaut Edwin "Buzz" Aldrin born, 1930	*. . . well,*
21	Sa.	Smoking in public places in N.Y.C. became illegal for women, 1908 • Tides {8.9 8.5	*you*
22	A	**3rd S. af. Ep.** • Britain's Queen Victoria died, 1901 • {8.9 8.1	*know.*
23	M.	☌♃☾ • Willie Mays elected to the Baseball Hall of Fame, 1979 • Tides {9.0 7.9	*So*
24	Tu.	–15°F Nashville, Tennessee, 1963 • *An ounce of patience is worth a pound of brains.* • {9.2 7.9	*take*
25	W.	**Conversion of Paul** • Mendelssohn's "Wedding March" played at Queen Victoria's daughter's wedding, 1858	*a*
26	Th.	**Sts. Timothy & Titus** • ☿ IN SUP. ☌ • Tides {10.0 8.4	*sunny*
27	Fr.	☾ RUNS LOW • ☌♀☾ • ♄ AT ☍ • Inventor Thomas Crapper died, 1910	*break,*
28	Sa.	**St. Thomas Aquinas** • Snow crushed theater roof, Washington, D.C., 1922 • {11.1 9.5	*then*
29	A	**4th S. af. Ep.** • Chinese New Year • **New** ● • {11.6 10.0	*look*
30	M.	☾ AT PERIG. • Raccoons mate now. • *The harder you fall, the higher you bounce.* • {11.8 —	*out*
31	Tu.	**Islamic New Year** • ☌♅☾ • Napier first car to go more than 100 mph (104.65), 1905	*below!*

Farmer's Calendar

■ Last winter, memorably, the first honest snowstorm came late, not 'til after the middle of January. When it came, however, it more than made up for its tardiness. After scaring themselves half to death for a couple of days, the TV weather forecasters found their habitual exaggeration fully justified: Over three days, a blast of snow and wind traveled from Minnesota to Maine and as far south as Washington, D.C. Airports were closed, highways were made impassable. The city of Boston virtually shut down. The blizzard was, an awed reporter noted, one of the ten biggest winter storms of the past century.

At this place, in the New England hill country, the snow began late on a Saturday afternoon and fell for about 12 hours. The next morning, I found it lying to the level of my knees—a little short of two feet deep. With a sigh, I loaded both barrels of the snow shovel and plodded forth to my labor of removal, only to find no labor but a blessing. Under a clear azure sky, a brisk wind whipped over plains and ridges of snow. And what snow it was: dry, fine, powdery, sparkling like diamond dust—and practically weightless. The stuff fairly flew off the shovel. My kind of snow, I thought. Two feet is more snow than anybody should have to move with nothing but a shovel, but if you must have two feet of snow to move, these are the two feet to have.

SKY WATCH ☆ *Mars is very close to the Moon on the 5th, one day before it crosses into Taurus. On the 6th, Mercury begins its best showing of the year and is easily seen in the fading evening twilight, especially before the 21st. Use binoculars to view orange Mercury very close to dim-green Uranus on the 14th. The Moon's orbit, experiencing an extreme tilt during 2006, will take it to unusual places: On the 8th, it leaves the zodiac and ventures into the northern constellation Auriga. Jupiter at midmonth rises by 1:00 A.M., while Saturn, high overhead, is out all night. The Moon is at its closest to the Earth for the year—when its surface is only 217,000 miles from ours, an extreme perigee—on the 27th.*

☽	First Quarter	5th day	1st hour	29th minute
○	Full Moon	12th day	23rd hour	44th minute
☾	Last Quarter	21st day	2nd hour	17th minute
●	New Moon	27th day	19th hour	31st minute

To use this page, see p. 92; for Key Letters, see p. 237; for Tide Corrections, see p. 234.
All times are given in Eastern Standard Time. ☞ **Bold = P.M.** ☞ Light = A.M.

Day of Year	Day of Month	Day of Week	Rises h. m.	Key	Sets h. m.	Key	Length of Day h. m.	Sun Fast m.	Declination of Sun ° '	High Tide Times Boston		Rises h. m.	Key	Sets h. m.	Key	Place	Age
32	1	W.	6 58	D	**4 59**	A	10 01	2	17 s.00	1	1¼	8 52	D	**9 05**	D	AQU	3
33	2	Th.	6 57	D	**5 00**	A	10 03	2	16 43	1¾	2	9 14	C	**10 21**	E	PSC	4
34	3	Fr.	6 56	D	**5 01**	A	10 05	2	16 25	2½	3	9 36	B	**11 35**	E	PSC	5
35	4	Sa.	6 55	D	**5 02**	A	10 07	2	16 07	3½	4	10 01	B	—	–	ARI	6
36	5	**A**	6 54	D	**5 04**	A	10 10	2	15 49	4¼	5	10 29	A	12 49	E	ARI	7
37	6	M.	6 52	D	**5 05**	A	10 13	2	15 31	5¼	6	11 03	A	2 01	E	TAU	8
38	7	Tu.	6 51	D	**5 06**	A	10 15	1	15 12	6¼	7¼	11 44	A	3 10	E	TAU	9
39	8	W.	6 50	D	**5 08**	B	10 18	1	14 53	7½	8¼	**12 34**	A	4 11	E	AUR	10
40	9	Th.	6 49	D	**5 09**	B	10 20	1	14 34	8½	9¼	**1 31**	A	5 04	E	AUR	11
41	10	Fr.	6 48	D	**5 10**	B	10 22	1	14 14	9¼	10	**2 34**	A	5 47	E	GEM	12
42	11	Sa.	6 46	D	**5 12**	B	10 26	1	13 55	10	10¾	**3 38**	B	6 22	E	CAN	13
43	12	**A**	6 45	D	**5 13**	B	10 28	1	13 35	10¾	11¼	**4 43**	B	6 49	E	CAN	14
44	13	M.	6 44	D	**5 14**	B	10 30	1	13 14	11½	11¾	**5 46**	C	7 12	E	LEO	15
45	14	Tu.	6 42	D	**5 15**	B	10 33	1	12 54	**12**	—	**6 48**	C	7 32	D	LEO	16
46	15	W.	6 41	D	**5 17**	B	10 36	1	12 33	12½	12½	**7 49**	D	7 50	D	LEO	17
47	16	Th.	6 40	D	**5 18**	B	10 38	2	12 13	1	1¼	**8 51**	D	8 07	C	VIR	18
48	17	Fr.	6 38	D	**5 19**	B	10 41	2	11 52	1½	1¾	**9 53**	E	8 25	B	VIR	19
49	18	Sa.	6 37	D	**5 20**	B	10 43	2	11 30	2¼	2½	**10 58**	E	8 44	B	VIR	20
50	19	**A**	6 35	D	**5 22**	B	10 47	2	11 09	2¾	3¼	—	–	9 07	B	VIR	21
51	20	M.	6 34	D	**5 23**	B	10 49	2	10 47	3½	4	**12 06**	E	9 34	A	LIB	22
52	21	Tu.	6 32	D	**5 24**	B	10 52	2	10 26	4¼	5	**1 16**	E	10 09	A	SCO	23
53	22	W.	6 31	D	**5 26**	B	10 55	2	10 04	5¼	6	**2 27**	E	10 55	A	OPH	24
54	23	Th.	6 29	D	**5 27**	B	10 58	2	9 42	6¼	7¼	**3 33**	E	11 54	A	SAG	25
55	24	Fr.	6 28	D	**5 28**	B	11 00	2	9 20	7½	8¼	**4 31**	E	**1 06**	A	SAG	26
56	25	Sa.	6 26	D	**5 29**	B	11 03	2	8 57	8½	9¼	**5 17**	E	**2 27**	B	SAG	27
57	26	**A**	6 25	D	**5 31**	B	11 06	3	8 19	9¼	10	**5 55**	E	**3 51**	B	CAP	28
58	27	M.	6 23	D	**5 32**	B	11 09	3	8 06	10¼	10¾	**6 25**	E	**5 14**	C	AQU	0
59	28	Tu.	6 21	D	**5 33**	B	11 12	3	7 s.50	11¼	11¾	**6 50**	D	**6 36**	D	AQU	1

FEBRUARY

FEBRUARY HATH 28 DAYS • 2006

The speckled sky is dim with snow,
The light flakes falter and fall slow. –John Townsend Trowbridge

Day of Month	Day of Week	Dates, Feasts, Fasts, Aspects, Tide Heights	Weather
1	W.	**St. Brigid** • ☾ ON EQ. • *He who would travel much should eat little.*	*Groundhogs*
2	Th.	**Candlemas** • **Groundhog Day** • ☾ AT ☊ • { 10.9 / 11.1	*see*
3	Fr.	♀ STAT. • U.S. copyright law began protecting music, 1831	*the*
4	Sa.	Shays's Rebellion, to aid the financial plight of farmers, failed, 1787 • Auspicious day for weddings. • { 10.6 / 9.6	*sun,*
5	**A**	**5th S. af. Ep.** • ☌♂☾ • Tides { 10.3 / 8.9	*then*
6	M.	☌♆☉ • Mr. Fred Rogers molded the 100 billionth Crayola crayon, 1996 • { 9.9 / 8.4	*duck*
7	Tu.	*The wise are too smart to deny their ignorance.* • Tides { 9.6 / 8.1	*it;*
8	W.	8°F in Jacksonville, Fla., 1835 • Jay Berwanger first to be drafted by NFL, 1936 • Tides { 9.5 / 8.1	*milder*
9	Th.	☾ RIDES HIGH • First Boeing 727 flight took place, 1963	*now,*
10	Fr.	Circus performer "General Tom Thumb" married Lavinia Warren, 1863 • Tides { 9.6 / 8.4	*but*
11	Sa.	☌♄☾ • First joint U.S.-Russian space shuttle mission completed, 1994 • { 9.8 / 8.6	*pouring*
12	**A**	**Septuagesima** • **Full Snow** ○ • Abe Lincoln born, 1809	*buckets!*
13	M.	☾ AT APO. • Ice floes in Gulf of Mexico, 1784 • ASCAP was founded, 1914 • { 10.0 / 9.0	*It*
14	Tu.	**Sts. Cyril & Methodius** • **Valentine's Day** • ☌☿♅	*feels*
15	W.	Susan B. Anthony born, 1820 • Winter's back breaks. • Tides { 9.2 / 9.8	*like*
16	Th.	☾ ON EQ. • ☾ AT ☋ • Benevolent and Protective Order of Elks founded, N.Y.C., 1868	*spring*
17	Fr.	♀ GR. BRIL. • Elvis Presley was awarded his first gold album, for *Elvis,* 1960 • { 9.3 / 9.3	*training:*
18	Sa.	*Abandon not your old clothes till you get your new.* • { 9.3 / 8.9	*Nope,*
19	**A**	**Sexagesima** • Thomas Edison's phonograph patented, 1878 • { 9.3 / 8.5	*snowing*
20	M.	**George Washington's Birthday (observed)** • ☌♃☾ • { 9.3 / 8.2	*and*
21	Tu.	George W. Bush's dog, Spotty (daughter of George H. W. Bush's dog, Millie), died, 2004 • Tides { 9.2 / 7.9	*raining.*
22	W.	G. Washington born, 1732 • Baseball manager "Sparky" Anderson born, 1934	*A*
23	Th.	☾ RUNS LOW • –18°F, Valley Head, Ala., 1905 • Tides { 9.6 / 8.1	*thaw*
24	Fr.	**St. Matthias** • ☌♀☾ • ☿ GR. ELONG. (18° EAST) • Tides { 10.0 / 8.6	*that's*
25	Sa.	Cassius Clay (later Muhammad Ali) won world heavyweight boxing championship, 1964 • { 10.5 / 9.2	*delightful,*
26	**A**	**Quinquagesima** • ☌♆☾ • Tides { 11.1 / 10.0	*then*
27	M.	**New** ● • ☾ AT PERIG. • 22nd Amendment, limiting U.S. presidents to two terms, ratified, 1951	*raw,*
28	Tu.	**Shrove Tuesday** • ☌☿☾ • *Many cares make the head white.* • { 11.8 / 11.1	*frightful!*

I hold it that a little rebellion, now and then, is a good thing, and as necessary in the political world as storms in the physical.
–Thomas Jefferson, third U.S. president

Farmer's Calendar

■ *February 10.* A bright, glittering winter day, the air strung so tight it twangs. Not a cloud, not the least hint of wind, except now and then when a puff pushes a dust of powder over the snowpack. The sun blinds, but it scarcely warms: It blazes off the snow and flashes from the icicles that fringe the frozen eaves. Still, it's more of a sun than we've seen in the past couple of months, and as it comes through the kitchen windows, it feels good.

So good that a calico cat who is old enough to know better is fooled. She sits in the window looking over the white world. Not for eight or ten weeks has she ventured out there, but today she feels a deep prompting to go forth. The warm, bright window, the lengthening shadows in the yard, the longer days persuade her that winter is past. She goes to the door, bats at it with her paw, and sets up a pitiful meowing. The door is opened for her, and out she goes.

So far, so good—but here's the thing: It's 15 below. The cat halts. She shakes herself, she shakes the snow off her feet, she fluffs up her fur. It's still 15 below. She's had enough. She returns to the kitchen door, bangs on it, meows, is admitted. Elapsed cat time outdoors: 30 seconds. That was half a minute too long. We're told to follow our instincts, our deep promptings, but sometimes our instincts are wrong. Winter isn't over yet, after all.

SKY WATCH ☆ *Mercury finishes its outstanding evening appearance during the first week of March, but it is much less bright than it was in February. Venus is dazzling, but not very high, in the predawn eastern sky. Mars, bright but fading, moves through Taurus. Saturn is still out most of the night and has a close meeting with the Moon on the 10th. Jupiter now rises before midnight and meets the Moon on the 18th. The vernal equinox brings the start of spring on the 20th, at 1:26 P.M. On the 29th, areas of Africa and Central Europe will experience an excellent four-minute total solar eclipse. By the next evening, North Americans will see the Moon as a smiling crescent directly above the sunset.*

☽	First Quarter	6th day	15th hour	16th minute
○	Full Moon	14th day	18th hour	35th minute
☾	Last Quarter	22nd day	14th hour	10th minute
●	New Moon	29th day	5th hour	15th minute

To use this page, see p. 92; for Key Letters, see p. 237; for Tide Corrections, see p. 234. All times are given in Eastern Standard Time. ☞ **Bold = P.M.** ☞ Light = A.M.

Day of Year	Day of Month	Day of Week	☀ Rises h. m.	Key	☀ Sets h. m.	Key	Length of Day h. m.	Sun Fast m.	Declination of Sun ° '	High Tide Times Boston	☽ Rises h. m.	Key	☽ Sets h. m.	Key	☽ Place	☽ Age
60	1	W.	6 20	D	**5 34**	B	11 14	3	7 s. 27	**12** —	7 14	C	**7 55**	E	PSC	2
61	2	Th.	6 18	D	**5 35**	B	11 17	3	7 05	12½ **12¾**	7 37	C	**9 14**	E	PSC	3
62	3	Fr.	6 17	D	**5 37**	B	11 20	4	6 42	1¼ **1¾**	8 01	B	**10 31**	E	PSC	4
63	4	Sa.	6 15	D	**5 38**	B	11 23	4	6 18	2 **2½**	8 29	A	**11 47**	E	ARI	5
64	5	**A**	6 13	D	**5 39**	B	11 26	4	5 55	3 **3½**	9 01	A	—	—	TAU	6
65	6	M.	6 12	D	**5 40**	B	11 28	4	5 32	3¾ **4½**	9 41	A	12 59	E	TAU	7
66	7	Tu.	6 10	D	**5 41**	B	11 31	4	5 09	4¾ **5¾**	10 28	A	2 05	E	AUR	8
67	8	W.	6 08	D	**5 43**	B	11 35	5	4 45	6 **6¾**	11 24	A	3 01	E	AUR	9
68	9	Th.	6 07	D	**5 44**	B	11 37	5	4 22	7 **7¾**	**12 25**	A	3 47	E	GEM	10
69	10	Fr.	6 05	D	**5 45**	B	11 40	5	3 58	8 **8¾**	**1 30**	A	4 24	E	CAN	11
70	11	Sa.	6 03	D	**5 46**	B	11 43	5	3 35	9 **9½**	**2 34**	B	4 54	E	CAN	12
71	12	**A**	6 02	C	**5 47**	B	11 45	6	3 11	9¾ **10¼**	**3 38**	B	5 18	E	LEO	13
72	13	M.	6 00	C	**5 48**	B	11 48	6	2 47	10¼ **10¾**	**4 40**	C	5 38	D	LEO	14
73	14	Tu.	5 58	C	**5 50**	B	11 52	6	2 24	11 **11¼**	**5 42**	D	5 57	D	LEO	15
74	15	W.	5 56	C	**5 51**	B	11 55	7	2 00	11½ 12	**6 43**	D	6 14	C	VIR	16
75	16	Th.	5 55	C	**5 52**	B	11 57	7	1 36	12¼ —	**7 46**	E	6 32	C	VIR	17
76	17	Fr.	5 53	C	**5 53**	B	12 00	7	1 13	12½ **12¾**	**8 50**	E	6 50	B	VIR	18
77	18	Sa.	5 51	C	**5 54**	B	12 03	7	0 49	1 **1½**	**9 57**	E	7 11	B	VIR	19
78	19	**A**	5 50	C	**5 55**	B	12 05	8	0 25	1½ **2**	**11 06**	E	7 37	A	LIB	20
79	20	M.	5 48	C	**5 57**	C	12 09	8	0 s. 02	2¼ **2¾**	—	—	8 08	A	LIB	21
80	21	Tu.	5 46	C	**5 58**	C	12 12	8	0 N. 22	3 **3¾**	12 16	E	8 49	A	SCO	22
81	22	W.	5 44	C	**5 59**	C	12 15	9	0 46	3¾ **4½**	1 22	E	9 42	A	SAG	23
82	23	Th.	5 43	C	**6 00**	C	12 17	9	1 10	4¾ **5¾**	2 21	E	10 46	A	SAG	24
83	24	Fr.	5 41	C	**6 01**	C	12 20	9	1 33	6 **6¾**	3 11	E	**12 01**	A	SAG	25
84	25	Sa.	5 39	C	**6 02**	C	12 23	9	1 57	7 **7¾**	3 50	E	**1 22**	B	CAP	26
85	26	**A**	5 37	C	**6 03**	C	12 26	10	2 20	8 **8¾**	4 22	E	**2 43**	C	CAP	27
86	27	M.	5 36	C	**6 04**	C	12 28	10	2 44	9 **9½**	4 49	D	**4 04**	D	AQU	28
87	28	Tu.	5 34	C	**6 06**	C	12 32	10	3 07	10 **10½**	5 13	D	**5 24**	D	AQU	29
88	29	W.	5 32	C	**6 07**	C	12 35	11	3 31	10¾ **11¼**	5 36	C	**6 44**	E	PSC	0
89	30	Th.	5 31	C	**6 08**	C	12 37	11	3 54	11¾ —	6 00	B	**8 03**	E	PSC	1
90	31	Fr.	5 29	C	**6 09**	C	12 40	11	4 N. 17	12 **12½**	6 26	B	**9 22**	E	ARI	2

MARCH HATH 31 DAYS • 2006

O Spring-time sweet!
The whole Earth smiles, thy coming to greet. –Unknown

Day of Month	Day of Week	Dates, Feasts, Fasts, Aspects, Tide Heights	Weather
1	W.	**Ash Wednesday** • ☾ AT ☊ • ☾ ON EQ. • Tides { 11.8 —	*The*
2	Th.	**St. Chad** • ☿ STAT. • *Love laughs at locksmiths.* • { 11.4 11.5	*plow-*
3	Fr.	Sing Sing prison, Ossining, N.Y., began taking prisoners' fingerprints, 1903 • Tides { 11.5 10.9	*man*
4	Sa.	♃ STAT. • Football coach Knute Rockne born, 1888 • { 11.2 10.2	*comes*
5	**A**	**1st S. in Lent** • Churchill's "Iron Curtain" speech, 1946 • Tides { 10.8 9.4	*and*
6	M.	**Pure Monday** • ☌♂☾ • Comedian Lou Costello born, 1906 • { 10.2 8.7	*then*
7	Tu.	**St. Perpetua** • First jazz recording released, 1917 • "Tiny" Tymm, 21-millionth Canadian, born, 1969	*re-*
8	W.	Ember Day • ☾ RIDES HIGH • Wheeled suitcase with collapsible towing handle patented, 1994	*treats;*
9	Th.	*The only perfect climate is in bed.* • Tides { 9.1 8.0	*it snows*
10	Fr.	Ember Day • ☌♄☾ • An earthquake near Long Beach, Calif., measured 6.4, 1933	*again,*
11	Sa.	Ember Day • ☿ IN INF. ☌ • Florida panther added to endangered list, 1967 • { 9.3 8.5	*and*
12	**A**	**Sunday of Orthodoxy** • ☾ AT APO. • Tides { 9.5 8.8	*he*
13	M.	Solar flare caused power grid failure of Hydro-Quebec in Canada, 1989 • Tides { 9.7 9.1	*repeats.*
14	Tu.	**Full Worm** ○ • **Eclipse** ☾ • Chipmunks emerge from hibernation now.	*Saint*
15	W.	Beware the ides of March. • ☾ ON EQ. • ☾ AT ☋ • Tides { 9.8 9.6	*Pat's*
16	Th.	Nathaniel Hawthorne's *The Scarlet Letter* published, 1850 • Tides { 9.7 —	*paraders*
17	Fr.	**St. Patrick** • Franklin D. Roosevelt married Anna Eleanor Roosevelt, 1905 • { 9.8 9.5	*better*
18	Sa.	British Parliament repealed the Stamp Act, 1766 • { 9.8 9.2	*wear*
19	**A**	**3rd S. in Lent** • ☌♃☾ • Explorer David Livingstone born, 1813	*waders.*
20	M.	**St. Joseph** • **Vernal Equinox** • Physicist Sir Isaac Newton died, 1727	*Sunny*
21	Tu.	First rock concert, held in Cleveland, Ohio, 1952 • { 9.6 8.3	*spells,*
22	W.	☾ RUNS LOW • Louis L'Amour, author of more than 100 books, born, 1908 • { 9.6 8.1	*then a*
23	Th.	*Half an orange tastes as sweet as a whole one.* • { 9.6 8.2	*soaking;*
24	Fr.	☿ STAT. • Ground-breaking ceremony for N.Y.C. subway system, 1900 • Tides { 9.7 8.5	*but*
25	Sa.	**Annunciation** • ☌♆☾ • ☌♀☾ • ♀ GR. ELONG. (47° WEST)	*through*
26	**A**	**4th S. in Lent** • ☌♆♀ • Tides { 10.5 9.8	*the*
27	M.	☌☿☾ • ☌♅☾ • Cherry trees planted in Washington, D.C., 1912 • { 11.0 10.6	*mud,*
28	Tu.	☾ ON EQ. • ☾ AT ☊ • ☾ AT PERIG. • Singer Maria von Trapp died, 1987	*crocuses*
29	W.	**New** ● • **Eclipse** ☉ • ♇ STAT. • Tides { 11.5 11.6	*are*
30	Th.	H. Lipman patented pencil and eraser combo, 1858 • { 11.4 —	*surely*
31	Fr.	*A dry March, wet April, and cool May Fill barn, cellar, and bring much hay.* • Tides { 11.8 11.0	*poking.*

Farmer's Calendar

■ A well-stocked winter feeder ought to be a peaceable place. The kindly owner has laid on plenty of everything and for every taste: seeds, grains, suet, even bread-crumbs—even, for heaven's sake, peanut butter. The birds never had it so good. Do they know this? Do they show in their conduct at the feeder a patient, grateful decorum?

By no means. The feeder is a war zone where tiny Pattons struggle bitterly, evidencing a level of natural aggression that would be terrifying if housed in bodies that weighed more than a few ounces. A chickadee is feasting on the sunflower seeds when another alights nearby. The first hurls itself at the newcomer, and the two of them go at each other like enraged tigers—until a squadron of goldfinches zooms in and drives the combatants off, supplanting their two-way battle with a chaotic free-for-all.

That the feeder, where mildness would surely have its reward, should be a theater of greed and violence is especially surprising given the lowly position of the antagonists. They are the bottom of the avian food chain, a meal for every cat, weasel, hawk, and owl in the neighborhood. Being weak, they ought to hang together, to share, to look out for one another. But no, they choose to squabble and fight instead. So we see in our winter visitors great charm, beauty, and peerless aerodynamics —united with a certain lack of moral intelligence.

THE FOURTH MONTH • 2006

SKY WATCH ☆ *This is the last hurrah for Orion and surrounding brilliant constellations as they hover in the southwest at nightfall. The brightest stars seem to vanish into the solar glare: They are setting four minutes earlier each evening, and the Sun is setting one to two minutes later. Mars moves into Gemini in midmonth, after meeting the Moon on the 3rd. The Moon has a conjunction with Saturn on the 6th and Jupiter on the 14th. Jupiter now rises by 10:00 P.M. and dominates the sky. Binoculars reveal a close conjunction of dazzling Venus and faint Uranus from the 18th to the 20th, especially on the 19th, an hour before sunrise. The Moon joins them on the 24th.*

☽	**First Quarter**	5th day	8th hour	1st minute
○	**Full Moon**	13th day	12th hour	40th minute
☾	**Last Quarter**	20th day	23rd hour	28th minute
●	**New Moon**	27th day	15th hour	44th minute

To use this page, see p. 92; for Key Letters, see p. 237; for Tide Corrections, see p. 234.

After 2:00 A.M. on April 2, Eastern Daylight Time is given. ☞ **Bold = P.M.** ☞ Light = A.M.

Day of Year	Day of Month	Day of Week	☼ Rises h. m.	Key	☼ Sets h. m.	Key	Length of Day h. m.	Sun Fast m.	Declination of Sun ° ′	High Tide Times Boston		☽ Rises h. m.	Key	☽ Sets h. m.	Key	☽ Place	☽ Age
91	1	Sa.	5 27	B	**6 10**	C	12 43	12	4N.40	12¾	**1½**	6 57	A	**10 39**	E	ARI	3
92	2	**A**	6 25	B	**7 11**	C	12 46	12	5 03	1½	**3¼**	8 34	A	—	–	TAU	4
93	3	M.	6 24	B	**7 12**	C	12 48	12	5 26	3½	**4¼**	9 20	A	12 50	E	TAU	5
94	4	Tu.	6 22	B	**7 13**	C	12 51	12	5 49	4¼	**5**	10 14	A	1 53	E	AUR	6
95	5	W.	6 20	B	**7 15**	D	12 55	13	6 12	5¼	**6¼**	11 15	A	2 44	E	GEM	7
96	6	Th.	6 19	B	**7 16**	D	12 57	13	6 35	6¼	**7¼**	**12 19**	A	3 25	E	GEM	8
97	7	Fr.	6 17	B	**7 17**	D	13 00	13	6 58	7½	**8¼**	**1 24**	B	3 57	E	CAN	9
98	8	Sa.	6 15	B	**7 18**	D	13 03	14	7 20	8½	**9**	**2 28**	B	4 22	E	LEO	10
99	9	**A**	6 13	B	**7 19**	D	13 06	14	7 43	9¼	**10**	**3 31**	C	4 44	D	LEO	11
100	10	M.	6 12	B	**7 20**	D	13 08	14	8 05	10¼	**10½**	**4 33**	C	5 03	D	LEO	12
101	11	Tu.	6 10	B	**7 21**	D	13 11	14	8 27	10¾	**11¼**	**5 34**	D	5 21	C	VIR	13
102	12	W.	6 09	B	**7 22**	D	13 13	15	8 49	11½	**11¾**	**6 37**	D	5 38	C	VIR	14
103	13	Th.	6 07	B	**7 24**	D	13 17	15	9 11	**12**	—	**7 41**	E	5 56	B	VIR	15
104	14	Fr.	6 05	B	**7 25**	D	13 20	15	9 32	12¼	**12¾**	**8 48**	E	6 17	B	VIR	16
105	15	Sa.	6 04	B	**7 26**	D	13 22	15	9 54	12¾	**1½**	**9 57**	E	6 41	A	LIB	17
106	16	**A**	6 02	B	**7 27**	D	13 25	16	10 15	1½	**2**	**11 07**	E	7 11	A	LIB	18
107	17	M.	6 00	B	**7 28**	D	13 28	16	10 36	2	**2¾**	—	–	7 49	A	SCO	19
108	18	Tu.	5 59	B	**7 29**	D	13 30	16	10 57	2¾	**3½**	12 15	E	8 37	A	OPH	20
109	19	W.	5 57	B	**7 30**	D	13 33	16	11 18	3½	**4½**	1 16	E	9 38	A	SAG	21
110	20	Th.	5 56	B	**7 31**	D	13 35	17	11 38	4½	**5¼**	2 08	E	10 48	A	SAG	22
111	21	Fr.	5 54	B	**7 33**	D	13 39	17	11 59	5½	**6¼**	2 49	E	**12 05**	B	CAP	23
112	22	Sa.	5 53	B	**7 34**	D	13 41	17	12 19	6½	**7½**	3 23	E	**1 23**	C	CAP	24
113	23	**A**	5 51	B	**7 35**	D	13 44	17	12 39	7¾	**8½**	3 50	E	**2 42**	C	AQU	25
114	24	M.	5 50	B	**7 36**	D	13 46	17	12 58	8¾	**9¼**	4 14	D	**3 59**	D	AQU	26
115	25	Tu.	5 48	B	**7 37**	D	13 49	18	13 18	9¾	**10¼**	4 37	C	**5 16**	E	PSC	27
116	26	W.	5 47	B	**7 38**	D	13 51	18	13 37	10¾	**11**	5 00	B	**6 35**	E	PSC	28
117	27	Th.	5 45	B	**7 39**	D	13 54	18	13 56	11½	**11¾**	5 24	B	**7 54**	E	ARI	0
118	28	Fr.	5 44	B	**7 40**	D	13 56	18	14 15	**12½**	—	5 53	B	**9 12**	E	ARI	1
119	29	Sa.	5 43	B	**7 42**	D	13 59	18	14 34	12½	**1¼**	6 27	A	**10 28**	E	TAU	2
120	30	**A**	5 41	B	**7 43**	D	14 02	18	14N.53	1½	**2**	7 09	A	**11 37**	E	TAU	3

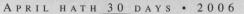

April hath 30 days • 2006

April is here!
Listen, a bluebird is caroling near! –Eben Eugene Rexford

Day of Month	Day of Week	Dates, Feasts, Fasts, Aspects, Tide Heights	Weather
1	Sa.	**All Fools'** • *Never offer to teach fish to swim.* • { 11.7 / 10.5	*Foolish,*
2	**A**	**5th S. in Lent** • **Daylight Saving Time begins, 2:00 A.M.** • { 11.3 / 9.9	*coolish,*
3	M.	**St. Richard of Chichester** • ☌♂☾ • Tides { 10.7 / 9.2	*winter's*
4	Tu.	☾ RIDES HIGH • President William Henry Harrison died of pneumonia a month after inauguration, 1841	*mulish.*
5	W.	♄ STAT. • Richard J. Daley elected as Chicago's 39th mayor, 1955 • Tides { 9.5 / 8.2	*It*
6	Th.	☌♄☾ • Snow-melting apparatus patented, 1869 • { 9.1 / 8.0	*ain't*
7	Fr.	Football's Tony Dorsett born, 1954 • *Little brooks make great rivers.*	*lovely;*
8	Sa.	☿ GR. ELONG. (28° WEST) • League of Nations assembled in Geneva for last time, 1946 • Tides { 8.9 / 8.4	*in*
9	**A**	**Palm Sunday** • ☾ AT APO. • Tides { 9.1 / 8.7	*Maine,*
10	M.	First Arbor Day celebration, held in Nebraska, 1872 • { 9.2 / 9.1	*it's*
11	Tu.	☾ ON EQ. • ☾ AT ☋ • Rattlesnake bit shopper in tree section of Okla. home-improvement store, 2004	*shovelly!*
12	W.	Space shuttle *Columbia* first launched, 1981 • { 9.5 / 9.8	*The*
13	Th.	**First day of Passover** • **Full Pink** ○ • President Thomas Jefferson born, 1743	*sun*
14	Fr.	**Good Friday** • Deadly tornado, St. Cloud, Minn., 1886 • Tides { 10.0 / 9.5	*is*
15	Sa.	☌♃☾ • Pres. Lincoln called for 75,000 Union militia volunteers, 1861 • { 10.1 / 9.4	*getting*
16	**A**	**Easter** • Two giant pandas arrived at the National Zoo, Wash., D.C., 1972 • { 10.2 / 9.2	*stronger;*
17	M.	**Easter Monday** • Business tycoon John P. Morgan born, 1837 • { 10.2 / 9.0	*days*
18	Tu.	☌⛢♀ • Actress Grace Kelly married Prince Rainier of Monaco in civil ceremony, 1956	*(though*
19	W.	☾ RUNS LOW • *Oxford English Dictionary* completed, 1928	*damp)*
20	Th.	Electron microscope demonstrated to public, 1940 • { 9.9 / 8.6	*are*
21	Fr.	Giants and Yankees played ball to raise funds for *Titanic* survivors, 1912 • Tides { 9.9 / 8.7	*getting*
22	Sa.	☌♆☾ • *When eager bites the thirsty flea, Clouds and rain you sure shall see.* • { 9.9 / 9.1	*longer.*
23	**A**	**2nd S. of Easter** • **Orthodox Easter** • ☌⛢☾	*Bees*
24	M.	☌♀☾ • *The Old Farmer's Almanac* founder, Robert B. Thomas, born, 1766	*buzzin'—*
25	Tu.	**St. Mark** • ☾ ON EQ. • ☾ AT ☊ • ☾ AT PERIG. • { 10.6 / 11.0	*but*
26	W.	☌☿☾ • First international satellite launched, 1962 • Tides { 10.8 / 11.5	*drizzles*
27	Th.	**New** ● • Expo '67 opened, Montreal, Quebec, 1967 • { 10.8 / 11.8	*by*
28	Fr.	*There is more than one way out of the woods.* • Tides { 10.7 / —	*the*
29	Sa.	Taylor, Tex., received 2 inches of rain in ten minutes, 1905 • Poplars leaf out about now. • { 11.8 / 10.4	*dozen,*
30	**A**	**3rd S. of Easter** • *Look and you shall find.* • { 11.5 / 10.0	*cousin.*

A mathematician is a device for turning coffee into theorems.
–Paul Erdos, Hungarian mathematician

Farmer's Calendar

■ Any house, if you have lived in it for a while, becomes a kind of laboratory or experiment station, where the passing seasons can be recorded and observed. The materials of which the house is built react to changing conditions, making the house a recording instrument of considerable sensitivity. How that instrument is to be read, though, isn't obvious. You have to learn it over time as years of residence add up.

On this place, for example, we measure the strength of the winter past by keeping track of a particular snow pile in an angle of the house. That corner faces north and east and gets no direct sun at all. It does get, over the course of the winter, the snow and ice slide from off the roof. As spring gains a hold and winter melts away, a moraine of snow hangs on in that cold corner. The date on which it at last disappears gives you a gauge of how tough the winter has been. Most years, the snow is gone by late April, but it has sometimes endured into June.

Around the same time that the dregs of the snow vanish, the door to the cellar stairs begins to stick. By midsummer it won't close at all, but Columbus Day will see it right. There's a picture in the sitting room that tilts out of straight in the spring, and the house has other mysterious leaks, creaks, and crotchets that must mean something—if I were acute enough to interpret them.

SKY WATCH ☆ *Jupiter reaches opposition on the 4th. However, it is at its brightest of the year and nearest to Earth one day later, when it shines at magnitude –2.0. Retrograding in Libra, it is out all night. The Moon meets Saturn on the 3rd and Jupiter on the 11th, before coming close to Venus on the 24th. It passes just to the right of Mercury in a conjunction on the 27th and meets Saturn again on the 31st. The odd tilt of the lunar orbit keeps the Moon extremely low during the midmonth period; in the northern parts of Canada and Alaska, it simply does not rise at all. Mars, fading all the while, crosses into Cancer at the end of the month and approaches Saturn.*

☽	First Quarter	5th day	1st hour	13th minute
○	Full Moon	13th day	2nd hour	51st minute
☾	Last Quarter	20th day	5th hour	20th minute
●	New Moon	27th day	1st hour	26th minute

To use this page, see p. 92; for Key Letters, see p. 237; for Tide Corrections, see p. 234.
All times are given in Eastern Daylight Time. ☞ **Bold** = P.M. ☞ Light = A.M.

Day of Year	Day of Month	Day of Week	Rises h. m.	Key	Sets h. m.	Key	Length of Day h. m.	Sun Fast m.	Declination of Sun ° '	High Tide Times Boston		Rises h. m.	Key	Sets h. m.	Key	Place	Age
121	1	M.	5 40	B	**7 44**	D	14 04	18	15 N.11	2¼	**3**	8 01	A	—	–	AUR	4
122	2	Tu.	5 38	B	**7 45**	D	14 07	19	15 29	3	**3¾**	9 01	A	12 34	E	AUR	5
123	3	W.	5 37	B	**7 46**	D	14 09	19	15 47	3¾	**4¾**	10 05	A	1 20	E	GEM	6
124	4	Th.	5 36	A	**7 47**	D	14 11	19	16 04	4¾	**5½**	11 11	B	1 56	E	CAN	7
125	5	Fr.	5 35	A	**7 48**	D	14 13	19	16 21	5¾	**6½**	**12 16**	B	2 25	E	CAN	8
126	6	Sa.	5 33	A	**7 49**	D	14 16	19	16 38	6¾	**7½**	**1 20**	C	2 48	E	LEO	9
127	7	**A**	5 32	A	**7 50**	D	14 18	19	16 55	7¾	**8¼**	**2 22**	C	3 08	D	LEO	10
128	8	M.	5 31	A	**7 52**	D	14 21	19	17 11	8½	**9**	**3 23**	D	3 26	C	LEO	11
129	9	Tu.	5 30	A	**7 53**	D	14 23	19	17 27	9½	**9¾**	**4 25**	D	3 43	C	VIR	12
130	10	W.	5 29	A	**7 54**	D	14 25	19	17 43	10¼	**10½**	**5 29**	E	4 01	B	VIR	13
131	11	Th.	5 27	A	**7 55**	D	14 28	19	17 58	11	**11**	**6 35**	E	4 21	B	VIR	14
132	12	Fr.	5 26	A	**7 56**	D	14 30	19	18 14	11½	**11¾**	**7 44**	E	4 44	B	LIB	15
133	13	Sa.	5 25	A	**7 57**	D	14 32	19	18 29	**12¼**	—	**8 55**	E	5 12	A	LIB	16
134	14	**A**	5 24	A	**7 58**	D	14 34	19	18 43	12¼	**1**	**10 05**	E	5 47	A	SCO	17
135	15	M.	5 23	A	**7 59**	E	14 36	19	18 57	1	**1¾**	**11 10**	E	6 33	A	OPH	18
136	16	Tu.	5 22	A	**8 00**	E	14 38	19	19 11	1¾	**2½**	—	–	7 31	A	SAG	19
137	17	W.	5 21	A	**8 01**	E	14 40	19	19 24	2½	**3¼**	12 05	E	8 39	A	SAG	20
138	18	Th.	5 20	A	**8 02**	E	14 42	19	19 38	3¼	**4¼**	12 49	E	9 55	B	CAP	21
139	19	Fr.	5 19	A	**8 03**	E	14 44	19	19 51	4¼	**5**	1 25	E	11 12	B	CAP	22
140	20	Sa.	5 18	A	**8 04**	E	14 46	19	20 03	5¼	**6**	1 54	E	**12 29**	C	AQU	23
141	21	**A**	5 18	A	**8 05**	E	14 47	19	20 15	6¼	**7**	2 18	D	**1 45**	D	AQU	24
142	22	M.	5 17	A	**8 06**	E	14 49	19	20 28	7½	**8**	2 40	C	**3 00**	D	PSC	25
143	23	Tu.	5 16	A	**8 07**	E	14 51	19	20 39	8½	**9**	3 02	C	**4 15**	E	PSC	26
144	24	W.	5 15	A	**8 08**	E	14 53	19	20 50	9½	**9¾**	3 25	B	**5 31**	E	PSC	27
145	25	Th.	5 14	A	**8 09**	E	14 55	19	21 01	10½	**10¾**	3 51	B	**6 49**	E	ARI	28
146	26	Fr.	5 14	A	**8 09**	E	14 55	19	21 11	11¼	**11½**	4 22	A	**8 05**	E	ARI	29
147	27	Sa.	5 13	A	**8 10**	E	14 57	19	21 21	**12¼**	—	5 01	A	**9 17**	E	TAU	0
148	28	**A**	5 12	A	**8 11**	E	14 59	18	21 31	12¼	**1**	5 49	A	**10 20**	E	TAU	1
149	29	M.	5 12	A	**8 12**	E	15 00	18	21 40	1	**1¾**	6 45	A	**11 12**	E	AUR	2
150	30	Tu.	5 11	A	**8 13**	E	15 02	18	21 49	1¾	**2½**	7 49	A	**11 53**	E	AUR	3
151	31	W.	5 11	A	**8 14**	E	15 03	18	21 N.58	2½	**3¼**	8 56	A	—	–	CAN	4

CALENDAR

MAY HATH 31 DAYS • 2006

The flowers in the breeze are swaying, swaying,
The whole wide world is out a-Maying. –Genevieve Mary Irons

Day of Month	Day of Week	Dates, Feasts, Fasts, Aspects, Tide Heights	Weather
1	M.	**Sts. Philip & James** • **May Day** • ☾ RIDES HIGH • { 11.1 9.5	*Warm*
2	Tu.	**St. Athanasius** • ☌♂☾ • First U.S. kindergarten for blind opened, 1887	*and*
3	W.	**Invention of the Holy Cross** • Washington, D.C., incorporated as a city, 1802	*stormy,*
4	Th.	☌♄☾ • ♃ AT ☍ • First Freedom Ride began, 1961 • Tides { 9.4 8.4	*bright*
5	Fr.	**Cinco de Mayo** • Hawaii's Kilauea erupted, 1973 • { 9.1 8.3	*and*
6	Sa.	Linus Yale Jr. received patent for a lock and key, 1851 • *Even the sharpest ear can not hear an ant singing.*	*cheery!*
7	**A**	**4th S. of Easter** • ☾ AT APO. • Tides { 8.8 8.7	*Get*
8	M.	**St. Julian of Norwich** • ☾ ON EQ. • World's fattest raccoon (~75 lbs.) died, 2004	*outside*
9	Tu.	**St. Gregory of Nazianzus** • ☾ AT ☋ • Tides { 8.9 9.4	*while*
10	W.	*You can't make bricks without straw.* • Tides { 9.0 9.7	*it*
11	Th.	James Monroe became first U.S. president to ride a steamboat, 1819 • **Three** • { 9.1 10.0	*lasts,*
12	Fr.	☌♃☾ • Tornado struck Xenia, Ohio, 1886 • **Chilly** • { 9.2 10.3	*dearie—*
13	Sa.	**Vesak** • **Full Flower** ○ • **Saints** • Tides { 9.2 —	*now*
14	**A**	**5th S. of Easter** • Singer Bobby Darin born, 1936 • { 10.4 9.2	*it's*
15	M.	*Where everyone goes, the grass never grows.* • { 10.6 9.2	*dreary.*
16	Tu.	☾ RUNS LOW • Congress approved minting the nickel, 1866 • Muppets creator Jim Henson died, 1990	*Cooling-*
17	W.	First coin-operated mailbox, the Mailomat, installed, 1939 • Boxer Sugar Ray Leonard born, 1956 • { 10.6 9.1	*off*
18	Th.	☿ IN SUP. ☌ • Tennessee Valley Authority created, 1933 • Tides { 10.5 9.1	*period:*
19	Fr.	**St. Dunstan** • ☌♆☾ • Author Oscar Wilde released from jail, 1897 • { 10.3 9.2	*dank*
20	Sa.	Homestead Act signed, 1862 • Cranberries in bud now. • Tides { 10.2 9.5	*and*
21	**A**	**Rogation S.** • ☌♅☾ • Tides { 10.0 9.8	*dismal,*
22	M.	**Victoria Day (Canada)** • ☾ ON EQ. • ☾ AT ☊ • ☾ AT PERIG. • ♆ STAT.	*but*
23	Tu.	*Better to be deprived of food for three days, than tea for one.* • Tides { 10.0 10.8	*blossoms*
24	W.	☌♀☾ • Steamer *Victoria* sank in Thames River, near London, Ontario, 1881 • { 10.0 11.2	*are*
25	Th.	**Ascension** • Hands Across America, 1986 • Tides { 10.0 11.4	*myriad!*
26	Fr.	Smallpox epidemic Boston, Mass., 1721 • Entertainer Al Jolson born, 1886 • { 10.0 11.5	*Showers—*
27	Sa.	**New** ● • Indianapolis, Ind., experienced its latest freeze on record, 1961 • { 9.9 —	*Decorate*
28	**A**	**1st S. af. Asc.** • First stamp auction in the U.S., 1870 • { 11.4 9.7	*heroes'*
29	M.	**Memorial Day (observed)** • ☾ RIDES HIGH • President John F. Kennedy born, 1917 • { 11.1 9.5	*graves*
30	Tu.	☌♂☾ • Lincoln Memorial dedicated, Washington, D.C., 1922 • Tides { 10.8 9.2	*with*
31	W.	**Visit. of Mary** • ☌♄☾ • *Moderate measures succeed best.* • { 10.3 9.0	*flowers.*

Farmer's Calendar

■ A spider makes its strange, busy way across a table. It's tiny, too small to have any particular color. It advances in little darts and dashes so quick that the eye can have trouble following them. It is no bigger than the lowercase "o" on this page, but even so, it partakes in the uncanniness of the spider kind.

There are about 3,500 species of spiders in North America, and every one of them is regarded with special misgivings. People don't like spiders, as a rule, but our response to them is complex. We have for spiders some of the same feelings we have for snakes: an odd union of fear and veneration—almost affection.

Why? Why are spiders so creepy—so much creepier than insects, which, in most respects, they so resemble? Surely, the answer is in their locomotion, their way of going. An insect on its six legs is not such an outlandish thing after all, not that different from an animal that goes on all fours. It's the extra pair of legs, numbers seven and eight, that makes the spider's gait that much more complex and alarming than the insect's. Again as with the snake, which seems to move without motion, it's the spider's progress, its odd, agitated movement, that makes us jump. Spiders have a sudden, nervous haste to their motion, resembling that of no other being. For this, for their originality, we distrust them.

SKY WATCH ☆ *This is an exciting planet month in the evening sky. For the first two weeks, Mercury has an especially good showing in evening twilight. Mars meets Saturn in Cancer. The ringed planet is in front of the lovely "Beehive" star cluster from the 1st to the 15th; use binoculars. Mars is there, too, from the 14th to 17th and is best viewed around 10:00 P.M. Impossibly dim Pluto is at opposition on the 16th in the constellation Serpens. Its lopsided oval orbit is now carrying the most distant planet even farther away at each opposition. The solstice ushers in summer on the 21st at 8:26 A.M. On the 27th, the Moon, Mercury, Saturn, and Mars all come together in Cancer and are fairly low in the fading evening twilight.*

☽ First Quarter	3rd day	19th hour	6th minute
○ Full Moon	11th day	14th hour	3rd minute
☾ Last Quarter	18th day	10th hour	8th minute
● New Moon	25th day	12th hour	5th minute

To use this page, see p. 92; for Key Letters, see p. 237; for Tide Corrections, see p. 234.
All times are given in Eastern Daylight Time. ☞ **Bold** = P.M. ☞ Light = A.M.

Day of Year	Day of Month	Day of Week	☼ Rises h. m.	Key	☼ Sets h. m.	Key	Length of Day h. m.	Sun Fast m.	Declination of Sun ° ′	High Tide Times Boston		☽ Rises h. m.	Key	☽ Sets h. m.	Key	☽ Place	☽ Age
152	1	Th.	5 10	A	**8 14**	E	15 04	18	22 N.06	3½	4¼	10 02	B	**12 24**	E	CAN	5
153	2	Fr.	5 10	A	**8 15**	E	15 05	18	22 14	4¼	5	11 07	C	**12 50**	E	LEO	6
154	3	Sa.	5 09	A	**8 16**	E	15 07	18	22 22	5	5¾	**12 10**	C	1 11	D	LEO	7
155	4	**A**	5 09	A	**8 17**	E	15 08	17	22 28	6	6½	**1 11**	D	1 30	D	LEO	8
156	5	M.	5 08	A	**8 17**	E	15 09	17	22 35	7	7½	**2 12**	D	1 48	C	VIR	9
157	6	Tu.	5 08	A	**8 18**	E	15 10	17	22 41	7¾	8¼	**3 15**	D	2 05	C	VIR	10
158	7	W.	5 08	A	**8 19**	E	15 11	17	22 47	8¾	9	**4 19**	E	2 24	B	VIR	11
159	8	Th.	5 08	A	**8 19**	E	15 11	17	22 53	9½	9¾	**5 27**	E	2 45	B	VIR	12
160	9	Fr.	5 08	A	**8 20**	E	15 12	16	22 58	10¼	10½	**6 38**	E	3 11	A	LIB	13
161	10	Sa.	5 07	A	**8 20**	E	15 13	16	23 03	11	11¼	**7 49**	E	3 44	A	SCO	14
162	11	**A**	5 07	A	**8 21**	E	15 14	16	23 07	11¾	12	**8 58**	E	4 26	A	OPH	15
163	12	M.	5 07	A	**8 21**	E	15 14	16	23 10	12½	—	**9 58**	E	5 20	A	SAG	16
164	13	Tu.	5 07	A	**8 22**	E	15 15	16	23 14	12¾	1½	**10 47**	E	6 27	A	SAG	17
165	14	W.	5 07	A	**8 22**	E	15 15	15	23 17	1½	2¼	**11 26**	E	7 42	B	SAG	18
166	15	Th.	5 07	A	**8 23**	E	15 16	15	23 19	2¼	3	**11 57**	E	9 01	B	CAP	19
167	16	Fr.	5 07	A	**8 23**	E	15 16	15	23 20	3¼	4	—	–	10 19	C	CAP	20
168	17	Sa.	5 07	A	**8 23**	E	15 16	15	23 23	4	4¾	12 22	D	11 35	D	AQU	21
169	18	**A**	5 07	A	**8 24**	E	15 17	15	23 25	5	5¾	12 45	D	**12 50**	D	PSC	22
170	19	M.	5 07	A	**8 24**	E	15 17	14	23 26	6	6¾	1 07	C	**2 04**	E	PSC	23
171	20	Tu.	5 07	A	**8 24**	E	15 17	14	23 26	7	7½	1 29	B	**3 18**	E	PSC	24
172	21	W.	5 08	A	**8 25**	E	15 17	14	23 26	8¼	8½	1 53	B	**4 34**	E	ARI	25
173	22	Th.	5 08	A	**8 25**	E	15 17	14	23 26	9¼	9½	2 22	A	**5 49**	E	ARI	26
174	23	Fr.	5 08	A	**8 25**	E	15 17	14	23 25	10¼	10¼	2 57	A	**7 02**	E	TAU	27
175	24	Sa.	5 09	A	**8 25**	E	15 16	13	23 24	11	11¼	3 40	A	**8 08**	E	TAU	28
176	25	**A**	5 09	A	**8 25**	E	15 16	13	23 23	12	12	4 33	A	**9 03**	E	AUR	0
177	26	M.	5 09	A	**8 25**	E	15 16	13	23 21	12¾	—	5 34	A	**9 48**	E	GEM	1
178	27	Tu.	5 10	A	**8 25**	E	15 15	13	23 19	12¾	1½	6 40	B	**10 23**	E	GEM	2
179	28	W.	5 10	A	**8 25**	E	15 15	12	23 16	1½	2¼	7 48	B	**10 51**	E	CAN	3
180	29	Th.	5 10	A	**8 25**	E	15 15	12	23 13	2¼	2¾	8 54	B	**11 14**	D	LEO	4
181	30	Fr.	5 11	A	**8 25**	E	15 14	12	23 N.09	3	3½	9 57	C	**11 34**	D	LEO	5

JUNE HATH 30 DAYS • 2006

Joy for the sturdy trees;
Fanned by each fragrant breeze. –Samuel Francis Smith

Day of Month	Day of Week	Dates, Feasts, Fasts, Aspects, Tide Heights	Weather
1	Th.	**Orthodox Ascension** • 39°F, Springfield, Ill., 2003 • {9.9 8.7	*Bang!*
2	Fr.	**Shavuot** • First soft landing of U.S. spacecraft *(Surveyor I)* on Moon, 1966 • {9.5 8.6	*Crash!*
3	Sa.	☾ at apo. • *A good life keeps off wrinkles.* • {9.1 8.6	*Lightning*
4	**A**	**Whit S. • Pentecost** • Tides {8.8 8.7	*flash!*
5	M.	**St. Boniface** • ☾ on Eq. • ☾ at ☋ • Tides {8.6 8.9	*Summer*
6	Tu.	D-Day, 1944 • Barbara Washburn reached summit of Alaska's Mt. McKinley, 1947 • {8.5 9.2	*enters*
7	W.	Ember Day • William Bruce Mumford first U.S. citizen hanged for treason, 1862 • {8.5 9.5	*with*
8	Th.	☌♃☾ • N.Y. Yankees retired Mickey Mantle's uniform, No. 7, 1969 • Tides {8.6 9.8	*a*
9	Fr.	Ember Day • *You can't grow figs from thistles.* • {8.7 10.1	*splash!*
10	Sa.	Ember Day • Singer Judy Garland born, 1922 • Pacific salmon migrate upriver. • {8.9 10.4	*Clear*
11	**A**	**Trinity • Orthodox Pentecost • Full Strawberry** ○	*and*
12	M.	**St. Barnabas** • ☾ runs low • Society of Unitarian Christians organized, 1796	*bright*
13	Tu.	Police required to inform suspects of their rights before questioning, 1966 • Tides {10.9 9.3	*for*
14	W.	**St. Basil** • Isaac Fisher Jr. patented sandpaper, 1834	*brides*
15	Th.	☌♆☾ • Composer Edvard H. Grieg born, 1843 • Tides {11.0 9.6	*and grooms.*
16	Fr.	☾ at perig. • ♇ at ☍ • 124°F, Mecca, Calif., 1917	*Golfers,*
17	Sa.	☌♂♄ • ☌♅☾ • French ship *Isère,* with Statue of Liberty in 214 crates, arrived in N.Y.C., 1885	*keep*
18	**A**	**Corpus Christi • Orthodox All Saints'** • ☾ on Eq. • ☾ at ☊	*your*
19	M.	♅ stat. • First Father's Day celebrated, Spokane, Wash., 1910 • Tides {10.0 10.4	*eyes*
20	Tu.	☿ gr. elong. (25° east) • *All is soon ready in an orderly house.* • {9.7 10.6	*on*
21	W.	**Summer Solstice** • First amendment to Canada's Constitution Act of 1982 took effect, 1984 • {9.5 10.8	*the*
22	Th.	**St. Alban** • ☌♀☾ • Hail, 18.75 inches in circumference, fell in Aurora, Nebr., 2003	*horizon;*
23	Fr.	Texas voted in favor of annexation by the U.S., 1845 • Butterfly weed in bloom now. • {9.3 11.0	*lightning*
24	Sa.	**Nativ. John the Baptist • Midsummer Day** • {9.3 10.9	*flickers,*
25	**A**	**3rd S. af. P.** • **New** ● • ☾ rides high • {9.3 10.8	*thunder*
26	M.	Opening ceremonies for St. Lawrence Seaway, 1959	*booms.*
27	Tu.	☌☿☾ • Hurricane Audrey reached landfall near Cameron Parish, La., 1957 • {10.7 9.1	*No*
28	W.	**St. Irenaeus** • ☌♂☾ • ☌♄☾ • Tides {10.5 9.1	*school!*
29	Th.	**Sts. Peter & Paul** • Peter Jones, first native Methodist missionary to Ojibwa, died, 1856	*That's*
30	Fr.	*Make not the sauce till you have caught the fish.* • {9.9 8.9	*cool!*

I don't have to look up my family tree, because I know that I'm the sap.
–Fred Allen, American comedian

Farmer's Calendar

■ News reports from Washington, D.C., over the past couple of years have identified a growing threat, a profound challenge to the executive branch of our government—indeed, to its political fundamentals. The threat comes not from strange and distant lands or from tumultuous peoples who wish us harm, but from an unlikely quarter: squirrels.

Gray squirrels, it seems, fairly overrun the grounds of the executive mansion. They gnaw trees, devour tulip bulbs, and generally mess up the environs of the White House, our preeminent national edifice.

What to do? Recent presidents have varied in their modes of squirrel control. Some have live-trapped squirrels and shown them the way out of town. Some have worked the supply side, handing out peanuts in hope that the squirrels would feed up and leave the landscaping alone. Most recently, dog-owning presidents have encouraged their pets to chase the squirrels away. Nothing works. The squirrels thrive.

They thrive on inconsistency. Here is the crux of the present affront to presidential power. The White House squirrels pose a critique of democratic government: It's changeable, it has difficulty projecting policy steadily into the future. King Louis XIV didn't have that problem, but we do. Meantime, the squirrels dig and the tulips weep.

SKY WATCH ☆ *The evening action fades as Saturn and Mercury fall into the Sun's glare. Mars, barely brighter than the North Star, postpones the inevitable by chugging into Leo and keeping just ahead of the Sun's glare; nonetheless, it is now low in the sky and scarcely worth watching. The Moon passes below the one remaining bright planet, Jupiter, on the 5th. From July 6th to 12th, the Moon stays very low. It remains below its normal path while passing through the lowest zodiac constellations. In the predawn sky, the crescent Moon meets Venus on the 22nd and 23rd. Mercury can be seen in that vicinity starting on the 30th. July's humidity helps backyard telescopes see sharp details on the Moon and Jupiter.*

☽	First Quarter	3rd day	12th hour	37th minute
○	Full Moon	10th day	23rd hour	2nd minute
☾	Last Quarter	17th day	15th hour	12th minute
●	New Moon	25th day	0 hour	31st minute

To use this page, see p. 92; for Key Letters, see p. 237; for Tide Corrections, see p. 234. All times are given in Eastern Daylight Time. ☞ **Bold** = P.M. ☞ Light = A.M.

Day of Year	Day of Month	Day of Week	Rises h. m.	Key	Sets h. m.	Key	Length of Day h. m.	Sun Fast m.	Declination of Sun ° '	High Tide Times Boston		Rises h. m.	Key	Sets h. m.	Key	Place	Age
182	1	Sa.	5 11	A	8 25	E	15 14	12	23 N.05	3¾	4¼	10 59	D	11 51	D	LEO	6
183	2	**A**	5 12	A	8 25	E	15 13	12	23 00	4½	5	12 00	D	—	–	VIR	7
184	3	M.	5 13	A	8 24	E	15 11	11	22 55	5¼	5¾	1 01	D	12 09	C	VIR	8
185	4	Tu.	5 13	A	8 24	E	15 11	11	22 50	6¼	6½	2 04	E	12 27	B	VIR	9
186	5	W.	5 14	A	8 24	E	15 10	11	22 45	7	7¼	3 10	E	12 47	B	VIR	10
187	6	Th.	5 15	A	8 24	E	15 09	11	22 39	8	8¼	4 18	E	1 10	B	LIB	11
188	7	Fr.	5 15	A	8 23	E	15 08	11	22 33	8¾	9	5 29	E	1 39	A	LIB	12
189	8	Sa.	5 16	A	8 23	E	15 07	11	22 26	9¾	9¾	6 39	E	2 17	A	SCO	13
190	9	**A**	5 16	A	8 22	E	15 06	10	22 19	10½	10¾	7 44	E	3 06	A	OPH	14
191	10	M.	5 17	A	8 22	E	15 05	10	22 11	11½	11½	8 39	E	4 08	A	SAG	15
192	11	Tu.	5 18	A	8 22	E	15 04	10	22 03	12¼	—	9 22	E	5 21	B	SAG	16
193	12	W.	5 19	A	8 21	E	15 02	10	21 55	12¼	1	9 57	E	6 41	B	CAP	17
194	13	Th.	5 19	A	8 20	E	15 01	10	21 47	1¼	1¾	10 25	D	8 03	B	CAP	18
195	14	Fr.	5 20	A	8 20	E	15 00	10	21 38	2	2¾	10 49	D	9 22	C	AQU	19
196	15	Sa.	5 21	A	8 19	E	14 58	10	21 28	3	3½	11 12	C	10 39	D	AQU	20
197	16	**A**	5 22	A	8 19	E	14 57	10	21 18	3¾	4½	11 34	B	11 54	E	PSC	21
198	17	M.	5 23	A	8 18	E	14 55	10	21 08	4¾	5¼	11 57	B	1 09	E	PSC	22
199	18	Tu.	5 24	A	8 17	E	14 53	9	20 58	5¾	6¼	—	–	2 24	E	ARI	23
200	19	W.	5 24	A	8 16	E	14 52	9	20 47	6¾	7¼	12 24	A	3 39	E	ARI	24
201	20	Th.	5 25	A	8 16	E	14 51	9	20 36	8	8¼	12 56	A	4 52	E	TAU	25
202	21	Fr.	5 26	A	8 15	E	14 49	9	20 24	9	9¼	1 36	A	5 59	E	TAU	26
203	22	Sa.	5 27	A	8 14	E	14 47	9	20 13	10	10	2 26	A	6 58	E	AUR	27
204	23	**A**	5 28	A	8 13	E	14 45	9	20 00	10¾	11	3 24	A	7 45	E	AUR	28
205	24	M.	5 29	A	8 12	E	14 43	9	19 47	11¾	11¾	4 28	A	8 23	E	GEM	29
206	25	Tu.	5 30	A	8 11	E	14 41	9	19 35	12½	—	5 35	B	8 53	E	CAN	0
207	26	W.	5 31	A	8 10	D	14 39	9	19 21	12½	1	6 41	B	9 17	E	CAN	1
208	27	Th.	5 32	A	8 09	D	14 37	9	19 08	1¼	1¾	7 46	C	9 38	D	LEO	2
209	28	Fr.	5 33	A	8 08	D	14 35	9	18 54	1¾	2¼	8 49	C	9 56	D	LEO	3
210	29	Sa.	5 34	A	8 07	D	14 33	9	18 40	2½	3	9 50	D	10 13	C	LEO	4
211	30	**A**	5 35	A	8 06	D	14 31	9	18 25	3¼	3½	10 50	D	10 31	C	VIR	5
212	31	M.	5 36	A	8 05	D	14 29	9	18 N.10	4	4¼	11 52	E	10 50	B	VIR	6

JULY HATH 31 DAYS • 2006

Come up! come up! for the world is fair
Where the merry leaves dance in the summer air. –M. Howitt

Day of Month	Day of Week	Dates, Feasts, Fasts, Aspects, Tide Heights	Weather
1	Sa.	**Canada Day** • ☾ at apo. • Lincoln Highway Association formed, 1913 • { 9.5 / 8.9	*Fire*
2	**A**	**4th S. af. P.** • ☾ on Eq. • ☾ at ☋ • { 9.1 / 8.9	*the*
3	M.	Dog Days begin. • ☿ stat. • ⊕ at aphelion • { 8.8 / 9.0	*rockets!*
4	Tu.	**Independence Day** • U.S.S. *Ranger* flew U.S. flag made from gowns, 1777 • { 8.5 / 9.1	*Sing*
5	W.	☌♃☾ • *You can't grow hair on a billiard ball.* • { 8.3 / 9.3	*the*
6	Th.	♃ stat. • First Atlantic crossing by a dirigible completed, Scotland to N.Y., 1919 • { 8.2 / 9.5	*anthem!*
7	Fr.	Ten inches of snow fell in Glacier National Park, Mont., 1981	*Bring*
8	Sa.	Francis M. Barrere received the first U.S. passport, 1796 • Ziegfeld Follies opened in New York City, 1907	*umbrellas*
9	**A**	**5th S. af. P.** • Canada's Official Languages Act adopted, 1969 • { 8.7 / 10.6	*to*
10	M.	**Full Buck** ○ • ☾ runs low • Wyoming became 44th state, 1890 • { 9.0 / 11.0	*the*
11	Tu.	*A hedge between keeps friendship green.* • Tides { 9.3 / —	*beach*
12	W.	Cornscateous air is everywhere. • Potter Josiah Wedgwood born, 1730 • Tides { 11.3 / 9.7	*and*
13	Th.	☾ at perig. • ☌♆☾ • Armadillos mate now. • { 11.5 / 10.0	*plant*
14	Fr.	Bastille Day • ☌♅☾ • *Mariner 4* delivered close-up photos of Mars, 1965 • { 11.4 / 10.3	*them!*
15	Sa.	**St. Swithin** • ☾ on Eq. • ☾ at ☊ • Black-eyed Susans in bloom now. • { 11.2 / 10.5	*Sip*
16	**A**	**6th S. af. P.** • F2 tornado, Grafton County, N.H., 1880 • { 10.8 / 10.6	*some*
17	M.	Disneyland opened in Anaheim, Calif., 1955 • Tides { 10.3 / 10.7	*lovely*
18	Tu.	☿ in inf. ☌ • Garden State Park racetrack opened, Cherry Hill, N.J., 1942	*lemonade,*
19	W.	Artist Edgar Degas born, 1834 • Don Gorske ate his 20,000th Big Mac in 32 years, 2004	*while*
20	Th.	U.S.S. *Machias,* first steel-hulled ship built in Maine, commissioned, 1893 • Tides { 9.0 / 10.5	*listening*
21	Fr.	Discovery of the tau neutrino, a subatomic particle, announced, 2000 • Adult gypsy moths emerge. • { 8.8 / 10.4	*to*
22	Sa.	**St. Mary Magdalene** • ☾ rides high • ☌♀☾ • Tides { 8.8 / 10.4	*the*
23	**A**	**7th S. af. P.** • *There's no corn without chaff.*	*nightly*
24	M.	Debut of Marvin the Martian in Bugs Bunny's *Haredevil Hare,* 1948 • Tides { 8.9 / 10.4	*cannonade!*
25	Tu.	**Sts. James & Christopher** • **New** ● • Canadian income tax introduced, 1917	*The*
26	W.	**St. Anne** • "Black Bart" made his first stagecoach robbery, Calif., 1875 • Tides { 10.3 / 9.1	*dew*
27	Th.	☌♂☾ • Discovery of insulin announced, 1921 • { 10.2 / 9.1	*point*
28	Fr.	☿ stat. • Tupperware inventor Earl S. Tupper born, 1907 • Tides { 10.0 / 9.2	*affects*
29	Sa.	**St. Martha** • ☾ on Eq. • ☾ at ☋ • ☾ at apo. • { 9.8 / 9.2	*our*
30	**A**	**8th S. af. P.** • *Truth is the daughter of time.* • { 9.5 / 9.2	*view-*
31	M.	**St. Ignatius of Loyola** • President Andrew Johnson died, 1875 • Tides { 9.1 / 9.2	*point.*

Farmer's Calendar

■ Each season is not only a span of time, which all creatures experience in common, but also a program, a plan of work, a set of tasks and traditions, that belong to each kind more particularly. What those tasks are and how they progress define the season as much as the calendar does.

By the end of July, our own human summer is most fully itself in its sensations, its associations, in the structure it imposes on our lives. Being outdoors, gardening, mowing the grass, getting out on the water, traveling: The activities that summer permits us, and those it demands of us, are now perfectly familiar and become the meaning of the season as much as any grand solar interval or pattern of weather. For us, moreover, that meaning has to do with a measure of freedom, of relative ease.

That's our summer, but perhaps it's ours alone. Summer for the birds, for example, though it occupies the same weeks, is a very different season. It's a hectic, exhausting race to hatch, rear, fledge, and launch the new generation. By our midsummer, that race is nearly run. The nests are abandoned; they begin to fall apart. The young of the year are mostly on their own. A few species—including some of the small songbirds—have already left for the south. When the human summer is fairly getting into top gear, the birds' summer is, for all practical purposes, over.

SKY WATCH ☆ *The Moon hovers above lone Jupiter on the 1st and the 29th. Saturn has its conjunction with the Sun on the 7th. Neptune's opposition on the 11th is hard to see, even with a telescope. The Perseid meteors are dimmed by a nearly full Moon on the 11th. In the predawn sky, Mercury and Venus in Gemini stay fairly close together during the first two weeks. Binoculars may show the conjunction of Mercury and Saturn on the 20th and 21st; fading Venus is just above them. The Moon joins them on the 22nd. Saturn and Venus are very close together on the 26th but difficult to view in the brightening dawn.*

☽	First Quarter	2nd day	4th hour	46th minute
○	Full Moon	9th day	6th hour	54th minute
☾	Last Quarter	15th day	21st hour	51st minute
●	New Moon	23rd day	15th hour	10th minute
☽	First Quarter	31st day	18th hour	56th minute

To use this page, see p. 92; for Key Letters, see p. 237; for Tide Corrections, see p. 234.
All times are given in Eastern Daylight Time. ☞ **Bold = P.M.** ☞ Light = A.M.

Day of Year	Day of Month	Day of Week	☼ Rises h. m.	Key	☼ Sets h. m.	Key	Length of Day h. m.	Sun Fast m.	Declination of Sun ° '	High Tide Times Boston		☽ Rises h. m.	Key	☽ Sets h. m.	Key	☽ Place	☽ Age
213	1	Tu.	5 37	A	**8 04**	D	14 27	9	17N.55	4¾	5	**12 55**	E	**11 11**	B	VIR	7
214	2	W.	5 38	A	**8 03**	D	14 25	9	17 40	5½	5¾	**2 01**	E	**11 37**	A	VIR	8
215	3	Th.	5 39	A	**8 01**	D	14 22	9	17 25	6¼	6½	**3 10**	E	—	–	LIB	9
216	4	Fr.	5 40	A	**8 00**	D	14 20	9	17 09	7¼	7½	**4 20**	E	12 09	A	SCO	10
217	5	Sa.	5 41	A	**7 59**	D	14 18	10	16 53	8¼	8½	**5 26**	E	12 52	A	OPH	11
218	6	**A**	5 42	A	**7 58**	D	14 16	10	16 36	9¼	9¼	**6 25**	E	1 47	A	SAG	12
219	7	M.	5 43	A	**7 56**	D	14 13	10	16 19	10	10¼	**7 14**	E	2 55	A	SAG	13
220	8	Tu.	5 44	A	**7 55**	D	14 11	10	16 02	11	11¼	**7 53**	E	4 13	B	CAP	14
221	9	W.	5 45	A	**7 54**	D	14 09	10	15 45	11¾	—	**8 24**	E	5 36	B	CAP	15
222	10	Th.	5 46	A	**7 52**	D	14 06	10	15 27	12	12¾	**8 51**	D	6 59	C	AQU	16
223	11	Fr.	5 47	A	**7 51**	D	14 04	10	15 10	12¾	1½	**9 14**	D	8 19	D	AQU	17
224	12	Sa.	5 48	A	**7 50**	D	14 02	10	14 52	1¾	2¼	**9 37**	C	9 38	D	PSC	18
225	13	**A**	5 49	A	**7 48**	D	13 59	11	14 34	2½	3	**10 00**	B	10 55	E	PSC	19
226	14	M.	5 50	A	**7 47**	D	13 57	11	14 15	3½	4	**10 27**	B	**12 12**	E	PSC	20
227	15	Tu.	5 52	B	**7 45**	D	13 53	11	13 57	4½	4¾	**10 57**	A	1 29	E	ARI	21
228	16	W.	5 53	B	**7 44**	D	13 51	11	13 38	5½	5¾	**11 35**	A	2 44	E	TAU	22
229	17	Th.	5 54	B	**7 42**	D	13 48	11	13 19	6½	6¾	—	–	3 53	E	TAU	23
230	18	Fr.	5 55	B	**7 41**	D	13 46	12	12 59	7¾	8	12 21	A	4 54	E	AUR	24
231	19	Sa.	5 56	B	**7 39**	D	13 43	12	12 40	8¾	9	1 17	A	5 45	E	AUR	25
232	20	**A**	5 57	B	**7 38**	D	13 41	12	12 20	9¾	9¾	2 19	A	6 25	E	GEM	26
233	21	M.	5 58	B	**7 36**	D	13 38	12	12 00	10½	10¾	3 25	A	6 56	E	CAN	27
234	22	Tu.	5 59	B	**7 35**	D	13 36	13	11 40	11¼	11½	4 31	B	**7 22**	E	CAN	28
235	23	W.	6 00	B	**7 33**	D	13 33	13	11 19	12	—	5 36	C	**7 43**	D	LEO	0
236	24	Th.	6 01	B	**7 32**	D	13 31	13	10 59	12	12½	6 40	C	**8 02**	D	LEO	1
237	25	Fr.	6 02	B	**7 30**	D	13 28	13	10 38	12¾	1¼	7 41	D	**8 20**	C	LEO	2
238	26	Sa.	6 03	B	**7 28**	D	13 25	14	10 17	1¼	1¾	8 42	D	**8 37**	B	VIR	3
239	27	**A**	6 04	B	**7 27**	D	13 23	14	9 56	2	2¼	9 43	E	**8 55**	B	VIR	4
240	28	M.	6 05	B	**7 25**	D	13 20	14	9 35	2¾	3	10 45	E	**9 15**	B	VIR	5
241	29	Tu.	6 06	B	**7 23**	D	13 17	14	9 14	3¼	3½	11 50	E	**9 38**	B	VIR	6
242	30	W.	6 07	B	**7 22**	D	13 15	15	8 52	4	4¼	**12 56**	E	**10 07**	A	LIB	7
243	31	Th.	6 08	B	**7 20**	D	13 12	15	8N.30	4¾	5	**2 04**	E	**10 44**	A	SCO	8

CALENDAR

AUGUST HATH 31 DAYS • 2006

'Tis the middle watch of a summer's night—
The Earth is dark, but the heavens are bright. –Joseph Rodman Drake

Day of Month	Day of Week	Dates, Feasts, Fasts, Aspects, Tide Heights	Weather
1	Tu.	**Lammas Day** • Astronomer Helen Battles Sawyer Hogg born, 1905 • Tides { 8.7 / 9.2	*Hot*
2	W.	☌♃☾ • *He goes farthest who knows not where he is going.* • Tides { 8.4 / 9.2	*enough*
3	Th.	American Canoe Association formed, Lake George, N.Y., 1880 • Gray squirrels have second litters now. • { 8.1 / 9.3	*to*
4	Fr.	Gestapo found Anne Frank, 1944 • 108°F, Spokane, Wash., 1961 • Tides { 8.0 / 9.5	*boil*
5	Sa.	*Little Orphan Annie* comic strip debuted, 1924 • Tides { 8.1 / 9.8	*your*
6	**A**	**Transfiguration** • ☾ RUNS LOW • ☿ GR. ELONG. (19° WEST)	*bunions;*
7	M.	☌♄☉ • *Le Griffon,* first ship to sail upper Great Lakes, entered Lake Erie, 1679 • { 8.8 / 10.8	*heap*
8	Tu.	**St. Dominic** • Performer G. A. Farini's stilts got caught as he walked the rapids above Niagara Falls, 1864	*those*
9	W.	**Full Sturgeon** ○ • ☌♆☾ • Henry David Thoreau's *Walden* published, 1854	*burgers*
10	Th.	**St. Lawrence** • ☾ AT PERIG. • *The smallest fishes bite the fastest.* • { 11.6 / 10.4	*with*
11	Fr.	**St. Clare** • Dog Days end. • ☾ AT ☊ • ☌⛢☾ • ♆ AT ☍	*fried*
12	Sa.	☾ ON EQ. • Isaac Singer's double-treadle sewing machine patented, 1851 • Tides { 11.6 / 11.1	*onions!*
13	**A**	**10th S. af. P.** • Explorer J. Cartier first heard word "kanata," 1535 • { 11.3 / 11.2	*We've*
14	M.	FDR and Winston Churchill signed the Atlantic Charter, 1941 • *Soft words win hard hearts.* • { 10.8 / 11.1	*an*
15	Tu.	**Assumption** • Columbus encountered cacao beans, 1502 • { 10.1 / 10.8	*inkling*
16	W.	A 1-pound, 15-ounce northern hogsucker set a Minnesota state fishing record, 1982 • Tides { 9.5 / 10.5	*of a*
17	Th.	Cat Nights commence. • *A cat pent up becomes a lion.* • { 8.9 / 10.2	*sprinkling.*
18	Fr.	Corn crops destroyed by hail, SE Iowa, 1925 • Plant patent No. 1 granted for climbing rose, 1949 • { 8.6 / 10.0	*Not*
19	Sa.	☾ RIDES HIGH • Carly Patterson won women's gymnastics all-around Olympic gold medal, 2004 • { 8.5 / 10.0	*a*
20	**A**	**11th S. af. P.** • ☌☿♄ • Ragweed in bloom. • { 8.6 / 10.0	*night*
21	M.	☌♀☾ • Christopher Robin Milne, son of *Winnie-the-Pooh* author, born, 1920 • Tides { 8.7 / 10.1	*to*
22	Tu.	William Sheppard patented a liquid soap, 1865 • Tides { 8.9 / 10.1	*fly*
23	W.	New ● • Actor Gene Kelly born, 1912 • Lyricist Oscar Hammerstein II died, 1960 • { 9.1 / —	*a*
24	Th.	**St. Bartholomew** • *If you wish another to keep your secret, first keep it yourself.* • { 10.1 / 9.3	*kite:*
25	Fr.	☾ AT ☋ • ☾ AT APO. • ☌♂☾ • Tides { 10.0 / 9.4	*Zeus*
26	Sa.	☾ ON EQ. • ☌♀♄ • Twentieth Century Fox offered Norma Jeane Baker her first studio contract, 1946	*and*
27	**A**	**12th S. af. P.** • Edwin Drake struck oil, Titusville, Pa., 1859 • { 9.6 / 9.5	*Thor*
28	M.	**St. Augustine of Hippo** • *Dry August, arid, warm, Doth harvest no harm.* • { 9.3 / 9.5	*are*
29	Tu.	**St. John the Baptist** • ☌♃☾ • Actress Ingrid Bergman born, 1915	*in*
30	W.	Thurgood Marshall became first African-American Supreme Court justice, 1967 • Tides { 8.6 / 9.4	*a*
31	Th.	First Neutrality Act signed, 1935 • Hummingbirds migrate south. • { 8.3 / 9.3	*fight!*

Farmer's Calendar

■ You have seen, during yard sale season, the forlorn little collections of articles piled at the roadsides with a crude sign propped against them: FREE. These are the unsold remainders of the long day's effort at household commerce. They are the lowest, poorest bottom of the unwanted. You might find a ratty recliner that doesn't recline (or unrecline); an old vacuum tube radio that was last heard from in 1957; a single bicycle tire, flat; a box of old *National Geographics,* mildewed. Days will pass, the rain will fall, and the Free pile will sit there, undiminished. At last the would-be seller will give up and cart the articles off to the dump. You can't give this stuff away.

You can't give it away, but it has always seemed to me to be a mistake to try to dispose of the useless by taking it out of the market entirely. After all, how much more abject is the junk in the Free pile than the junk that has been successfully sold around and beside it? Not much more, I suggest. The astute seller, rather than trying to give away his remnants, would put up a sign advertising them for, say, one dollar; he would assign them not much value, but value nonetheless. My guess is, they'd move. Unaccountably, people will accept for a price what they disdain for nothing. In the sea of the Free pile and the yard sale, the ship of Supply and Demand sails into shoal waters.

C
A
L
E
N
D
A
R

SKY WATCH ☆ *Use binoculars to view Uranus as it reaches opposition on the 5th. Bright light from the nearby Moon will make it difficult to see. Fading Venus sinks in the predawn east; Saturn, crossing into Leo, rises just ahead of morning twilight. The Moon will keep it company on the 18th. A partial lunar eclipse on the 7th can not be seen from North America. Jupiter alone remains in the evening sky, but it becomes quite low by month's end. On the 22nd, the Moon, at apogee, is at its farthest from the Earth for the year—248,000 miles. Autumn officially begins with the equinox on the 23rd, at 12:03 A.M. The month's highlight may be the Milky Way, which splits the midnight sky from the 18th through the 24th.*

○	Full Moon	7th day	14th hour	42nd minute
☾	Last Quarter	14th day	7th hour	15th minute
●	New Moon	22nd day	7th hour	45th minute
☽	First Quarter	30th day	7th hour	4th minute

To use this page, see p. 92; for Key Letters, see p. 237; for Tide Corrections, see p. 234.
All times are given in Eastern Daylight Time. ☞ **Bold** = P.M. ☞ Light = A.M.

Day of Year	Day of Month	Day of Week	☀ Rises h. m.	Key	☀ Sets h. m.	Key	Length of Day h. m.	Sun Fast m.	Declination of Sun ° '	High Tide Times Boston	☾ Rises h. m.	Key	☾ Sets h. m.	Key	☾ Place	☾ Age
244	1	Fr.	6 09	B	7 18	D	13 09	15	8 N.09	5¾ 6	3 11	E	11 32	A	SCO	9
245	2	Sa.	6 11	B	7 17	D	13 06	16	7 47	6¾ 7	4 12	E	—	–	SAG	10
246	3	**A**	6 12	B	7 15	D	13 03	16	7 25	7¾ 8	5 04	E	12 33	A	SAG	11
247	4	M.	6 13	B	7 13	D	13 00	16	7 03	8¾ 9	5 46	E	1 45	A	SAG	12
248	5	Tu.	6 14	B	7 12	D	12 58	17	6 41	9¾ 10	6 21	E	3 05	B	CAP	13
249	6	W.	6 15	B	7 10	D	12 55	17	6 18	10½ 10¾	6 49	D	4 27	B	CAP	14
250	7	Th.	6 16	B	7 08	D	12 52	17	5 56	11¼ 11¾	7 14	D	5 49	C	AQU	15
251	8	Fr.	6 17	B	7 06	D	12 49	18	5 34	12¼ —	7 38	C	7 11	D	PSC	16
252	9	Sa.	6 18	B	7 05	C	12 47	18	5 11	12½ 1	8 01	B	8 31	E	PSC	17
253	10	**A**	6 19	B	7 03	C	12 44	18	4 48	1½ 1¾	8 27	B	9 51	E	PSC	18
254	11	M.	6 20	B	7 01	C	12 41	19	4 26	2¼ 2½	8 57	A	11 11	E	ARI	19
255	12	Tu.	6 21	B	6 59	C	12 38	19	4 03	3¼ 3½	9 33	A	12 29	E	ARI	20
256	13	W.	6 22	B	6 58	C	12 36	19	3 40	4¼ 4½	10 17	A	1 43	E	TAU	21
257	14	Th.	6 23	B	6 56	C	12 33	20	3 17	5¼ 5½	11 10	A	2 49	E	AUR	22
258	15	Fr.	6 24	B	6 54	C	12 30	20	2 54	6¼ 6½	—	–	3 43	E	AUR	23
259	16	Sa.	6 25	B	6 52	C	12 27	21	2 31	7¼ 7½	12 11	A	4 26	E	GEM	24
260	17	**A**	6 26	B	6 51	C	12 25	21	2 07	8½ 8½	1 17	A	5 00	E	CAN	25
261	18	M.	6 27	B	6 49	C	12 22	21	1 44	9¼ 9½	2 23	B	5 27	E	CAN	26
262	19	Tu.	6 28	B	6 47	C	12 19	22	1 21	10¼ 10¼	3 28	B	5 50	D	LEO	27
263	20	W.	6 29	C	6 45	C	12 16	22	0 58	10¾ 11	4 32	C	6 09	D	LEO	28
264	21	Th.	6 31	C	6 44	C	12 13	22	0 34	11½ 11¾	5 34	C	6 26	D	LEO	29
265	22	Fr.	6 32	C	6 42	C	12 10	23	0 N. 11	12 —	6 34	D	6 44	C	VIR	0
266	23	Sa.	6 33	C	6 40	C	12 07	23	0 S. 12	12¼ 12½	7 35	D	7 01	B	VIR	1
267	24	**A**	6 34	C	6 38	C	12 04	23	0 36	1 1¼	8 37	E	7 20	B	VIR	2
268	25	M.	6 35	C	6 36	C	12 01	24	0 59	1½ 1¾	9 41	E	7 42	B	VIR	3
269	26	Tu.	6 36	C	6 35	C	11 59	24	1 23	2¼ 2¼	10 47	E	8 09	A	LIB	4
270	27	W.	6 37	C	6 33	C	11 56	24	1 46	2¾ 3	11 54	E	8 43	A	LIB	5
271	28	Th.	6 38	C	6 31	B	11 53	25	2 09	3½ 3¾	1 00	E	9 26	A	SCO	6
272	29	Fr.	6 39	C	6 29	B	11 50	25	2 33	4¼ 4½	2 02	E	10 20	A	OPH	7
273	30	Sa.	6 40	C	6 28	B	11 48	25	2 S. 56	5¼ 5½	2 56	E	11 25	A	SAG	8

SEPTEMBER

SEPTEMBER HATH 30 DAYS • 2006

My schoolroom lies on the meadow wide,
Where under the clover the sunbeams hide. –Katharine Lee Bates

Day of Month	Day of Week	Dates, Feasts, Fasts, Aspects, Tide Heights	Weather
1	Fr.	☿ IN SUP. ☌ • Orchestra conductor Seiji Ozawa born, 1935 • Tides { 8.1 / 9.3	*It's*
2	Sa.	☾ RUNS LOW • Vice President Theodore Roosevelt advised, "Speak softly and carry a big stick," 1901	*gonna*
3	**A**	**13th S. af. P.** • Abolitionist Frederick Douglass escaped slavery, 1838 • { 8.2 / 9.9	*be*
4	M.	**Labor Day** • *Blow not against the hurricane.* • { 8.6 / 10.4	*a*
5	Tu.	☌♆☾ • ♇ STAT. • ♅ AT ☍ • Tides { 9.2 / 10.9	*sauna.*
6	W.	Cal Ripken Jr. played his 2,131st consecutive baseball game, surpassing Lou Gehrig's record, 1995 • { 9.9 / 11.4	*School*
7	Th.	**Full Corn** ○ • **Eclipse** ☾ • ☾ AT PERIG. • ☌♅☾	*returns,*
8	Fr.	☾ ON EQ. • ☾ AT ☊ • *Genesis* return capsule, with solar wind samples, crashed, 2004	*but*
9	Sa.	**St. Omer** • Canadian swimmer Marilyn Bell became first person to swim across Lake Ontario, 1954	*kids*
10	**A**	**14th S. af. P.** • New leader for Jamestown colony, Va., 1608 • { 11.5 / 11.7	*don't*
11	M.	**Sts. Protus & Hyacinth** • Terrorist attacks on United States, 2001 • { 11.1 / 11.6	*wanna.*
12	Tu.	Poet Elizabeth Barrett eloped with Robert Browning, 1846 • Singer Johnny Cash died, 2003	*Hurricane*
13	W.	*An egg today is better than a hen tomorrow.* • Tides { 9.8 / 10.8	*threat,*
14	Th.	**Holy Cross** • First lighthouse in North America, Boston Light, was lit, 1716 • { 9.2 / 10.2	*we*
15	Fr.	☾ RIDES HIGH • ☌♂☿ • Landscape architect Andre Le Notre died, 1700 • { 8.7 / 9.8	*bet.*
16	Sa.	Many reported appearance of lake monster Ogopogo in Lake Okanagan in B.C., 1926 • Tides { 8.4 / 9.6	*Up*
17	**A**	**15th S. af. P.** • U.S. Constitution signed, 1787 • Tides { 8.4 / 9.6	*north,*
18	M.	☌♄☾ • First nighttime skywriting in U.S., 1937 • { 8.6 / 9.6	*it's*
19	Tu.	*A good soil yields good fruit.* • Frogs' eggs fell from the sky, Berlin, Conn., 2003 • { 8.9 / 9.7	*wet.*
20	W.	**St. Eustace** • Ember Day • The "Adirondack tornado" traveled 275 miles, 1845	*Cool*
21	Th.	**St. Matthew** • ☾ AT ☋ • Tolkien's *The Hobbit* published, 1937 • { 9.4 / 9.8	*and*
22	Fr.	Ember Day • **New** ● • **Eclipse** ☉ • ☾ ON EQ. • ☾ AT APO.	*dry*
23	Sa.	Ember Day • **Rosh Hashanah** • Harvest Home • **Autumnal Equinox** • { 9.8 / 9.8	*and*
24	**A**	**16th S. af. P.** • **First day of Ramadan** • ☌☿☾	*providential;*
25	M.	*Never tickle the nose of a sleeping bear.* • Tides { 9.4 / 9.8	*then*
26	Tu.	☌♃☾ • First temple of the Shriners opened, 1872 • Tides { 9.2 / 9.8	*potentially*
27	W.	**St. Vincent de Paul** • Cyclist Clara Hughes born, 1972	*torrential!*
28	Th.	Explorer Juan Rodríguez Cabrillo discovered San Diego Bay in Calif., 1542 • Tides { 8.6 / 9.6	*Raincoats*
29	Fr.	**St. Michael** • Hurricane hit SE Louisiana, with wind gusts up to 140 mph, 1915 • Tides { 8.3 / 9.5	*are*
30	Sa.	**St. Sophia** • ☾ RUNS LOW • Woodchucks hibernate now.	*essential!*

Good teaching is one-fourth preparation and three-fourths theater.
–Gail Godwin, American writer

Farmer's Calendar

■ They tell you that cutting your own firewood warms you twice. It's a lie, but it's a witty lie. It's one of those lies that has truth in its pocket; it's a lie because it's more than true, not less. Therefore, in reflecting on its deception, you can not only avoid error, you can also learn.

As anybody who has done it knows too well, cutting your own wood warms you not twice, but three, four, ten, twenty times. The implication that you work up a mild and pleasing heat in procuring a year's worth of fuel and then forget about firewood until you kindle a blaze to cheer a cold winter night is fanciful. The woodcutter each year pits himself against a level of mass, weight, and inertia that is truly gigantic. Indeed, assuming that you own a chainsaw, *cutting* your wood is the least of the job. The real work of getting your fuel is in moving the stuff from one place to another. You will lift and shift every stick. And again. And again. And then again. The warming you get from the combustion of all this matter comes as an anticlimax.

Therefore, when an advocate of antique ways tries to float this warms-you-twice canard by you, reflect. Not all lies are untrue. Here, the lie isn't in what he's telling you, but in what he's not. If you fall from a great height into a vat of vegetable soup, you'll get a carrot in your ear. But you'll get more than that.

THE TENTH MONTH • 2006

SKY WATCH ☆ *This is the year's worst month for planets. Mars finally reaches conjunction and slips behind the Sun on the 23rd. By month's end, Jupiter will be difficult to view as it vanishes into the Sun's glare, as does Venus. Mercury is barely visible above the horizon, making its meeting with Venus from the 20th through the 31st challenging to view. The Moon is so far south that, when one day old on the 23rd, it sets before the Sun; the two-day-old Moon is equally impossible to see. These are the lowest, hardest-to-see crescent Moons in 18 years. Only Saturn is easily visible, but it doesn't rise until 2:30 A.M. The medium-intensity Orionid meteors add some sparkle to the sky on the 21st.*

○	**Full Moon**	6th day	23rd hour	13th minute
☾	**Last Quarter**	13th day	20th hour	26th minute
●	**New Moon**	22nd day	1st hour	14th minute
☽	**First Quarter**	29th day	16th hour	25th minute

To use this page, see p. 92; for Key Letters, see p. 237; for Tide Corrections, see p. 234.
After 2:00 A.M. on October 29, Eastern Standard Time is given. ☞ **Bold = P.M.** ☞ Light = A.M.

Day of Year	Day of Month	Day of Week	☼ Rises h. m.	Key	☼ Sets h. m.	Key	Length of Day h. m.	Sun Fast m.	Declination of Sun ° ′	High Tide Times Boston	☽ Rises h. m.	Key	☽ Sets h. m.	Key	☽ Place	☽ Age
274	1	**A**	6 41	C	**6 26**	B	11 45	26	3 s.19	6¼ 6½	3 41	E	—	–	SAG	9
275	2	M.	6 42	C	**6 24**	B	11 42	26	3 42	7¼ 7½	4 17	E	12 40	B	CAP	10
276	3	Tu.	6 44	C	**6 23**	B	11 39	26	4 06	8¼ 8½	4 47	E	1 58	B	CAP	11
277	4	W.	6 45	C	**6 21**	B	11 36	27	4 29	9¼ 9½	5 13	D	3 19	C	AQU	12
278	5	Th.	6 46	C	**6 19**	B	11 33	27	4 52	10 10½	5 37	D	4 39	D	AQU	13
279	6	Fr.	6 47	C	**6 17**	B	11 30	27	5 15	11 11¼	6 00	C	5 59	D	PSC	14
280	7	Sa.	6 48	C	**6 16**	B	11 28	28	5 38	11¾ —	6 25	B	7 20	E	PSC	15
281	8	**A**	6 49	C	**6 14**	B	11 25	28	6 01	12¼ 12½	6 53	B	8 42	E	ARI	16
282	9	M.	6 50	C	**6 12**	B	11 22	28	6 24	1 1¼	7 27	A	10 04	E	ARI	17
283	10	Tu.	6 51	C	**6 11**	B	11 20	28	6 46	2 2¼	8 09	A	11 23	E	TAU	18
284	11	W.	6 52	C	**6 09**	B	11 17	29	7 09	2¾ 3	9 01	A	**12 35**	E	TAU	19
285	12	Th.	6 54	C	**6 07**	B	11 13	29	7 32	3¾ 4	10 01	A	1 36	E	AUR	20
286	13	Fr.	6 55	C	**6 06**	B	11 11	29	7 54	4¾ 5	11 06	A	2 24	E	GEM	21
287	14	Sa.	6 56	D	**6 04**	B	11 08	29	8 17	5¾ 6	—	–	3 02	E	GEM	22
288	15	**A**	6 57	D	**6 03**	B	11 06	30	8 39	7 7	12 13	B	3 31	E	CAN	23
289	16	M.	6 58	D	**6 01**	B	11 03	30	9 01	8 8	1 19	B	3 55	D	LEO	24
290	17	Tu.	6 59	D	**5 59**	B	11 00	30	9 23	8¾ 9	2 24	C	4 15	D	LEO	25
291	18	W.	7 01	D	**5 58**	B	10 57	30	9 45	9½ 9¾	3 26	C	4 33	D	LEO	26
292	19	Th.	7 02	D	**5 56**	B	10 54	31	10 07	10¼ 10½	4 27	D	**4 50**	C	VIR	27
293	20	Fr.	7 03	D	**5 55**	B	10 52	31	10 28	10¾ 11¼	5 28	D	**5 08**	B	VIR	28
294	21	Sa.	7 04	D	**5 53**	B	10 49	31	10 49	11½ 11¾	6 29	E	**5 26**	B	VIR	29
295	22	**A**	7 05	D	**5 52**	B	10 47	31	11 11	**12** —	7 33	E	**5 48**	B	VIR	0
296	23	M.	7 07	D	**5 50**	B	10 43	31	11 32	12½ 12½	8 38	E	**6 13**	A	LIB	1
297	24	Tu.	7 08	D	**5 49**	B	10 41	31	11 52	1 1¼	9 45	E	**6 45**	A	LIB	2
298	25	W.	7 09	D	**5 47**	B	10 38	31	12 13	1¾ 1¾	10 52	E	**7 25**	A	SCO	3
299	26	Th.	7 10	D	**5 46**	B	10 36	32	12 34	2½ 2½	11 55	E	**8 15**	A	OPH	4
300	27	Fr.	7 11	D	**5 45**	B	10 34	32	12 54	3¼ 3¼	**12 51**	E	**9 16**	A	SAG	5
301	28	Sa.	7 13	D	**5 43**	B	10 30	32	13 14	4 4	**1 38**	E	**10 26**	A	SAG	6
302	29	**A**	6 14	D	**4 42**	B	10 28	32	13 34	4 4	**1 16**	E	**10 41**	B	SAG	7
303	30	M.	6 15	D	**4 40**	B	10 25	32	13 53	5 5	**1 47**	E	**11 57**	B	CAP	8
304	31	Tu.	6 16	D	**4 39**	B	10 23	32	14 s.13	6 6¼	**2 13**	D	—	–	AQU	9

OCTOBER HATH 31 DAYS • 2006

O wise little birds, how do ye know
The way to go? –Harriet McEwen Kimball

Day of Month	Day of Week	Dates, Feasts, Fasts, Aspects, Tide Heights	Weather
1	**A**	**17th S. af. P.** • First agricultural fair in the U.S., Pittsfield, Mass., 1810 • { 8.2 / 9.6	*It's*
2	M.	**Yom Kippur** • Bob Shaw set NFL record with five touchdown catches, 1950 • { 8.5 / 9.9	*fine*
3	Tu.	☌♆☾ • *Never look for a worm in the apple of your eye.*	*out*
4	W.	**St. Francis of Assisi** • ☌♅☾ • Artist Frederic Remington born, 1861	*for*
5	Th.	☾ ON EQ. • ☾ AT ☊ • Marc Garneau became first Canadian in space, 1984 • { 10.5 / 11.2	*dryin'*
6	Fr.	**Full Harvest** ○ • ☾ AT PERIG. • *All happiness is in the mind.* • { 11.2 / 11.4	*out.*
7	Sa.	**Sukkoth** • The rose became the official floral emblem of U.S., 1986 • Tides { 11.8 / —	*A*
8	**A**	**18th S. af. P.** • Acadian deportation in progress, 1755 • Tides { 11.4 / 12.0	*little*
9	M.	**Columbus Day** • **Thanksgiving Day (Canada)** • Tides { 11.1 / 12.0	*more*
10	Tu.	Washington, D.C., had its earliest measurable snow of the century, 1979 • Tides { 10.7 / 11.7	*rain's*
11	W.	Premiere of first radio quiz show in the U.S., *Professor Quiz*, 1936 • Timber rattlesnakes move to winter dens. • { 10.1 / 11.2	*no*
12	Th.	☾ RIDES HIGH • 100 mph winds in Oreg., 1962 • { 9.5 / 10.6	*strain—*
13	Fr.	Copyright for "Happy Birthday to You" melody registered, 1893 • Tides { 9.0 / 10.0	*What?*
14	Sa.	*The pumpkin vine never bears watermelons.* • { 8.6 / 9.5	*Another*
15	**A**	**19th S. af. P.** • U.S. Dept. of Transportation established, 1966	*hurricane!*
16	M.	☌♄☾ • 7.1 Hector Mine earthquake, Calif., 1999	*Autumn's*
17	Tu.	**St. Ignatius of Antioch** • ☿ GR. ELONG. (25° EAST) • { 8.7 / 9.2	*stirring*
18	W.	**St. Luke** • Russia formally transferred Alaskan territory to U.S., 1867 • Tides { 9.0 / 9.3	*carillon*
19	Th.	☾ ON EQ. • ☾ AT ☋ • ☾ AT APO. • Cornwallis surrendered at Yorktown, Va., 1781 • { 9.3 / 9.4	*of*
20	Fr.	The Town Clock in Halifax, Nova Scotia, began keeping time, 1803 • Tides { 9.6 / 9.5	*colors*
21	Sa.	*A smart mouse has more than one hole.* • Tides { 9.9 / 9.4	*swells,*
22	**A**	**20th S. af. P.** • New ● • Artist N. C. Wyeth born, 1882	*while*
23	M.	☌♂☉ • Bryn Mawr College opened, 1885 • { 9.3 / 10.1	*trick-*
24	Tu.	☌♃☾ • ☌☿☾ • *Rain at seven, Fine at eleven.* • Tides { 9.2 / 10.1	*or-*
25	W.	☌♃☿ • Poet G. Chaucer died, 1400 • Tides { 9.0 / 10.0	*treaters*
26	Th.	Little brown bats hibernate now. • Minimum wage raised to 75¢ per hour, 1949 • { 8.8 / 9.9	*carry*
27	Fr.	☾ RUNS LOW • ♀ IN SUP. ☌ • Red Sox won the World Series, 2004 • { 8.6 / 9.8	*on*
28	Sa.	**Sts. Simon & Jude** • ☌♃☿ • ☿ STAT. • Tides { 8.4 / 9.7	*and*
29	**A**	**21st S. af. P.** • **Daylight Saving Time ends, 2:00 A.M.** • ♆ STAT.	*ring*
30	M.	☌♆☾ • Spectacular northern lights display seen as far south as Florida, 2003 • Tides { 8.6 / 9.7	*our*
31	Tu.	**All Hallows' Eve** • **St. Wolfgang** • Nevada became 36th state, 1864 • { 9.0 / 9.9	*bells.*

Farmer's Calendar

■ For all their richness and variety, the autumn colors have a profound stillness. They are frozen, unmoving. On the brilliant hillsides, under the high blue sky, the colors change but they hardly stir. The effect is to bring a certain gravity to the season, a solemnity, like a single note long held, sounded on a great organ.

The spectacle of the autumn leaves is therefore a tableau, not a dance. Until they fall. Then, for a few days, the fixed and stately show of leaf color gives way to a shimmering ballet. You're walking down a road in the woods when, suddenly, the air all around you fills with falling yellow leaves, golden leaves, cascading down like weightless doubloons. They flicker in the soft autumn light as they slip to earth through the air, numberless as raindrops.

I am always reminded of one of those famous ticker tape parades down Broadway with which New York City receives the nation's greatest heroes. The hero and the city fathers proceed down the avenue while people in the tall buildings to either side let fall a vast shower of ribbon, confetti, and paper. The air, the whole world, turns into a glittering dome as the parade passes, just as in a moment of leaf fall on a country road—with the difference that, to enjoy the latter show, you don't need to have done great deeds. All you need to do is be there.

THE ELEVENTH MONTH • 2006

SKY WATCH ☆ *The evening sky is now nearly empty of planets, with Jupiter reaching conjunction with the Sun on the 21st. Venus is technically back, but it is actually too low to be easily observed. One bright spot this month is Saturn, which now rises by 11:00 P.M. at midmonth in Leo. However, the real highlight this month is the first transit of Mercury visible throughout North America in decades. Specially equipped solar telescopes or binoculars with strong appropriate filters (always use eye protection when viewing solar events) will show the innermost planet march across the Sun's face on the 8th. Orion and the brilliant winter stars return this month, rising well before midnight.*

○	**Full Moon**	5th day	7th hour	58th minute
☾	**Last Quarter**	12th day	12th hour	45th minute
●	**New Moon**	20th day	17th hour	18th minute
☽	**First Quarter**	28th day	1st hour	29th minute

To use this page, see p. 92; for Key Letters, see p. 237; for Tide Corrections, see p. 234.
All times are given in Eastern Standard Time. ☞ **Bold = P.M.** ☞ Light = A.M.

Day of Year	Day of Month	Day of Week	☼ Rises h. m.	Key	☼ Sets h. m.	Key	Length of Day h. m.	Sun Fast m.	Declination of Sun ° '	High Tide Times Boston		☽ Rises h. m.	Key	☽ Sets h. m.	Key	☽ Place	☽ Age
305	1	W.	6 18	D	**4 38**	B	10 20	32	14 s. 32	6¾	**7¼**	**2 37**	D	1 15	C	AQU	10
306	2	Th.	6 19	D	**4 37**	B	10 18	32	14 51	7¾	**8¼**	**3 00**	C	2 32	D	PSC	11
307	3	Fr.	6 20	D	**4 35**	B	10 15	32	15 10	8¾	**9¼**	**3 23**	B	3 50	E	PSC	12
308	4	Sa.	6 21	D	**4 34**	B	10 13	32	15 29	9½	**10**	**3 49**	B	5 10	E	PSC	13
309	5	**A**	6 22	D	**4 33**	B	10 11	32	15 47	10¼	**11**	**4 21**	A	6 32	E	ARI	14
310	6	M.	6 24	D	**4 32**	B	10 08	32	16 05	11¼	**11¾**	**4 59**	A	7 54	E	ARI	15
311	7	Tu.	6 25	D	**4 31**	B	10 06	32	16 23	**12**	—	**5 47**	A	9 12	E	TAU	16
312	8	W.	6 26	D	**4 29**	A	10 03	32	16 40	12¾	**12¾**	**6 45**	A	10 20	E	AUR	17
313	9	Th.	6 27	D	**4 28**	A	10 01	32	16 57	1½	**1¾**	**7 51**	A	11 15	E	AUR	18
314	10	Fr.	6 29	D	**4 27**	A	9 58	32	17 14	2½	**2½**	**8 59**	A	11 58	E	GEM	19
315	11	Sa.	6 30	D	**4 26**	A	9 56	32	17 31	3¼	**3½**	**10 07**	B	**12 32**	E	CAN	20
316	12	**A**	6 31	D	**4 25**	A	9 54	32	17 47	4¼	**4½**	**11 13**	B	**12 58**	E	CAN	21
317	13	M.	6 32	D	**4 24**	A	9 52	31	18 03	5¼	**5½**	—	–	**1 19**	D	LEO	22
318	14	Tu.	6 34	D	**4 23**	A	9 49	31	18 19	6¼	**6½**	12 16	C	**1 38**	D	LEO	23
319	15	W.	6 35	D	**4 23**	A	9 48	31	18 34	7	**7¼**	1 17	D	**1 56**	C	LEO	24
320	16	Th.	6 36	D	**4 22**	A	9 46	31	18 50	7¾	**8¼**	2 18	D	**2 13**	C	VIR	25
321	17	Fr.	6 37	D	**4 21**	A	9 44	31	19 04	8½	**9**	3 19	E	**2 31**	B	VIR	26
322	18	Sa.	6 39	D	**4 20**	A	9 41	31	19 18	9¼	**9¾**	4 22	E	**2 52**	B	VIR	27
323	19	**A**	6 40	D	**4 19**	A	9 39	30	19 32	9¾	**10½**	5 27	E	**3 16**	A	VIR	28
324	20	M.	6 41	D	**4 19**	A	9 38	30	19 46	10½	**11**	6 34	E	**3 46**	A	LIB	0
325	21	Tu.	6 42	D	**4 18**	A	9 36	30	19 59	11	**11¾**	7 42	E	**4 24**	A	SCO	1
326	22	W.	6 44	D	**4 17**	A	9 33	30	20 12	11¾	—	8 48	E	**5 11**	A	OPH	2
327	23	Th.	6 45	D	**4 17**	A	9 32	29	20 24	12½	**12½**	9 47	E	**6 10**	A	SAG	3
328	24	Fr.	6 46	D	**4 16**	A	9 30	29	20 37	1	**1¼**	10 36	E	**7 18**	A	SAG	4
329	25	Sa.	6 47	D	**4 15**	A	9 28	29	20 49	2	**2**	11 17	E	**8 31**	B	SAG	5
330	26	**A**	6 48	D	**4 15**	A	9 27	28	21 00	2¾	**2¾**	11 49	E	**9 46**	B	CAP	6
331	27	M.	6 49	E	**4 14**	A	9 25	28	21 11	3½	**3¾**	**12 16**	E	**11 01**	C	CAP	7
332	28	Tu.	6 50	E	**4 14**	A	9 24	28	21 22	4½	**4¾**	**12 40**	D	—	–	AQU	8
333	29	W.	6 52	E	**4 14**	A	9 22	28	21 32	5½	**5¾**	**1 02**	C	12 16	D	PSC	9
334	30	Th.	6 53	E	**4 13**	A	9 20	27	21 s. 42	6½	**7**	**1 24**	C	1 31	D	PSC	10

In slack wind of November
The fog forms and shifts. –Christina Georgina Rossetti

Farmer's Calendar

Day of Month	Day of Week	Dates, Feasts, Fasts, Aspects, Tide Heights	Weather
1	W.	**All Saints'** • ♂☉☾• Five-mile-long Mackinac Bridge, Mich., opened, 1957	*Dripping*
2	Th.	**All Souls'** • ☾ ON EQ. • ☾ AT �♉ • Spruce Goose plane flew 1 mile, 194/ • { 10.3 / 10.4 }	*and*
3	Fr.	☾ AT PERIG. • Canada's first bank opened, 1817 • { 11.0 / 10.7 }	*flaking,*
4	Sa.	*If you don't have what you like,* Good time to gather *you must like what you have.* milkweed pods for crafts.	*then*
5	**A**	**22nd ☉. af. ℙ.** • **Full Beaver** ◯ • Tides { 11.9 / 10.7 }	*sunny*
6	M.	Inventor of basketball, *Genius, like water,* James Naismith, born, 1861 *will find its level.* • { 12.0 / 10.5 }	*for*
7	Tu.	Election Day • UN approved formation of United Nations Emergency Force, 1956 • { 11.9 / — }	*raking.*
8	W.	☾ IN INF. ♂ • ☿ TRANSIT OVER ☉ • Tides { 10.2 / 11.5 }	*Showers*
9	Th.	☾ RIDES HIGH • *A fox should not be of the jury at a goose's trial.*	*ample;*
10	Fr.	Mammoth storm in Minnesota produced record-breaking low pressure, 1998 • Tides { 9.2 / 10.3 }	*now*
11	Sa.	**St. Martin of Tours** • **Veterans Day** • Sadie Hawkins Day • { 8.8 / 9.7 }	*a*
12	**A**	**23rd ☉. af. ℙ.** • Indian Summer • ♂♄☾• { 8.6 / 9.3 }	*sample*
13	M.	The Wall of Vietnam Veterans Memorial dedicated, 1982	*of*
14	Tu.	Journalist Nellie Bly left N.Y.C. for tour around the world in 72 days, 1889 • Tides { 8.5 / 8.8 }	*what's*
15	W.	☾ ON EQ. • ☾ AT �♉ • ☾ AT APO. • Lobsters move to offshore waters. • { 8.7 / 8.8 }	*to*
16	Th.	Louis Riel, leader of Métis resistance vs. Canada, hanged, 1885 • *After black clouds, clear weather.* • { 9.0 / 8.8 }	*come!*
17	Fr.	**St. Hugh of Lincoln** • ☿ STAT. • Crab apples are ripe now. • { 9.4 / 8.9 }	*Mild,*
18	Sa.	William Tell shot apple off son's head, 1307 • Tides { 9.7 / 8.9 }	*but*
19	**A**	**24th ☉. af. ℙ.** • ♂☉☾• Edsel car discontinued, 1959	*glum.*
20	M.	**New** ● • �♅ STAT. • Photos required for U.S. passports, 1914 • Tides { 10.1 / 9.0 }	*Just*
21	Tu.	♂♃☉ • Truman became first U.S. president to ride underwater in a submarine, 1946	*enough*
22	W.	*Eat at pleasure,* Humpback whales mi- *drink by measure.* grate to Hawaii now. • Tides { 10.3 / — }	*snow*
23	Th.	**St. Clement** • **Thanksgiving** • ☾ RUNS LOW • Tides { 8.9 / 10.3 }	*for*
24	Fr.	Suspected JFK assassin Lee Harvey Oswald murdered, 1963 • Tides { 8.8 / 10.3 }	*tracking—*
25	Sa.	☿ GR. ELONG. (20° WEST) • Robert S. Ledley granted patent for CAT scan, 1975 • Tides { 8.8 / 10.2 }	*or*
26	**A**	**25th ☉. af. ℙ.** • ♂♇☾• First lion exhibited in America, 1716	*packing*
27	M.	The "Portland storm" brought 27 inches of snow to New London, Conn., 1898 • Tides { 8.9 / 9.9 }	*it away*
28	Tu.	♂☉☾ • U.S. bill signed allowing states to set own speed limits, 1995 • Tides { 9.2 / 9.8 }	*on*
29	W.	☾ ON EQ. • ☾ AT �♉ • Pong coin-operated video game debuted, 1972 • { 9.6 / 9.7 }	*Turkey*
30	Th.	**St. Andrew** • *A heavy November snow will last until April.*	*Day!*

Life is a combination of magic and pasta.
–Federico Fellini, Italian film director

■ With the painful and protesting reluctance of a rusty hinge, the lazy householder turns again to his seasonal tasks. Procrastination ends at last. The leaves, the storm windows, the outdoor furniture, the tangled garden hose, the half-frozen garden itself—all these and many more must be attended to. Stiffly, slowly, not without creaks and groans, the work begins.

As it proceeds, however, the ordeal of the fall chores reveals a curious dynamic, a kind of automatic acceleration that lightens the whole job—maybe too much so. First, you do the things that must be done (the storm windows); then you do the things that might as well be done (the leaves); then those that it's nice to have done (the garden). You might call it a day at this point, but by now you're hooked. Your former inertia overcome—indeed, annihilated—you plunge on. You do jobs that never needed to be done and progress to others that, frankly, should have been omitted.

We have in action here a fundamental principle of behavior, hitherto little understood. Its algebraic expression might be $B = 1/t$, where B is the benefit of work and t is the time a worker has been at his tasks. The idea is that benefit is inversely proportional to time spent. It's a formula as rigorous, as inexorable, as Universal Gravitation, and in this humble space it has found its Newton. I call it the Iron Law of Puttering.

THE TWELFTH MONTH • 2006

SKY WATCH ☆ *There's lots to see this month: A wonderfully tight Mercury/Mars/Jupiter conjunction stands low in the predawn twilight on the 9th. The next morning, Mercury and Jupiter are extremely close together, and Mercury remains visible during the whole first half of the month. Jupiter emerges from the solar glare as a morning star and crosses into Scorpius. Venus appears in the evening sky, although it is still low during twilight. Saturn rises by 9:30 P.M. at midmonth and is near the Moon on the 9th. The Geminid meteor showers should be visible before midnight on both the 13th and 14th. Winter officially arrives with the solstice on the 21st, at 7:22 P.M.*

○	Full Moon	4th day	19th hour	25th minute
☾	Last Quarter	12th day	9th hour	32nd minute
●	New Moon	20th day	9th hour	1st minute
☽	First Quarter	27th day	9th hour	48th minute

To use this page, see p. 92; for Key Letters, see p. 237; for Tide Corrections, see p. 234.
All times are given in Eastern Standard Time. ☞ **Bold = P.M.** ☞ Light = A.M.

Day of Year	Day of Month	Day of Week	☼ Rises h. m.	Key	☼ Sets h. m.	Key	Length of Day h.	m.	Sun Fast m.	Declination of Sun °	'	High Tide Times Boston		☽ Rises h. m.	Key	☽ Sets h. m.	Key	☽ Place	☽ Age
335	1	Fr.	6 54	E	**4 13**	A	9	19	27	21 s.	51	7¼	**8**	**1 48**	B	2 47	E	PSC	11
336	2	Sa.	6 55	E	**4 13**	A	9	18	26	22	00	8¼	**9**	**2 16**	B	4 05	E	ARI	12
337	3	**A**	6 56	E	**4 12**	A	9	16	26	22	09	9¼	**9¾**	**2 50**	A	5 26	E	ARI	13
338	4	M.	6 57	E	**4 12**	A	9	15	26	22	17	10	**10¾**	**3 34**	A	6 45	E	TAU	14
339	5	Tu.	6 58	E	**4 12**	A	9	14	25	22	25	10¾	**11½**	**4 27**	A	7 58	E	TAU	15
340	6	W.	6 59	E	**4 12**	A	9	13	25	22	32	11¾	—	**5 30**	A	9 00	E	AUR	16
341	7	Th.	7 00	E	**4 12**	A	9	12	24	22	39	12¼	**12½**	**6 39**	B	9 50	E	GEM	17
342	8	Fr.	7 01	E	**4 12**	A	9	11	24	22	45	1¼	**1¼**	**7 50**	B	10 28	E	CAN	18
343	9	Sa.	7 02	E	**4 12**	A	9	10	24	22	51	2	**2**	**8 58**	B	10 58	E	CAN	19
344	10	**A**	7 02	E	**4 12**	A	9	10	23	22	57	2¾	**3**	**10 03**	C	11 22	D	LEO	20
345	11	M.	7 03	E	**4 12**	A	9	09	23	23	02	3¾	**3¾**	**11 06**	C	11 42	D	LEO	21
346	12	Tu.	7 04	E	**4 12**	A	9	08	22	23	06	4½	**4¾**	—	–	**12 00**	D	LEO	22
347	13	W.	7 05	E	**4 12**	A	9	07	22	23	10	5¼	**5¾**	12 07	D	**12 17**	C	VIR	23
348	14	Th.	7 06	E	**4 12**	A	9	06	21	23	14	6¼	**6½**	1 07	D	**12 35**	B	VIR	24
349	15	Fr.	7 07	E	**4 13**	A	9	06	21	23	17	7	**7½**	2 09	E	**12 55**	B	VIR	25
350	16	Sa.	7 07	E	**4 13**	A	9	06	20	23	20	7¾	**8¼**	3 13	E	**1 17**	B	VIR	26
351	17	**A**	7 08	E	**4 13**	A	9	05	20	23	22	8½	**9¼**	4 19	E	**1 45**	A	LIB	27
352	18	M.	7 09	E	**4 14**	A	9	05	19	23	24	9¼	**10**	5 27	E	**2 19**	A	LIB	28
353	19	Tu.	7 09	E	**4 14**	A	9	05	19	23	25	10	**10½**	6 35	E	**3 04**	A	SCO	29
354	20	W.	7 10	E	**4 14**	A	9	04	18	23	26	10¾	**11¼**	7 37	E	**4 00**	A	SAG	0
355	21	Th.	7 11	E	**4 15**	A	9	04	18	23	26	11¼	—	8 31	E	**5 06**	A	SAG	1
356	22	Fr.	7 11	E	**4 15**	A	9	04	17	23	26	12	**12**	9 16	E	**6 20**	B	SAG	2
357	23	Sa.	7 11	E	**4 16**	A	9	05	17	23	26	12¾	**12¾**	9 51	E	**7 36**	B	CAP	3
358	24	**A**	7 12	E	**4 17**	A	9	05	16	23	25	1½	**1¾**	10 20	E	**8 52**	C	CAP	4
359	25	M.	7 12	E	**4 17**	A	9	05	16	23	23	2¼	**2½**	10 45	D	**10 07**	D	AQU	5
360	26	Tu.	7 12	E	**4 18**	A	9	06	15	23	22	3¼	**3½**	11 07	D	**11 21**	D	AQU	6
361	27	W.	7 13	E	**4 19**	A	9	06	15	23	19	4	**4½**	11 28	C	—	–	PSC	7
362	28	Th.	7 13	E	**4 19**	A	9	06	14	23	16	5	**5½**	11 51	B	12 35	E	PSC	8
363	29	Fr.	7 13	E	**4 20**	A	9	07	14	23	12	6	**6½**	**12 17**	B	1 51	E	PSC	9
364	30	Sa.	7 13	E	**4 21**	A	9	08	13	23	08	7	**7¾**	**12 47**	A	3 08	E	ARI	10
365	31	**A**	7 13	E	**4 22**	A	9	09	13	23 s.	04	8	**8¾**	**1 26**	A	4 25	E	TAU	11

DECEMBER HATH 31 DAYS • 2006

The icicles now fringe the trees
That swayed in summer's gentle breeze. –Dora Read Goodale

Day of Month	Day of Week	Dates, Feasts, Fasts, Aspects, Tide Heights	Weather
1	Fr.	☾ AT PERIG. • Rosa Parks arrested for not giving her bus seat to a white passenger, 1955 • { 10.6 / 9.8	*Snow*
2	Sa.	St. Viviana • Touro Synagogue, oldest in U.S., dedicated, Newport, R.I., 1763 • { 11.1 / 9.9	*lightly*
3	**A**	**1st S. of Advent** • Probe *Pioneer 10* reached Jupiter, 1973	*falls*
4	M.	**Full Cold** ○ • New Haven, Conn., received 20 inches of snow, 1786 • { 11.6 / 9.9	*outside*
5	Tu.	*A good example is the best sermon.* • Tides { 11.6 / 9.8	*the*
6	W.	St. Nicholas • ☾ RIDES HIGH • ♄ STAT. • Tides { 11.5 / —	*malls*
7	Th.	St. Ambrose • **National Pearl Harbor Remembrance Day** • { 9.6 / 11.1	*on*
8	Fr.	Popeye creator, Elzie Crisler Segar, born, 1894 • { 9.4 / 10.7	*shoppers*
9	Sa.	☌♂☿ • Quebec adopted new coat of arms, 1939 • Tides { 9.1 / 10.2	*making*
10	**A**	**2nd S. of Advent** • ☌♃☿ • ☌♄☾	*cell phone*
11	M.	☌♂♃ • Cold air stopped Big Ben clock, 1981 • Winterberry fruits especially showy now. • { 8.7 / 9.1	*calls.*
12	Tu.	☾ AT ☋ • Pa. became second state in Union, 1787 • { 8.6 / 8.7	*It's*
13	W.	St. Lucia • ☾ ON EQ. • ☾ AT APO. • *A merry host makes merry guests.*	*cold*
14	Th.	Halcyon Days • Meteorite fell in Weston, Conn., 1807 • Tides { 8.7 / 8.3	*out;*
15	Fr.	Bill of Rights ratified, 1791 • "Great Blizzard" in Prairie provinces, 1964 • { 8.9 / 8.2	*"The*
16	Sa.	First day of Chanukah • Novelist Jane Austen born, 1775	*Nut-*
17	**A**	**3rd S. of Advent** • First official NFL championship game, 1933	*cracker's*
18	M.	☌♂☾ • ☌♃☾ • ☌♇☉ • Pres. Woodrow Wilson married Edith B. Galt, 1915	*sold*
19	Tu.	*He who would live in peace and at ease, Must not speak all he knows, nor judge all he sees.* • { 10.0 / 8.7	*out!"*
20	W.	Ember Day • **New** ● • ☾ RUNS LOW • Tides { 10.3 / 8.8	*Opening*
21	Th.	St. Thomas • **Winter Solstice** • Four-day snowstorm began, Portland, Oreg., 1892	*presents*
22	Fr.	Ember Day • Beware the Pogonip. • Tides { 9.0 / 10.7	*is*
23	Sa.	Ember Day • ☌♆☾ • G. Washington resigned army commission, 1783 • { 9.1 / 10.7	*always*
24	**A**	**4th S. of Advent** • Little League Baseball admitted girls, 1974	*a*
25	M.	**Christmas Day** • ☌♅☾ • Tides { 9.4 / 10.4	*thrill—*
26	Tu.	St. Stephen • **Boxing Day (Canada)** • **First day of Kwanzaa** • ☾ ON EQ. • ☾ AT ☊	*'007's*
27	W.	St. John • ☾ AT PERIG. • Rubber rationing began in U.S., 1941 • { 9.8 / 9.7	*got*
28	Th.	Holy Innocents • First chewing gum patent granted, 1869	*a*
29	Fr.	Fred Newton completed 1,826-mile swim in Mississippi River, Minn. to La., 1930 • Tides { 10.3 / 9.2	*license*
30	Sa.	Social reformer Amelia Bloomer died, 1894 • The Arroyo Seco Pkwy., California's first freeway, officially opened, 1940	*to*
31	**A**	**1st S. af. Ch.** • *Years know more than books.* • { 10.7 / 9.1	*chill!*

Farmer's Calendar

■ In recent times, as the season for building and other outdoor projects draws to an end, a last flurry of construction has come to mark the dwindling year—an access of shelter-making that is dedicated, busy, and, at first, a little odd. I refer to the rearing of elaborate houses to protect the shrubs, hedges, and other plantings that adorn our dwellings.

We are not talking here about flimsy shelters thrown up just anyhow. The preferred form in these parts is a sturdy A-frame made of 2x4 stringers and ties of 1x4 stock at the lightest. Such a structure big enough to keep snow and ice from breaking down a good-size yew or rosebush has real weight and takes some building. It all seems a bit extreme. Sure, you build for your family, for your livestock, even for your dogs. Do you really have to build for your rhododendrons?

Formerly, these shrub castles were hardly seen. Twenty years ago, only the grandest places had them. There, perhaps, is a hint of the reason for the recent annual frenzy of plant-protection: Everybody's place is grand today—grand, at least, in expense. Nowadays, those hybrid honeysuckles come from a Garden Center, where you must leave serious money in exchange for serious botany. Come December, therefore, as you immure your fothergilla in lumber, don't be hard on yourself. You're not crazy; you're protecting your investment.

Glossary of Almanac Oddities

■ Many readers have expressed puzzlement over the rather obscure notations that appear on our **Right-Hand Calendar Pages, 97–123.** These "oddities" have long been fixtures in the Almanac, and we are pleased to provide some definitions. (Once explained, they may not seem so odd after all!)

–Beth Krommes

Ember Days: The Almanac traditionally marks the four periods formerly observed by the Roman Catholic and Anglican churches for prayer, fasting, and the ordination of clergy. These Ember Days are the Wednesdays, Fridays, and Saturdays that follow in succession after (1) the First Sunday in Lent; (2) Whitsunday–Pentecost; (3) the Feast of the Holy Cross, September 14; and (4) the Feast of St. Lucia, December 13. The word *ember* is perhaps a corruption of the Latin *quatuor tempora,* "four times."

Folklore has it that the weather on each of the three days foretells the weather for the next three months; that is, for September's Ember Days, Wednesday forecasts the weather for October, Friday for November, and Saturday for December.

Distaff Day (January 7): This was the first day after Epiphany, when women were expected to get back to their spinning. (Plough Monday was the day the men returned to work; every few years, Distaff Day and Plough Monday fall on the same day.) A distaff is the staff for holding the flax or wool in spinning, and it symbolized the domestic sphere. "The distaff side" indicated the women. One proverb notes that "Yule is come and Yule is gone, and we have feasted well; so Jack must to his flail again and Jenny to her wheel."

Plough Monday (January): The first Monday after Epiphany was called Plough Monday because it was the day that men returned to their plough, or daily work, after the Christmas holiday. It was customary for farm laborers to draw a plough through the village, soliciting money for a "plough-light," which was kept burning in the parish church all year. In some areas, the custom of blessing the plough is maintained.

Three Chilly Saints (May): Mamertus, Pancras, and Gervais were three early Christian saints. Because their feast days, on May 11, 12, and 13, respectively, are traditionally cold, they have come to be known as the Three Chilly Saints. An old French saying translates to: "St. Mamertus, St. Pancras, and St. Gervais do not pass without a frost."

Midsummer Day (June 24): Although it occurs near the summer solstice, to the farmer this day is the midpoint of the growing season, halfway between planting and harvest and an occasion for festivity. The English church considered it a "Quarter Day," one of the four major divisions of the liturgical year. It also marks the feast day of St. John the Baptist.

Cornscateous Air (July): First used by early almanac makers, this term signifies

warm, damp air. Though it signals ideal climatic conditions for growing corn, it also poses a danger to those affected by asthma, pneumonia, and other respiratory problems.

Dog Days (July 3–August 11): These are the hottest and most unhealthy days of the year. Also known as Canicular Days, their name derives from the Dog Star, Sirius. The traditional period of Dog Days is the 40 days beginning July 3 and ending August 11, coinciding with the heliacal (at sunrise) rising of Sirius.

Lammas Day (August 1): From the Old English "hlaf maesse," meaning "loaf mass," Lammas Day marked the beginning of the harvest. Traditionally, loaves of bread were baked from the first-ripened grain and brought to the churches to be consecrated. Eventually, "loafmass" became "Lammas." In Scotland, Lammastide fairs became famous as the time when trial marriages could be made. These marriages could end after a year with no strings attached.

Cat Nights Begin (August 17): This term harks back to the days when people believed in witches. An old Irish legend says that a witch could turn into a cat and regain herself eight times, but on the ninth time, August 17, she couldn't change back, hence the saying: "A cat has nine lives." Because August is a "yowly" time for cats, this may have prompted the speculation about witches on the prowl in the first place.

Harvest Home (September): In Europe and Britain, the conclusion of the harvest each autumn was once marked by festivals of fun, feasting, and thanksgiving known as "Harvest Home." It was also a time to hold elections, pay workers, and collect rents. These festivals usually took place around the time of the autumnal equinox. Certain groups in this country, particularly the Pennsylvania Dutch, have kept the tradition alive.

St. Luke's Little Summer (October): A spell of warm weather that occurs about the time of the saint's feast day, October 18, this period is sometimes referred to as Indian summer.

Indian Summer (November): A period of warm weather following a cold spell or a hard frost, Indian summer can occur between St. Martin's Day (November 11) and November 20. Although there are differing dates for its occurrence, for more than 200 years the Almanac has adhered to the saying "If All Saints' brings out winter, St. Martin's brings out Indian summer." As for the origin of the term, some say that it comes from the early Native Americans, who believed that the condition was caused by a warm wind sent from the court of their southwestern god, Cautantowwit.

Halcyon Days (December): About 14 days of calm weather follow the blustery winds of autumn's end. The ancient Greeks and Romans believed them to occur around the time of the winter solstice, when the halcyon, or kingfisher, was brooding. In a nest floating on the sea, the bird was said to have charmed the wind and waves so that the waters were especially calm during this period.

Beware the Pogonip (December): The word *pogonip* is a meteorological term used to describe an uncommon occurrence—frozen fog. The word was coined by Native Americans to describe the frozen fogs of fine ice needles that occur in the mountain valleys of the western United States and Canada. According to their tradition, breathing the fog is injurious to the lungs. ☐☐

Black Listed Cancer Treatment Could Save Your Life

As unbelievable as it seems, the key to stopping many cancers has been around for over 30 years. Yet it has been banned. Blocked. And kept out of your medicine cabinet by the very agency designed to protect your health—the FDA.

In 1966, the senior oncologist at a prominent New York hospital rocked the medical world when he developed a serum that **"shrank cancer tumors in 45 minutes!"** 90 minutes later they were gone... Headlines hit every major paper around the world. Time and again this life saving treatment worked miracles, but the FDA ignored the research and hope he brought and shut him down.

You read that right. He was not only shut down—but also forced out of the country where others benefited from his discovery. How many other treatments have they been allowed to hide?

Decades ago, European research scientist Dr. Johanna Budwig, a six-time Nobel Award nominee, discovered a totally natural formula that not only protects against the development of cancer, but has helped people all over the world diagnosed with incurable cancer—now lead normal lives.

After 30 years of study, Dr. Budwig discovered that the blood of seriously ill cancer patients was deficient in certain substances and nutrients. Yet, healthy blood always contained these ingredients. It was the lack of these nutrients that allowed cancer cells to grow wild and out of control.

It has been shown that by simply eating a combination of two natural and delicious foods (found on page 134) not only can cancer be prevented—but in some cases it was actually healed! "Symptoms of cancer, liver dysfunction, and diabetes were completely alleviated." Remarkably, what Dr. Budwig discovered was a totally natural way for eradicating cancer.

However, when she went to publish these results so that everyone could benefit—**she was blocked by manufacturers with heavy financial stakes!** For over 10 years now her methods have proved effective—yet she is denied publication—blocked by the giants who don't want you to read her words.

What's more, the world is full of expert minds like Dr. Budwig who have pursued cancer remedies and come up with remarkable natural formulas and diets that work for hundreds and thousands of patients. *How to Fight Cancer & Win* author William Fischer has studied these methods and revealed their secrets for you—so that you or someone you love may be spared the horrors of conventional cancer treatments.

As early as 1947, Virginia Livingston, M.D., isolated a cancer-causing microbe. She noted that every cancer sample analyzed contained it.

This microbe—a bacteria that is actually in each of us from birth to death—multiplies and promotes cancer when the immune system is weakened by disease, stress, or poor nutrition. Worst of all, the microbes secrete a special hormone protector that short-circuits our body's immune system—allowing the microbes to grow undetected for years. No wonder so many patients are riddled with cancer by the time it is detected. But there is hope even for them...

Throughout the pages of *How to Fight Cancer & Win* you'll meet real people who were diagnosed with cancer—suffered through harsh conventional treatments—turned their backs on so called modern medicine—only to be miraculously healed by natural means! Here is just a sampling of what others have to say about the book.

"We purchased *How to Fight Cancer & Win*, and immediately my husband started following the recommended diet for his just diagnosed colon cancer. He refused the surgery that our doctors advised. Since following the regime recommended in the book he has had no problems at all, cancerwise. If not cured, we believe the cancer has to be in remission."   —*Thelma B.*

"As a cancer patient who has been battling lymphatic cancer on and off for almost three years now, I was very pleased to stumble across *How to Fight Cancer & Win*. The book was inspiring, well-written and packed with useful information for any cancer patient looking to maximize his or her chances for recovery."   —*Romany S.*

"I've been incorporating Dr. Budwig's natural remedy into my diet and have told others about it. Your book is very informative and has information I've never heard about before. Thanks for the wonderful information."   —*Molly G.*

Claim your book today and you will be one of the lucky few who no longer have to wait for cures that get pushed "underground" by big business and money hungry giants.

To get your copy of *How to Fight Cancer & Win* go to www.agorahealthbooks.com/alm8 or call **1-888-821-3609 and ask for code P6F92** to order by credit card. Or write "Fight Cancer—Dept. P6F92" on a plain piece of paper with your name, address, phone number (in case we have a question about your order) and mail it with a check for $19.95 plus $5.00 shipping to: **Agora Health Books, Dept. P6F92, P.O. Box 925 Frederick, MD 21705-9838**

If you are not completely satisfied, return the book within one year for a complete and total refund—no questions asked. This will probably be the most important information you and your loved ones receive—so order today!

ID#P6F92

Holidays and Observances

For Movable Religious Observances, see page 95.

Jan. 17	Benjamin Franklin's Birthday		June 17	Bunker Hill Day *(Suffolk Co., Mass.)*
Jan. 19	Robert E. Lee Day *(Ark., Fla., Ky., La., S.C.)*		June 18	Father's Day
			June 19	Emancipation Day *(Tex.)*
Feb. 2	Groundhog Day Guadalupe-Hidalgo Treaty Day *(N.Mex.)*		June 20	West Virginia Day
			July 1	Canada Day
Feb. 12	Abraham Lincoln's Birthday		July 24	Pioneer Day *(Utah)*
Feb. 14	Valentine's Day		Aug. 7	Colorado Day Civic Holiday *(Canada)*
Feb. 15	Susan B. Anthony's Birthday *(Fla., Wis.)*		Aug. 16	Bennington Battle Day *(Vt.)*
Feb. 28	Mardi Gras *(Baldwin & Mobile counties, Ala.; La.)*		Aug. 19	National Aviation Day
			Aug. 26	Women's Equality Day
Mar. 2	Texas Independence Day		Sept. 9	Admission Day *(Calif.)*
Mar. 7	Town Meeting Day *(Vt.)*		Sept. 10	Grandparents Day
Mar. 15	Andrew Jackson Day *(Tenn.)*		Sept. 17	Citizenship Day
Mar. 17	St. Patrick's Day Evacuation Day *(Suffolk Co., Mass.)*		Oct. 2	Child Health Day
			Oct. 9	Leif Eriksson Day Native Americans Day *(S.Dak.)* Thanksgiving Day *(Canada)*
Mar. 27	Seward's Day *(Alaska)*			
Apr. 2	Pascua Florida Day		Oct. 18	Alaska Day
Apr. 17	Patriots Day *(Maine, Mass.)*		Oct. 24	United Nations Day
Apr. 21	San Jacinto Day *(Tex.)*		Oct. 31	Halloween Nevada Day
Apr. 22	Earth Day			
Apr. 28	National Arbor Day		Nov. 4	Will Rogers Day *(Okla.)*
May 1	May Day		Nov. 7	Election Day
May 5	Cinco de Mayo		Nov. 11	Remembrance Day *(Canada)*
May 8	Truman Day *(Mo.)*		Nov. 19	Discovery Day *(Puerto Rico)*
May 14	Mother's Day		Nov. 24	Acadian Day *(La.)*
May 16	Census Day *(Canada)*		Nov. 26	John F. Kennedy Day *(Mass.)*
May 20	Armed Forces Day		Dec. 7	National Pearl Harbor Remembrance Day
May 22	National Maritime Day Victoria Day *(Canada)*			
			Dec. 15	Bill of Rights Day
June 5	World Environment Day		Dec. 17	Wright Brothers Day
June 11	King Kamehameha I Day *(Hawaii)*		Dec. 26	Boxing Day *(Canada)* First day of Kwanzaa
June 14	Flag Day			

Federal Holidays

Jan. 1	New Year's Day		July 4	Independence Day
Jan. 16	Martin Luther King Jr.'s Birthday *(observed)*		Sept. 4	Labor Day
			Oct. 9	Columbus Day *(observed)*
Feb. 20	George Washington's Birthday *(observed)*		Nov. 11	Veterans Day
			Nov. 23	Thanksgiving Day
May 29	Memorial Day *(observed)*		Dec. 25	Christmas Day

2005

January
S	M	T	W	T	F	S
						1
2	3	4	5	6	7	8
9	10	11	12	13	14	15
16	17	18	19	20	21	22
23	24	25	26	27	28	29
30	31					

February
S	M	T	W	T	F	S
		1	2	3	4	5
6	7	8	9	10	11	12
13	14	15	16	17	18	19
20	21	22	23	24	25	26
27	28					

March
S	M	T	W	T	F	S
		1	2	3	4	5
6	7	8	9	10	11	12
13	14	15	16	17	18	19
20	21	22	23	24	25	26
27	28	29	30	31		

April
S	M	T	W	T	F	S
					1	2
3	4	5	6	7	8	9
10	11	12	13	14	15	16
17	18	19	20	21	22	23
24	25	26	27	28	29	30

May
S	M	T	W	T	F	S
1	2	3	4	5	6	7
8	9	10	11	12	13	14
15	16	17	18	19	20	21
22	23	24	25	26	27	28
29	30	31				

June
S	M	T	W	T	F	S
			1	2	3	4
5	6	7	8	9	10	11
12	13	14	15	16	17	18
19	20	21	22	23	24	25
26	27	28	29	30		

July
S	M	T	W	T	F	S
					1	2
3	4	5	6	7	8	9
10	11	12	13	14	15	16
17	18	19	20	21	22	23
24	25	26	27	28	29	30
31						

August
S	M	T	W	T	F	S
	1	2	3	4	5	6
7	8	9	10	11	12	13
14	15	16	17	18	19	20
21	22	23	24	25	26	27
28	29	30	31			

September
S	M	T	W	T	F	S
				1	2	3
4	5	6	7	8	9	10
11	12	13	14	15	16	17
18	19	20	21	22	23	24
25	26	27	28	29	30	

October
S	M	T	W	T	F	S
						1
2	3	4	5	6	7	8
9	10	11	12	13	14	15
16	17	18	19	20	21	22
23	24	25	26	27	28	29
30	31					

November
S	M	T	W	T	F	S
		1	2	3	4	5
6	7	8	9	10	11	12
13	14	15	16	17	18	19
20	21	22	23	24	25	26
27	28	29	30			

December
S	M	T	W	T	F	S
				1	2	3
4	5	6	7	8	9	10
11	12	13	14	15	16	17
18	19	20	21	22	23	24
25	26	27	28	29	30	31

2006

January
S	M	T	W	T	F	S
1	2	3	4	5	6	7
8	9	10	11	12	13	14
15	16	17	18	19	20	21
22	23	24	25	26	27	28
29	30	31				

February
S	M	T	W	T	F	S
			1	2	3	4
5	6	7	8	9	10	11
12	13	14	15	16	17	18
19	20	21	22	23	24	25
26	27	28				

March
S	M	T	W	T	F	S
			1	2	3	4
5	6	7	8	9	10	11
12	13	14	15	16	17	18
19	20	21	22	23	24	25
26	27	28	29	30	31	

April
S	M	T	W	T	F	S
						1
2	3	4	5	6	7	8
9	10	11	12	13	14	15
16	17	18	19	20	21	22
23	24	25	26	27	28	29
30						

May
S	M	T	W	T	F	S
	1	2	3	4	5	6
7	8	9	10	11	12	13
14	15	16	17	18	19	20
21	22	23	24	25	26	27
28	29	30	31			

June
S	M	T	W	T	F	S
				1	2	3
4	5	6	7	8	9	10
11	12	13	14	15	16	17
18	19	20	21	22	23	24
25	26	27	28	29	30	

July
S	M	T	W	T	F	S
						1
2	3	4	5	6	7	8
9	10	11	12	13	14	15
16	17	18	19	20	21	22
23	24	25	26	27	28	29
30	31					

August
S	M	T	W	T	F	S
		1	2	3	4	5
6	7	8	9	10	11	12
13	14	15	16	17	18	19
20	21	22	23	24	25	26
27	28	29	30	31		

September
S	M	T	W	T	F	S
					1	2
3	4	5	6	7	8	9
10	11	12	13	14	15	16
17	18	19	20	21	22	23
24	25	26	27	28	29	30

October
S	M	T	W	T	F	S
1	2	3	4	5	6	7
8	9	10	11	12	13	14
15	16	17	18	19	20	21
22	23	24	25	26	27	28
29	30	31				

November
S	M	T	W	T	F	S
			1	2	3	4
5	6	7	8	9	10	11
12	13	14	15	16	17	18
19	20	21	22	23	24	25
26	27	28	29	30		

December
S	M	T	W	T	F	S
					1	2
3	4	5	6	7	8	9
10	11	12	13	14	15	16
17	18	19	20	21	22	23
24	25	26	27	28	29	30
31						

2007

January
S	M	T	W	T	F	S
	1	2	3	4	5	6
7	8	9	10	11	12	13
14	15	16	17	18	19	20
21	22	23	24	25	26	27
28	29	30	31			

February
S	M	T	W	T	F	S
				1	2	3
4	5	6	7	8	9	10
11	12	13	14	15	16	17
18	19	20	21	22	23	24
25	26	27	28			

March
S	M	T	W	T	F	S
				1	2	3
4	5	6	7	8	9	10
11	12	13	14	15	16	17
18	19	20	21	22	23	24
25	26	27	28	29	30	31

April
S	M	T	W	T	F	S
1	2	3	4	5	6	7
8	9	10	11	12	13	14
15	16	17	18	19	20	21
22	23	24	25	26	27	28
29	30					

May
S	M	T	W	T	F	S
		1	2	3	4	5
6	7	8	9	10	11	12
13	14	15	16	17	18	19
20	21	22	23	24	25	26
27	28	29	30	31		

June
S	M	T	W	T	F	S
					1	2
3	4	5	6	7	8	9
10	11	12	13	14	15	16
17	18	19	20	21	22	23
24	25	26	27	28	29	30

July
S	M	T	W	T	F	S
1	2	3	4	5	6	7
8	9	10	11	12	13	14
15	16	17	18	19	20	21
22	23	24	25	26	27	28
29	30	31				

August
S	M	T	W	T	F	S
			1	2	3	4
5	6	7	8	9	10	11
12	13	14	15	16	17	18
19	20	21	22	23	24	25
26	27	28	29	30	31	

September
S	M	T	W	T	F	S
						1
2	3	4	5	6	7	8
9	10	11	12	13	14	15
16	17	18	19	20	21	22
23	24	25	26	27	28	29
30						

October
S	M	T	W	T	F	S
	1	2	3	4	5	6
7	8	9	10	11	12	13
14	15	16	17	18	19	20
21	22	23	24	25	26	27
28	29	30	31			

November
S	M	T	W	T	F	S
				1	2	3
4	5	6	7	8	9	10
11	12	13	14	15	16	17
18	19	20	21	22	23	24
25	26	27	28	29	30	

December
S	M	T	W	T	F	S
						1
2	3	4	5	6	7	8
9	10	11	12	13	14	15
16	17	18	19	20	21	22
23	24	25	26	27	28	29
30	31					

CALENDAR

BOO! Scaring Up

BY LYNN SMYTHE

Bring forth the raisins and the nuts—
Tonight All-Hallows' Spectre struts
Along the moonlit way.
—John Kendrick Bangs,
American humorist (1862–1922)

Why Is It Called "Halloween"?

The origin of Halloween and many of its customs can be traced to Samhain (pronounced *sow*-in, which rhymes with *cow*-in), an ancient pagan Celtic festival that was celebrated in what is now Great Britain to mark the end of harvesttime and the beginning of the new year. The two-day celebration began at sundown on October 31. The ancient Celts believed that the veil between the worlds of the living and the dead was at its thinnest during Samhain, thereby making it a good time to communicate with the deceased and to divine the future.

Following the triumph of the Holy Roman Empire over Celt-occupied lands in the 1st century A.D., the Romans incorporated many of the Celtic traditions, including Samhain, with their own. Eight hundred years later, the Roman Catholic Church further modified Samhain, designating November 1 as All Saints' Day, in honor of all Catholic saints. It was celebrated with a mass, bonfires, and people costumed as angels and saints parading through the villages.

November 1 was also known as All Hallows' Day ("hallow" means to sanctify or make holy). October 31 was called All Hallows' Eve. Over time, All Hallows' Eve was shortened to Hallows' Eve, which became Hallows Evening, which became Hallowe'en and, eventually, Halloween.

Witches on Broomsticks

In the Middle Ages, women labeled as witches (from the Anglo-Saxon word *wicce,* or "wise one") practiced divination. Such a woman would curl up near a fireplace and go into a trancelike state by chanting, meditating, or using hallucinogenic herbs. When she came out of the trance, she would reveal her dreams or predictions. Superstitious people believed that these women flew out of their chimneys on broomsticks and terrorized the countryside with their magical deeds.

Bobbing for Apples

The Roman festival for Pomona, the goddess of fruit and orchards, was celebrated around November 1. Romans believed that the first person to

HAPPY HALLOWEEN! For seasonal advice and craft and recipe ideas, plus a Halloween puzzle, go to **Almanac.com/extras.**

he Ancient Traditions of Halloween

catch a bobbing apple with his or her teeth would be the first to marry in the new year. They also believed that apple peels held the secret to true love. The lovelorn would peel an apple in one long, unbroken piece and throw it over his or her shoulder while being spun around. The shape of the peel on the ground represented the first initial of the peeler's true love.

The Jack-o'-lantern

Turnip lanterns predate pumpkins as jack-o'-lanterns. In ancient Ireland, revelers would hollow out large turnips (or potatoes or beets), carve frightening designs into them, and light them from within with a candle or a piece of smoldering coal. They then placed the lanterns in the windows and doorways of their homes, in the belief that the carvings would scare off evil spirits and welcome deceased loved ones inside.

Irish immigrants arriving in the New World during the early 1800s found the larger, easier-to-carve pumpkins ready substitutes for turnips.

Costumes

During Samhain, superstitious country folk would disguise themselves with animal skins and masks made from sailcloth or linen. In costume they would go outdoors and make lots of noise, in an effort to fool troublesome spirits into thinking they were one of them or to scare them away.

Tricks or Treats

An extra place was set at the table during Samhain as an offering to deceased loved ones. In addition, food was placed outside, near the doorway, to appease bothersome spirits who might otherwise play a trick on the inhabitants, such as tipping over containers of milk.

Today's trick-or-treating dates from the Middle Ages, when poor people collected baked goods called "soul cakes" from the wealthy—a practice also called going-a-souling. In exchange for cakes, the poor promised to pray for the giver's deceased loved ones. □□

Lynn Smythe writes from the Palm Beaches in Florida.

Your Ambition Suits You to a T

by Sonja Hakala

■ Isn't the uniqueness of handwriting remarkable? In English-speaking cultures, we all use the same 26 letters and are all taught the same basic letter shapes—the roundness of an O or the vertical rise of a T. Yet as soon as we master the alphabet, we each press our pen to paper in our own individual ways.

Over the past 100 years, scientific research has proved that personality traits can be discerned through the analysis of handwriting patterns. A graphologist, someone who analyzes handwriting professionally, looks at patterns throughout a piece of writing, not just individual letters, to find indications of personality traits. Such characteristics include slant, the use of margins, the size of a signature, and individual letters—and that's just the beginning. There are thousands of strokes, shapes, and traits, far too many to describe here, but this is a start.

In order to analyze your own handwriting, grab a blank piece of paper and pen a few sentences. It doesn't matter what you write, just that you move your pen from left to right the way you normally do. When you get to the bottom of the page, sign your name.

Ready? Let's see what your handwriting reveals about you. (Just remember that these are only a few of hundreds of examples and traits.)

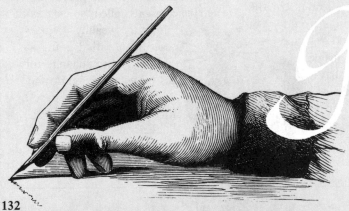

Slant

■ Which way does your handwriting slant? Slant indicates your degree of emotional expression.

Most people are right-handed and most handwriting is done from left to right, so the natural slant of letters on a page is slightly to the right, or inclined. The more inclined the writing, the more expressive and extroverted the writer. A leftward slant, or reclined writing, indicates emotional reserve. Vertical letters are a sign of someone who is emotionally independent and keeps "cool."

What about lefties? The indications are the same. Assuming that you are able to adjust your position to the pen and writing surface, you will produce the slant that matches your emotional expression.

Just for fun, try slanting your writing in the opposite direction of what you normally do. It feels strange, doesn't it?

Inclined

*To thine own self be tr
And it shall follow as t
night the day —.*

Very reclined

*This is a fun evening so
I am in my late-ish*

Vertical

*Outside of the prune-industry
press, I've seen very little copy on
our show during the past few months*

Margins

■ The page is space, and the way you fill the page indicates how you approach the world. Balanced writing in the middle of a page indicates poise, control, and awareness of social boundaries. A wide left margin indicates avoidance of the past, a communicative nature, and courage in facing life. A wide right margin indicates fear of the future and oversensitivity.

Me, Me, Me, I, I, I

■ In graphology, one of the most important keys to personality is the personal pronoun I. Among other things, the letter I is an indicator of a person's self-image.

A capital I that is printed when all the rest of the writing is in cursive indicates someone who is a clear, constructive thinker and independent by nature.

▶ $\mathcal{I}$

A stick figure I is a sign of independence and maturity, someone who's culturally aware.

▶ |

An I with a tall, inflated upper loop indicates an outgoing person who enjoys the spotlight or someone with imagination.

▶ φ

c o n t i n u e d

Crossed t's and Dotted i's

■ Cursive writing allows us to move from one letter to the next as quickly and efficiently as possible. This forward motion gets interrupted by t bars and i dots, however, and it's that interruption that makes these letters so interesting to graphologists.

Examine the small t's in your sample. Your t bar tells how willpower and personal drive are expressed in your life.

The higher the bar, the more important your goals.

The longer the t bar, the stronger your willpower.

An ascending t bar indicates optimism and ambition.

A descending t bar indicates fear and hopelessness.

A t bar that sits on the left side of the stem indicates procrastination.

A t bar that sits on the right side of the stem indicates impulsiveness and enthusiasm.

An inverted t bar indicates fickleness.

A looped or knotted t bar indicates persistence and tenacity.

Now survey your dotted i's . . .

■ Where is the dot in relation to the stem? The location of the i dot relates to the intellect and aspirations; it reveals your practicality.

A round dot placed over the stem indicates orderliness, a good memory, and concentration.

A round dot high above the stem indicates imagination and enthusiasm. If the dot is very light, it's a sign of spirituality.

The absence of a dot indicates absent-mindedness and carelessness.

A sharp dash reveals a lively wit and an original mind.

c o n t i n u e d

Love calendar lore? Find more at Almanac.com.

Hills and Valleys

■ Look through your writing sample for examples of the small letters m, n, and r; they will indicate what kind of thinker you are.

Sharp points are characteristic of a penetrating, fast, and intuitive thinker. The sharper and higher the points, the more vivid and rapid the comprehension.

Upside-down v's or spade shapes reveal a critical, investigative, and thirsty mind.

Roundness indicates a careful and creative mind that uses observations and proven facts to draw logical conclusions.

Overly rounded tops on m's, n's, and r's suggest childish tendencies and immaturity, and indicate someone who yields easily and follows rules.

Sharp needle points with very round connectors indicate someone conflicted between a keen mind and a yielding nature.

Single Letters

Small a's and o's open at the top: openness, generosity, frankness, and sincerity if they're open just a bit. Gaping openings could suggest talkativeness.

Small a's and o's tightly closed: cautiousness.

A wide loop in the small e: talkativeness.

A Greek e (lowercase epsilon): refinement and culture.

A large upper loop in an f: lots of ideas but little follow-through. A large lower loop: practicality.

An f with a return stroke to the left: fluency of thought, a quick mind.

The figure-eight g: adaptability, rapidity of thought, intuition, and sense of humor.

The figure-nine g: mathematical ability, good judgment.

Tall spike at the top of the p: argumentative, contentious.

A small r that is squared at the top, called a craftsman's r: manual dexterity.

A small s printed within cursive writing: someone who reads a lot.

136

c o n t i n u e d

2006

Signatures

■ Your signature expresses the way you want to be seen by others. Look at the signature on your sample. How does it compare in size to the lines above it?

If your signature is the same size and style as your writing sample, you are natural and unself-conscious in public and in private.

If your signature is a little bigger than the sample, you want to be recognized as an important person. Pride, self-confidence, and self-esteem are evident.

If your signature is smaller than the sample, you are modest, perhaps introverted or shy, and someone who treasures privacy.

Now put all these traits together: What does your handwriting say about you?

Vermont's **Sonja Hakala,** is the editor of *Patchwork Prose: Quilts, Quilters and Their Stories,* scheduled for publication in 2007 by Thomas Dunne Books of St. Martin's Press.

WRITE AGAIN!
Find this fascinating? For more examples of letters and the traits they reveal, go to **Almanac.com/extras.**

The Same but Different

■ These three men have the same first name but different personalities. Each writer's strokes reveal his own specific traits.

BILL BRYSON, AUTHOR. The B in Bryson is larger than the B in Bill, indicating that family is very important to him. The leftward slant shows that he is comfortable working alone for periods of time. Light writing indicates that he likes to pace himself and have ample lead time on assignments. The long downstroke on the y shows a desire to finish what he starts and not give up. He can be counted on to complete what he agrees to, while he tries to balance work and family.

BILL CLINTON, 42ND U.S. PRESIDENT. The B in Bill is larger then the C in Clinton, indicating that he feels important and confident. Sharp points indicate a razor-sharp and quick mind. The i dots are small slashes pointed to the right, showing quick wit. Dark, heavy writing indicates enduring stamina and an ability to function well under high-pressure circumstances. He thrives in difficult situations and can hold his own with the "best and brightest" of people.

BILL GATES, MICROSOFT FOUNDER. The very heavy, dark writing shows endurance and great passion. Pressure, long work hours, deadlines, and crises energize him rather than deter him from his mission. He is strongly opinionated and not intimidated by anyone. The t crossed fairly high on the stem shows clear, high, and yet realistic goals. The l's going high into the upper zone show strategic thinking for the future. Believe in him or not, but if you don't, get out of the way because he is coming through.

–analysis above: Judith A. Piani, traitsecrets.com

Diabetes Healing Secret

Here's important news for anyone with diabetes. A remarkable book is now available that reveals medically tested principles that can help normalize blood sugar <u>naturally</u> ...and greatly improve the complications associated with diabetes. People report **better vision, more energy, faster healing, regained feeling in their feet**, as well as a reduction of various risk factors associated with other diseases.

It's called *"How to Reverse Diabetes"* and it was researched, developed and written by a leading nutrition specialist. It shows you exactly how nature can activate your body's built-in healers once you start eating the right combination of foods. It can work for both Type I and Type II diabetes and people report it has helped reduce their insulin resistance. It can give diabetics control of their lives and a feeling of satisfaction that comes from having normal blood sugar profiles.

The results speak for themselves. *"How to Reverse Diabetes"* is based on research that many doctors may not be aware of yet. It tells you which delicious foods to eat and which to avoid. It also warns you of the potential danger of certain so-called "diabetes" diets. Diabetics are calling this program "very outstanding"..."a tremendous help"... and saying it made "a difference in my life." *"How to Reverse Diabetes"* is based on documented scientific principles that can help:

• **Eliminate ketones and give you more abundant energy**
• **Make blood sugar levels go from High Risk to Normal**
• **Stimulate scratches and scrapes to heal faster**

• **Improve eyesight**
• **Improve your balance**
• **Help numb feet regain a level of feeling**
• **Reverse neuropathy and resultant heel ulcers**

Improvement may be seen in other areas as well, such as **lower blood pressure, lower cholesterol** and **reduced triglyceride levels**. There may also be a reduction of other risk factors associated with: **heart attacks, stroke, retinopathy, kidney damage**.

What's more, it may help improve **short term memory** and make you feel **more alert** and **no longer chronically tired**. Improvements of **double vision** or *diplopia* may also be experienced.

If you or someone you know have diabetes, this could be the most important book you'll ever read. As part of a special introductory offer, right now you can order a special press run of *"How to Reverse Diabetes"* for only $12.95 plus $2.00 shipping. It comes with a 90 day money back guarantee. If you are not 100% satisfied, simply return it for a <u>full refund...no questions asked</u>.

Order an extra copy for family or friend and SAVE. You can order 2 for only $20 total.

HERE'S HOW TO ORDER:

Simply PRINT your name and address and the words "Reverse Diabetes" on a piece of paper and mail it along with a check or money order to: Diabetes Health Publishers, Dept. DR286, P.O. Box 8347, Canton, OH 44711. VISA or MasterCard send card number and expiration date. Act now. Orders are fulfilled on a first come, first served basis. ©2005 Diabetes Health

Winners in the 2005 Essay Contest

My Remodeling Disaster

We bought our old farmhouse after many visits to Downeast Maine. After moving in, remodeling included siding an enclosed porch. We decided to use cedar shingles. What could be more prototypically New England? Determined to fit in, I decided to do the job myself, as would a Mainer.

I began on the road-facing side, and soon had the first bundle firmly nailed in place. "Nice work," said the neighborly local from his pickup. "Darn nice work. Shame the shingles are upside-down."

Sixty square feet of shingling, neatly applied, level . . . and upside-down! I stuttered for justification. "No chance to check how it's done," I gasped. As if there were no examples around! In fact, the entire rear side of our house is shingled. I thanked him. Suppose I had finished the five remaining bundles?

To the hardware store for a nail puller. Didn't help; the heads were firmly nailed, deep. I dug out those nails, one by one, using a combination of knife, chisel, and side cutters.

I relaid the shingles, neatly, level, butt end down. Got it right this time, after the entire community heard about the newcomer who had nailed his shingles upside down. —*Ron Pesha, Lubec, Maine*

My wife and I decided to convert our attached garage into a family room. It would make a perfect weekend project.

The first day, I prepared two 2x4x8s to frame the door opening. I placed the 2x4s on the ground on edge, forming a 90-degree angle at one end. As I swung the hammer, one of the 2x4s fell, making me miss the nail and hit the index finger on my left hand. The force burst the tip of the finger open, splattering the wall with flesh and blood.

The pain was excruciating, all the way to the doctor's office. He gave me a tetanus shot and pain pills, and bandaged the finger.

Ten days later, I decided to start again. While I was squatting down, my two-year-old daughter ran up to me and hugged me, so I lost my balance and fell backwards. This time, I got a piece of board nailed to my left elbow.

The doctor sympathetically said that no additional treatment was needed; I already had pain pills and a tetanus shot. But he highly recommended hiring a contractor.

Today, my wife and I enjoy our family room. The contractor did a fine job.

—*Guadalupe E. Garces, Corpus Christi, Texas*

(continued)

Long-term care coverage for under $100 per month

The number one reason most Americans don't buy long-term care insurance is the perception that the premiums are too high. However, if you're willing to cover a portion of the cost of care using some of your own income or assets, chances are you can get a policy for under $100 per month.

Normally, consumers look to insure 100% of the cost of care in their area. The current national average is $198 per day, or over $72,000 per year.* However, an alternative strategy is to purchase less coverage—say 50% to 80%—and, in the event you need care, pay the difference with your own money.

"My dad needed care for over four years and if we'd had a policy that paid even $1500 per month towards the ongoing expense, it would have made it a lot easier," says Bob Burke, a broker who sells long-term care policies in the Phoenix area.

In general, long-term care coverage makes sense for people with a net worth of $100,000 to $2 million. Those with less will exhaust their assets and qualify for Medicaid; those with more can generally fund their own care.

Consider an elimination period—the time before your benefits begin—of 90 days. This approach lowers your cost—in some cases, by

Smart Money Tip

as much as 30% per year. Equally important, insist on insurers rated "A" or better by A.M. Best.

With over 100 policies on the market—each with different benefits, premiums and application requirements—it pays to comparison shop. According to respected *Money Magazine* financial editor, Jean Chatzky, "Your best bet is to get quotes from at least three companies." In addition, you should consider a policy with at least a three-year term—the average time people need care.

If you'd like to receive three quotes with just one call, Long-Term Care Quote[SM] will provide them—free of charge. The company—which has been recommended in *Consumers Digest, Kiplinger's, The Wall Street Journal* and on NBC—will ask for basic information on your age, health and location, then shop up to 15 top-rated carriers on your behalf. You'll get details and quotes on three low-cost, high-quality policies—at least one of which will be under $100 per month (assuming you're younger than 70)—plus a copy of *The Consumer's Guide to Long-Term Care Insurance*. And no agent will visit without your permission.

To request your free information kit and personalized quotes, call 1-800-587-3279.

*Genworth Financial Cost of Care Survey, 1/13/05; Writing agent Robert W. Davis, CA License #0B78024. All inquiries will be kept strictly confidential. Not yet available in KS or TX.

Winners in the 2005 Essay Contest (continued)

Third Prize

Years ago, my wife and I decided to divorce. We owned a house together and, when we split, even though we were divorced, she asked me—and I, her—to help look for a new dwelling. I bought a house; she, a condo. This is where disaster and romance met.

The condo had great structure, but the inside was beyond words—stained, marred, worn, and smelly. Could we turn this into a place to live? I convinced her that we could do the work!

We tackled the job, starting with fumigating. Then, we removed enough carpet, molding, plumbing, and garbage to fill a 30-yard dumpster. The hours of cleaning, painting, tiling, and flooring went on. We saw each other more than if we had been living together. House hunting and then remodeling, evenings and weekends, turned out to be like dates. The work, sweat, and long hours were therapy.

Turns out we fell in love. The great remodeling disaster turned into the best disaster of our lives. We remarried a few months later and I made a new best friend.

–Cliff Thorne, Canby, Oregon

Honorable Mention

My husband and I decided to do a quick "pick up" in our little trailer's kitchen. We went to the store and purchased some "make it stone" spray in aerosol cans to paint the backboards around the sink, cupboards, and stove. We carefully cleaned the surfaces and then taped off all the edges with newspaper. We even covered the stovetop in paper.

It was turning out beautifully. We were almost done. As my husband leaned over the stove to finish the backboard . . . whooooosh! We had forgotten to shut off the propane, and the pilot light had ignited the fumes!

Quickly, we managed to beat out the flames and, with trembling hands and thumping heart, my husband raced out to shut off the propane. Fortunately, we did not have any lasting damage or any signs of fire. We just had to repaint the backboard behind the stove and clean up the splatters where we had beaten out the flames.

–Donna Bettenson, Campbell River, British Columbia

□□

Announcing the 2006 Essay Contest

MY MARRIAGE PROPOSAL

In 200 words or less, please tell us about the funny, touching, or wacky way that you or your spouse proposed marriage.

ESSAY AND RECIPE CONTEST RULES
Cash prizes (first prize, $100; second prize, $75; third prize, $50) will be awarded for the best original essay on the subject "My Marriage Proposal" and for the best recipe using rice (amateur cooks only, please). All entries become the property of Yankee Publishing, which reserves all rights to the material. The deadline for entries is Friday, January 27, 2006. Label "Essay Contest" or "Recipe Contest" and send to The Old Farmer's Almanac, P.O. Box 520, Dublin, NH 03444; or e-mail essaycontest@yankeepub.com or recipecontest@yankeepub.com. Include your name, mailing address, and e-mail address. Winners will be announced in *The 2007 Old Farmer's Almanac* and on our Web site, Almanac.com.

TOYS

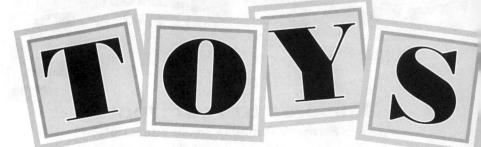

That Have Withstood the Test of Time

Technology may be taking some of the fun out of life. According to a *New York Times* report, sales of toys dropped 2 percent in 2004, in part because "kids are getting older, younger." They are turning to video games, the Internet, and cable TV at an increasingly earlier age. Meanwhile, a select few toys have survived shifting cultural changes. Chances are good that you've played with at least one of these and can attest to its appeal.

A WAY TO PLAY WITH YOUR FOOD

In 1951, a man named George Lerner, apparently seeing potential in the idea that kids like to play with their food, approached Hassenfeld Brothers (later shortened to Hasbro), a Providence, Rhode Island, manufacturer of pencils, pencil boxes, and stationery. Lerner offered the company a set of plastic noses, eyes, ears, and other facial features. These, he explained, were meant for children to stick into a potato; the end result would be a toy.

The management was initially skeptical, but their interest in becoming more involved in the toy market (during World War II, they had manufactured and marketed junior air-warden kits) helped persuade them to take a chance on Lerner's idea. They decided to market it as the **MR. POTATO HEAD FUNNY-FACE KIT.** To introduce the kit, they took advantage of a relatively new medium—television—and in so doing, made history: When Mr. Potato Head appeared in a commercial on *The Jackie Gleason Show* in 1952, it became the first toy to be advertised on TV.

Mr. Potato Head was instantly popular, and its success led Hasbro to expand the line with the introduction of Mrs. Potato Head, a son named Spud, and a daughter named Yam. By 1964, as a result of the public's preference for quick-fix foods (such as french fries) and new toy safety laws (which frowned upon the toy pieces' sharp points), Hasbro introduced the plastic potato body that is familiar today.

CONTINUED

Mrs. Potato Head (left) and Mr. Potato Head, c. 1950s

–Hasbro, Inc.

THE SILLY SYNTHETIC

The now-famous matter known as SILLY PUTTY came into being as a result of a World War II government contract to develop an inexpensive synthetic rubber. James Wright, an engineer at General Electric's New Haven, Connecticut, laboratory, was working on this very challenge in 1943 when he combined boric acid and silicone oil and found that the

Original Silly Putty and egg container

resulting amalgam seemed in some ways superior to natural rubber. The puttylike material bounced, stretched, and retained its properties over a wide range of temperatures. Nonetheless, the U.S. War Production Board was not impressed and decided that it didn't suit their needs.

Wright and his friends found the substance highly entertaining, however, and soon it was making the rounds at local cocktail parties. At one such affair, Ruth Fallgatter, a New Haven toy-store owner, and an ambitious advertising copywriter named Peter Hodgson were taken with it. The two decided to include the irresistible material in Fallgatter's holiday catalog. It was a top-seller, but despite this fact, Fallgatter decided to discontinue the product. Hodgson was

not put off so easily. "I would have had to be blind not to see the possibilities," he later said.

After borrowing $147, Hodgson bought a batch of the seemingly useless matter from General Electric. He considered 15 different names, finally settling on Silly Putty, and began trying to market it, with limited success.

Silly Putty might have remained an obscure novelty if it had not been written about in the "Talk of the Town" column in *The New Yorker* magazine in 1950. The article, which described the product's popularity at Doubleday bookstores in New York City, resulted in a flood of orders. (One account claims that Hodgson received 250,000 orders within three days.) Adults' enthusiasm for Silly Putty continued into the mid-1950s, when the stuff became equally popular with children.

FROM A SIMPLE SPRING

It was an otherwise normal day at a shipyard in Philadelphia in 1945 for marine engineer Richard James as he was work-

Original metal Slinky

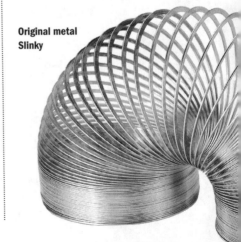

ing to find a way to dampen shipboard vibrations caused by heavy weather or the firing of guns. When one of the many steel torsion springs James was experimenting with happened to fall off a table and "walk," he took notice.

That night, he took the spring home, showed it to his wife, Betty, and said, "I think there could be a toy in this." She agreed and began scouring a dictionary for a word that would describe the simple coil. Eventually, she settled on **SLINKY**. Meanwhile, the couple's children had shared the spring with their friends, and it had become a neighborhood phenomenon, further assuring the Jameses that they were onto something.

Richard James arranged for a local machine shop to manufacture 400 of the springs. Then he convinced Gimbel's department store in Philadelphia to let him put on a demonstration in the toy department. Unsure of what the response would be, Betty James and a friend stood on the periphery, ready to draw attention to the new product and ensure that it had at least two customers.

They needn't have worried: Shortly after Richard James showed how the Slinky walked down stairs, shuffled from hand to hand, and made that distinctive

Striped Wham-O Hula Hoops

"slinkity" sound, the table was mobbed by customers, and the supply sold in 90 minutes. The fame and popularity of the Slinky grew from there, and, since its inception, there have been more than 250 million sold.

A USE FOR WAISTED ENERGY

In 1948, aspiring entrepreneurs Arthur Melin and Richard Knerr were producing inexpensive slingshots in a garage and trying to launch a business they had named Wham-O, after the sound a slingshot makes. One day, a friend mentioned that while visiting Australia, he had observed schoolchildren twirling bamboo hoops around their waists during gym class. Melin and Knerr decided to try to adapt the obscure Australian fad to the American market and produced prototypes in colorful plastic.

After recruiting a few local children to "test-spin" their new product,

147

the pair was convinced that they had a good idea. They could not have imagined the widespread obsession for their **HULA HOOP** (named for the traditional Hawaiian dance) that followed during the next ten years.

By 1958, at the height of hulamania, their company was producing 20,000 hoops per day. But because Wham-O could not secure a patent for a mere plastic hoop, several other companies seized the opportunity to flood the market with their own versions, with names like Spin-a-Hoop and Hoop-D-Doo. Whatever the name, more than 15 million hoops were sold that year. Their popularity also inspired a short-lived hit record called "The Hula Hoop Song," by Teresa Brewer.

■ A CONSTRUCTION CRAZE

When A. C. Gilbert graduated from Yale Medical School in 1909, he did not pursue a career in medicine. Instead, he devoted his energies to educating and entertaining children with what he called "good, clean fun." A longtime magic buff who had performed magic shows to help pay his tuition, he formed the Mysto Manufacturing Company (later known as the A. C. Gilbert Company) to produce magic kits.

One day, Gilbert was on a train when he looked out the window and noticed workmen positioning and riveting steel beams. He decided to develop a kit consisting of miniature beams, bolts, pulleys, and even motors, with which children could build small-scale towers, bridges, and the like. By 1913, he was ready to market the kit, which he called The Mysto Erector Structural Steel Builder, and set up a national advertising campaign, the first for any toy.

Over the next 50 years, Gilbert's company sold 30 million **ERECTOR SETS,** as they came to be known. By the time of his death in 1962, Gilbert held 150 patents, but the Erector Set is his most famous—and constructive—contribution to the world of toys.

A 1931 Erector Set, the largest ever made

Jeff Baker's work has appeared in the *Oxford American, Yankee* Magazine, *The New York Times Magazine,* and other publications. His only bad toy memory is of a tragically unproductive ant farm.

–photo: from the collection of Joel Perlin

Why Some

Are Fun Forever

According to Chris Byrne, whose 26 years as a marketing consultant to toy companies have made him known as "The Toy Guy," toys last because of how we creatively express ourselves with them: "Toys come to life only when played with. They require the interaction not just of a physical being but of an imaginative, creative intelligence. Because each of us has that, we can use these toys to create our own individual experiences. The toys become a reflection of ourselves, and the play is a vital form of expression. You can pick up any of these toys at any time and have a satisfying experience, alone or with others. But the primary reason I think these toys remain irresistible is that people never grow out of that essentially creative question: I wonder what I can do with this?" □□

PLAYTIME

If you thought this was fun, you'll love learning about two toys that failed the test of time. Speaking of tests, we have one that will challenge your knowledge of classic toys. Interested? Go to **Almanac.com/extras**.

What Do You Wan

Choosing the right school can help you turn your favorite pastime into the career of your dreams.

D eciding what to do for a living is one of the most important decisions you'll ever make. Although it's not as simple as "follow your passion and the money will follow," the process of choosing a career becomes less daunting when job seekers focus on their own unique interests, skills, and goals.

Here are some "uncommon" schools that will prepare you for a new vocation or help you turn a lifelong interest into the career of your dreams. You'll also find a list of occupations that are expected to be in demand, as well as a sampling of jobs ranked by their "prestige power."

ZOOKEEPER

If you've always been wild about animal husbandry, animal science, endangered species preservation, or just animals in general, then check out . . .

- Millbrook School, Millbrook, New York, the only U.S. secondary school with an on-site zoo

- **CURRICULUM:** The school's Trevor Zoo is a living biology class. As an accredited member of the American Zoo and Aquarium Association (AZA) and the Species Survival Plan (SSP), the zoo participates in international breeding programs for endangered species.

- **CLASS SIZE:** 240 students total; about 40 volunteer at the zoo

-illustrated by David Austin Cl

to Be?

■ **PREREQUISITES:** Admission is based on Secondary School Admission Test (SSAT) scores, academic standing, teacher recommendations, an application essay, and a personal interview.

■ **CAREER TIP:** The zoo experience also helps liberal arts students round out their studies.

Class Notes

"From being able to work with endangered species, watch animal surgeries, and hang around with our zoo veterinarian, I've learned more than a person at my age should have a right to," says 17-year-old Lacey Ogden, the infirmary curator. Lacey's responsibilities include feeding the animals "enrichment foods" (such as peanut butter treats to the foxes) to keep the animals' lives interesting.

STUNTPERSON

If you'd jump at the chance to be a professional stunt performer or theatrical fight scene choreographer, then consider the . . .

■ International Stunt School, Seattle, Washington

■ **CURRICULUM:** Eleven instructors provide 150 hours of training (in

weaponry, stair falls, and unarmed combat) during a three-week period. Students focus on specific stunt skills, such as those involving fire, horses, or edged weapons.

■ **CLASS SIZE:** About 45 students per session

■ **PREREQUISITES:** The minimum age is 20; younger students who possess the maturity, discipline, and precision needed to succeed are accepted on an individual basis. Previous gymnastic, martial arts, or auto racing experience is beneficial.

■ **CAREER TIP:** Be realistic about your abilities. Former student Daniel Ford Beavis, 29, says that everyone has a fear of something. For him, it is a fear of horses—both getting on them and falling off of them. "What [Director

Dave] Boushey teaches you is to be honest. Don't say that you can do something if you can't," he says.

C l a s s   N o t e s

At home in Saskatoon, Saskatchewan, Beavis choreographs fight scenes for local theater groups. "We do a lot of Shakespeare," he says. "Simple fights aren't too difficult—they're basically a slap, a punch, and a fall."

HOTEL CONCIERGE

If the idea of catering to guests' needs as a concierge at a luxury hotel or resort has always made you feel comfortable, then look into the . . .

- Merici International Concierge Institute, Montreal, Quebec

- **CURRICULUM:** An intensive six-month program, including a nine-week internship

- **CLASS SIZE:** 40 to 45 students are enrolled and trained each year

- **PREREQUISITES:** A smile in your voice and a can-do attitude

- **CAREER TIP:** The one phrase that is not in a concierge's vocabulary (unless in reply to a request to break the law) is "I'm sorry, I can't arrange that," says Suzanne Cayer, development manager at the Institute. Successful concierges develop the ability to network with other concierges

and people in luxury goods and service businesses (jewelers, yacht companies, private airline companies, limousine services, and florists, among others).

C l a s s   N o t e s

Virginia Casale, a concierge at a Montreal hotel and an Institute teacher, was once asked to make travel arrangements for two husky puppies. Within eight hours, she had arranged for a limousine to pick up the puppies at their farm in upstate New York and deliver them (adorned with red bows and accompanied by appropriate paperwork and a dictated love letter) to the Plaza Hotel in New York City—with help from her professional network.

CARTOONIST

If you feel that being a cartoon artist, graphic designer, storyteller, illustrator, or graphic novelist would draw out the best in you, then try . . .

- The Center for Cartoon Studies, White River Junction, Vermont

- **CURRICULUM:** Classes in graphic design, illustration, and publishing, with field trips to Montreal, Boston, and New York to visit professionals in those fields

- **CLASS SIZE:** 20 students admitted per year

- **PREREQUISITES:** A portfolio of work, including an essay and an illustrated comic story (minimum: two pages) starring you, a snowman, and a piece of fruit

- **CAREER TIP:** Previous formal training in visual arts is not mandatory. Applicants have included recent high school graduates, older students with doctorate degrees (in non–arts-related areas), and graphic arts professionals.

C l a s s   N o t e s

"What we're looking for," says Managing Director Michelle Ollie, "is the ability to tell a story."

PILOT OR ASTRONAUT

If you don't mind having your career plans up in the air and would like to get involved in commercial aviation or exploring space, then file a flight plan for . . .

- Aviation High School, Highline School District, Seattle, Washington

- **CURRICULUM:** Standard high school courses—science, math, reading, language arts—are taught as they relate to flying and aviation.

- **CLASS SIZE:** 100 students per grade

- **PREREQUISITES:** A passion for the field and a personal interview. Academic achievement is not the top priority. Principal Reba Gilman says that the interview often is the key factor in determining acceptance.

- **CAREER TIP:** Principal Gilman says that the school is just the kind of educational experience you want all children to have. "You want kids to be thinkers and researchers. Teachers shouldn't be handing them the information." This school provides students with the skills they need to "take off" on their own.

C l a s s   N o t e s

Kevin Thompson first dreamed of becoming an airline pilot at the age of six, when he took his first airplane flight. When he saw a newspaper ad announcing the opening of Aviation High School, he knew it was a perfect choice for him. Thompson, who plans to get his pilot's license when he turns 17, admits that he "slacked off" in math before enrolling in Aviation High. "This year, I can't do that," he says.

continued

HELP WANTED

HIGH IN DEMAND

The following Top Ten occupation categories are projected to have the greatest number of job openings through 2012:

Occupation	Projected number of new jobs
Registered nurses	623,000
Postsecondary teachers	603,000
Retail salespeople	596,000
Customer service representatives	460,000
Combined food preparation and serving workers, including fast food	454,000
Cashiers (except gaming)	454,000
Janitors and cleaners (except maids and housekeeping cleaners)	414,000
General and operations managers	376,000
Waiters and waitresses	367,000
Nurse's aides, orderlies, and attendants	343,000

–adapted from the Bureau of Labor Statistics, U.S. Department of Labor

HIGH IN RESPECT

The following vocations are ranked according to their "prestige power," as perceived by the percentage of the adults polled:

Occupation	Percentage of adults	Occupation	Percentage of adults
Scientist	57	Military officer	46
Fireman	55	Police officer	42
Doctor	52	Priest/minister/clergyman	38
Teacher	49	Member of Congress	30
Nurse	47	Engineer	28

–Harris Interactive, 2003

□□

Martie Majoros is the research editor of *The Old Farmer's Almanac.*

Get Working!

Not really sure of what you want to be? Take a quiz to determine your career strengths and learn about current and future career trends at **Almanac.com/extras,** where you can also find stuff about a taxidermy school.

Good for What Ails You

☞ CENTURIES-OLD SOLUTIONS FOR ORDINARY PAINS AND COMMON DISCOMFORTS • *compiled by Sarah Perreault*

Nothing should be thrown away, so long as it is possible to make use of it, however trifling that use may be.

–Lydia Maria Child,
American author (1802–1880)

Every year, people spend millions of dollars on commercial products to improve their health and well-being. They have probably never heard of Lydia Maria Child. In the early 1800s, Mrs. Child compiled a collection of household hints and home remedies in a book titled *American Frugal Housewife*, which she dedicated to those "who are not ashamed of economy." These are among her recommendations:

■ **If you cut yourself while cooking,** apply molasses to the wound to bind it temporarily.

■ **For relief from a toothache,** apply a poultice made of gingerroot to your cheek on the side of the tooth pain.

■ **To take down swellings** and/or relieve the pain of arthritis, apply a soft poultice of stewed white beans to the bothersome area. Place the poultice in a thin muslin bag and apply, replacing the contents every hour or two.

■ **To extract a corn from your foot,** attach half of a cranberry or a small piece of lemon to the corn before going to bed. (Make sure that the open side of the fruit is on the corn.) Remove in the morning. Repeat this process, using new fruit, for several nights, and the corn will be drawn out.

■ **Use boiled potatoes to cleanse the hands.** They work as well as common soap and keep the skin soft and healthy.

■ **Stricken with an ingrown toenail?** Clip the nail as near to the flesh as possible. When the corner of the nail can be raised up out of the flesh, keep it from reentering by putting a tuft of fine lint under it.

■ **For a sudden attack of croup,** bathe the neck with bear's grease. (Out of bear? Goose grease, or any kind of oily grease, is as good.)

■ **To soothe the discomfort of a strained muscle,** rub an ointment made from common earthworms (fish bait) on the swollen area.

■ **Troubled by cracked lips?** Massage them with a dab of earwax (preferably your own). □□

How to Make a Marriage Las

(OR MORE)

Commonsense advice from five siblings who have done it. ■ by Mark L. Hoffman

If scientists have yet to stumble upon a genetic link between longevity, love, and loyalty, perhaps they are looking in the wrong place. They have only to look in Reading, Pennsylvania, home to many members of the Janikowski clan. Seven couples in three generations of that family have celebrated golden wedding anniversaries. We asked one generation— five siblings—to share their secrets.

1. Put the needs of the other first. "I learned not to expect the best all the time, that sometimes you have to settle," says Julia.

2. Don't let money ruin your relationship. "One person has to handle the finances," says Frances. "In our case, it was me."

3. Learn how to get along. "I shared a bed with my sister for years," says Jessie. "We would argue and push each other around, but we still had to live together peaceably."

4. Respect each other's privacy. "Give each other a lot of space. Develop interests outside of each other," says Paul, who plays golf. His wife, Rickie, plays tennis.

5. Get to know your partner before you start a family. "Don't get married and have kids right away. As soon as the kids come, they dominate your life and you have less time for each other," says Julia.

6. Never move in with your in-laws. "When you live in someone else's house, you can wind up losing all sense of privacy and sense of individuality. Everything is theirs. Nothing is yours," says Jessie, who lived with her in-laws while her husband was overseas during World War II.

7. Set aside time for each other. "The family that plays together stays together," says Paul.

8. Grow together, not apart. "Learn to recognize each other's needs and realize that those needs are going to change," warns Stanley. "Marriage requires a lot of adjustments."

9. Encourage your spouse to live out his or her dreams. "My husband had a lot of jobs during our life together. It

50 Years

Few can top this for wedded bliss:

The Janikowski siblings and spouses on July 6, 2002.
Front row, left to right: Rickie Jannis, Paul Jannis,
Sophia Janikowski, Frances Blekicki, Julia Woolf, and
Jim Woolf; *back row:* Stanley Janikowski, Paul Sockel,
and Jessie Sockel.

wasn't easy," says Frances. "He opened a store. I didn't think it was a good idea. Sure enough, three years later, we lost the business. I let him do it, even though I had no faith in it. Why? Because I loved him and felt he deserved the chance."

10. Make up and move on. "Learn to forgive and forget. Tomorrow will bring its own set of problems," advises Frances.

11. Be honest. "There should be no secrets. Keeping secrets shows a lack of trust and respect," says Jessie.

12. Trust your instincts. Love at first sight really happens. All five Janikowskis say they knew the first time they met their future partner that they were going to spend the rest of their lives together.

Mark L. Hoffman, from Lancaster County in Pennsylvania, was a writer for numerous national magazines. He was lucky in love, but unlike the Janikowskis, it took him three times to get it right.

■ Frances Janikowski Blekicki, 88, was married to Walter for 58 years.

■ Jessie Janikowski Sockel, 86, has been married to Paul for 64 years.

■ Paul Jannis, 84, has been married to Rickie for 59 years. (Paul changed his last name to make it easier for people to pronounce.)

■ Julia Janikowski Woolf, 79, has been married to Jim for 57 years.

■ Stanley Janikowski, 75, has been married to Sophia for 53 years.

■ Their parents, Stanley and Cecilia Janikowski, were married for 51 years.

■ Their grandparents Paul and Frances Poziemski were married for 52 years.

EAT YOUR

by Laurel Vukovic

BURDOCK
(*Arctium* spp.)

I recently had dinner at a restaurant where I was served a salad of wild greens that included dandelion, purslane, and chickweed. It was delicious. You probably think of these plants as pesky weeds, but they were once valued for both their culinary and medicinal uses. Perhaps it's time to rediscover their virtues.

Forage With Care

When gathering wild foods, always be certain that you can accurately identify the plant. Never take wild plants from areas that have been treated with chemicals, and don't gather plants close to roadsides, as they may have been contaminated by exhaust fumes.

Burdock prefers full sun and grows in empty lots, parks, backyards, and fields throughout North America—except near the seashore or in the Deep South.

It has large (up to two feet long), coarse, heart-shape leaves with wavy edges. The stem and leaves are covered with tiny hairs, which give the plant a distinct sandpaper-like texture. It's a biennial, producing a rosette of leaves in the first year. In the second year, it sends up a tall (up to eight feet), multibranched stalk topped with purple, thistlelike flowers. (If you have ever brushed against burdock, then you know the tenacity of the bristly brown burrs that crown the plant.) Its taproot can

WEEDIES

grow up to four feet long and three inches in diameter; it has a brown, barklike surface, with a creamy white interior and a taste similar to that of artichoke.

Dig burdock roots in the fall of the first year, or in the spring of the second year before the plant sends up its flower stalk. To clean the root, scrub under running water with a coarse vegetable brush. Don't eat the leaves; they are extremely bitter.

Pasta With Burdock Root and Mushrooms

8 ounces linguine
2 tablespoons extra-virgin olive oil
1 small red onion, thinly sliced
2 cloves garlic, minced
1 cup burdock root cut into thin matchstick pieces
1/2 cup thinly sliced red bell pepper
1/2 cup thinly sliced mushrooms
1/2 teaspoon salt
1/2 teaspoon dried oregano
1/8 teaspoon red pepper flakes
3/4 cup water
1 1/2 teaspoons cornstarch blended with 1/4 cup water
2 tablespoons chopped parsley
1/2 cup grated Parmesan cheese

■ Cook pasta in boiling, salted water according to package directions, drain, and keep warm. While pasta is cooking,

A SWISS ENGINEER NAMED GEORGE DE MESTRAL USED *BURDOCK BURRS* AS HIS INSPIRATION TO INVENT WHAT EVENTUALLY CAME TO BE KNOWN AS VELCRO.

heat oil in a large nonstick skillet over medium heat. Sauté onion for 2 minutes, add garlic, and sauté for an additional minute. Add burdock, red bell pepper, mushrooms, and salt, and cook for 6 to 8 minutes, or until burdock begins to brown. Add oregano, red pepper flakes, and water. Bring to a boil, cover, and reduce heat to low. Simmer vegetables for 6 to 8 minutes, or until burdock is tender. Add cornstarch mixture and parsley, and cook for 1 to 2 minutes, until sauce is slightly thickened. Serve over pasta, and sprinkle with grated Parmesan. **Serves 2.**

DANDELION
(Taraxacum officinale)

There's probably not a lawn or garden in North America lacking the sunny yellow flower heads of dandelion. Although the plants are remarkably tenacious and will grow even through sidewalk cracks, they prefer richer soil and full sun to partial shade.

The leaves of dandelion are smooth, and each flower grows as a single stalk

THE COMMON NAME *"DANDELION"* COMES FROM THE FRENCH *DENTS DE LION*, MEANING "LION'S TEETH"—A REFERENCE TO THE JAGGED LEAVES. ACCORDING TO FOLKLORE, YOU CAN GET RID OF WARTS BY APPLYING THE MILKY SAP OF A DANDELION STEM TO THEM.

directly from the base of the plant. The leaves have toothed margins and may be up to 16 inches long. Dandelion leaves are tastiest in the early spring, before the plant flowers. Leaves gathered later tend to be bitter.

Dandelion Greens With Warm Turkey Bacon Dressing

4 cups tender dandelion greens, washed and dried
2 tablespoons extra-virgin olive oil
1/2 pound turkey bacon, cut into 1/2-inch pieces
2 tablespoons finely chopped red onion
1/4 cup balsamic vinegar
1 teaspoon Dijon-style mustard
1/4 cup feta cheese, drained
black pepper, to taste

■ Cut or tear the dandelion greens into bite-size pieces. Place into a large salad bowl. Sauté the bacon in olive oil over moderate heat until it is done. Remove bacon, and add red onion to the skillet. Sauté 3 to 5 minutes, until the onion softens. Add vinegar and mustard

to the skillet along with the bacon, and bring to a boil, stirring constantly. Pour the hot dressing over the greens, toss to coat, and crumble the feta over the top. Season with freshly ground black pepper. Serve immediately. **Serves 2 to 4.**

LAMB'S-QUARTER
(Chenopodium album)

Lamb's-quarter grows throughout North America, with the exception of extreme northern areas. You'll find it in "disturbed" soil in parks, in backyards, and along roadsides.

Sometimes called wild spinach or pigweed, lamb's-quarter is a relative of cultivated spinach and beets. The plant generally grows from one to three feet tall, but it can grow to six feet or more under ideal conditions—in sun or partial shade. The lower leaves are triangular or diamond-shape, and have toothed edges. The upper leaves are narrow and toothless. The undersides of the leaves have a powdery white coating. Collect the entire plant when it is about six inches tall, or harvest the leaves and tender tips of larger plants from spring through fall.

Lamb's-Quarter Frittata

8 cups young lamb's-quarter leaves, washed and chopped
2 cloves garlic, minced
2 tablespoons olive oil, divided
2 scallions, thinly sliced
1/2 cup diced roasted red bell pepper
1/2 cup crumbled feta cheese
1/4 cup grated Parmesan cheese
1/4 teaspoon salt
1/4 teaspoon freshly ground black pepper
6 eggs, beaten

■ Preheat oven to 325°F. In a large nonstick skillet, sauté the chopped lamb's-quarter leaves and garlic in ½ tablespoon of olive oil over medium heat until the greens are wilted. Remove the mixture from skillet and cool. Drain excess liquid from greens and place them in a bowl. Add scallions, red bell pepper, feta, and Parmesan. Season with salt and pepper. Stir the beaten eggs into the mixture. On top of the stove, heat the remaining 1½ tablespoons of oil in a medium-large nonstick skillet with an ovenproof handle. Swirl the oil around the sides of the pan to coat the entire pan. When the oil is hot, pour the egg mixture into the skillet and immediately turn the heat to medium-low. Cook, undisturbed, for several minutes,

LAMB'S-QUARTER WAS CALLED

"LAMMAS QUARTER'S HERB" IN ANCIENT

ENGLAND BECAUSE IT BLOOMS

AROUND AUGUST 1, THE DATE OF THE

PAGAN HARVEST FESTIVAL OF LAMMAS.

until the sides begin to set. Transfer skillet to the oven, and bake for approximately 20 to 25 minutes, until the frittata is golden brown on top and firm. **Serves 4.**

(continued)

PURSLANE
(Portulaca oleracea)

Purslane can be found throughout North America. This low-growing, fleshy, succulent annual thrives in sandy soil that gets plenty of sun.

The leaves are light green, smooth, flat, paddle-shape, and approximately one to two inches long. The stems and undersides of the leaves are reddish. Radiating from the center, the stems create numerous branches that hug the ground. The entire plant can grow up to one foot in diameter. In midsummer, it produces tiny yellow flowers with four to six petals. Purslane is tastiest when its leaves and stems are small. Harvest from spring through summer.

–Hunt Institute for Botanical Documentation, Carnegie Mellon University, Pittsburgh, PA

NATIVE TO THE MIDDLE EAST AND INDIA, *PURSLANE'S* LATIN SPECIES NAME, *OLERACEA,* MEANS "EDIBLE VEGETABLE."

Potato Salad With Purslane

6 medium red new potatoes (about 3 pounds), scrubbed
2 cups washed and chopped purslane
1 medium red onion, finely chopped
1 small cucumber, finely chopped
1/4 cup finely chopped parsley
1/2 cup mayonnaise
1/2 cup plain yogurt
1/4 cup apple cider vinegar (or more, to taste)
2 teaspoons stone-ground mustard
1/2 to 1 teaspoon salt, to taste
black pepper, to taste

■ Cut potatoes into bite-size pieces. Boil in salted water until just tender (about 15 minutes), drain, and rinse in cold water. Combine potatoes, purslane, onion, cucumber, and parsley in a large bowl. Mix together mayonnaise, yogurt, vinegar, mustard, and salt. Add to vegetables and mix gently. Add pepper, and adjust seasonings to taste. **Serves 6.** ☐☐

Laurel Vukovic enjoys edible weeds in southern Oregon. She is the author of several books, including *Herbal Healing Secrets for Women* (Prentice Hall, 2000).

HUNGRY FOR MORE?

For advice about finding and using red clover and chickweed, plus information on the health benefits of all of these plants, go to **Almanac.com/extras.**

Table of Measures

APOTHECARIES'
1 scruple = 20 grains
1 dram = 3 scruples
1 ounce = 8 drams
1 pound = 12 ounces

AVOIRDUPOIS
1 ounce = 16 drams
1 pound = 16 ounces
1 hundredweight = 100 pounds
1 ton = 2,000 pounds
1 long ton = 2,240 pounds

LIQUID
4 gills = 1 pint
63 gallons = 1 hogshead
2 hogsheads = 1 pipe or butt
2 pipes = 1 tun

DRY
2 pints = 1 quart
4 quarts = 1 gallon
2 gallons = 1 peck
4 pecks = 1 bushel

LINEAR
1 hand = 4 inches
1 link = 7.92 inches
1 span = 9 inches
1 foot = 12 inches
1 yard = 3 feet
1 rod = 5½ yards
1 mile = 320 rods = 1,760 yards = 5,280 feet
1 Int. nautical mile = 6,076.1155 feet
1 knot = 1 nautical mile per hour
1 fathom = 2 yards = 6 feet
1 furlong = ⅛ mile = 660 feet = 220 yards
1 league = 3 miles = 24 furlongs
1 chain = 100 links = 22 yards

SQUARE
1 square foot = 144 square inches
1 square yard = 9 square feet
1 square rod = 30¼ square yards = 272¼ square feet
1 acre = 160 square rods = 43,560 square feet
1 square mile = 640 acres = 102,400 square rods
1 square rod = 625 square links
1 square chain = 16 square rods
1 acre = 10 square chains

CUBIC
1 cubic foot = 1,728 cubic inches
1 cubic yard = 27 cubic feet
1 cord = 128 cubic feet
1 U.S. liquid gallon = 4 quarts = 231 cubic inches
1 Imperial gallon = 1.20 U.S. gallons = 0.16 cubic foot
1 board foot = 144 cubic inches

KITCHEN
3 teaspoons = 1 tablespoon
16 tablespoons = 1 cup
1 cup = 8 ounces
2 cups = 1 pint
2 pints = 1 quart
4 quarts = 1 gallon

To convert Fahrenheit and Celsius:
$$°C = (°F - 32) \times \tfrac{5}{9}$$
$$°F = (°C \times \tfrac{9}{5}) + 32$$

Metric Conversions

LINEAR
1 inch = 2.54 centimeters
1 centimeter = 0.39 inch
1 meter = 39.37 inches
1 yard = 0.914 meter
1 mile = 1.61 kilometers
1 kilometer = 0.62 mile

SQUARE
1 square inch = 6.45 square centimeters
1 square yard = 0.84 square meter
1 square mile = 2.59 square kilometers
1 square kilometer = 0.386 square mile

1 acre = 0.40 hectare
1 hectare = 2.47 acres

CUBIC
1 cubic yard = 0.76 cubic meter
1 cubic meter = 1.31 cubic yards

HOUSEHOLD
½ teaspoon = 2 mL
1 teaspoon = 5 mL
1 tablespoon = 15 mL
¼ cup = 60 mL
⅓ cup = 75 mL
½ cup = 125 mL
⅔ cup = 150 mL
¾ cup = 175 mL
1 cup = 250 mL

1 liter = 1.057 U.S. liquid quarts
1 U.S. liquid quart = 0.946 liter
1 U.S. liquid gallon = 3.78 liters
1 gram = 0.035 ounce
1 ounce = 28.349 grams
1 kilogram = 2.2 pounds
1 pound = 0.45 kilogram

Food

A Wok on the Wild Side

Chinese food is one of the most popular ethnic fares in North America. Would you have guessed that there are more than 44,000 Asian-American restaurants in the United States and Canada? Interestingly, too, according to a study done in 2001 by the Center for Culinary Development, a research company in San Francisco, 39 percent of American youngsters ages 10 to 13 prefer Chinese food to any other ethnic type. (Mexican was second, at 21 percent.)

This got us to thinking about Chinese cuisine, which in turn found us pondering the intriguing names of the dishes: Who was General Tso? Are Crossing the Bridge Noodles strictly an on-the-go dish? Are there actually twigs in Bird's Nest Soup? Read on, then taste and see.

身体好

(good health)

by Sarah Perreault

164

General Tso's Chicken

General Tso Tsung-t'ang (1812–1885) gained fame as a powerful military leader for the Qing Dynasty (1644–1911) during the greatest upheaval in 19th-century China—the 14-year Taiping Rebellion, which claimed millions of lives. He destroyed the Taiping rebels in numerous provinces, put down the Nien Rebellion (led by antigovernment outlaws), and then marched his army west to conquer Muslim rebels in Chinese Turkestan.

General Tso loved food, especially meat, and many feasts were prepared in his honor. All of the cooks prepared tantalizing dishes, but the general was not an easy man to please. Jacqueline Newman, editor of *Flavor and Fortune,* a magazine dedicated to the art and science of Chinese cuisine, says that during a banquet in 1875, General Tso was served generous helpings of every entrée. One of his fellow citizens at the banquet asked him, "Old friend, at one seating how can you devour so much meat? It is as the old saying goes: A general's fame is as big as his appetite. I hope that stomach of yours can live up to your fame."

Chinese literature assumes that fried spiced chicken was the general's favorite dish, so some creative chef (whose identity is now lost to history) named this dish after him. We think you'll agree that the general's chicken is indeed fit for a hero.

1 1/2 cups chicken broth
1 1/2 cups cornstarch, divided
1/4 cup water
1 1/2 teaspoons minced garlic
1 1/2 teaspoons minced fresh ginger
3/4 cup sugar
3/4 cup soy sauce, divided
1/4 cup white vinegar
1/4 cup white wine
2 1/2 pounds boneless chicken (dark meat best, but white meat OK, too), cut into large chunks or tenders

1 teaspoon white pepper
1 egg, lightly beaten
1 cup peanut (preferred) or vegetable oil, plus 2 tablespoons additional oil for deep frying
2 cups sliced scallions
16 small dried hot peppers

Heat the chicken broth in a small saucepan to just below boiling. In a medium bowl, mix ½ cup of the cornstarch with water. Add garlic, ginger, sugar, ½ cup of the soy sauce, vinegar, wine, and the chicken broth. Stir until sugar dissolves. Refrigerate until needed. In a separate bowl, mix chicken, remaining ¼ cup of soy sauce, and white pepper. Stir in egg. Add remaining 1 cup of cornstarch and mix until chicken pieces are coated evenly. Add 1 cup of peanut or vegetable oil to help keep the chicken pieces separate. Divide into small quantities and deep-fry at 350°F until crispy. Drain on a wire rack. Place 2 tablespoons of oil in a wok or deep frying pan and heat over medium-high heat. Add onions and dried peppers. Stir-fry briefly. Remove sauce from refrigerator, stir, and add to wok. Place chicken in sauce and cook until sauce thickens. Serve with white rice. **Makes 4 to 6 servings.**

Ants, Lions, and Birds' Nests

The Chinese often name a dish for a memorable incident, the dish's appearance, or its contents. Here are a few more:

■ **ANTS CLIMBING A TREE** contains morsels of ground beef or pork that play the parts of ants, while noodles stand in as the tree.

■ **LION'S HEAD MEATBALLS** are very large meatballs, approximately the size of tennis balls, served with cabbage meant to simulate a lion's mane.

■ The nests of swiftlets, tiny birds found throughout Southeast Asia, are used to make the stock of **BIRD'S NEST SOUP.** The swiftlet makes its nest from strands of its own gummy saliva instead of from twigs and straw. The most precious of these is the first nest of the season (swiftlets often build as many as three per year to replace ones that are stolen), which may be red-tinged because of regurgitated flecks of blood mixed in with the saliva. Obtaining these nests is not easy, as the birds build them in caves on high cliffs. Some people have been known to risk their lives in trying to get a nest; others have trained monkeys or other animals to fetch them. Once a nest is cleaned of any feathers and debris, it is added to the soup, where it breaks into short, noodlelike strands. Chinese history tells of Zheng Ho (1371–1433), a famous navigator during the Ming Dynasty (1368–1644), who searched for trade routes in the South Seas. Of the many treasures he brought back from his numerous voyages, swiftlets' nests were the most exotic and rare. Today, a single swiftlet's nest can range in price from $5 to $300, depending on the quality, and a bowl of Bird's Nest Soup may cost as much as $60. However, many restaurants in western cultures replace the actual swiftlet's nest with noodles.

CONFUCIUS SAYS . . .

Try the Kung Pao Chicken recipe at **Almanac.com/extras**. While you're there, learn about the origin of fortune cookies and check out your Chinese birth year profile.

Mu Shu Pork

The "mu shu" in Mu Shu Pork refers to the flowers of either the cassia or olive tree. This dish evokes nature, using tree ears (edible mushrooms) and lily buds (unopened flowers of daylilies). Most recipes also contain bits of scrambled egg, symbolic of yellow flowers. Note: Lily buds, tree ears, and mu shu pancakes are available at Asian food markets; if desired or necessary, you can use dried mushrooms to replace lily buds or tree ears.

1/3 cup dried lily buds
1/3 cup dried tree ears
2 tablespoons peanut oil
1 boneless pork chop
(4 ounces), cut into
Julienne strips
2 large eggs, lightly beaten
2 1/2 cups shredded
Chinese cabbage
1/2 cup chopped water
chestnuts
1 teaspoon minced garlic
2 teaspoons soy sauce
1/4 teaspoon salt

1/4 teaspoon pepper
2 scallions, cut into 1-inch
pieces
8 mu shu pancakes
hoisin sauce

Rinse lily buds and tree ears in cold water. Cover with cold water and soak 1 hour or until soft. Drain well and pat dry; chop. Set aside. Heat peanut oil in a large skillet or wok over medium-high heat. Add pork and stir-fry 2 minutes; transfer to a small bowl. Add eggs to skillet and stir-fry until cooked. Remove from skillet and add to pork. Add lily buds, tree ears, cabbage, water chestnuts, and garlic to skillet. Stir-fry about 2 minutes. Stir in pork and eggs; add soy sauce, salt, pepper, and scallions. Cook 1 minute or until thoroughly heated. Brush pancakes with hoisin sauce. Place pork mixture in center, roll up, and serve. **Makes 4 servings.**

Crossing the Bridge Noodles

T he story behind Crossing the Bridge Noodles is a sweet tale of love and devotion. Legend has it that sometime during the Qing Dynasty, in Mengzi County, a scholar chose to live away from his wife while preparing for his imperial civil service examinations. Each evening, the scholar's loyal wife brought him his favorite meals, crossing a long bridge to get to her husband's study chambers. Each time she made the trek, she noticed that the food was no longer hot when she reached her destination. It is said that on one trip over the bridge, the scholar's wife fainted. When she awoke, she found that the noodle soup she was carrying was still warm. The hot food pleased the scholar, and his wife spread the word of her discovery—that a layer of fat on the surface of the soup had kept it warm.

Those disinclined to believe the tale of the scholar and his wife claim that the recipe's name derives from the arc or "bridge" created when the cook pours the noodles into the broth containing the meat and fish.

Scholar or not, you can use this dish to bridge the gap between Chinese cuisine and your kitchen.

1 teaspoon rice wine
1/4 teaspoon minced fresh ginger
1/8 teaspoon salt, plus 1/2 teaspoon
1/2 teaspoon soy sauce
3 ounces skinned and boned chicken breast
3 ounces skinned fish fillet
3 ounces shrimp, peeled and deveined
2 cups loosely packed spinach

9 ounces very fine Chinese noodles
6 cups chicken broth
1/2 teaspoon MSG (optional)

C ombine rice wine, ginger, ⅛ teaspoon salt, and soy sauce in a small bowl. Set aside. Slice chicken, fish, and shrimp in paper-thin slices; add to rice wine mixture. Set aside. Cook spinach in boiling water for 30 seconds; drain. Plunge into ice water to stop cooking process; drain and set aside. Cook noodles in boiling water 4 minutes or until done. Drain and set aside. Bring chicken broth to a boil; add ½ teaspoon salt and MSG, if desired. (Some recipes call for including 5 tablespoons of chicken fat at this stage, but we have omitted it to make for a healthier dish.) Boil 1 minute. Immediately add chicken, fish, and shrimp to broth. Add noodles. Remove from heat and let stand 1 minute. Top with spinach. Serve in individual bowls. **Makes 4 servings.** □□

Sarah Perreault, assistant editor of *The Old Farmer's Almanac,* prefers Sesame Chicken to Bird's Nest Soup, but is willing to try anything once.

Winners in the 2005 Recipe Contest

Oatmeal

SWEDISH OATMEAL PANCAKES

2 cups old-fashioned rolled oats
2 cups buttermilk, plus more as needed
1/2 cup flour
2 tablespoons sugar
1 teaspoon baking powder
1 teaspoon baking soda
2 large eggs, lightly beaten
4 tablespoons unsalted butter, melted
canola oil for cooking
1 large pear, cored, peeled, and thinly sliced
1/4 cup lightly toasted sliced almonds

In a large bowl, combine oats and 2 cups buttermilk. Soak at least 30 minutes. In a medium bowl, combine the dry ingredients. Stir them into oat mixture. Mix in eggs and melted butter. Batter should be thick; add 1 or 2 tablespoons more buttermilk if it's too thick to pour. Coat a nonstick or well-seasoned griddle with canola oil and heat it over medium heat. Pour out batter in ¼-cup portions. Place a few pear slices and almonds on each pancake. Cook until browned on bottom, 2 to 3 minutes. Flip and cook for 2 to 3 minutes more. Serve with butter and maple syrup. **Serves 4 to 6.**

–Diane Halferty, Corpus Christi, Texas

SPICY GLAZED MEATBALLS

1 pound lean ground beef
1/2 cup old-fashioned rolled oats
1/2 teaspoon seasoned salt
1/2 teaspoon black pepper
2 tablespoons minced onion
2 teaspoons Worcestershire sauce
1/4 cup milk

GLAZE:
1 cup raspberry jam
1 tablespoon white vinegar
1/3 cup prepared mustard

Preheat oven to 400°F. In a large bowl, mix all meatball ingredients together with a wooden spoon until well combined. Shape into 1-inch balls. Coat a large skillet with nonstick cooking spray. Cook meatballs in a single layer over medium heat for 10 to 15 minutes, turning occasionally to brown on all sides. Drain well and place in a single layer in a 9x12-inch baking dish. Purée jam and vinegar together in a food processor or blender until smooth. Place jam mixture and mustard in a microwave-safe bowl, stir to blend, and microwave on high for 2 to 3 minutes, or until jam is melted. Spoon the mixture over the meatballs. Bake for 15 minutes until glazed. Serve warm. **Serves 4 to 6.**

–Mary Shivers, Ada, Oklahoma

STUFFED CHICKEN BREASTS

VINAIGRETTE:
5 tablespoons chopped Italian parsley
1 teaspoon chopped thyme
3 tablespoons chopped tarragon

1 garlic clove, minced
1/4 cup extra-virgin olive oil
8 tablespoons rice wine vinegar or red
     wine vinegar

4 tablespoons butter
1 medium sweet onion, minced
2 garlic cloves, minced
1/2 cup quick-cooking oatmeal
1/2 cup pine nuts, toasted
salt and pepper, to taste
4 boneless chicken breasts, with skin on
cotton string
1/4 cup canola oil

Combine vinaigrette ingredients in a bottle or a bowl. Reserve.

In a medium bowl, mix butter, onion, garlic, oatmeal, pine nuts, salt, and pepper. Reserve. Lay chicken breasts on their sides and, with a small paring knife, slice through each, making a pocket. Do not cut through the bottom or the top of the breast. Stuff each pocket with onion mixture. Wind each breast with string, stretching the chicken skin over the pocket opening to hold the stuffing in place. Tie to secure. Season with salt and pepper. Heat the oil in a skillet over medium-high heat and put in the chicken, skin side down. Cover the pan. Cook 10 to 12 minutes, then turn breasts over, cover the pan again, and cook for 10 more minutes. Chicken is done when it is pierced and the juices run clear. Remove chicken from skillet and place on a platter. Immediately drizzle with herb vinaigrette, reserving some to serve at the table. Cut off the string before serving. **Serves 4.**

–Ginger Moreno, Rancho Palo Verdes, California

Honorable Mention

NORTHERN BANANA PUDDING

2 bananas, sliced
3/4 cup old-fashioned rolled oats
1 cup milk
2 eggs
1/4 cup maple syrup, plus some for topping
1 tablespoon butter, melted
1 teaspoon salt
cinnamon, nutmeg, or cloves to taste

Preheat oven to 350°F. Mix all ingredients in a bowl. Pour mixture into a small, ovenproof pan. Bake about one hour, depending on the size of your pan and how dark you like the pudding. Remove from the oven. Drizzle extra maple syrup over hot pudding. Top with your favorite oatmeal granola and cream or milk. Eat it hot, but don't burn your mouth! **Serves 2 to 3.**

–Joe Fiala, Weare, New Hampshire

**Announcing the 2006
Recipe Contest: Rice**

Send us your best recipe using rice. (Amateur cooks only, please.) See page 142 for contest rules.

HAVE IT YOUR WAY

It seems that just about everybody likes oatmeal. We received more than 200 oatmeal recipes, including 50 for cookies, with "mix-ins" such as dried cranberries, currants, raisins, dates, pecans, walnuts, macadamia nuts, crunchy peanut butter, chocolate chips, toffee pieces, butterscotch morsels, crystallized ginger, canned pumpkin, marshmallows, cornflakes, and coconut. For a few of the cookie recipes as well as recipes for other oatmeal dishes, go to **Almanac.com/extras.**

THE TOUGHEST JOB IN SPORTS

The ice hockey goal seems an innocent place in the moments before a game. Seconds before the opening face-off at center ice, the goalie skates over to the net, pivots on his blades, and crouches. The moment the referee drops the puck and the game begins, the goalie becomes a target. He is under attack. "No role in team sport has such violence associated with it," writes Douglas Hunter in *A Breed Apart, An Illustrated History of Goaltending* (Triumph Books, 1995).

Few would disagree. The goalie's job is to patrol the crease, a designated area in front of the net, and stop the puck (a six-ounce, one-inch-thick disk of vulcanized rubber) as it hurtles toward the net, sometimes reaching speeds

Boston Bruins goalie Gerry Cheevers attempts a save on Toronto Maple Leaf Paul Henderson.

of 115 mph. Dunc Wilson, of the National Hockey League (NHL) Vancouver Canucks, compared being hit by a puck to being struck by a sledgehammer. During one game, he took the first shot square in the mask—and it knocked him out. Other goalies draw a parallel to bullets. After a puck clipped his side, Detroit Red Wing Manny Legace said, "The shot felt like it went through my chest, like I had a hole in my body." NHL Hall-of-Famer Jacques Plante described his job simply as "like being shot at."

No athlete in any sport goes into a game so bulletproofed. Thick pads cover the goalie's legs. A chest protector and elbow and shoulder pads beneath his jersey swell his size until he resembles the rotund Michelin Man. On one hand, he wears a flexible "catching" mitt with which to snare pucks; on the other, a stiff, heavy "blocking glove" with which both to hold the extra-wide goalie stick and to deflect inbound pucks on that side. His throat is protected by a special collar or by a polycarbonate throat shield that dangles from his mask. His face is hidden behind the iron face bars of a helmet or beneath a fiberglass mask built to withstand the force of pucks slamming into it—as well as slower missiles. A hard-boiled egg thrown from the stands once knocked out Lorne "Gump" Worsley,

—DiMaggio-Kalish/Hockey Hall of Fame

Boston Bruins goalie Gerry Cheevers painted stitch marks on his mask after every game, indicating where he had been struck by a puck or stick.

Montreal Maroons goalie Clint Benedict wore a face mask in 1930—but abandoned it when he found that it blocked his vision.

—James Rice/Hockey Hall of Fame

171

another Hall of Famer. He also had to dodge cups of beer, soup cans, a dead rabbit, a dead octopus, a folding chair, and a cheese sandwich wrapped in brown paper. Former Boston Bruins coach Don Cherry spoke for all who have ever guarded the net when he once said, "There is no such thing as painless goaltending."

Indeed. For years, goalies didn't wear face masks during games. Clint Benedict of the Montreal Maroons was the first pro to wear one, in 1930, but they never became popular. The supermacho ethos of goalies dictated that they accept pain as part of the sport. Many dutifully spilled their teeth onto the ice like marbles. Lorne Chabot, a veteran of five

NHL teams, always shaved before a game because, he said, "I stitch better when smooth."

In 1956, Jacques Plante began wearing a mask during Montreal Canadiens practices, but his coach, Toe Blake, forbade him to wear it during a game. Blake thought that the mask signified weakness and cowardice. Of course, Blake, a former forward, had never been on the receiving end of a slap shot. On November 1, 1959, Plante took a puck flush on the face for what was to be the last time. In the dressing room, where his face was being stitched, he told Blake that he would not play again without some face protection. Ultimately Blake acquiesced, and Plante began wearing a mask.

During a practice in the 1968–69 season, then–Boston Bruins goalie Gerry Cheevers came up with an idea to show just how valuable masks really were. After every game, he painted stitch or scar marks on his, indicating where he had been struck by a puck or stick. By the end of a season, he usually ran out of space after 200 or so stitches had been recorded.

Though masks were never made mandatory, it has been more than 30 years since a goalie has played in an NHL game without one. As Clint

-Imperial Oil-Turofsky/Hockey Hall of Fame

Bill Durnan (left, with Maurice "Rocket" Richard) won the Vezina Trophy as the NHL's top netminder six times.

Canadien Ken Dryden started his warm-ups by shooting a puck at his own net and missing, hoping that the bad karma would spread to opposing players.

Malarchuk can attest, however, its presence doesn't guarantee freedom from injury. On March 22, 1989, St. Louis Blues right winger Steve Tuttle charged toward Malarchuk, who was in goal for the Buffalo Sabres. Tuttle drew back his stick and fired a shot. The puck sped through the crease just as Malarchuk sprawled on the ice to stop it. At that instant, Tuttle was sent flying as he was tripped by a defenseman. One of his skates sliced through Malarchuk's neck, slashing the jugular vein. As blood pooled on the ice, three players who witnessed the accident vomited, and two spectators suffered heart attacks. Only the quick action of doctors and trainers— and more than 300 stitches—saved Malarchuk's life.

The outcome of a hockey game can rest almost entirely on the shoulders of the goalie, which means that the stress and pressure involved can be seriously daunting. Lloyd Percival, author of *The Hockey Handbook* (McClelland & Stewart, 1997) and founder of Canada's famed Fitness Center Institute, claimed that before a Stanley Cup playoff game, many goaltenders experience a level of anxiety that most people feel only once or twice in a lifetime—say, before a serious operation.

Consider the experiences of these three players. Bill Durnan won the Vezina Trophy (for being the NHL's best goalie) six times as a Canadien, yet the demands of carrying his team buckled his spirit, and he quit during the 1950 Stanley Cup playoffs against the New York Rangers—after surrendering 10 goals in three games. "I couldn't sleep. I couldn't keep my meals down," he told reporters. "I felt that nothing was worth that kind of agony." (The Rangers won the series.)

Wilfred Cude, then of the Canadiens, experienced similar strain one night after a game toward the end of the 1941 season. He arrived home for dinner with his nerves shot. Apparently unaware of his distress, his wife served him a steak. Cude threw the meat against the dining room wall, saying, "If that thing comes down, I'm quitting." The meat slithered to the floor, and he left the goal crease for good.

Then there was Frank McCool. Named NHL rookie of the year in 1945, McCool recorded three straight shutouts while leading the Toronto Maple Leafs to the 1945 Stanley Cup championship. Yet he played only two years. It seemed that "Ulcers," as he was appropriately nicknamed, became

Terry Sawchuk, who holds the record for the most shutouts in NHL history, abruptly retired at age 27 in 1957, saying that he couldn't take the emotional strain.

SCORE!

To learn more about legendary NHL goalies and find other hockey trivia, go to **Almanac.com/extras.**

nearly doubled over from stomach pain almost every time he took the ice.

Talent offers little protection from the stress of the job, even for Hall of Famers. Terry Sawchuk, who holds the record for the most shutouts in NHL history (103), abruptly retired at age 27 in 1957, saying that he couldn't take the emotional strain. He was coaxed back onto the ice for the next season but played most games thereafter with his back in knots.

Glenn Hall's record 552 consecutive NHL games earned him the nickname "Mr. Goalie," but he was also famous for his nervous stomach. He became nauseous so often before and during games that he kept a spit bucket at his team's bench and sipped a stomach-soothing tea between periods. That was the only way he could endure a game, or what he described as "sixty minutes of hell."

Considering the pressure on goalies, it should come as no surprise that they are among the most ritualistic and superstitious of athletes. They will watch videotapes of saves but not of goals allowed; to do so might invite more goals. Canadien Ken Dryden always started his warm-ups by shooting a puck at his own net and missing; he hoped that the bad karma would spread to opposing players. Before a game, 18-year NHL veteran Tony Esposito talked to no one—not family, friends, or even teammates—as he tried to block all thoughts of failure from his mind. Patrick Roy, who retired from the Colorado Avalanche in 2003, kept a puck in a secret place and brought it out to bounce on the locker-room floor between periods for good luck.

So, why do it? Why endure the pain, take the risks, put your life on the line? Because a goalie has the potential to be the hero in every game. Don Cherry put it this way: "If a football team has the worst quarterback, it can still win. You can have the worst pitcher in baseball, but if the other guys on the team can get enough hits, you'll win. But [in hockey,] if you don't have a good goaltender, you're dead." ☐☐

Mel Allen, executive editor of *Yankee* Magazine, writes on a variety of topics for *The Old Farmer's Almanac.*

How to Teach

OLD CHICKENS NEW TRICKS

by Sophia Yin, D.V.M.

Your hens are the most

profitable stock you have if

you treat them rightly. When

they are troublesome, . . .

train them so that they will

follow you like a dog and

then just at night take them

out on a walk.

–The Old Farmer's Almanac
archives, 1865

–illustrated by Paul Meisel

W hile backyard poultry farmers know the joys of raising chickens and gathering tasty eggs, most would probably be surprised to learn that the seemingly simple chicken could actually be smarter than their dog. Well, sort of. It's easy and fun to train chickens and, in many cases, faster than training a dog. All you need is a hungry chicken and chicken feed, such as pellet or scratch, or special food treats.

These tricks consist of many little steps, but because chickens peck quickly and love to eat, you'll get lots of practice in a short period of time—which will lead to very fast learning. Best of all, you and your friends will soon learn to appreciate your chicken for her mind as well as her eggs.

1. Come When Called

■ Use food that your chicken loves but gets only during these training sessions (tiny pieces of hot dog work well). Hold the food in your hand or place it in a small measuring cup that you can deliver quickly. Start by placing the food right next to your chicken and giving her a few treats to make sure she's hungry. (You'll know this when she immediately eats what you put in front of her.) Now hide the food by holding it up high or behind your back. Say your chicken's name and immediately deliver the food so that she gets it within one second. Allow only one to two pecks, or she'll get full too quickly. Do this twice a day, in the morning and in the afternoon, in three five-minute sessions with five-minute breaks in between.

After several five-minute sessions, switch to saying your chicken's name when she's looking down or away from you, before swiftly delivering the food so that it appears in front of her, out of

Once your chicken understands that she'll get a reward for particular behaviors, you will have established a pattern that can be used to teach other tricks.

the blue. After a day or two, she'll start to associate the sound of her name with the delivery of food. You'll know this because she'll automatically look toward you and the food whenever she hears her name.

Next, increase the distance by standing several feet away, calling her name, and immediately presenting the food. Your chicken should run right over.

Once she masters that, try adding distractions, such as practicing in new locations or scattering her regular, boring food on the ground when she knows you have treats. If you call her and she ignores you, she's not hungry or the distraction is too intense; don't keep calling her, or she'll learn to ignore you. Instead, decrease the intensity of the distraction or try her later in the day when she's hungry. Pretty soon, your chicken will come when called better than most dogs.

2. Touch a Target With the Beak

■ Use a pencil with a big eraser on the end for your target. Tape a small piece of feed onto the eraser and hold the eraser in front of the chicken. When your chicken pecks at the feed, immediately give her a treat from your hand or measuring cup. Remove the target for a few seconds, then repeat.

Once she can touch the target immedi-

178

ately upon presentation nine out of ten times when it's held one to two inches from her beak, you can repeat this step without the food taped to the target. You'll have to be fast at your food delivery to ensure that you reward the first correct peck.

When your chicken is able to consistently peck the target without food taped on it, gradually increase the distance at which you present the target. Start by presenting it about three inches away and build up to several feet. Once your chicken understands that she'll get a reward for particular behaviors, you will have established a pattern that can be used to teach other tricks.

3. Pick a Card

■ This is a trick that most dogs will never be taught, and it only takes a couple of days to teach it to your chicken. In this trick, you'll teach your chicken to distinguish the queen of hearts or another favorite card from all the others in a deck of cards.

Tape a small piece of feed on the center of the queen of hearts, and then hold the card out for your chicken to see. When she pecks at the food, quickly give her a treat. Repeat, until she automatically pecks the card as soon as she sees the picture on it. Next, remove the treat taped to the card and repeat. When your chicken pecks consistently, the next step is to present the card an inch or so lower until your chicken

Gradually lower the card until your chicken will peck it when it's on the ground. Now you're ready to teach her to peck only the queen of hearts.

immediately pecks consistently at the lower height. Gradually lower the card until she'll peck it when it's on the ground and even run several feet to peck it. Now you're ready to teach her to peck only the queen of hearts and not the other cards.

Start by placing a number (not face) card from a black suit several inches from the queen of hearts, but have the queen of hearts slightly closer so that your chicken is more likely to peck it. Each time she pecks the queen of hearts, reward her and then move the cards around. Ignore pecking of the incorrect card. Gradually place the cards closer and closer, as long as she's pecking the correct card.

Repeat each step until she consistently chooses the right card. Next, add more black number cards and repeat. (Yes, chickens *do* see in color.)

Once she can pick out the queen of hearts from among a pile of black number cards, you can repeat the process, first with black face cards, such as the king of clubs and the jack of spades, then with red number cards, and finally with red face cards. She'll have the most trouble with the queen of diamonds, so when you get to this step, practice with just the queen of diamonds and queen of hearts.

The final step is to add all of the cards together. Start with several cards at a time spread far apart, with the queen of hearts a little easier to reach. Then gradually place the cards closer together, with the queen of hearts in the midst of the others. Pretty soon, your chicken will be an ace at picking out the right card, and your friends will be amazed to see your biddy doing your bidding.

Everywhere a Chick-Chick

If you're thinking about raising a few chickens in your backyard, you are not alone:

■ The number of poultry raised on small farms has increased by about 12 percent since 1997, according to the most recent (2002) USDA Agricultural Census.

■ Membership in the American Poultry Association (APA) has increased from 1,500 in 1994 to over 4,000 in 2004, and youth membership is up to 800 nationwide.

■ Backyard enthusiasts prefer rare and heritage breeds, especially Lamona, Salmon Faverolles, and Chanticleer Java, reports the APA.

□□

Sophia Yin, D.V.M., is an applied animal behaviorist, animal trainer, and lecturer in domestic animal behavior at University of California, Davis. She uses chicken training to demonstrate the principles of learning in animals.

> **WING IT**
> Want to teach your chicken to spin in a circle, jump in the air, and fly from place to place? See instructional videos of these tricks and learn how to hypnotize a chicken at **Almanac.com/extras.**

Gestation and Mating Table

	Proper Age for First Mating	Period of Fertility (years)	Number of Females for One Male	Period of Gestation (days) AVERAGE	RANGE
Ewe	90 lb. or 1 yr.	6		147 / 151[1]	142–154
Ram	12–14 mo., well matured	7	50–75[2] / 35–40[3]		
Mare	3 yr.	10–12		336	310–370
Stallion	3 yr.	12–15	40–45[4] / Record 252[5]		
Cow	15–18 mo.[6]	10–14		283	279–290[7] 262–300[8]
Bull	1 yr., well matured	10–12	50[4] / Thousands[5]		
Sow	5–6 mo. or 250 lb.	6		115	110–120
Boar	250–300 lb.	6	50[2] / 35–40[3]		
Doe goat	10 mo. or 85–90 lb.	6		150	145–155
Buck goat	Well matured	5	30		
Bitch	16–18 mo.	8		63	58–67
Male dog	12–16 mo.	8	8–10		
Queen cat	12 mo.	6		63	60–68
Tom cat	12 mo.	6	6–8		
Doe rabbit	6 mo.	5–6		31	30–32
Buck rabbit	6 mo.	5–6	30		

[1]For fine wool breeds. [2]Hand-mated. [3]Pasture. [4]Natural. [5]Artificial. [6]Holstein and beef: 750 lb.; Jersey: 500 lb. [7]Beef; 8–10 days shorter for Angus. [8]Dairy.

Incubation Period of Poultry (days)
Chicken. 21
Duck 26–32
Goose 30–34
Guinea 26–28

Maximum Life Span of Animals in Captivity (years)
Cat (domestic). 34
Chicken (domestic). 25
Dog (domestic) 29

Duck (domestic) 23
Goat (domestic). 20
Goose (domestic) 20
Horse 62
Rabbit . . . . 18+

	Estral/Estrous Cycle (including heat period) AVERAGE	RANGE	Length of Estrus (heat) AVERAGE	RANGE	Usual Time of Ovulation	When Cycle Recurs if Not Bred
Mare	21 days	10–37 days	5–6 days	2–11 days	24–48 hours before end of estrus	21 days
Sow	21 days	18–24 days	2–3 days	1–5 days	30–36 hours after start of estrus	21 days
Ewe	16½ days	14–19 days	30 hours	24–32 hours	12–24 hours before end of estrus	16½ days
Goat	21 days	18–24 days	2–3 days	1–4 days	Near end of estrus	21 days
Cow	21 days	18–24 days	18 hours	10–24 hours	10–12 hours after end of estrus	21 days
Bitch	24 days		7 days	5–9 days	1–3 days after first acceptance	Pseudo-pregnancy
Cat		15–21 days	3–4 days, if mated	9–10 days, in absence of male	24–56 hours after coitus	Pseudo-pregnancy

Tracker's Guide

Off for a walk in the woods? Keep an eye out for signs of these woodland creatures • text compiled by Sarah Perreault

–illustrated by Erick Ingraham

Gray Wolf

- **Habitat:** Forests, deserts, plains, mountains, tundra
- **Weight:** Males, 85 to 115 pounds; females, 50 to 100 pounds
- **Height:** 26 to 32 inches at shoulder
- **Length:** 50 to 70 inches
- **Diet:** Deer, elk, caribou, bison, cattle, sheep, beaver, rabbits, rodents, grasses, nuts, berries
- **Territory:** North central, northwestern (including Alaska), and southwestern United States; Canada

Striped Skunk

- **Habitat:** Woodlands, grasslands, farmland, suburbs
- **Weight:** Males, 3 to 11 pounds; females, 2 to 8 pounds
- **Height:** 6 to 8 inches at shoulder
- **Length:** 21 to 26 inches
- **Diet:** Mice, shrews, eggs, grubs and other insects, nuts, fruit, garbage
- **Territory:** Throughout the United States, except the arid Southwest; southern Canada

Snowshoe Hare

- **Habitat:** Forests, fields, riversides, swamps
- **Weight:** 2 to 4 pounds, on average
- **Height:** 12 to 18 inches
- **Length:** 15 to 20 inches, on average
- **Diet:** Grass, clover, dandelions, raspberry and blackberry shoots, twigs, woody plants
- **Territory:** Northern United States; most of Canada

Moose

- **Habitat:** Recently burned areas with willow and birch shrubs; dense forests; timberline plateaus; riversides
- **Weight:** Males, 1,200 to 1,600 pounds; females, 800 to 1,300 pounds
- **Height:** 76 inches at shoulder, on average
- **Length:** 90 to 120 inches
- **Diet:** Willow, cottonwood, fir trees; aquatic plants
- **Territory:** Northern United States; Canada

Tracks are not to scale.

CHILLING SCREAMS IN THE DEAD OF NIGHT. LONG, CURVED CLAWS THAT CAN DISEMBOWEL A PORCUPINE WITH SURGICAL PRECISION. THE WORST CATFIGHT YOU'VE EVER HEARD—EXCEPT THAT ONE OF THE COMBATANTS ISN'T A CAT. IT'S A FISHER.

Your Kitty's

New Worst Enemy

BY SALLY ROTH

Three to four feet long from its twitching nose to the tip of its luxurious tail, the fisher looks big and cuddly, something like a cross between a giant-size black Persian cat and a baby bear. Looks can be deceptive. Under all that long, thick, dark brown fur is a body that rarely tops 12 pounds, and usually weighs in at about half that. And forget cuddly. The fisher—big brother of the weasel clan, Mustelidae—is one of the most efficient killers in the forest.

Nearly wiped out due to overtrapping years ago, when a single pelt was worth a month's wages, fishers are ba-a-a-ack with a vengeance. In Massachusetts, New Hampshire, Michigan, and other areas where fishers were reintroduced decades ago in an effort to restore biodiversity, it's a success story—a success, that is, unless you happen to be a kitty cat. Filet-of-feline is now a prime choice in some areas.

A case in point: Bloodcurdling wails woke Robin Peters of Goffstown, New Hampshire, with a jolt at 4:00 A.M. one June morning. Cats fighting outside, she figured. Knowing that Shadow, a family kitty with pretty black-and-white fur and a penchant for perching on the windowsill, was indoors, she went back to sleep.

The next morning, Peters discovered that Shadow had been nabbed right out of her living room.

"To see that screen, it was like a bear was in here!" said Peters. Claw marks in the aluminum siding showed how the fisher had scrambled up to the window screen, ripped a hole to enter—and exited with Shadow in its clutches. Tufts of black and white fur in the screen and across the yard spelled out an unhappy ending for Peters's kitty.

"She loved to sit in that window, serenading the Moon," says Peters. "When I think that I actually heard the whole thing...." She trails off, regretful and angry. "It was like a murder. Like a murderer came into the house."

Peters had prior evidence of the predator's presence. She had noticed fisher tracks in the snow close to her house in wintertime. The distinctive, 2½- to 3-inch-wide, five-toed paw prints, about as big as those of a good-size dog, are noticeably wider than tall. Each toe imprint is tipped with claw marks.

CONTINUED

The fisher (Martes pennanti)

–photo: Daniel J. Cox/NaturalExposures.com

Most folks in fisher country know little about these predators, which, at least until recently, have rarely strayed from the forests. Now that fishers seem to be changing their modus operandi, getting to know the habits of these wild neighbors can help you keep your pets from becoming prey.

Hearing or seeing a fisher or spotting its tracks means that it's likely to be back, because fishers are creatures of habit. They patrol regular routes through their territory, sniffing in sheds, hollow logs, and any other likely hiding place for a warm-blooded animal. They're solitary types, with each fisher claiming its own territory of 10 to 150 square miles.

On the ground, snowshoe hares are the main dish du jour—or more accurately, du soir—for these mostly nocturnal predators who have a nose and a doggedness for following scent trails that rival those of the best hounds.

But fishers are also supremely agile climbers. (They climb like a cat, and it's no wonder that fishers are called "fisher cats" in many places.) In the trees, it's hapless porcupines that become the target. Stumble across a dead porky on its back, its insides partly eaten, and you can bet that you've found the remains of a fisher's meal. Check any scat you come across in porcupine habitat, too; if it contains quills, it's likely from a fisher.

The fisher vs. porcupine battle is an astounding face-off. Unfortunately for ol' Porky, that's in the literal as well as figurative sense. A porcupine's face is nearly free of the painful barbed quills that armor its body, and that's where the fisher attacks. Lightning-fast slashes to the vulnerable face with those rapier claws soon disable the porcupine, and the rest is gravy—or innards, shall we say, because the internal organs are the first part of the animal the fisher devours. The predator revisits the carcass over the next few days until the skin is picked so clean of meat that trappers acknowledge that they couldn't have done a better job.

Porky has a fighting chance if he can reach the end of a branch before the fisher. With back turned to the danger, he clings and waits out the onslaught. But if he doesn't reach the end of the branch fast enough, the fisher simply leapfrogs over him and turns the pursuit into an ambush.

On the ground, the porcupine's last-ditch defense is parking its face against a tree trunk.

The "Cat's" Meow

Fishers are still a target of trappers in northern and mountainous areas where the animals roam. These days, a lush fisher pelt brings about $30 to $50, a far cry from the heyday of the fur, when a good skin could fetch $400.

Coats made from the soft, dense fur that once kept its original owners cozy during cold winters are also sold at furriers and online auctions, for $5,000 and up. Should you happen to win the Miss New Hampshire contest, you'll most likely receive a fisher fur coat created from pelts donated by trappers in the state.

Encountering this, the fisher merely springs higher onto the trunk, reverses its position, and then descends headfirst, snarling and spitting and scaring all but the most stalwart porcupine away from its barky refuge.

It's no wonder that somewhere along the line, fishers seem to have figured out that domestic felines, hissy fits and all, are much easier pickings for breakfast than barbed quills. Those whose cats disappear in the night can take some small comfort in knowing that fishers kill prey other than porcupines with a single swift bite to the neck.

Where the Wild Things Are

Fishers once prowled from Alaska to California, across Canada and the northern United States, down through the Rockies, throughout the Northeast—almost everywhere that forests are deep and winters are cold and snowy.

Trappers soon learned how simple it is to lure a fisher into a trap, and that was the beginning of the end. By the 1930s, fishers were going, going, gone from many of their homelands.

Thanks to reintroduction efforts, fisher screams are once again sending chills up the spine in many areas. However, they remain nearly nonexistent in California, Oregon, and Washington today.

In New England and some northern areas, fishers appear to be adapting all too well to the folks who move into once-wild woodsy areas. They've been spotted in backyards in broad daylight. They've been photographed under raised decks and in garden sheds. And their tracks show that towns and suburbia are now included in their territories. They've become

Top Cats

In Fall 2003, New Hampshire's newly formed double-A baseball team conducted a "Name the Team" contest. Three thousand ideas were submitted. Thirteen thousand fans voted. The winner, by 22 votes, was New Hampshire Fisher Cats.

so used to humans that they've even been spotted eating pet food that's been left outside and rummaging through garbage.

As word spreads about cats that disappear in the night, it's all too easy for feline owners to get frantic, and for others to worry about their dogs—or their kids. Thankfully, there's no need to worry about Junior or your golden Lab; they aren't likely to be attacked by a six-pound predator.

As for vanishing cats, unless the evidence shows otherwise, it's likely that fishers are often taking an unfair rap for the work of coyotes, which are much more abundant than fishers and notorious takers of small pets.

To stay on the safe side of prowling predators, keep your pets indoors unless you're closely supervising them. And—for extra insurance—close your windows at night. ☐☐

Sally Roth, author of nature and gardening books, lives in Washougal, Washington, where fishers are long gone but cougars and bears still roam.

Climate

The world is warming!

Glaciers are melting!

Oceans are rising!

And it's all our fault!

Sound familiar?

However alarming, though, these headlines—which usually go on to blame fossil fuel use and carbon gases—are but one-half of a scientific debate that has been raging for decades.

Unfortunately, if you are limited to this information only, you are missing a much more complicated and interesting story. Yes, the North Pole is getting warmer, but the South Pole (specifically, central Antarctica) is get-

Change:
BEHIND THE HEADLINES

ting slightly cooler. Temperatures in cities are soaring. Temperatures in the tropical Pacific are dropping. The global climate is changing—and there is no simple answer for what is shifting the world's weather. Here are five factors that play a role.

by Evelyn Browning-Garriss

1 Model Misbehavior

Early climate scientists used computer models to understand weather. Many of these early models dated from the 1950s, when scientists such as Edward Teller, father of the hydrogen bomb, were promoting atomic energy and the "Atoms for Peace" program. Their competition was carbon fuels: gas, oil, and coal. The scientists created models showing that burning these fuels produced gases that would trap the warmth from the Sun in Earth's atmosphere, just as glass traps warmth within a greenhouse.

The earliest climate models assumed that most of the factors that influenced the global climate, such as solar radiation, rarely changed. Man's behavior was deemed to be the major variable; therefore, if the climate changed, it was man's fault. When there was acid rain, it was due to utilities burning coal. When there was global warming, it was due to man-made greenhouse gas emissions.

continued

By 1971, satellite readings began to challenge these views. Previously, most computer models had used temperature measurements that dated from 1880 and were almost entirely land-based, mostly from cities and later from airports. Satellite readings were able to show temperatures at many spots on the globe, from mountaintops to the centers of the oceans. The long-term temperature record showed global warming; the satellites showed extreme heating in cities (creating urban "heat islands"), less warming in other areas, and cooling in some regions. For at least a couple of decades, the modelers and satellite scientists argued about whether global warming even existed, each claiming that the others' readings were flawed.

These days, most scientists agree that Earth has been warming, especially since the 1980s. They also agree that some warming is due to natural causes and some is due to human activity. However, scientists still disagree on how much the globe is heating up, as well as on how much of this change in temperature is mankind's doing.

Sun Cycles

2 Probably the biggest arguments are about the Sun and its impact on Earth's climate. Most scientists—but not all—agree that for thousands of years the planet's climate warmed and cooled in conjunction with long-term cycles of solar activity. What they don't agree on is how much the Sun is influencing climate change now.

The Sun provides the energy to run the weather machine. Compared to most stars, the Sun is fairly stable—so boring and reliable that life has been able to bubble along on Earth for over a billion years. "Stable" is a relative term, however. The Sun constantly goes through cycles of activity—some short, some lasting for centuries. The best known of these are the sunspot cycles, which last 11 years, on average, from start to finish.

Each sunspot cycle starts at a solar minimum, when the Sun is quiet, or relatively inactive. As the Sun becomes increasingly active, it generates more radiation, until it reaches a solar maximum, a peak of activity. During this period, it is covered with more than a hundred dark,

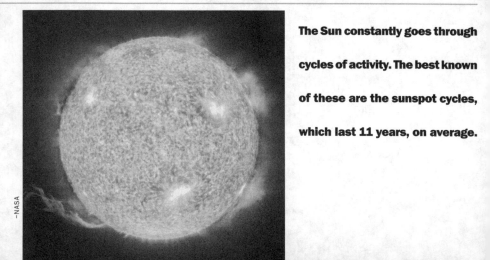

–NASA

The Sun constantly goes through cycles of activity. The best known of these are the sunspot cycles, which last 11 years, on average.

Scientists have known since the days of Benjamin Franklin that volcano ash affects global climate. The ash darkens the skies and less sunshine reaches Earth.

swirling sunspots—huge magnetic storms ejecting giant flares of superheated, polarized gases. Solar flares and storms become frequent. The Sun radiates more ultraviolet energy, and the temperature of Earth's upper atmosphere doubles. Solar winds accelerate and blow away cosmic rays that would normally create clouds that block sunlight and cool Earth's lower atmosphere. As the cycle progresses toward a new solar minimum, the activity dies down.

The Sun also seems to have long periods during which consecutive sunspot cycles are either quiet or unusually active. During the quiet periods, we have undergone global cooling; the "Little Ice Age" during the Middle Ages is one example of this. From approximately 1645 to 1715, there were almost no sunspots, even during solar maximums.

More recently, the Sun has been going through a period of more active consecutive sunspot cycles. Solar activity has increased .05 percent per decade since the 1970s, and during the current cycle there have been days when more than 200 stormy sunspots raged on the Sun. According to the Max Planck Institute for Solar System Research in Lindau, Germany, the Sun is more active now than it has been in the last 8,000 years. At the same time, according to surface measurements, Earth has warmed .5°C (.9°F) over the past century.

How much of that warmth is due to the Sun?

This is where the arguing gets fierce. Some scientists claim that the changes in the Sun are too small and haven't lasted long enough to be responsible for Earth's rising temperatures. Others say that the Sun played a part in the warming in the early 1900s, but is not responsible for the explosive warming since 1980. Still others point out that the Sun has been getting more active over the past 60 years and claim that it is a major factor in global warming. The next solar maximum is expected in 2010, and the only thing more fierce than the continuing arguments about its effect on Earth will probably be the Sun itself.

Ash and Aerosols

3 Scientists have known since the days of Benjamin Franklin that volcano ash affects global climate. The ash darkens the skies, and less sunshine reaches Earth. For example, the 1815 eruption of

Mt. Tambora in Indonesia was followed by "the Year Without a Summer," 1816. In 1991, huge clouds of ash from the eruption of Mt. Pinatubo in the Philippines covered most of the globe. By the following year, global temperatures had fallen by .5°C (.9°F) and more than a foot of snow had fallen on Canadian wheat fields—in August.

The impacts of large volcano eruptions last for years. Volcanic ash and chemicals mix with water vapor, creating clouds. Later, the ash and debris rain out. Following the Pinatubo explosion, there were massive spring rains over North America in 1993, and all or parts of nine midwestern states were covered with waters from the worst Mississippi River flooding in a century.

Scientists have discovered that volcanic dust is not the only material in the air that changes the weather. The sky is filled with floating materials called aerosols (from dust to smoke to man-made pollution), which amount to as much as a billion tons per year. Such pollution also includes "bio-aerosols"—dandruff, dead skin cells, plant pollen and spores, fur particles, and other bits of biological detritus. Some of these aerosols reflect sunlight, cooling the atmosphere, while others absorb heat.

Some pose other problems. For example, giant clouds of aerosols can rise over the Sahara and be carried by winds as far as Florida, where they fertilize the water with iron and contribute to the formation of deadly "red tides"—blooms of reddish algae that grow in the water and kill fish. Asian aerosols have sometimes forced Pacific Northwest states to issue air pollution advisories. It's all very complicated.

Like volcanic dust, aerosol debris affects rain and snowfall. Water condenses around the particles, forming drops too tiny to fall out as rain. Winds can carry the droplets hundreds, even thousands, of miles before they collect enough moisture to fall. That's why Florida farmers, for example, sometimes find layers of red African sand in the bottom of buckets after a heavy rain.

Ocean Currents

4 The Sun radiates energy. The dusts and clouds determine how much energy reaches Earth. The ocean currents carry the warmth around the globe. The most famous of these are the warm El Niño and cool La Niña, tropical Pacific currents that influence global weather patterns and can bring heat waves, floods,

Tropical Pacific Ocean currents influence global weather patterns and can bring heat waves, floods, and drought.

and drought. There are other larger and slower patterns of currents that also change the climate. In two of these patterns—the Pacific Decadal Oscillation (PDO) and the Atlantic Multidecadal Oscillation (AMO)—ocean currents that flow from the warmer latitudes toward the North Pole have become more active. The currents are flowing faster and carrying more warm water north. This heavy activity began in the late 1990s, warming areas around the North Pole, North America, Europe, and East Asia. The increase of warm water brought higher temperatures and changed global precipitation patterns.

Just as El Niños come and go, so too do the PDO and AMO ocean patterns change every 20 to 30 years. From the mid-1970s through most of the 1990s, currents in both oceans flowed more slowly, bringing benign, stable weather to North America. Between 1995 and 1999, the pattern in both oceans changed. The new patterns are similar to those that caused huge droughts from California to the grain belts of the Midwest in the 1930s and 1950s. These are also the patterns that coincide with extremely busy Atlantic hurricane seasons. (Remember 2004?)

5 The Greenhouse Effect

Nature is not the only force shaping the weather. Man has an impact on the environment, especially his immediate surroundings. How much man-made greenhouse gases heat the entire globe is controversial; the fact that these greenhouse gases are turning cities into urban heat islands is not.

Storms tend to be heaviest east of large cities, where the hot urban air collides with cooler rural temperatures.

We all know that buildings, streets, and sidewalks absorb solar heat; they also absorb heat created by man's energy use. As cities have grown and energy use has increased, urban areas have grown warmer—.5°C (.9°F) warmer in each decade since World War II. This has resulted in urban heat islands, places where the temperature range of a central city differs from its rural surroundings. This difference has been shown to be from as little as 2.2°C (4°F) in St. Louis, Missouri, to as much as 10°C (18°F) in Mexico City. How hot can a city get? Recent satellite observations have shown us that temperatures in southern and western U.S. cities are reaching as high as 66.6°C (150°F) on inner-city rooftops and 48.9°C (120°F) on streets and parking lots.

Heat islands warp natural rainfall

patterns. Hot air during the day reduces rainfall on the cities and their surroundings. Then, at night, warm air radiated from the urban centers rises and mixes with pollution aerosols. Moisture collects around the pollution particles (similar to the way it forms around the ash aerosols mentioned earlier), forming clouds of tiny droplets that are then blown away by wind. Throughout the U.S. Midwest, storms tend to be heaviest east of large cities, where the hot urban air, carried on the prevailing westerly winds, collides with cooler rural temperatures. Scientists have reported that along the East Coast it rains more on the weekends, because most cities generate fewer pollution aerosols on Saturday and Sundays. (The fact that there are fewer aerosols means that each particle can absorb more moisture. These larger droplets fall rather than blow away.)

Skeptics claim that much of the global warming we have seen reflects the increased use and reradiation of energy in local heat islands and is not a worldwide phenomenon.

The Big Picture

Despite the sometimes provocative headlines, experts are not sure how much Earth is warming or why it is doing so. Carbon gases such as carbon monoxide (CO), carbon dioxide (CO_2), and methane (CH_4) are partially responsible, especially in metropolitan areas, but other factors are shaping Earth's climate as well—the Sun, the oceans, natural gases, clouds, and dust. The world is constantly changing and so is its climate. Mankind is not in charge.

Evelyn Browning-Garriss, editor of the *Browning Newsletter,* has been writing, speaking, and consulting about the social and economic impact of climate change for more than 30 years. She tracks weather trends and cycles from her office in New Mexico.

Weird Weather Events

As the global climate continues to change, we are seeing some truly strange weather. For example . . .

■ Hurricanes and typhoons are supposed to be impossible on the equator. Storms swirl counterclockwise in the Northern Hemisphere and clockwise in the Southern Hemisphere. Therefore, there is no way to have one storm that overlaps the equator and has its winds blowing "properly" on both sides. Yet on December 27, 2001, Typhoon Vamei raged along the equator, damaging several U.S. naval vessels before slamming into the Malay Peninsula.

■ One of the most publicized strange weather events was the European heat wave of August 2003. Cities throughout France, Italy, Germany, and the United Kingdom recorded their highest temperatures ever. More than 20,000 people died.

■ On March 26, 2004, satellites showed, for the first time in recorded history, a hurricane off the coast of Brazil! The Brazilian weather service reported that tropical storms in the South Atlantic are impossible, so the government refused to issue an alert. The hurricane hit Santa Catarina without warning and killed at least 38 people.

■ From 2000 to 2005, drought has plagued western states and provinces. Massive wildfires have blazed through the region. British Columbia reported that its drought was the worst in 400 years, and the Colorado River Basin that serves California and the Southwest reported its driest conditions in 500 years.

–Superstock, Inc.

■ Warmer temperatures are not just producing drought; they are distorting precipitation patterns around the globe, too. Moscow experienced its warmest January on record in 2005, so warm that bears awoke from hibernation months ahead of schedule. On January 27, however, winter returned and Moscow was hit with 12 inches of snow over a four-day period. The snowfall accumulation during January of that year was twice what that city normally averages for that month.

■ Even the nature of precipitation seems to be changing. In July 2004, scientists discovered the biggest raindrops ever recorded, with diameters about one-quarter that of a golf ball, over both Brazil and the Marshall Islands. The drops were so big that when they fell, they weren't configured as teardrops or spheres. Instead, air resistance caught their undersides and turned them into tiny, jellyfish-like shapes.

■ As the lower air warms, the stratosphere is simultaneously cooling. This produces huge hailstones. Spain was hit with basketball-size hail in January 2000. Globally, more than 50 huge hailstones have been reported in recent years, some weighing 25 to 35 pounds. The largest ever reported, weighing 440 pounds, fell in Brazil.

■ On December 30, 2004, snow fell on the United Arab Emirates for the first time in many years. In March 2005, Jammu, India, reported its greatest snowfall ever.

■ In 2005, Australia recorded its coldest February day in history (remember, this is summertime Down Under). The continent was plagued by storms and floods, and Melbourne recorded its heaviest rainfall since records began in 1856. –E. B.-G.

□ □

CURRENT NEWS

For more on world weather patterns, go to **Almanac.com/extras**.

MAKE IT METRIC. For help in converting measurements in this article to metric, see the Table of Measures.

How We Predict the Weather

■ **We derive our weather forecasts from** a secret formula that was devised by the founder of this Almanac, Robert B. Thomas, in 1792. Thomas believed that weather on Earth was influenced by sunspots, which are magnetic storms on the surface of the Sun.

–Beth Krommes

Over the years, we have refined and enhanced that formula with state-of-the-art technology and modern scientific calculations. We employ three scientific disciplines to make our long-range predictions: solar science, the study of sunspots and other solar activity; climatology, the study of prevailing weather patterns; and meteorology, the study of the atmosphere. We predict weather trends and events by comparing solar patterns and historical weather conditions with current solar activity.

Our forecasts emphasize temperature and precipitation deviations from averages, or normals. These are based on 30-year statistical averages prepared by government meteorological agencies and updated every ten years. The most-recent tabulations span the period 1971 through 2000.

We believe that nothing in the universe happens haphazardly, that there is a cause-and-effect pattern to all phenomena. However, although neither we nor any other forecasters have as yet gained sufficient insight into the mysteries of the universe to predict the weather with *total* accuracy, our results are almost always *very* close to our traditional claim of 80 percent.

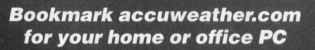

General Weather Report and Forecast

To see maps of the forecasts, turn to page 64.

W E A T H E R

This winter, the northeastern half of the country will be colder than normal, while the southwestern half will be milder than normal. Snowfall will be well above normal from Boston to Washington, D.C., and in the lee of the Great Lakes, but below normal in most other parts of the country. Summer will be hot in the west and the northeast, but relatively cool in most other parts of the country.

Last winter, our forecasts were accurate on many points. Among the highlights: In the Northeast and Atlantic Corridor, it was snowier than normal, with below-normal temperatures, and a mild midwinter was followed by a cold March. In the Southeast, the latter part of winter was colder than normal. In Florida, the winter was colder than normal on average, with March the most below normal. In the Upper Midwest and Heartland, the midwinter was mild (although milder than we predicted), and March was cold. The Deep South saw above-normal temps in the first part of winter, with below-normal temps in March. Much of the High Plains and Intermountain regions had above-normal temps. In the far west, the winter temps were relatively mild. January was the wettest month, on average, across the Pacific Southwest.

The trends we missed included warmer-than-normal temps in the first part of winter in the Southeast, the Upper Midwest, and the Heartland; the overall trend for the winter in Texas; and the rain in the far west, where the storm track was south of where we expected it to be, bringing more rain to the Pacific Southwest and less to the Pacific Northwest than we forecast.

Last winter's weather factors included a weak El Niño in the Pacific Ocean, which allowed wild swings in the weather in much of the country. The cool water near Florida, left by a concentration of hurricanes there, led to a more stable pattern than we expected for much of the winter in the southeast.

Factors in the 2005–06 winter weather will again include a pattern of wild weather swings. Without a strong La Niña or El Niño, the Atlantic Ocean grows more important as a major factor in the weather. With a relatively warm Atlantic and a continued trend of warmer-than-normal arctic temps, cold air will build over the center of the continent, resulting in a colder-than-normal winter in the northeast. That will also bring a southwesterly jet stream flow that will cause above-normal temps, on average, from the western states into the High Plains.

November through March will be colder than normal in most areas east of the Mississippi River and warmer than normal to its west. Snowfall will be above normal in the northeast and in the southern High Plains, but below normal in most other areas.

April and May will be cooler than normal in most of the country. Rainfall will be above normal in the northeastern quarter of the country, the Heartland, and the Pacific Northwest, and below normal in most other places.

June through August will be cooler than normal from the Heartland into the Southeast, and hotter than normal in most other areas. Rainfall will be above normal in the Northeast, from northern Florida to Richmond, in the Lower Lakes and southern Deep South, and from Texas northward to the Heartland and southern High Plains. Rainfall elsewhere will be generally below normal.

September and October will be warmer than normal in the Pacific Southwest and from the Lower Lakes eastward to the Northeast and southward into Florida and cooler than normal in most other areas. Precipitation will be above normal from the Intermountain region eastward to the Upper Midwest and southward to Texas, in the Lower Lakes, and along the northern and central Atlantic. Elsewhere, precipitation will be below normal.

U.S. Weather Regions

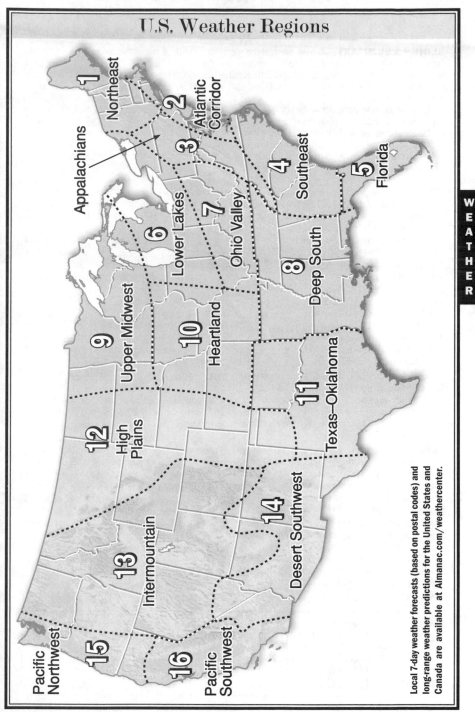

1 Northeast
2 Atlantic Corridor
3 Appalachians
4 Southeast
5 Florida
6 Lower Lakes
7 Ohio Valley
8 Deep South
9 Upper Midwest
10 Heartland
11 Texas–Oklahoma
12 High Plains
13 Intermountain
14 Desert Southwest
15 Pacific Northwest
16 Pacific Southwest

W
E
A
T
H
E
R

Local 7-day weather forecasts (based on postal codes) and long-range weather predictions for the United States and Canada are available at Almanac.com/weathercenter.

Northeast

REGION 1 SUMMARY: Although much of the winter season will be milder than normal, December and January will be exceptionally cold. Winter-season temperatures will be near normal in Maine, but a degree or two colder than normal elsewhere, on average. Snowfall will be below normal in the northwest, but above normal elsewhere. A big snowstorm will hamper Christmas travel, with other major snowstorms in mid-December and the first half of March.

Temperatures in April and May will be below normal, on average, with above-normal precipitation. Expect snow in early April, and very warm temperatures in early May.

The summer season will be hotter and wetter than normal, although there will not be a prolonged heat wave. The hottest periods will be in mid-July and early and late August.

September and October will be exceptionally mild, with very warm periods in early and mid-September. Rainfall will be near normal in the east and below normal in the west.

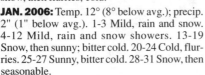

NOV. 2005: Temp. 42° (6° above avg. north; 2° above south); precip. 2" (1.5" below avg.). 1-4 Cold; sunny, then rain. 5-11 Mild; sunny, then showers. 12-16 Sunny, mild. 17-19 Seasonable, showers. 20-24 Showers and flurries. 25-30 Sunny, mild.

DEC. 2005: Temp. 23° (1° above avg. northeast; 7° below southwest); precip. 3" (avg.). 1-5 Cold, flurries. 6-8 Snow, cold. 9-14 Seasonable, flurries. 15-18 Snowstorm, very cold. 19-23 Cold; snow showers. 24-31 Heavy snow, then flurries; cold.

JAN. 2006: Temp. 12° (8° below avg.); precip. 2" (1" below avg.). 1-3 Mild, rain and snow. 4-12 Mild, rain and snow showers. 13-19 Snow, then sunny; bitter cold. 20-24 Cold, flurries. 25-27 Sunny, bitter cold. 28-31 Snow, then seasonable.

FEB. 2006: Temp. 26° (5° above avg.); precip. 3" (1" above avg. north; avg. south). 1-4 Sunny, mild, then snow. 5-7 Sunny, seasonable. 8-13 Turning mild; snow, then rain showers. 14-16 Sunny, mild. 17-21 Heavy snow north, rain south. 22-28 Mild, rain and snow.

MAR. 2006: Temp. 31° (2° below avg.); precip. 3" (avg.). 1-3 Heavy snow. 4-6 Sunny, cold. 7-10 Snowstorm, cold. 11-16 Cold, flurries. 17-22 Rain and snow showers, then sunny, warm. 23-31 Seasonable, showers and flurries.

APR. 2006: Temp. 42° (3° below avg.); precip. 3.5" (0.5" below avg. east; 1" above west). 1-8

Cold, snow. 9-14 Chilly; snow north, showers south. 15-23 Seasonable, showers. 24-30 Cool, showers.

MAY 2006: Temp. 55° (1° below avg.); precip. 4.5" (1" above avg.). 1-3 T-storms, warm. 4-9 Sunny; seasonable, then warm. 10-18 Cool, showers. 19-24 Heavy rain, chilly. 25-31 Seasonable, showers.

JUNE 2006: Temp. 65° (1° above avg. northeast; 1° below southwest); precip. 3.5" (avg.). 1-7 Warm, t-storms. 8-13 Sunny, cool. 14-19 Seasonable, t-storms. 20-24 Sunny, warm. 25-30 T-storms, then cool.

JULY 2006: Temp. 70° (avg.); precip. 4" (1" below avg. north; 1" above south). 1-12 Seasonable; scattered t-storms. 13-17 Sunny, hot. 18-24 Warm, showers. 25-31 Sunny, comfortable.

AUG. 2006: Temp. 69.5° (2.5° above avg.); precip. 4" (2" above avg.). 1-4 Sunny, hot. 5-11 T-storms, then cooler. 12-18 Seasonable, showers. 19-22 Heavy t-storms, warm. 23-25 Sunny, warm. 26-31 Hot, humid; severe t-storms.

SEPT. 2006: Temp. 63° (4° above avg.); precip. 3.5" (2" above avg. east; 2" below west). 1-8 Very warm, t-storms. 9-13 Sunny, cool. 14-20 Warm; t-storms north. 21-24 Sunny, cool. 25-30 Rain, then mild.

OCT. 2006: Temp. 52° (4° above avg.); precip. 2.5" (1" below avg.). 1-7 Sunny, warm. 8-11 Showers, then cool. 12-19 Sunny; warm, then seasonable. 20-25 Mild, showers. 26-31 Sunny, cool; then mild, showers.

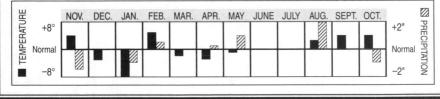

Atlantic Corridor

REGION 2 SUMMARY: Winter-season temperatures will be one degree below normal, on average, with above-normal precipitation in most of the region. Snowfall will be much greater than normal just about everywhere. The biggest snowfalls will be in early December and the second half of January, with other snowy periods in late December and early February. Temperatures will be relatively mild in November, the first half of January, and February, but colder than normal in December and exceptionally cold in the second half of January.

April and May will be cooler than normal, on average, although there will be warm temperatures in mid-April and early and late May. Rainfall will be above normal.

June will be quite pleasant overall, with below-normal rainfall and near-normal temperatures. July and August will be hotter than normal, with the hottest periods in mid-July and early and late August.

September and October will bring very mild temperatures, on average, but hurricanes will threaten the region around the middle of each month.

NOV. 2005: Temp. 50.5° (4° above avg. north; 1° above south); precip. 1.5" (2" below avg.). 1-4 Rain, chilly. 5-11 Sunny, mild. 12-16 Sunny, seasonable. 17-22 Rain, then sunny; mild. 23-27 Showers, then sunny; cool. 28-30 Sunny, mild.

DEC. 2005: Temp. 32° (6° below avg.); precip. 4" (1" above avg.). 1-4 Sunny, cold. 5-8 Heavy snow, then sunny; cold. 9-14 Showers, then sunny; cool. 15-22 Rain, then sunny; cold. 23-26 Heavy rain and wet snow. 27-31 Sunny, seasonable.

JAN. 2006: Temp. 26° (7° below avg.); precip. 4" (0.5" above avg.). 1-8 Sunny, seasonable. 9-12 Seasonable; snow north, rain south. 13-20 Heavy snow, bitter cold. 21-25 Sunny, very cold. 26-31 Heavy snow, cold.

FEB. 2006: Temp. 40° (7° above avg.); precip. 4" (0.5" below avg. north; 2" above south). 1-6 Rain and snow, seasonable. 7-11 Mild, showers. 12-16 Rain, then sunny. 17-21 Warm, rain. 22-24 Showers. 25-28 Sunny, warm.

MAR. 2006: Temp. 42° (1° below avg.); precip. 5" (1" above avg.). 1-5 Warm, then cold; rain to snow. 6-9 Mild; snow north, rain south. 10-14 Chilly, rain. 15-18 Chilly; heavy rain. 19-24 Sunny, mild. 25-31 Chilly; rain, then sunny.

APR. 2006: Temp. 50° (2° below avg.); precip. 5" (1.5" above avg.). 1-3 Sunny, cool. 4-10 Chilly, rain. 11-15 Sunny, cool. 16-20 Very warm, t-storms. 21-30 Rain, then sunny; cool.

MAY 2006: Temp. 61.5° (0.5° below avg.); precip. 4.5" (1" above avg. north; 0.5" below south). 1-3 T-storms, very warm. 4-10 Showers, warm. 11-18 Sunny, cool. 19-25 Cool; rain, then sunny. 26-31 Warm; scattered t-storms.

JUNE 2006: Temp. 70.5° (0.5° below avg.); precip. 3" (0.5" below avg.; 1" below south). 1-8 Warm, humid; scattered t-storms. 9-13 Sunny, cool nights. 14-21 Seasonable, t-storms. 22-24 Sunny, warm. 25-30 T-storms, then cooler.

JULY 2006: Temp. 76.5° (1° below avg. north; 2° above south); precip. 4" (1" above avg. north; 1" below south). 1-6 T-storms; then sunny, comfortable. 7-11 Warm, t-storms. 12-22 Hot, humid; sunny, then t-storms. 23-31 Seasonable; t-storms, then sunny.

AUG. 2006: Temp. 78° (4° above avg.); precip. 3" (1" below avg.). 1-5 Sunny, hot, humid. 6-12 T-storms, then sunny; seasonable. 13-22 Warm, t-storms. 23-31 Hot, humid; t-storms.

SEPT. 2006: Temp. 70° (3° above avg.); precip. 4" (3" above avg. east; 2" below west). 1-7 Sunny, hot. 8-12 Rain, then sunny; cool. 13-17 Hurricane threat. 18-21 Hot; rain north. 22-25 Sunny, cool. 26-30 Heavy rain, chilly.

OCT. 2006: Temp. 60° (4° above avg.); precip. 2.5" (1" below avg.). 1-7 Sunny, warm. 8-11 Rain, then sunny; cool. 12-16 Hurricane threat. 17-23 Sunny, seasonable. 24-31 Very warm, showers.

Boston
Hartford
New York
Philadelphia
Baltimore
Atlantic City
Washington
Richmond

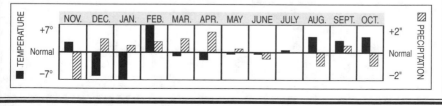

Appalachians

REGION 3 SUMMARY: The winter season will be colder than normal, on average, with above-normal snowfall. Most of the snow and cold will come during December and January, when temperatures will be seven or eight degrees below normal, on average. The rest of the season will be much milder, with near-normal temperatures in November and March and a very mild February. The coldest periods will be in mid-December and mid- and late January. The heaviest snow will occur in early and mid-December, mid- and late January, and early March.

April will start with a late-season snowstorm in the north, and temperatures will be relatively cool for most of the month. May will be a bit cooler and drier than normal.

June will be a bit cooler than normal, on average, and then temperatures will be hotter than normal through most of August. Rainfall will be below normal, especially in the south.

September and October will be warmer than normal, with much-below-normal rainfall in September and near-normal rainfall in October.

NOV. 2005: Temp. 44° (1° above avg.); precip. 1.5" (2" below avg.). 1-4 Chilly, showers. 5-8 Sunny, cool. 9-16 Mild, showers. 17-22 Rain, then sunny; warm. 23-27 Showers, then sunny; cool. 28-30 Sunny, mild.

DEC. 2005: Temp. 27° (7° below avg.); precip. 2.5" (0.5" below avg.). 1-4 Cold, flurries. 5-13 Snowstorm, then sunny; cold. 14-18 Very cold, snow. 19-26 Rain south, snow north; seasonable. 27-31 Sunny, seasonable.

JAN. 2006: Temp. 20° (8° below avg.); precip. 2.5" (0.5" below avg.). 1-5 Sunny, seasonable. 6-12 Seasonable, rain and snow showers. 13-21 Bitter cold, occasional snow. 22-26 Sunny, cold. 27-31 Cold; heavy snow, then sunny.

FEB. 2006: Temp. 35° (7° above avg.); precip. 2.5" (avg.). 1-7 Seasonable; heavy snow south, then sunny. 8-13 Mild, showers. 14-17 Rain, seasonable. 18-21 Windy, mild, showers. 22-24 Seasonable, showers. 25-28 Warm, showers.

MAR. 2006: Temp. 36° (3° below avg.); precip. 3" (avg.). 1-5 Chilly, rain and snow. 6-13 Cold, rain and snow showers. 14-18 Cool; snow north, rain south. 19-23 Mild, showers. 24-31 Rain, then flurries; cool.

APR. 2006: Temp. 46° (4° below avg.); precip. 4" (0.5" above avg.). 1-7 Cold; snow north, heavy rain south. 8-14 Rain, then sunny;

chilly. 15-19 T-storms, then sunny; warm. 20-30 Rain, then sunny; chilly.

MAY 2006: Temp. 59° (1° below avg.); precip. 3" (1" below avg.). 1-6 Seasonable, t-storms. 7-10 Sunny, warm. 11-15 Cool, showers. 16-19 Sunny, cool. 20-27 Cool, showers. 28-31 Sunny, warm.

JUNE 2006: Temp. 66.5° (1.5° below avg.); precip. 3.5" (0.5" below avg.). 1-7 Very warm, t-storms. 8-12 Sunny, cool. 13-20 T-storms, cool. 21-25 Sunny, very warm. 26-30 T-storms; hot, then seasonable.

JULY 2006: Temp. 74° (1° above avg.); precip. 3" (0.5" above avg. north; 1.5" below south). 1-5 Sunny, comfortable. 6-12 Seasonable, t-storms. 13-19 Hot, t-storms. 20-24 Sunny, hot. 25-31 T-storms, warm.

AUG. 2006: Temp. 73.5° (2.5° above avg.); precip. 3" (0.5" below avg.). 1-6 T-storms, very warm. 7-13 Sunny, seasonable. 14-20 T-storms, warm. 21-31 Hot, humid; afternoon t-storms.

SEPT. 2006: Temp. 66° (2° above avg.); precip. 2" (1.5" below avg.). 1-8 Sunny, hot. 9-14 Cool, showers. 15-19 Sunny, hot. 20-25 Sunny, cool. 26-30 Rain, then sunny; cool.

OCT. 2006: Temp. 56° (3° above avg.); precip. 2.5" (1" below avg. north; 0.5" above south). 1-7 Sunny, warm. 8-11 Showers, cool. 12-15 Rain, heavy south. 16-22 Cool, showers. 23-31 Warm, showers.

Elmira
Scranton
Harrisburg
Frederick
Roanoke
Asheville

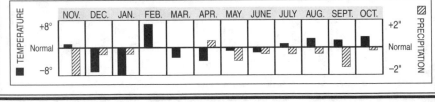

Southeast

REGION 4 SUMMARY: Temperatures will average about one degree colder than normal from November through March, with cold temperatures during the heart of winter but relatively mild temperatures early and late in the season. The coldest periods will occur in mid-December and mid-January. Snow and ice are most likely in the second half of January, when a few storms will bring a wintry mix to northern and interior parts of the region. Winter precipitation will be above normal.

April and May will be cooler than normal, with a damp April followed by a drier-than-normal May.

The summer season will be a bit cooler than normal, on average, with a cool June and then near-normal temperatures in July and August. The hottest weather will occur in mid- to late July. Rainfall will be a bit greater than normal, with widespread heavy thunderstorms in mid-August.

September and October will be much drier than normal, with below-normal temperatures in September and above-normal temperatures in October.

NOV. 2005: Temp. 55.5° (0.5° above avg.); precip. 1" (2" below avg.). 1-5 Cool, showers. 6-12 Warm; sunny, then showers. 13-20 Sunny, warm. 21-27 Showers, then sunny; cool. 28-30 Sunny, mild.

DEC. 2005: Temp. 42° (5° below avg.); precip. 2.5" (1" below avg.). 1-4 Sunny, colder. 5-8 Rain, then sunny; cold. 9-14 Showers, then sunny; cold. 15-19 Rain; then sunny, very cold. 20-23 Sunny, seasonable. 24-31 Rain, then sunny; chilly.

JAN. 2006: Temp. 38.5° (6.5° below avg.); precip. 4" (1" below avg. north; avg. south). 1-6 Sunny, cold. 7-9 Rain, mild. 10-13 Seasonable; sunny, then rain. 14-18 Very cold; snow north, sunny south. 19-24 Cold; snow north, rain south. 25-27 Sunny, seasonable. 28-31 Cold; snow north, rain south.

FEB. 2006: Temp. 52° (6° above avg.); precip. 8" (4" above avg.). 1-5 Cold; rain and snow, then sunny. 6-11 Sunny, warm. 12-19 Warm; heavy rain. 20-24 Seasonable, showers. 25-28 Sunny, warm.

MAR. 2006: Temp. 55° (1° below avg. north; 1° above south); precip. 5.5" (1" above avg.). 1-5 Rain, then sunny; cool. 6-8 Mild, rain. 9-15 Rain; cool north, warm south. 16-24 Sunny; cool, then warm. 25-31 Heavy rain, then sunny; cool.

APR. 2006: Temp. 59° (4° below avg.); pre-

cip. 4" (1" above avg.). 1-9 Cool; heavy rain. 10-19 Sunny; cool, then warm. 20-24 T-storms, then sunny; cool. 25-30 Showers, then sunny; seasonable.

MAY 2006: Temp. 69° (2° below avg.); precip. 2.5" (1" below avg.). 1-6 Warm, t-storms. 7-14 Sunny, seasonable. 15-20 Cool, showers. 21-28 Sunny; cool, then warm. 29-31 Warm, t-storms.

JUNE 2006: Temp. 74° (3° below avg.); precip. 5.5" (1" above avg.). 1-8 Warm; scattered t-storms. 9-15 Rain, cool. 16-22 Cool, t-storms. 23-30 Sunny, seasonable.

JULY 2006: Temp. 80.5° (1° above avg. east; 2° below west); precip. 4" (1" below avg.). 1-8 Cool; scattered t-storms. 9-16 Warm, t-storms. 17-27 Sunny, hot. 28-31 T-storms, seasonable.

AUG. 2006: Temp. 79° (avg.); precip. 7" (2" above avg.). 1-4 Showers, seasonable. 5-11 Comfortable; t-storms south. 12-20 Cool; heavy t-storms. 21-31 Warm; scattered t-storms.

SEPT. 2006: Temp. 72.5° (1.5° below avg.); precip. 1.5" (3" below avg.). 1-7 Warm; sunny north, t-storms south. 8-14 Cool; sunny, then showers. 15-24 Sunny; warm, then cool. 25-30 Rain, then sunny; cool.

OCT. 2006: Temp. 66° (2° above avg.); precip. 1" (2" below avg.). 1-7 Sunny, seasonable. 8-13 Showers, then sunny; cool. 14-22 Rain, then sunny; cool. 23-31 Sunny, then showers; warm.

Raleigh
Columbia
Atlanta
Savannah

W
E
A
T
H
E
R

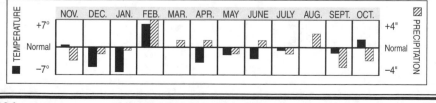

Florida

REGION 5 SUMMARY: Temperatures from November through March will be near normal in the north and about one degree below normal in the south, on average. The coldest weather will occur in mid-December and mid-January, but there will not be a severe freeze in central Florida. Rainfall will be a bit below normal, with the stormiest period in the first week of January.

April and May will be a bit cooler and drier than normal, with an extended period of sunny, warm weather in the first half of May.

June through August will feature near-normal temperatures, with above-normal rainfall in the north and near- to below-normal rainfall in the south. July will be much drier than normal, but June and August will have above-normal rainfall. The hottest periods will occur in the first and last thirds of July.

September and October will be much drier than normal. Temperatures will be near normal, on average, although mid-September will be particularly hot. There is only a slight chance of a tropical storm or hurricane.

NOV. 2005: Temp. 71° (2° above avg.); precip. 1" (1.5" below avg.). 1-10 Cool, then warm; scattered showers. 11-18 Sunny, warm. 19-23 Warm, humid; scattered showers. 24-30 Sunny, cool.

DEC. 2005: Temp. 58° (5° below avg.); precip. 1.5" (1" below avg.). 1-4 Sunny, mild. 5-8 Showers, then cold. 9-14 Rain, then sunny; cool. 15-19 Showers, then sunny; cool. 20-26 Mild, showers. 27-31 Sunny, cool.

JAN. 2006: Temp. 57° (4° below avg.); precip. 4.5" (2" above avg.). 1-8 T-storms; mild, then cool. 9-17 Sunny, cold. 18-20 Cool; showers north. 21-24 Rain, cool. 25-31 Sunny, then rain; cool.

FEB. 2006: Temp. 65° (6° above avg. north; 2° above south); precip. 2.5" (1" above avg. north; 1" below south). 1-7 Cool; t-storms, then sunny. 8-11 Sunny, mild. 12-19 Warm, humid, t-storms. 20-24 Sunny, warm. 25-28 Showers, warm.

MAR. 2006: Temp. 68° (1° above avg.); precip. 2.5" (0.5" below avg.). 1-6 Sunny; warm, then cool. 7-15 Warm, t-storms. 16-22 Sunny, seasonable. 23-26 T-storms, warm. 27-31 Sunny, cool.

APR. 2006: Temp. 70° (1° below avg.); precip. 1.5" (avg. north; 2" below south). 1-6 Seasonable, t-storms. 7-10 Seasonable; t-storms north. 11-21 Sunny; cool, then warm. 22-25

T-storms, then sunny; cool. 26-30 Warm, t-storms.

MAY 2006: Temp. 77° (avg.); precip. 4" (1" below avg. north; 1" above south). 1-4 T-storms, cool. 5-16 Sunny, warm. 17-24 T-storms; seasonable, then cool. 25-31 Seasonable; sunny north, t-storms south.

JUNE 2006: Temp. 80.5° (0.5° below avg.); precip. 9.5" (3" above avg.). 1-10 Seasonable, t-storms. 11-17 Scattered t-storms. 18-22 Warm, humid; heavy t-storms. 23-30 Seasonable; scattered t-storms.

JULY 2006: Temp. 83° (1° above avg.); precip. 3.5" (3" below avg.). 1-6 Seasonable, t-storms. 7-11 Sunny, hot. 12-20 Seasonable, t-storms. 21-25 Sunny, hot. 26-31 Warm, t-storms.

AUG. 2006: Temp. 81° (avg.); precip. 8" (2" above avg. north; 1" below south). 1-6 Warm; scattered t-storms. 7-16 T-storms, seasonable. 17-23 Scattered t-storms, seasonable. 24-31 Sunny, warm.

SEPT. 2006: Temp. 79.5° (1° below avg. north; 0.5° above south); precip. 3" (4" below avg.). 1-7 Warm; scattered t-storms. 8-12 Cool; heavy t-storms. 13-21 Sunny, hot. 22-30 Scattered t-storms; cooler north.

OCT. 2006: Temp. 75° (avg.); precip. 1" (3" below avg.). 1-8 Seasonable, t-storms. 9-19 Sunny, cool. 20-31 Warm, showers.

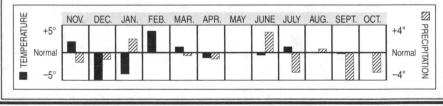

Lower Lakes

REGION 6 SUMMARY: The season's wintry weather will be short but powerful. After a relatively mild November, December and January will be exceptionally cold, with frequent snowfalls, heavy in the east. Then, winter will break and February will be unusually mild. Temperatures in March will be a bit below normal, on average. Snowfall will be above normal in the east and below normal in most other parts of the region. The coldest periods will be in mid-December and from mid- through late January. The heaviest widespread snowfall will occur in late January, with other major snowfalls in early, mid-, and late December; in mid-January; and in early March.

April and May will be cool, on average, with above-normal precipitation and snowfall several times in the first half of April. The summer season will be cooler than normal, with near-normal rainfall. June will be particularly cool, but hot weather will dominate from late August into early September. The hottest periods will occur in mid-July and late August.

Temperatures in September and October will average two degrees above normal, with near- or slightly above-normal rainfall.

NOV. 2005: Temp. 43° (3° above avg.); precip. 2" (1" below avg.). 1-4 Cold, rain and snow. 5-8 Sunny, warm. 9-14 Showers, then sunny. 15-22 Showers, then sunny; warm. 23-25 Cold; lake snows. 26-30 Mild; sunny, then rain.

DEC. 2005: Temp. 22° (7° below avg.); precip. 2.5" (0.5" above avg. east; 2" below west). 1-7 Cold; lake snows. 8-12 Seasonable; snow showers. 13-18 Snow, very cold. 19-25 Cold, flurries. 26-31 Seasonable; heavy snow east.

JAN. 2006: Temp. 16.5° (10° below avg. east; 5° below west); precip. 1.5" (1" below avg.). 1-12 Seasonable, flurries. 13-26 Bitter cold, lake snows. 27-31 Snowstorm, cold.

FEB. 2006: Temp. 32° (8° above avg.); precip. 3" (avg. north; 2" above south). 1-6 Seasonable, flurries. 7-10 Mild; snow east. 11-18 Mild; rainy periods. 19-22 Colder; rain, then snow. 23-28 Mild; sunny, then rain.

MAR. 2006: Temp. 34° (2° below avg.); precip. 3.5" (0.5" above avg.). 1-7 Cold, rain and snow. 8-11 Seasonable, rain and snow showers. 12-16 Mild, rain. 17-20 Cold; snow east. 21-31 Mild; then cold, snow showers.

APR. 2006: Temp. 43° (4° below avg.); precip. 5.5" (2" above avg.). 1-12 Chilly, periods of rain and snow. 13-19 Mild, rain. 20-30 Cool, showers.

MAY 2006: Temp. 56° (2° below avg.); precip. 3.5" (avg.). 1-8 Warm; rain, then sunny. 9-15 Cool, rain. 16-18 Sunny, mild. 19-24 Chilly, rain. 25-31 Seasonable; t-storms, then sunny.

JUNE 2006: Temp. 63.5° (3.5° below avg.); precip. 3" (0.5" below avg.). 1-7 Warm, t-storms. 8-13 Sunny, cool. 14-19 T-storms, cool. 20-23 Sunny, warm. 24-30 T-storms, then cool.

JULY 2006: Temp. 71° (avg. east; 2° below west); precip. 4.5" (1" above avg.). 1-6 Sunny; cool, then seasonable. 7-13 Seasonable, t-storms. 14-19 Warm, t-storms. 20-23 Sunny, warm. 24-31 T-storms, seasonable.

AUG. 2006: Temp. 72° (2° above avg.); precip. 4" (avg.). 1-5 T-storms, warm. 6-12 Sunny, seasonable. 13-20 Warm, t-storms. 21-31 Hot; scattered t-storms.

SEPT. 2006: Temp. 65° (2° above avg.); precip. 4.5" (1" above avg.). 1-5 Sunny, hot. 6-9 T-storms, turning cooler. 10-13 Sunny, cool. 14-18 Sunny, very warm. 19-23 T-storms, then sunny.

OCT. 2006: Temp. 54° (2° above avg.); precip. 2" (0.5" below avg.). 1-6 Sunny, warm. 7-10 Rain, chilly. 11-12 Sunny, warm. 13-18 Rain, then cool. 19-27 Mild, rain. 28-31 Sunny, cool.

Map labels: Syracuse, Rochester, Milwaukee, Detroit, Buffalo, Chicago, Cleveland, Indianapolis

Side tab: WEATHER

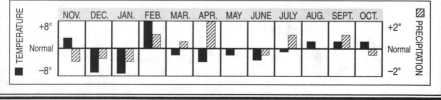

Ohio Valley

REGION 7 SUMMARY: Winter-season temperatures will be about a degree colder than normal, on average, due to a very cold December and January. The coldest temperatures will occur in mid-December and mid- to late January. February will be quite mild, followed by a near-normal March. Precipitation will be near or a bit below normal, with much-above-normal snowfall in the northeast and near-normal snowfall elsewhere. The snowiest periods will be in mid- and late December, mid- and late January, and mid-February.

April and May will be much cooler than normal, with near-normal precipitation in the east and above-normal precipitation in the west.

Temperatures in the summer season will be about a degree below normal, on average, with a cool June followed by a near-normal July and a hot August. The hottest temperatures will occur in late July and late August.

September and October will be warmer than normal, with near-normal rainfall. September will start hot, but temperatures after the month's first week will be near normal, on average. October will start and end with mild temperatures, with cool temperatures in the month's middle.

NOV. 2005: Temp. 48° (3° above avg.); precip. 2.5" (1" below avg.). 1-4 Rain, chilly. 5-9 Sunny, warm. 10-15 Rain, then sunny; mild. 16-21 Rain, then sunny; warm. 22-26 Cold, snow showers. 27-30 Sunny, mild.

DEC. 2005: Temp. 28° (7° below avg.); precip. 2" (1" below avg.). 1-4 Sunny, cold. 5-7 Snow, then very cold. 8-13 Cold, snow showers. 14-18 Snow, then bitter cold. 19-27 Snowstorm, cold. 28-31 Sunny, mild.

JAN. 2006: Temp. 23° (8° below avg.); precip. 2" (1" below avg.). 1-5 Cold, snow showers. 6-12 Mild; snow north, rain south. 13-21 Snowstorm, then snow showers; bitter cold. 22-26 Sunny, cold. 27-31 Snowstorm, cold.

FEB. 2006: Temp. 40° (8° above avg.); precip. 5" (1" above avg. east; 3" above west). 1-4 Cold, snow showers. 5-10 Sunny, mild. 11-18 Rain, mild. 19-22 Snow, seasonable. 23-28 Warm, t-storms.

MAR. 2006: Temp. 43.5° (0.5° below avg.); precip. 4" (avg.). 1-4 Chilly, rain and snow. 5-9 Seasonable; rain, then sunny. 10-14 Chilly, rain and snow. 15-18 Rain, seasonable. 19-21 Sunny, warm. 22-25 Showers, cool. 26-31 Chilly; snow, then sunny.

APR. 2006: Temp. 50° (4° below avg.); precip. 4.5" (1" above avg.). 1-7 Rain, cool. 8-13 Cold, rain and snow. 14-19 T-storms, warm.

Pittsburgh • Cincinnati • Louisville • Charleston

20-27 Rain, then sunny; cool. 28-30 Rain.

MAY 2006: Temp. 60° (3° below avg.); precip. 6" (0.5" below avg. east; 3" above west). 1-8 T-storms, warm. 9-15 Cool; rain, then sunny. 16-23 Sunny, then rain; chilly. 24-31 Warm; t-storms, then sunny.

JUNE 2006: Temp. 68° (4° below avg.); precip. 3" (1" below avg.). 1-8 T-storms, warm. 9-13 Sunny, cool. 14-19 Cool, t-storms. 20-23 Sunny, warmer. 24-30 Warm, t-storms.

JULY 2006: Temp. 75° (1° below avg.); precip. 6" (2" above avg.). 1-5 Sunny, cool. 6-13 Rain, cool. 14-19 Warm; heavy t-storms. 20-31 Hot, then seasonable; scattered t-storms.

AUG. 2006: Temp. 76° (2° above avg.); precip. 1.5" (2" below avg.). 1-4 T-storms, warm. 5-13 Sunny, seasonable. 14-19 T-storms, seasonable. 20-25 Sunny, hot. 26-31 Hot, humid, t-storms.

SEPT. 2006: Temp. 68° (1° above avg.); precip. 3" (avg.). 1-7 Hot; scattered t-storms. 8-12 Sunny, cool. 13-19 Very warm; sunny, then t-storms. 20-24 Sunny; cool, then warm. 25-30 Rain, then sunny; cool.

OCT. 2006: Temp. 59° (3° above avg.); precip. 2.5" (avg.). 1-6 Sunny, warm. 7-9 Cool, t-storms. 10-12 Sunny, warm. 13-15 Chilly, rain and wet snow. 16-18 Sunny, mild. 19-23 Rain, then sunny. 24-31 Warm, t-storms.

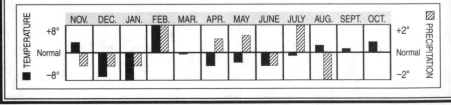

Deep South

REGION 8 SUMMARY: Temperatures will be much colder than normal from mid-December through January, but the remainder of the winter season will be relatively mild. Precipitation will be below normal in the north, but much above normal in the south. The best chances for snow and ice will be around Christmas and in the second half of January in the north. Ice may occur as far south as Shreveport, Jackson, and Montgomery in late January.

April and May will be very cool, with below-normal rainfall. The first half of April will be particularly cool.

The summer season will start cool, with June temperatures four to five degrees below normal, on average, and below-normal temperatures in early July. Temperatures from mid-July into early August will be close to normal, on average, followed by cool temperatures in the latter half of August. Rainfall will be below normal in the north, but much greater than normal in the south.

September and October will be cooler than normal, on average, with below-normal rainfall. The hottest temperatures will occur in mid-September.

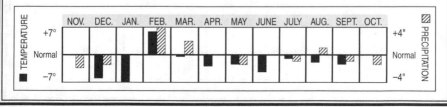

NOV. 2005: Temp. 55° (1° below avg. north; 1° above south); precip. 3" (2" below avg.). 1-6 Cool; rain north. 7-12 Mild, t-storms. 13-17 Warm; sunny, then rain. 18-23 Warm, showers. 24-30 Sunny, cold.

DEC. 2005: Temp. 41° (6° below avg.); precip. 3.5" (1.5" below avg.). 1-5 Rain, seasonable. 6-13 Rain, then sunny; cold. 14-17 Rain; then sunny, very cold. 18-25 Cool, rain; snow northwest. 26-31 Sunny, cold.

JAN. 2006: Temp. 37° (7° below avg.); precip. 5" (3" below avg. north; 3" above south). 1-4 Rain, then sunny; cold. 5-8 Rain, mild. 9-11 Sunny. 12-16 Rain, then sunny; cold. 17-25 Snow and ice north, rain south; then sunny, cold. 26-31 Chilly, rain.

FEB. 2006: Temp. 52° (6° above avg.); precip. 9" (2" above avg. north; 6" above south). 1-10 Sunny; cool, then warm. 11-18 Warm; heavy t-storms. 19-24 Seasonable; rain, then sunny. 25-28 Warm, t-storms.

MAR. 2006: Temp. 55.5° (0.5° below avg.); precip. 8" (2" above avg.). 1-5 Rain, then sunny; cool. 6-14 Seasonable, t-storms. 15-20 Sunny, cool. 21-25 Heavy t-storms. 26-31 Cool; sunny, then showers.

APR. 2006: Temp. 60° (3° below avg.); precip. 4.5" (1" above avg. north; 1" below south).

1-9 Cool, t-storms. 10-19 Sunny; cool, then warm. 20-30 T-storms, then sunny.

MAY 2006: Temp. 68.5° (2.5° below avg.); precip. 3.5" (1.5" below avg.). 1-7 Rain, then sunny; cool. 8-16 T-storms north, sunny south. 17-22 T-storms, then sunny; cool. 23-31 Warm; sunny, then t-storms.

JUNE 2006: Temp. 73.5° (4.5° below avg.); precip. 5" (2" below avg. north; 2" above south). 1-9 Seasonable; scattered t-storms. 10-20 Cool, t-storms. 21-30 Warm; sunny, then t-storms.

JULY 2006: Temp. 81° (1° below avg.); precip. 4" (1" below avg.; 4" above south). 1-4 Sunny, cool. 5-11 Warm; heavy t-storms. 12-20 Warm; scattered t-storms. 21-31 Warm; sunny, then t-storms.

AUG. 2006: Temp. 79° (2° below avg.); precip. 5.5" (1" below avg. north; 3" above south). 1-7 Warm, t-storms. 8-13 Sunny, warm. 14-21 Cool; t-storms south. 22-31 Warm, t-storms.

SEPT. 2006: Temp. 73.5° (2.5° below avg.); precip. 3.5" (1" below avg.). 1-7 Warm, humid, t-storms. 8-14 Sunny, cool. 15-20 Sunny, warm. 21-30 T-storms, then sunny; cool.

OCT. 2006: Temp. 65° (1° above avg. north; 1° below south); precip. 1.5" (1.5" below avg.). 1-7 T-storms, then sunny; warm north, seasonable south. 8-17 Sunny, cool. 18-23 Sunny, then t-storms. 24-31 Showers; warm, then cool.

Upper Midwest

REGION 9 SUMMARY: The winter season will be one to two degrees milder than normal, on average, with below-normal snowfall and near-normal precipitation. The coldest periods will occur in mid-December and mid-January. The biggest snowstorm will occur in late February, with other snowy periods in late November, mid-February, and early March.

April will be very chilly, with several snowfalls. May will be warmer, especially in the west.

The summer season will feature near-normal temperatures, on average. It will be a bit cooler in the east and a bit hotter than normal in the west. The hottest temperatures will occur in late June, late July, and mid-August. Rainfall will be below normal, with a dry June followed by near-normal rainfall in July and August.

After a hot start, September will be cooler than normal, on average, with above-normal rainfall. October will be a bit milder than normal, with above-normal rainfall. The month will end with the season's first wintry weather.

NOV. 2005: Temp. 30° (2° above avg.); precip. 2.5" (0.5" above avg.). 1-5 Flurries, cool. 6-10 Sunny, mild. 11-20 Snow; then sunny, mild. 21-25 Snow, then sunny; cold. 26-30 Mild; rain east, snow west.

DEC. 2005: Temp. 11° (3° below avg.); precip. 0.5" (0.5" below avg.). 1-6 Snow showers, then sunny; cold. 7-12 Snow showers, seasonable. 13-16 Sunny, very cold. 17-21 Snow, then very cold. 22-25 Sunny, mild. 26-29 Cold; snow showers. 30-31 Sunny, mild.

JAN. 2006: Temp. 7° (2° below avg.); precip. 0.5" (0.5" below avg.). 1-11 Sunny, mild. 12-19 Snow, then sunny; very cold. 20-31 Cold, flurries.

FEB. 2006: Temp. 19° (8° above avg.); precip. 1.5" (1" above avg. east; 0.5" below west). 1-7 Sunny, mild. 8-12 Snow, seasonable. 13-16 Sunny, mild. 17-23 Snow; then sunny, mild. 24-28 Snowstorm.

MAR. 2006: Temp. 28.5° (2° below avg. east; 5° above west); precip. 2" (0.5" above avg.). 1-4 Snow showers, seasonable. 5-14 Sunny; seasonable east, mild west. 15-21 Mild, rain and wet snow. 22-28 Sunny, chilly. 29-31 Cool, rain and snow.

APR. 2006: Temp. 36° (5° below avg.); precip. 2.5" (0.5" above avg.). 1-4 Sunny, cool. 5-11 Chilly, rain and snow. 12-18 Seasonable; rain east, wet snow west. 19-26 Sunny, chilly. 27-30 Seasonable; sunny, then t-storms.

MAY 2006: Temp. 54.5° (3° below avg. east; 2° above west); precip. 2.5" (0.5" below avg.). 1-7 T-storms; warm east, cool west. 8-14 Cool; t-storms east, sunny west. 15-24 Sunny, seasonable. 25-31 T-storms, then sunny; warm.

JUNE 2006: Temp. 64° (3° below avg. east; 3° above west); precip. 2" (2" below avg.). 1-6 Warm, t-storms. 7-11 Sunny, seasonable. 12-16 Cool, t-storms. 17-21 Sunny, seasonable. 22-25 Hot, t-storms. 26-30 Sunny, seasonable.

JULY 2006: Temp. 67° (2° below avg.); precip. 3.5" (avg.). 1-9 Cool; sunny, then t-storms. 10-17 Seasonable, t-storms. 18-24 Warm; scattered t-storms. 25-31 Sunny; seasonable east, hot west.

AUG. 2006: Temp. 68° (1° above avg.); precip. 3" (0.5" below avg.). 1-6 Cool; t-storms, then sunny. 7-11 Sunny, hot. 12-16 T-storms, then sunny; seasonable. 17-21 Seasonable, t-storms. 22-26 Sunny, hot. 27-31 T-storms, seasonable.

SEPT. 2006: Temp. 54° (4° below avg.); precip. 4" (1" above avg.). 1-8 T-storms; hot, then cool. 9-15 Warm; sunny, then t-storms. 16-24 Cool; sunny, then rain. 25-30 Sunny; cool, then very warm.

OCT. 2006: Temp. 47° (1° above avg.); precip. 3.5" (1" above avg.). 1-6 Rain, seasonable. 7-15 Sunny, warm. 16-23 Rain, seasonable. 24-26 Sunny, warm. 27-31 Rain, then flurries; cold.

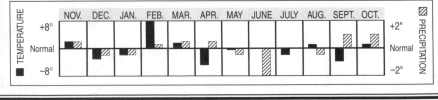

Heartland

REGION 10 SUMMARY: Temperatures in the winter season will be milder than normal, and precipitation will be above normal in the northwest and below normal in the southeast. While most of the region will have below-normal snowfall, snowfall in the area from St. Louis to eastern Iowa will be a bit above normal. The heaviest snow will fall in late January, with other snowstorms in late December, mid-January, and early March. The coldest periods will be in mid-December and mid- and late January.

April and May will be very cool, with above-normal rainfall. Watch for a late-season snowstorm in early April.

The summer will bring temperatures two to three degrees cooler than normal, on average. The hottest temperatures will occur in late July and late August. Rainfall will be below normal in June and August and above normal in July.

Despite a hot start, September will be cooler than normal, on average. Rainfall will be near normal in the east, while heavy rains will bring flooding to the west. October will be rainy, with temperatures near or a bit milder than normal.

NOV. 2005: Temp. 46° (4° above avg.); precip. 2" (0.5" below avg.). 1-5 Rain; then sunny, cold. 6-9 Warm; sunny, then t-storms. 10-16 Seasonable; sunny, then rain. 17-21 Sunny, warm. 22-26 Rain, then sunny; cool. 27-30 T-storms, warm.

DEC. 2005: Temp. 28° (2° below avg.); precip. 1" (0.5" below avg.). 1-3 Sunny, cold. 4-7 Cold, rain and snow. 8-13 Sunny, seasonable. 14-18 Snow, cold. 19-26 Mild; showers, then sunny. 27-31 Rain and snow, then warm.

JAN. 2006: Temp. 24° (1° above avg. northwest; 5° below southeast); precip. 0.5" (0.5" below avg.). 1-7 Sunny, mild. 8-12 Mild; snow north, rain south. 13-18 Cold; snow, then sunny. 19-23 Snow, then sunny; cold. 24-26 Sunny, mild. 27-31 Cold; snow, then sunny.

FEB. 2006: Temp. 35° (6° above avg.); precip. 3.5" (2" above avg.). 1-10 Sunny; cold, then warm. 11-15 Rain, then sunny; colder. 16-19 Rain, then sunny. 20-23 Chilly, snow showers. 24-28 Snow north; heavy t-storms, warm south.

MAR. 2006: Temp. 40.5° (2.5° below avg.); precip. 3.5" (3" above avg. northwest; 1" below southeast). 1-3 Chilly; snow north, rain south. 4-7 Snow north, heavy rain south. 8-11 Sunny, seasonable. 12-15 Chilly; snow north, rain south. 16-20 Sunny, mild. 21-26 Rain; then sunny, cold. 27-31 Chilly, showers.

APR. 2006: Temp. 49° (5° below avg.); precip. 5.5" (2" above avg.). 1-6 Chilly, rain and snow. 7-11 Chilly, rain and snow showers. 12-18 Warm, t-storms. 19-23 Cool, showers. 24-30 T-storms, cool.

MAY 2006: Temp. 62° (2° below avg.); precip. 4" (1" below avg. northwest; 2" above southeast). 1-8 Mainly dry north, heavy rain south; then sunny, warm. 9-22 Cool; t-storms, then sunny. 23-31 Seasonable, t-storms.

JUNE 2006: Temp. 70° (3° below avg.); precip. 3.5" (1" below avg.). 1-6 Sunny, warm. 7-12 T-storms, then sunny; cool. 13-20 Cool; showers north. 21-30 Seasonable, t-storms.

JULY 2006: Temp. 75° (3° below avg.); precip. 7" (3" above avg.). 1-5 Sunny, cool. 6-12 T-storms, then sunny; seasonable. 13-19 Heavy t-storms, cool. 20-25 Warm; t-storms north. 26-31 Seasonable; t-storms, then sunny.

AUG. 2006: Temp. 75° (1° below avg.); precip. 2.5" (1" below avg.). 1-6 Seasonable, t-storms. 7-11 Sunny, seasonable. 12-17 T-storms, cool. 18-26 Sunny, hot. 27-31 T-storms, seasonable.

SEPT. 2006: Temp. 64° (3° below avg.); precip. 5" (avg. east; 3" above west). 1-5 Sunny, hot. 6-13 Flooding rains, then sunny; cool. 14-23 T-storms, then sunny; cool. 24-30 T-storms, then sunny; cool.

OCT. 2006: Temp. 56.5° (0.5° above avg.); precip. 4.5" (1.5" above avg.). 1-6 Warm; sunny, then t-storms. 7-11 Sunny, seasonable. 12-16 Rain, then sunny; cool. 17-21 T-storms, then sunny; seasonable. 22-27 T-storms, warm. 28-31 Sunny, cold.

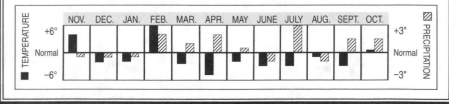

Texas–Oklahoma

REGION 11 SUMMARY: November through March will be wetter than normal, with near-normal temperatures. The coldest periods will occur in early and late December and mid- and late January. Snowfall will be greater than normal across the north, with snow or ice likely in early and late December, mid- to late January, and early February.

April and May will be much drier than normal, with near-normal temperatures in April and slightly above-normal temperatures in May.

The summer will be relatively cool, with temperatures three degrees below normal, on average, in the north and one degree below normal in the south. The hottest periods will occur in mid- and late July and late August.

September will be cooler and wetter than normal, with a hurricane threat in the first third of the month. Temperatures in October will be near normal, on average, with above-normal rainfall in the north and below-normal rainfall in the south.

NOV. 2005: Temp. 59° (3° above avg.); precip. 2.5" (0.5" below avg.). 1-5 Sunny, cool. 6-11 Warm, t-storms. 12-16 T-storms, seasonable. 17-22 Sunny, turning very warm. 23-27 T-storms, then sunny; cool. 28-30 Warm, rain.

DEC. 2005: Temp. 44° (4° below avg.); precip. 4.5" (2" above avg.). 1-8 Cold; snow north, rain south. 9-17 Sunny, cool. 18-21 Sunny, mild. 22-25 Cool; snow north, rain south. 26-31 Cool; sunny, then rain.

JAN. 2006: Temp. 43° (3° below avg.); precip. 2.5" (0.5" above avg.). 1-9 Seasonable; rain, then sunny. 10-12 Sunny, warm. 13-18 Cool, rain. 19-22 Cold; snow north, rain south. 23-27 Sunny; cold, then mild. 28-31 Rain, chilly.

FEB. 2006: Temp. 50° (4° above avg.; 0.5° above south); precip. 1" (1" below avg.; 0.5" above north). 1-4 Cool; snow north, rain south. 5-13 Warm; sunny, then t-storms. 14-18 Rain. 19-23 Sunny, cool. 24-28 Warm, t-storms.

MAR. 2006: Temp. 59° (avg. north; 2° above south); precip. 3.5" (1" above avg.). 1-4 Rain, then sunny; cool. 5-11 Warm; sunny, then t-storms. 12-14 Rain, cool. 15-21 Sunny, warm. 22-29 Showers, then sunny; seasonable. 30-31 Rain.

APR. 2006: Temp. 66° (1° below avg. north; 1° above south); precip. 1" (2" below avg.). 1-5 Rain, cool. 6-11 Sunny, cool. 12-21 Sunny, warm. 22-30 Warm; t-storms, then sunny.

MAY 2006: Temp. 73.5° (0.5° above avg.); precip. 3" (2" below avg.). 1-7 Showers, then sunny; cool. 8-16 Showers, then sunny; warm. 17-20 T-storms, cool. 21-26 Sunny, warm. 27-31 Warm; t-storms north.

JUNE 2006: Temp. 78° (avg. south; 4° below north); precip. 7" (3" above avg.). 1-6 Seasonable; rain south. 7-10 Seasonable; rain north. 11-13 Cool; heavy t-storms. 14-17 Sunny. 18-25 Warm; t-storms, then sunny. 26-30 Seasonable, t-storms.

JULY 2006: Temp. 82° (2° below avg. north; avg. south); precip. 5" (2" above avg.). 1-8 T-storms, cool. 9-13 Sunny, warm. 14-21 T-storms, cool. 22-28 Sunny, seasonable. 29-31 Seasonable, rain.

AUG. 2006: Temp. 79° (3° below avg.); precip. 1.5" (1" below avg.). 1-8 Rain, cool. 9-14 Cool; sunny north, rain south. 15-19 Cool; rain, then sunny. 20-25 Sunny north, rain south. 26-31 T-storms, seasonable.

SEPT. 2006: Temp. 73° (3° below avg.); precip. 5.5" (2" above avg.). 1-4 Warm; rain south. 5-9 Hurricane threat. 10-17 Sunny, seasonable. 18-24 T-storms, then sunny; warm. 25-30 T-storms, then sunny; cool.

OCT. 2006: Temp. 67° (avg.); precip. 4.5" (2" above avg. north; 1.5 below south). 1-6 Warm; t-storms north. 7-16 Sunny, cool. 17-20 Showers, seasonable. 21-25 Sunny, warm. 26-31 T-storms, cool.

Oklahoma City ⊙

Dallas ⊙

Houston ⊙

San Antonio ⊙

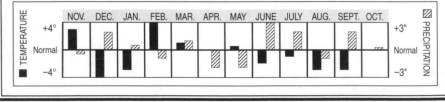

High Plains

REGION 12 SUMMARY: Winter-season temperatures will be near normal, on average, across the south. The north will be exceptionally mild—six degrees above normal, on average. Precipitation and snowfall will be below normal in the north and above normal in the south. The snowiest periods will occur in late November, mid-December, late February, and mid- and late March. The coldest temperatures will occur in mid-December, mid-January, and mid-February.

April will be chilly in the north, with a snowstorm in midmonth. The south will be relatively mild and dry. May will be mild, with near-normal rainfall.

The summer will be hot and dry across the north, with near-normal temperatures and rainfall in the south. The hottest temperatures will occur in early and late June, mid- and late July, and mid-August. Watch for sharply colder weather in late August, with heavy, wet snow in the foothills.

September and October will be cooler than normal, with near- to above-normal precipitation, and snow in mid- and late October.

NOV. 2005: Temp. 37° (1° above avg.); precip. 1" (avg.). 1-4 Snow, then sunny; cold. 5-9 Sunny, mild. 10-17 Snow showers, then sunny; seasonable. 18-21 Sunny, warm. 22-25 Snow, then sunny. 26-30 Snow, cold.

DEC. 2005: Temp. 27° (4° above avg. north; 4° below south); precip. 0.5" (avg.). 1-6 Snow showers, cold. 7-12 Sunny; cold, then mild. 13-16 Snow, cold. 17-20 Sunny, mild. 21-26 Snow showers, cold. 27-31 Sunny, mild.

JAN. 2006: Temp. 28° (8° above avg. north; 2° below south); precip. 0.1" (0.4" below avg.). 1-11 Flurries; then sunny, warm. 12-17 Snow showers, then sunny; seasonable. 18-23 Flurries, cold. 24-27 Sunny, mild. 28-31 Mild north, snow south.

FEB. 2006: Temp. 33.5° (10° above avg. north; 3° above south); precip. 0.5" (avg.). 1-6 Flurries; then sunny, warm. 7-13 Snow showers, cold. 14-20 Snow showers, seasonable. 21-23 Sunny, cold. 24-28 Snow, seasonable.

MAR. 2006: Temp. 41.5° (6° above avg. north; 1° above south); precip. 1.5" (0.5" below avg. north; 1.5" above south). 1-6 Flurries. 7-10 Sunny, warm. 11-14 Mild north, heavy snow south. 15-20 Mild; sunny, then showers. 21-25 Chilly; snow south. 26-31 Rain, then snow.

APR. 2006: Temp. 46.5° (4° below avg. north; 1° above south); precip. 1.5" (1" above avg. north; 1" below south). 1-8 Chilly, rain and

snow showers. 9-15 Sunny; cool, then warm. 16-21 Cool, snow and rain. 22-30 Cool; sunny, then rain.

MAY 2006: Temp. 60° (2° above avg.); precip. 2.5" (1" below avg. north; 1" above south). 1-6 Showers; cool north, warm south. 7-14 Seasonable, t-storms. 15-31 Mostly sunny, with scattered t-storms; warm.

JUNE 2006: Temp. 70.5° (7° above avg. north; avg. south); precip. 1.5" (1" below avg.). 1-7 Hot; scattered t-storms. 8-13 Cool; scattered t-storms. 14-19 Sunny, warm. 20-24 Hot; scattered t-storms. 25-30 Sunny, warm.

JULY 2006: Temp. 72° (avg.); precip. 2" (1" below avg. north; 1" above south). 1-8 Cool, t-storms. 9-12 Sunny, hot. 13-16 T-storms, cool. 17-25 Warm, t-storms. 26-31 Sunny, hot.

AUG. 2006: Temp. 72.5° (3° above avg. north; avg. south); precip. 2" (1" below avg. north; 1" above south). 1-4 Warm; scattered t-storms. 5-16 Seasonable, t-storms. 17-24 Sunny; hot north, seasonable south. 25-31 T-storms, then cold; snow west.

SEPT. 2006: Temp. 56° (5° below avg.); precip. 2.5" (1" above avg.). 1-9 Chilly; rain, then sunny. 10-15 Chilly, rain. 16-23 Cold, rain and snow. 24-30 Sunny, turning mild.

OCT. 2006: Temp. 47° (2° below avg.); precip. 1" (avg.). 1-7 Showers, then sunny; seasonable. 8-14 Sunny, mild. 15-21 Snow north; sunny, mild south. 22-31 Cold; snow north, rain south.

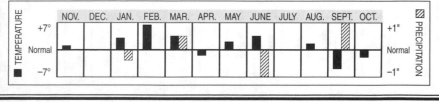

Intermountain

REGION 13 SUMMARY: The winter season will be mild, with temperatures two to three degrees above normal, on average. Temperatures in November and early December will be near or a bit cooler than normal; mid-December through March will bring exceptionally mild temperatures, on average. Snowfall through the region will be well below normal, with slightly below-normal precipitation. The coldest temperatures will occur in early and late December, with the snowiest weather occurring in late November, late January, mid- and late February, and early March.

April and May will be a bit cooler than normal, with near-normal precipitation.

The summer will be hot, with much-below-normal rainfall. The hottest temperatures will occur in mid-June, mid- and late July, and mid-August.

September and October will be cool, with temperatures each month four degrees below normal, on average. Precipitation will be a bit above normal in September and then near normal in October, with the season's first significant snowfall in late October.

NOV. 2005: Temp. 39.5° (2° above avg. east; 1° below west); precip. 2" (0.5" above avg.). 1-6 Cool, showers. 7-14 Mild; rain north. 15-19 Mild; rain north, sunny south. 20-24 Snow, then sunny; cool. 25-30 Chilly, rain and snow showers.

DEC. 2005: Temp. 29° (2° below avg.); precip. 0.5" (1" below avg.). 1-9 Sunny, cold. 10-17 Snow showers, then sunny; mild. 18-25 Snow showers, seasonable. 26-31 Sunny, cold.

JAN. 2006: Temp. 36° (6° above avg.); precip. 1" (0.5" below avg.). 1-10 Mild; showers north, sunny south. 11-18 Sunny, seasonable. 19-31 Rain and snow, then sunny; mild.

FEB. 2006: Temp. 36° (3° above avg.); precip. 1.5" (avg.). 1-5 Warm, rain. 6-11 Mild, rain and snow showers. 12-18 Snow, then sunny; seasonable. 19-23 Chilly, rain and snow showers. 24-28 Snow, cold.

MAR. 2006: Temp. 45° (3° above avg.); precip. 1.5" (avg.). 1-6 Seasonable; rain and snow north. 7-11 Mild; showers north. 12-21 Turning colder; showers, then snow. 22-31 Sunny; mild, then cool.

APR. 2006: Temp. 47° (2° below avg.); precip. 1" (avg.). 1-9 Chilly, rain and snow showers. 10-18 Mild, then colder; rain and snow showers north. 19-25 Sunny; mild, then cool. 26-30 Chilly, rain.

MAY 2006: Temp. 58° (1° above avg.); precip. 1.5" (0.5" below avg. east; 1" above west). 1-5 Showers; cool north, warm south. 6-11 Showers, cool. 12-18 Sunny, warm. 19-31 T-storms, then sunny; warm.

JUNE 2006: Temp. 71° (5° above avg.); precip. 0.1" (0.4" below avg.). 1-7 Warm; showers north, sunny south. 8-19 Sunny, hot. 20-30 T-storms, then sunny; seasonable.

JULY 2006: Temp. 76° (3° above avg.); precip. 0.3" (0.5" below avg. east; avg. west). 1-5 Sunny, warm. 6-15 Warm; scattered t-storms. 16-24 T-storms, then sunny; warm. 25-31 Sunny, then t-storms; hot north, seasonable south.

AUG. 2006: Temp. 74° (2° above avg.); precip. 1" (avg.). 1-6 Warm, t-storms south. 7-11 Cool, t-storms. 12-16 Sunny, hot. 17-23 T-storms, seasonable. 24-31 Cool; showers, then sunny.

SEPT. 2006: Temp. 58° (4° below avg.); precip. 1.5" (0.5" above avg.). 1-3 Showers, mild. 4-9 Sunny, cool. 10-21 Showers, then sunny; cool. 22-30 Seasonable; showers, then sunny.

OCT. 2006: Temp. 47° (4° below avg.); precip. 1" (avg.). 1-5 Rain, chilly. 6-14 Sunny, mild. 15-21 Showers, seasonable. 22-31 Cool; rain and snow, then sunny.

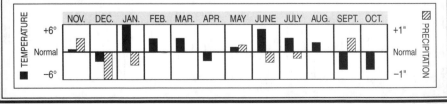

Desert Southwest

REGION 14 SUMMARY: Precipitation in the winter season will be below normal, with temperatures about a degree above normal, on average, from California into Arizona and about a degree below normal, on average, from New Mexico into Texas. Snowfall will be above normal in Texas and New Mexico, but near or below normal elsewhere, with the snowiest periods in early December and mid- to late March. The coldest temperatures will occur in early December, with other cold periods in mid- and late December and late January.

Rainfall in April and May will be below normal, with temperatures a bit below normal in the west and above normal in the east.

The summer season will see near-normal temperatures in the east and be hot in the west. Rainfall will be above normal in June and August and below normal in July. The hottest temperatures will occur in mid-June, the first half of July, and early August.

September and October will be cooler and drier than normal.

NOV. 2005: Temp. 55° (avg.); precip. 0.2" (0.3" below avg.). 1-18 T-storms, then sunny; seasonable. 19-21 Warm; scattered t-storms. 22-26 Sunny, seasonable. 27-30 T-storms, then sunny; cool.

DEC. 2005: Temp. 44° (5° below avg. east; 1° below west); precip. 0.1" (0.4" below avg.; 1" below east). 1-7 Cold; snow east, showers west. 8-15 Sunny, cool. 16-22 Sunny, mild. 23-31 Showers, then sunny; cool.

JAN. 2006: Temp. 48.5° (1° below avg. east; 4° above west); precip. 0.3" (0.2" below avg.). 1-7 Sunny, seasonable. 8-14 Sunny, mild. 15-21 Chilly, rain and snow showers east; mild, showers west. 22-28 Sunny, mild. 29-31 Cool; rain and snow showers east.

FEB. 2006: Temp. 50° (avg.); precip. 0.2" (0.3" below avg.). 1-9 Sunny; mild, then cool. 10-15 Showers, then sunny; cool. 16-22 Cool; rain and snow showers east, sunny west. 23-25 Sunny, mild. 26-28 Sunny east, showers west.

MAR. 2006: Temp. 58° (1° above avg.); precip. 0.6" (0.5" above avg. east; 0.2" below west). 1-8 Sunny; cool, then warm. 9-13 Cool, showers. 14-21 Sunny; mild, then cool. 22-24 Chilly, rain; snow central. 25-29 Sunny; cool, then warm. 30-31 T-storms east, sunny west.

APR. 2006: Temp. 64° (avg.); precip. 0.2" (0.3" below avg.). 1-6 Cool; scattered showers.

7-13 Sunny; cool, then warm. 14-21 Sunny; cool, then seasonable. 22-30 Sunny; warm, then cool.

MAY 2006: Temp. 73° (2° above avg. east; 2° below west); precip. 0.1" (0.4" below avg.). 1-9 Sunny; warm, then cool. 10-14 Sunny, warm. 15-20 Seasonable; scattered t-storms. 21-31 Sunny, seasonable.

JUNE 2006: Temp. 85° (0.5° above avg. east; 4° above west); precip. 1" (0.5" above avg.). 1-4 Sunny, warm. 5-8 Very warm; t-storms east, sunny west. 9-14 T-storms east; sunny, hot west. 15-19 Sunny, hot. 20-30 Scattered t-storms; very warm, then cooler.

JULY 2006: Temp. 89° (2° above avg.); precip. 1" (0.5" below avg.). 1-4 Seasonable; t-storms east, sunny west. 5-15 Hot; scattered t-storms. 16-31 Seasonable; scattered t-storms.

AUG. 2006: Temp. 83° (2° below avg.); precip. 2" (0.5" above avg.). 1-4 Hot; scattered t-storms. 5-17 Seasonable, t-storms. 18-21 Sunny, hot. 22-31 T-storms, then sunny; cooler.

SEPT. 2006: Temp. 75° (3° below avg.); precip. 0.5" (0.5" below avg.). 1-12 Cool; scattered t-storms. 13-24 Sunny; cool, then seasonable. 25-30 Sunny; cool east, seasonable west.

OCT. 2006: Temp. 65° (2° below avg.); precip. 0.5" (0.5" below avg.). 1-6 Cool; scattered t-storms. 7-20 Sunny; warm, then seasonable. 21-31 T-storms, then sunny; cold.

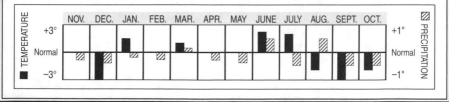

Pacific Northwest

REGION 15 SUMMARY: Winter-season temperatures will be milder than normal, on average, with above-normal rainfall and below-normal snowfall. January will be especially mild, with a couple of sunny periods in midmonth. The best chances for snow are in mid-November and late February. The coldest periods will occur in early and mid-December and late February. The stormiest periods will occur in mid-November, late December, early January, and early and mid- to late February.

April and early May will be cooler and wetter than normal, with little sunshine. The remainder of May will be warmer and drier than normal.

The summer season will feature abundant sunshine, with above-normal temperatures and below-normal rainfall. The hottest temperatures will occur in early to mid-June, early July, and early August.

September and October will be cooler than normal, with below-normal rainfall in September and above-normal rainfall in October.

NOV. 2005: Temp. 47° (avg.); precip. 10.5" (4" above avg.). 1-3 Showers, cool. 4-13 Stormy; heavy rain. 14-16 Snow north, rain south. 17-19 Heavy rain. 20-23 Sunny, cool. 24-30 Rain, then sunny; cool.

DEC. 2005: Temp. 41° (avg. north; 1.5° below south); precip. 4.5" (2" below avg.). 1-3 Sunny, cool. 4-13 Rain, mild. 14-17 Misty, seasonable. 18-28 Cool; rain, then sunny. 29-31 Heavy rain.

JAN. 2006: Temp. 49.5° (7.5° above avg.); precip. 7.5" (avg. south; 3" above north). 1-11 Rain, windy, mild. 12-16 Sunny; mild, then cool. 17-21 Rain, then sunny; mild. 22-31 Rain, mild.

FEB. 2006: Temp. 46° (2° above avg.); precip. 10" (5" above avg.). 1-5 Stormy; heavy rain. 6-12 Rain, seasonable. 13-15 Rain, windy. 16-22 Sunny, then heavy rain. 23-28 Cold, rain and snow.

MAR. 2006: Temp. 49° (2° above avg.); precip. 5.5" (1" above avg.). 1-6 Rain, seasonable. 7-13 Rain, mild. 14-20 Rain, seasonable. 21-25 Sunny, mild. 26-31 Rain, then sunny; seasonable.

APR. 2006: Temp. 47° (3° below avg.); precip. 4" (1" above avg.). 1-4 Misty, cool. 5-10 Rain, seasonable. 11-18 Cool, rain. 19-21

Sunny, cool. 22-30 Rain; mild, then cool.

MAY 2006: Temp. 55.5° (0.5° above avg.); precip. 2" (avg.). 1-8 Rain, cool. 9-13 Sunny, warm. 14-23 Seasonable, showers. 24-29 Sunny, warm. 30-31 Rain.

JUNE 2006: Temp. 61.5° (1.5° above avg.); precip. 0.5" (1" below avg.). 1-5 Cool, showers. 6-11 Sunny, hot. 12-22 Sunny, seasonable. 23-30 T-storms, cool.

JULY 2006: Temp. 67° (3° above avg.); precip. 0.1" (0.4" below avg.). 1-6 Sunny, hot. 7-15 T-storms, then sunny; warm. 16-25 T-storms, then sunny; seasonable. 26-31 Sunny, warm.

AUG. 2006: Temp. 67° (2° above avg.); precip. 1.5" (0.5" above avg.). 1-7 Sunny, hot. 8-11 Seasonable, t-storms. 12-16 Sunny, warm. 17-20 Seasonable, t-storms. 21-25 Warm; sunny, then showers. 26-31 Seasonable; scattered showers.

SEPT. 2006: Temp. 60.5° (0.5° below avg.); precip. 0.5" (1" below avg.). 1-7 Sunny; cool, then warm. 8-15 Showers, seasonable. 16-21 Sunny, cool. 22-24 Cool; showers north. 25-30 Mild; sunny, then showers.

OCT. 2006: Temp. 52° (2° below avg.); precip. 3.5" (0.5" above avg.). 1-6 Rain, cool. 7-12 Sunny; warm, then cool. 13-22 Rain, cool. 23-28 Cool; rain, then sunny. 29-31 Sunny, cool.

Map labels: Seattle, Portland, Eugene, Eureka

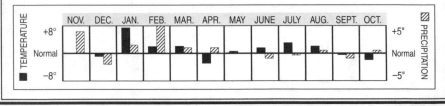

Pacific Southwest

REGION 16 SUMMARY: The winter season will be warmer than normal in most of the region, but a bit cooler than normal in The Valley. Rainfall will be near normal in the north and below normal in the south. Mountain snowfall will be below normal. The stormiest periods will occur in mid- to late November, mid-January, early and mid-February, and mid-March. The coldest temperatures will occur in early and late December.

Temperatures in April and May will be a bit cooler than normal, with near-normal rainfall.

Temperatures in the summer will average two to three degrees warmer than normal, with little, if any, rainfall in most places. The hottest periods will occur in early to mid-June, early and late July, and late August.

September will feature unusually warm temperatures and abundant sunshine, with the best chance for rain in early to midmonth. October will be warmer and drier than normal, with hot temperatures in midmonth.

NOV. 2005: Temp. 57° (1° below avg.); precip. 3" (3" above avg. north; avg. south). 1-4 Sunny, seasonable. 5-8 T-storms, seasonable. 9-15 Seasonable; showers north. 16-25 Sunny, then showers; cool. 26-30 Sunny, cool.

DEC. 2005: Temp. 51° (4° below avg. east; avg. west); precip. 0.5" (1.5" below avg.). 1-3 Sunny, cool. 4-9 Seasonable; showers north. 10-14 Showers, mild. 15-31 Sunny; cool north, seasonable south.

JAN. 2006: Temp. 56.5° (1° above avg. northeast; 6° above southwest); precip. 2.5" (0.5" below avg.). 1-5 Sunny; seasonable north, mild south. 6-13 Cloudy, cool north; sunny, warm south. 14-20 Mild, showers. 21-27 Seasonable; showers north, sunny south. 28-31 Sunny, seasonable.

FEB. 2006: Temp. 56° (1° below avg. northeast; 3° above southwest); precip. 1" (2" below avg.). 1-9 Mild; showers north, sunny south. 10-13 Sunny; seasonable north, warm south. 14-21 Sunny north, t-storms south. 22-24 Sunny, seasonable. 25-28 Showers north; sunny, warm south.

MAR. 2006: Temp. 58° (1° above avg.); precip. 2.5" (1" above avg. north; 1" below south). 1-8 Seasonable; showers north. 9-11 Showers. 12-16 Seasonable; showers north, sunny south. 17-22 Rain, cool. 23-26 Sunny; seasonable north, warm south. 27-31 Sunny, warm north; sprinkles south.

APR. 2006: Temp. 59.5° (0.5° below avg.); precip. 0.5" (avg. north; 1" below south). 1-5

Sunny, mild. 6-11 Showers, then sunny; mild. 12-17 Cool, showers. 18-30 Seasonable; sunny, then showers.

MAY 2006: Temp. 62° (2° below avg.); precip. 0.5" (avg.). 1-11 Showers, then sunny; cool. 12-20 Showers north, sunny south. 21-31 Cool; scattered showers.

JUNE 2006: Temp. 70° (2° above avg.); precip. 0" (0.1" below avg.). 1-7 Mostly cloudy coast; sunny inland. 8-11 Sunny, hot north; sprinkles south.12-20 Sunny, very warm. 21-30 Sunny; seasonable coast, cool inland.

JULY 2006: Temp. 74° (3° above avg.); precip. 0.1" (0.1" above avg.). 1-5 Sunny, hot. 6-8 Cloudy, seasonable. 9-14 Sunny, warm. 15-24 Warm; mostly cloudy coast, sunny inland. 25-27 Sunny, seasonable. 28-31 Hot; t-storms.

AUG. 2006: Temp. 74° (2° above avg.); precip. 0.1" (avg.). 1-6 Warm; scattered t-storms. 7-11 Sunny, seasonable. 12-13 Warm, t-storms. 14-20 Warm; scattered t-storms north, sunny south. 21-31 Sunny; seasonable, then hot.

SEPT. 2006: Temp. 70° (avg.); precip. 0.3" (0.3" above avg. north; 0.1" below south). 1-6 Sunny, warm. 7-11 Cool; scattered t-storms. 12-16 Seasonable; sunny inland, cloudy coast. 17-20 Sunny, warm. 21-30 Sunny, warm north; mostly cloudy, seasonable south.

OCT. 2006: Temp. 66° (1° above avg.); precip. 0.1" (0.4" below avg.). 1-6 Seasonable; scattered t-storms. 7-10 Sunny, hot. 11-18 Sunny, seasonable. 19-24 Showers north, sunny south. 25-31 T-storms, then sunny.

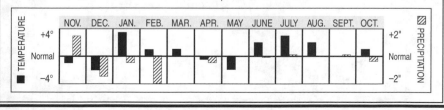

In the Wake of

Lost lore from the aftermath of San Francisco's 1906 disaster.

a Quake

At 5:12 A.M. on Wednesday, April 18, 1906, an earthquake woke up residents of San Francisco and tossed them from their beds. The 45-second jolt (later estimated to have been between 7.8 and 8.3 on the Richter scale) caused chimneys to fall and china to shatter, but most of the city's wooden structures—especially those built on solid ground—remained largely intact and in fairly good condition.

Hardest hit were structures built on former wetlands that had been filled in with garbage, rubble from past fires, and even the remains of ships abandoned during the 1849 gold rush. South of Market Street, on ground reclaimed from the Mission Bay Swamp, a dozen residential hotels sank or collapsed, crushing sleeping inhabitants. The business and wholesale districts north of Market Street, which were constructed primarily of brick and stone, suffered heavy damage, too. Among them was the new city hall, which collapsed and left its steel skeleton sticking above the rubble like a birdcage.

(continued)

The Fairmont Hotel *(top)* suffered heavy interior damage, while the Hall of Justice *(foreground)* was hit even harder.

by **Kimberly Green**

~photos: Gladys Hansen Museum in San Francisco, unless otherwise noted

When the earth stopped shaking, few people realized that San Francisco's cataclysm had only just begun. Almost immediately, downed power cables, broken gas lines, and damaged chimneys ignited widespread fires. Worse, the quake had cracked the city's massive clay water mains, leaving firefighters virtually without water. Tales of the disaster are legend; here are a few you may not have heard.

Quake Quirk

■ **Charles F. Richter** *(below)* developed the Richter scale in 1935 at the California Institute of Technology as a mathematical

—California Institute of Technology Archives

device to compare the size of earthquakes (not to measure the damage they wrought). Quakes of 8 or more are considered "great"; the scale has no upper limit.

The Fire Vibrated

T he fire burned for 72 hours, at times consuming one city block every 30 minutes and eventually charring more than four square miles. Towers of smoke billowed a mile high. The flames reached 2,700°F; even using saltwater lines from the bay and wearing protective wet bags, firefighters couldn't get near the fire. Some observers claimed that the fire could actually be felt as "vibrations like the rumbling of a steam boiler or the passing of several streetcars."

A SURVIVOR'S STORY

"Go back to bed!"

■ "Reaching the room [in the boarding house], I found the man standing dumb and speechless, and the woman, as she saw me, cried out, 'Oh, Mr. Greenberg!' and fainted away. I kicked the man to arouse him, and caught up a pitcher of water from the sideboard and dashed it on the woman, reviving her, and telling them to go back to bed, as that was the safest plan. There was no use running on the street for fear of getting killed from falling debris. . . .

"Remember, the house was still shaking, and I did all this in my underwear."

–David Greenberg, resident

Left: "The Great Fire" of 1906 destroyed 28,000 buildings and killed 3,000 people.
Below left: San Franciscans hurry to escape the firestorm that engulfed their city.
Below right: A man poses among the ruins.

Dynamite Fueled the Flames

C ity and military authorities attempted to create a firebreak using dynamite and gunpowder. But, inexperienced with explosives, they sometimes failed to check the wind or anticipate the direction of the fire before blasting buildings. Instead of creating a firebreak, they often sent flaming debris to neighboring blocks, spreading the fire faster and farther.

Cars to the Rescue!

D ebris-clogged streets were impassable for horses and wagons. Cablecar tracks were twisted and blocked by rubble, which was of no matter as power stations had been destroyed anyway. The few streetcars that survived the fire soon sheltered refugee families, who used the platforms for porches and bell straps for laundry lines.

With their relatively high clearance, automobiles could maneuver over or around rubble and climb San Francisco's steep hills. Cars were pressed into service as ambulances and hearses. Because telegraph and telephone systems were down, automobiles also carried messages along a fragmented mile-long fire line. Services were so badly needed that the speed limit was temporarily eliminated.

A SURVIVOR'S STORY

"Everything I Know Is Up *Here*"

■ "'Everything I own is burning up: my library, my drawings, plans, office furnishings, and all my architectural equipment. But everything I know is up *here*,' my father said, as he put his finger lightly to his brow."

–Eleanor Deering Matthews, recalling her father's words during the fire

(continued)

Crowd and Class Control

Half the city's population—over 200,000 people—fled their homes, trudging up and down the city's steep hills and "slipping on the cinder-coated sidewalk . . . as if it had been coated with ice." Refugees packed into every public square, cemetery, and park, with an estimated 50,000 to 90,000 in Golden Gate Park alone. At first, people of different classes and ethnicities crowded together on park benches and rubbed elbows in bread lines. Within days, however, enough ugly bias returned to force the Chinese refugees into segregated camps.

A SURVIVOR'S STORY

Found Money

■ "I was quite a junk picker. . . . We would sell window weights, copper wires, and copper boilers [to junk dealers]. When we started to dig around, we found five-dollar pieces melted together, which we sold for the gold. Everybody did this; it was another gold rush."

–*Aurelio de Crespi, who was 10 years old in 1906*

Postage Not Paid

In the chaos of evacuation, notes between families and friends appeared in unlikely places: on old shutters and pieces of furniture, in trees. The Post Office required no stamps and accepted letters written on anything—soup can labels, paper bags, rags, old cuffs, any scrap of paper. One man wrote to his mother on his removable shirt collar.

Scarce Food and Hot Cash

By April 21, much of the city's food had been consumed by flames or hungry refugees. Trains chugged into the area with bread from Utah, oranges from Los Angeles, raisins from Fresno, and beef from Tacoma. Other cities and states shipped blankets, cots, clothing, drugs, and tons of flour.

Even after the threat of famine had ceased, food was rationed and shops remained closed. Money was also in short supply, as every bank in the city had burned; for weeks, their fireproof vaults were too hot to open.

A SURVIVOR'S STORY

"Curlinary" Arts

■ "I did all the cooking, and on Mama's curling iron stove. I don't know how I ever did it, but somehow it just came. . . . I made all kinds of soups, salads, and creamed crab, oysters, etc., and cooked meats, vegetables, and potatoes, and you can bet we ate and made up for the starvation period."

–Mabel Coxe, in a letter to her brother

Left: Two hundred thousand earthquake refugees camped out in tents provided by the army.

Right: A family cooks on a stove rescued from a damaged home.

Below: Amidst their salvaged possessions, another family pauses for the camera.

S o l e s   S a v e d

Many foot-weary San Franciscans soon sported obsolete army boots. Local army warehouses held 84,000 pairs of outdated russet shoes, which the local quartermaster general gave out to the needy.

S i d e w a l k   K i t c h e n s

Until their damaged chimneys received an inspector's blessing, home owners had to cook outdoors. Consequently, woodstoves, coal stoves, enormous laundry stoves, and even small bedroom stoves were hauled out onto the sidewalks. In time, those kitchens grew more elaborate, as cooks added worktables, cupboards, and windscreens. In fact, on May 2, the *San Francisco Chronicle* declared that overbuilt kitchens, loaded with "inflammable fripperies," posed a public menace!

O h ,   R a t s !

Like their human counterparts, San Francisco's considerable rat population fled before the flames. Fearing bubonic plague, city health officials offered 15 cents a rat—dead or alive. Soon residents

219

turned up with rodents in everything from butterfly nets to gopher traps. "[W]hat a perplexing problem this creates when every kid in the neighborhood discovers that rats are salable," reporter Grover Tracy wrote. In short time, some 150,000 rats were exterminated.

The "Great" Debate

P rior to 1906, California entrepreneurs had avoided public discussion of earthquakes, fearing that it would hurt business and discourage investment. After the disaster, James Horsburgh Jr., an agent for Southern Pacific Railroad, wrote to chambers of commerce throughout the state, explaining, "We do not believe in advertising the earthquake. The real calamity in San Francisco was undoubtedly the fire." Likewise, in late April, the San Francisco Real Estate Board passed a resolution saying that "the great fire" should be used instead of "the great earthquake" when referring to the disaster. Acts of God, such as earthquakes, could wreak havoc on real estate values, whereas the familiar threat of fire could be minimized by improved building codes and emergency preparedness. □□

Kimberly Green is an English teacher who lives in Moscow, Idaho. Her great-grandmother was a survivor of the 1906 earthquake.

QUAKY QUESTIONS

To learn more about earthquakes, go to **Almanac.com/extras**.

Go to the Edge of the Earth

■ Point Reyes National Seashore offers an interpretive earthquake trail near Olema, 30 miles north of San Francisco. Visitors can find a section of fence displaced almost 20 feet by the 1906 quake and straddle the two tectonic plates that form the San Andreas Fault, with noticeably different rock on each side. On the west is the Pacific Plate, which contains large amounts of granite and Monterey shale and is drifting northwestward at approximately one to two inches a year. On the east, the North American Plate is primarily "Franciscan Formation," composed of graywacke, shale, conglomerate, and chert, and is moving ever so slightly westward.

–G. K. Gilbert

The San Andreas fault line is clearly visible in this 1906 photo. Today, visitors can still straddle the two tectonic plates.

When Time Stands Still

■ Each year on April 18, at 5:12 A.M. exactly, hundreds gather to commemorate the 1906 earthquake with a moment of silence at Lotta's Fountain on Market Street. For information about attending this year's centennial commemoration, e-mail sfisno1@aol.com.

The Roads Most Traveled

As America's interstate

system celebrates

its 50th anniversary,

join us on this

informational journey

through highway

history, trivia, and lore.

by Alice Cary

IKE'S GRAND IDEA

On July 7, 1919, 81 U.S. Army vehicles left Washington, D.C., and headed for San Francisco on a trip that was to prove historic: They were the first transcontinental motor convoy. One of those taking part was Lt. Col. Dwight D. "Ike" Eisenhower. The convoy traveled along a transcontinental route known as the Lincoln Highway (a series of connecting roadways, hardly a highway in today's terms), averaging 58 miles each day at a speed of about 5 miles per hour. They completed the journey in what was a record-setting pace—62 days—but along the way soldiers had to deal with breakdowns, deep mud and sand, broken bridges, and weather delays.

Later, during World War II, General Eisenhower got a firsthand look at Germany's

Above: *General Lucius D. Clay shows President Eisenhower a map of the proposed interstate highway system.*

Right: *On August 2, 1956, Missouri became the first state to start interstate construction, when it began work on I-70 in St. Charles County.*

autobahn expressway and how easily troops moved on it. He grew determined to create a similar highway network in the United States.

U.S. politicians and officials had begun seriously considering an interstate highway system in the 1930s, and in 1941, President Franklin D. Roosevelt had appointed a committee to more closely examine national needs. Various acts were passed, but the big challenge lay in financing such a large project.

When Eisenhower became president in 1953, he was able to convince others that interstate funding was a national, not a state, issue; that interstate highways made sense for national security; and that the project would also create an immense number of jobs. His personal campaign culminated on June 29, 1956, when, while recuperating from intestinal surgery at Walter Reed Medical Center, he signed the Federal Aid Highway Act of 1956.

On October 15, 1990, the roadway—some 46,726.36 miles long—was officially named the Dwight D. Eisenhower System of Interstate and Defense Highways.

Today, interstates comprise only one percent of the total road mileage in America, yet carry more than 20 percent of our traffic.

THE ULTIMATE ROAD SHOW

■ To help the public understand how interstate highways might work, General Motors created an exhibit called "Futurama" for the 1939 New York World's Fair. GM enlisted Broadway producer and designer Norman Bel Geddes to design its seven-acre exhibit, which quickly became the fair's most popular attraction.

–New York Public Library

The now-familiar cloverleaf design of highway entrances and exits was unveiled for the first time at the 1939 World's Fair.

Visitors sat on 600 upholstered, moving chairs to listen to 16 minutes of narration and view a model of a cross section of the country as it might be in 1960, complete with 14-lane superhighways and experimental homes and farms. The scenery included a million scaled-down trees, a half-million model buildings, and 50,000 teardrop-shape cars, trucks, and buses.

Futurama showed how interstate highways would improve our lives. Vehicles would travel as fast as 100 miles per hour, with radio beams in the cars making sure that they didn't get too close to each other. Traffic would be tiered in cities, with a bottom service level for getting to and from parking lots. Bel Geddes predicted that cars of the future would be able to cross the country in 24 hours.

continued

CONSTRUCTION, NUCLEAR-STYLE

In 1963, engineers working on I-40 across California's Mojave Desert considered using 22 buried atomic bombs to obliterate the 1,200-foot mountains that stood in the way. Not only would $8 million in construction costs be saved, but also the Atomic Energy Commission thought that the blast might publicize peaceful uses of nuclear energy.

In 1965, the idea was dropped because scientists couldn't accurately predict how long after the blast it would be safe for workers to return to the area to build the new road.

Among the proposed interstate highway marker designs submitted were those from (clockwise from top) Minnesota, North Carolina, Nevada, and New York.

D E T O U R S   A N D   D I V E R S I O N S

LAND O' LAKES. While creating a section of I-80 through Nebraska's Platte River Valley in the 1960s, highway engineers worked with state environmental organizations to create a "Chain of Lakes"—more than 50—to be used for recreational purposes.

PANTHER PATHWAY. Florida's Alligator Alley, I-75, connects Naples and Miami. When the roadway was upgraded from a two-lane highway to an interstate, engineers installed special underpasses just for Florida panthers to try to help preserve the endangered state animal.

SAVING FACE. Granite Staters feared that construction blasting of I-93 in New Hampshire might damage the state symbol, "The Old Man of the Mountain," a 40-foot-tall natural granite outcropping in the shape of an old man's face. Workers used

The final design selected was based on proposals from Texas (below) and Missouri (bottom).

carefully measured blasts to create the Franconia Notch Parkway, which opened in 1988. (The Old Man collapsed from natural causes in May 2003.)

FEATHERY FINANCING. Before 1956, financing roads was often a tricky business. For example, the construction of a bridge over the Tombigbee River at Demopolis, Alabama, was partly financed by—of all things—a rooster sale. The event was the brainchild of a creative fund-raiser named Frank Derby. On August 15, 1919, 5,000 roosters were auctioned to the public, the proceeds going to road building.

Though it's officially the Memorial Bridge, locals have always called this span the Rooster Bridge. A legislative act in 1959 made the nickname official and stipulated that in the future any span across the river at that point will bear the same title.

MILE BY MILE

■ The longest interstate is I-90, running from Seattle, Washington, to Boston, Massachusetts, for 3,020.54 miles.

■ The shortest two-digit interstate is I-73, running 12.27 miles between Emery and Greensboro, North Carolina.

■ Three-digit highways are usually auxiliary spurs or peripheral belt lines that are relatively short. I-878 in New York City has a length of only seven-tenths of a mile, or 3,696 feet.

■ Interstates running east and west are designated with even numbers, while north-and-south ones have odd-numbered identifications.

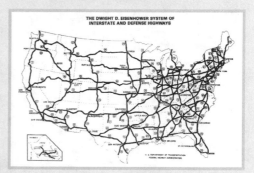

Although the original plan called for 41,000 miles of interstate highway, more mileage was eventually added.

TRAFFIC LIGHTS OUT

The last stoplight along an interstate route was removed from an intersection along I-90 in Wallace, Idaho, in 1991. Citizens threw a gala funeral, putting it in a coffin and ushering it away in a horse-drawn hearse as bagpipes played and a 21-gun salute was fired.

WHY WE DRIVE ON THE RIGHT. In 1792, Pennsylvania legislators voted to establish a turnpike from Lancaster to Philadelphia. The law mandated that travel would be on the right-hand side—the first official ruling on the matter in the New World.

continued

ROADWAYS BY RAKEMAN

When an artist named Carl Rakeman started working for the U.S. Bureau of Public Roads in 1921, few imagined what an impact he would have. Over the next 30 years, Rakeman painted more than 100 scenes depicting the history of American trails, roads, and highways, ranging from cobblestone streets in a Maine village in 1625 and the Pony Express to the Lincoln Highway in 1913 and the Pennsylvania Turnpike in 1945. His work is believed to be the most complete illustrated history of American highway development.

The San Francisco–Oakland Bay Bridge, as depicted by Carl Rakeman in 1939. Construction of the bridge began on July 3, 1933; it opened on November 12, 1936.

MILE ZERO. In 1919, when the U.S. Army sent its first convoy of military vehicles across the country, a Mile Zero marker was dedicated on the Ellipse near the White House South Lawn.

On June 4, 1923, that marker was replaced with a hip-high permanent stone. Today that stone, which was inspired by the Golden Milestone at the Roman Forum, is little more than a curiosity, and from time to time, as the Ellipse area is updated, the National Park Service considers removing it.

AMERICANS ON THE MOVE

■ As Americans fell in love with cars and driving, our landscape changed forever. Drag racing, car washes, truck stops, rest areas, and drive-in movie theaters all became part of our culture. The real estate adjacent to interstate exits became the proving ground for fast-food restaurants, as well as motel and service station chains. Here are brief glimpses at a few pioneers.

SLEEP TIGHT. In 1951, Kemmons Wilson, a successful Memphis home builder and former movie theater owner, took his family on a vacation to Washington, D.C., that he would never forget. He found it nearly impossible to find clean, reliable places to stay with his children. A year later, in Memphis, he opened his first motel—the Holiday Inn, which offered free lodging for kids, modern rooms with air conditioning, kennels, and a swimming pool. To announce the inn, Wilson developed a 50-foot-high, green-and-yellow "Great Sign" that resembled a movie marquee. He put his mother, Ruby "Doll" Wilson, in charge of interior decorating.

TRAVEL BACK

To view images of Futurama and the paintings of Carl Rakeman, go to **Almanac.com/extras.**

Wilson took an assembly-line approach to building his motels and by 1960 had over 100. As recreational vehicles became popular, he also opened a string of Trav-L-Parks that featured pools and miniature golf for camping families.

Kemmons Wilson and his distinctive sign, which was easily recognizable by motorists.

ORANGE ROOFS. In 1925, Howard Johnson (his real name) opened a drug and ice cream store in Quincy, Massachusetts. By 1935, he had 25 such roadside restaurants in that state. In 1940, he won a contract for 11 locations along the Pennsylvania Turnpike, and after World War II, he arranged for a similar presence along the Ohio and New Jersey turnpikes.

In 1954, the entrepreneur decided to add lodging to his restaurants, beginning in Savannah, Georgia. Soon, buildings with a bright-orange roof became a friendly sight for travelers across the nation.

FILL 'ER UP!

The increase in highway travel in the late 1940s prompted the creation of new types of gas stations. Some included self-serve pumps and girls on roller skates taking money and making change. Eventually, entrepreneurs developed mega–truck stops such as Wyoming's Little America, which featured dozens of pumps as well as dining, lodging, and entertainment facilities. Oil companies also jumped on the bandwagon, and signs for Mobil, Shell Oil, Phillips 66, and Texaco service stations popped up everywhere along America's interstates.

–Little America

The original Little America, built in 1934 and boasting four pumps, was a far cry from today's huge travelers' oasis along I-80.

"ARE WE THERE YET?" When you're on a trip and asked this for the umpteenth time, stall your questioner(s) with this riddle from the Old Farmer:

Q: What can go for thousands of miles and never move?

A: The interstate!

Alice Cary, a frequent contributor to *The Old Farmer's Almanac,* writes about popular culture.

227

Best Fishing Days and Times

■ **The best times to fish are when the fish are naturally most active. The Sun,** Moon, tides, and weather all influence fish activity. For example, fish tend to feed more at sunrise and sunset. During a full Moon, tides are higher than average and fish tend to feed more. However, most of us go fishing when we can get the time off, not because it is the best time. But there *are* best times, according to fishing lore:

The Best Days for 2006, when the Moon is between new and full:

January 1–14

Jan. 29–Feb. 12

Feb. 27–Mar. 14

Mar. 29–Apr. 13

Apr. 27–May 13

May 27–Jun. 11

Jun. 25–Jul. 10

Jul. 25–Aug. 9

Aug. 23–Sept. 7

Sept. 22–Oct. 6

Oct. 22–Nov. 5

Nov. 20–Dec. 4

December 20–31

■ **One hour before and one hour after high tides, and one hour before and one hour after low tides. (The times of high tides for Boston are given on pages 96–122; also see pages 234–235. Inland, the times for high tides correspond with the times when the Moon is due south. Low tides are halfway between high tides.)**

■ During the "morning rise" (after sunup for a spell) and the "evening rise" (just before sundown and the hour or so after).

■ **When the barometer is steady or on the rise. (But even during stormy periods, the fish aren't going to give up feeding. The smart fisherman will find just the right bait.)**

■ When there is a hatch of flies—caddis flies or mayflies, commonly. (The fisherman will have to match *his* fly with the hatching flies or go fishless.)

■ **When the breeze is from a westerly quarter rather than from the north or east.**

■ When the water is still or rippled, rather than during a wind.

Tackle-Box Checklist

✔ Fishing line

✔ Bobbers

✔ Swivels, to keep fishing line from twisting

✔ Leaders

✔ Sinkers

✔ Different sizes of hooks

✔ Pliers, to help remove hooks

✔ Stringer, to hold all the fish you catch

✔ Sharp knife

✔ Ruler/scale

✔ Flashlight

✔ First-aid kit

✔ Insect repellent

✔ Sunscreen

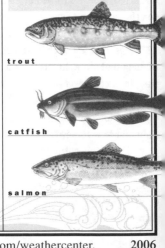

trout

catfish

salmon

Astrological Timetable

The following month-by-month chart is based on the Moon's sign and shows the
best days each month for certain activities. —*Celeste Longacre*

	JAN.	FEB.	MAR.	APR.	MAY	JUNE	JULY	AUG.	SEPT.	OCT.	NOV.	DEC.
Quit smoking	16, 21	18, 26	17, 26	23, 26	19, 24	16, 20	13, 17	13, 22	10, 19	16, 21	12, 17	10, 15
Begin diet to lose weight	16, 21	18, 26	17, 26	23, 26	19, 24	16, 20	13, 17	13, 22	10, 19	16, 21	12, 17	10, 15
Begin diet to gain weight	3, 7, 30	3, 12	2, 11	8, 12	5, 10	2, 6, 29	4, 31	27, 28	6, 24	3, 30	4, 27	1, 24, 28
Cut hair to discourage growth	16, 20, 21	16, 17, 18	15, 16, 17	27, 28	25, 26	21, 22	18, 19	14, 15	11, 12	15, 16, 20, 21	6, 16, 17	13, 14, 15
Cut hair to encourage growth	4, 5, 31	4, 5	3, 4, 10, 11	1, 7, 8	4, 5, 9, 10	1, 2, 5, 6	3, 4, 30, 31	26, 27, 28	23, 24	5, 6	1, 28, 29	2, 3, 29, 30
Have dental care	17, 18, 19	14, 15	13, 14	9, 10, 11	7, 8	3, 4, 30	1, 2, 27, 28, 29	24, 25	20, 21	17, 18, 19	14, 15	11, 12
End projects	27, 28	25, 26	27, 28	25, 26	25, 26	23, 24	23, 24	21, 22	20, 21	20, 21	18, 19	18, 19
Start projects	30, 31	1, 2	30, 31	28, 29	28, 29	26, 27	26, 27	24, 25	23, 24	23, 24	21, 22	21, 22
Entertain	15, 16	11, 12, 13	10, 11, 12	7, 8	4, 5	1, 2, 28, 29	25, 26	21, 22, 23	17, 18, 19	15, 16	11, 12	8, 9, 10
Go camping	25, 26	21, 22	20, 21	17, 18	14, 15	10, 11	8, 9	4, 5, 31	1, 28, 29	25, 26	21, 22	18, 19, 20
Plant aboveground crops	3, 4, 12, 13	9, 10	8, 9	4, 5	2, 3, 12	8, 9, 26, 27	5, 6	2, 3	25, 26	4, 5, 23, 24	1, 28, 29	25, 26
Plant belowground crops	22, 23, 24	19, 20, 27	18, 19, 27, 28	14, 15, 23, 24	20, 21	17, 18	14, 15, 23, 24	10, 11, 19, 20	8, 15, 16	12, 13	9, 10, 19	6, 7, 16, 17
Destroy pests and weeds	6, 7	2, 3	1, 2, 29, 30	25, 26	22, 23, 24	19, 20	16, 17	12, 13	9, 10	6, 7	3, 4, 30	1, 27, 28
Graft or pollinate	12, 13, 14	9, 10	8, 9	4, 5	2, 3, 29, 30	25, 26, 27	23, 24	19, 20	15, 16	12, 13, 14	9, 10	6, 7
Prune to encourage growth	6, 7	2, 3, 11, 12	1, 2, 10, 11	7, 8	4, 5	1, 2, 10	8, 9, 26	4, 5, 31	1, 28, 29	6, 25, 26	3, 4, 30	1, 27, 28
Prune to discourage growth	15, 16, 25, 26	21, 22	20, 21	17, 18	15, 23, 24	19, 20	16, 17	12, 13	9, 18, 19	15, 16	11, 12	18, 19
Harvest above-ground crops	8, 9	4, 5	3, 4, 13	1, 9, 10	7, 8	3, 4	1, 2, 28, 29	6, 7, 24, 25	3, 4, 30	1, 27, 28	23, 24	2, 3, 29, 30
Harvest below-ground crops	27, 28	14, 15, 23, 24	23, 24	19, 20	16, 17, 25, 26	12, 13, 21, 22	18, 19	14, 15	11, 12, 20, 21	8, 9	14, 15	11, 12
Cut hay	6, 7	2, 3	1, 2, 29, 30	4, 5	4, 5	19, 20	16, 17	12, 13	9, 10	6, 7	3, 4, 30	1, 27, 28
Begin logging	27, 28	23, 24	23, 24	19, 20	16, 17	12, 13	10, 11	6, 7	3, 4, 30	1, 27, 28	23, 24, 25	21, 22
Set posts or pour concrete	27, 28	23, 24	23, 24	19, 20	16, 17	12, 13	10, 11	6, 7	3, 4, 30	1, 27, 28	23, 24, 25	21, 22
Breed	22, 23, 24	19, 20	18, 19	14, 15	12, 13	8, 9	5, 6	2, 3, 29, 30	25, 26	22, 23, 24	19, 20	16, 17
Wean	16, 21	18, 26	17, 26	23, 26	19, 24	16, 20	13, 17	13, 22	10, 19	16, 21	12, 17	10, 15
Castrate animals	1, 2, 29, 30	25, 26	25, 26	21, 22	18, 19	15, 16	12, 13	8, 9	5, 6	2, 3, 29, 30	26, 27	23, 24
Slaughter livestock	22, 23, 24	19, 20	18, 19	14, 15	12, 13	8, 9	5, 6	2, 3, 29, 30	25, 26	22, 23, 24	18, 19, 20	16, 17

Secrets of the Zodiac

■ Ancient astrologers believed that each astrological sign influenced a specific part of the body. The first sign of the zodiac—Aries—was attributed to the head, with the rest of the signs moving down the body, ending with Pisces at the feet.

Astrology vs. Astronomy

■ Astrology is a tool we use to time events according to the astrological placements of the Sun, the Moon, and eight planets in the 12 signs of the zodiac. Astronomy, on the other hand, is the study of the actual placement of the known planets and constellations, taking into account the precession of the equinoxes. The placement of the planets in the signs of the zodiac is not the same astrologically and astronomically. The Moon's astrological place is given in **Gardening by the Moon's Sign, page 231;** its astronomical place is given in the **Left-Hand Calendar Pages, 96–122.**

Modern astrology is a study of synchronicities. The planetary movements do not cause events; rather, they explain the path, or "flow," that events tend to follow. Astrologers use the current relationship of the planets and your personal birth chart to determine the best possible times for you to carry out your plans.

The dates in the **Astrological Timetable, page 229,** are based on the astrological passage of the Moon. However, other planets also influence us, so it's best to consider all indicators before making any major decisions.

When Mercury Is Retrograde

■ Sometimes from our perspective, the other planets appear to be traveling backward through the zodiac. (All heavenly bodies move forward. An optical illusion makes them seem as if they are moving backward.) We call this *retrograde motion.*

Mercury's retrograde periods, which

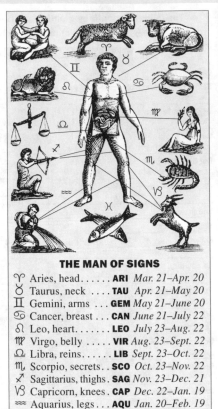

THE MAN OF SIGNS

♈ Aries, head......	**ARI**	*Mar. 21–Apr. 20*
♉ Taurus, neck	**TAU**	*Apr. 21–May 20*
♊ Gemini, arms ...	**GEM**	*May 21–June 20*
♋ Cancer, breast ...	**CAN**	*June 21–July 22*
♌ Leo, heart.......	**LEO**	*July 23–Aug. 22*
♍ Virgo, belly	**VIR**	*Aug. 23–Sept. 22*
♎ Libra, reins......	**LIB**	*Sept. 23–Oct. 22*
♏ Scorpio, secrets..	**SCO**	*Oct. 23–Nov. 22*
♐ Sagittarius, thighs.	**SAG**	*Nov. 23–Dec. 21*
♑ Capricorn, knees..	**CAP**	*Dec. 22–Jan. 19*
♒ Aquarius, legs...	**AQU**	*Jan. 20–Feb. 19*
♓ Pisces, feet......	**PSC**	*Feb. 20–Mar. 20*

occur three or four times a year, can cause our plans to go awry. However, this is an excellent time to reflect on the past. Intuition is high during these periods and coincidences can be extraordinary.

When Mercury is retrograde, astrologers advise us to be flexible, allow extra time for travel, and avoid signing contracts. It's helpful to review projects and plans because we may see them in a new perspective at these times, but it's best to wait until Mercury is direct again to make any final decisions.

In 2006, Mercury will be retrograde from March 2–25, July 4–29, and October 28–November 18. *–Celeste Longacre*

Gardening by the Moon's Sign

■ The placement of the planets through the signs of the zodiac is not the same in astrology and astronomy. The *astrological* placement of the Moon, by sign, is given in the table below. Its *astronomical*, or actual, placement is given in the **Left-Hand Calendar Pages, 96–122.**

For planting, the most fertile Moon signs are the three water signs: Cancer, Scorpio, and Pisces. Good second choices are Taurus, Virgo, and Capricorn. Weeding and plowing are best done when the Moon occupies Aries, Gemini, Leo, Sagittarius, or Aquarius. Insect pests can also be handled

at these times. Transplanting and grafting are best done under a Cancer, Scorpio, or Pisces Moon.

Pruning is best done under an Aries, Leo, or Sagittarius Moon, with growth encouraged during waxing (from the day of new to the day of full Moon) and discouraged during waning (from the day after full to the day before new Moon). For the dates of the Moon's phases, see **pages 96–122.**

Clean out the garden shed when the Moon occupies Virgo. Build or repair fences and permanent garden beds when Capricorn predominates.

Moon's Place in the Astrological Zodiac 2005–06

	Nov.	Dec.	Jan.	Feb.	Mar.	Apr.	May	June	July	Aug.	Sept.	Oct.	Nov.	Dec.
1	SCO	SAG	AQU	PSC	ARI	TAU	GEM	LEO	VIR	SCO	SAG	CAP	PSC	ARI
2	SCO	SAG	AQU	ARI	ARI	GEM	CAN	LEO	VIR	SCO	CAP	AQU	PSC	TAU
3	SAG	CAP	PSC	ARI	TAU	GEM	CAN	VIR	LIB	SCO	CAP	AQU	ARI	TAU
4	SAG	CAP	PSC	TAU	TAU	CAN	LEO	VIR	LIB	SAG	CAP	PSC	ARI	GEM
5	SAG	AQU	ARI	TAU	GEM	CAN	LEO	LIB	SCO	SAG	AQU	PSC	TAU	GEM
6	CAP	AQU	ARI	GEM	GEM	CAN	VIR	LIB	SCO	CAP	AQU	ARI	TAU	CAN
7	CAP	PSC	ARI	GEM	GEM	LEO	VIR	LIB	SAG	CAP	PSC	ARI	GEM	CAN
8	AQU	PSC	TAU	GEM	CAN	LEO	VIR	SCO	SAG	AQU	PSC	TAU	GEM	LEO
9	AQU	ARI	TAU	CAN	CAN	VIR	LIB	SCO	SAG	AQU	ARI	TAU	CAN	LEO
10	PSC	ARI	GEM	CAN	LEO	VIR	LIB	SAG	CAP	PSC	ARI	GEM	CAN	LEO
11	PSC	TAU	GEM	LEO	LEO	VIR	SCO	SAG	CAP	PSC	TAU	GEM	LEO	VIR
12	ARI	TAU	CAN	LEO	LEO	LIB	SCO	CAP	AQU	ARI	TAU	CAN	LEO	VIR
13	ARI	TAU	CAN	LEO	VIR	LIB	SCO	CAP	AQU	ARI	GEM	CAN	VIR	LIB
14	TAU	GEM	CAN	VIR	VIR	SCO	SAG	AQU	PSC	TAU	GEM	CAN	VIR	LIB
15	TAU	GEM	LEO	VIR	LIB	SCO	SAG	AQU	PSC	TAU	CAN	LEO	VIR	LIB
16	GEM	CAN	LEO	LIB	LIB	SAG	CAP	AQU	ARI	GEM	CAN	LEO	LIB	SCO
17	GEM	CAN	VIR	LIB	LIB	SAG	CAP	PSC	ARI	GEM	LEO	VIR	LIB	SCO
18	GEM	LEO	VIR	LIB	SCO	SAG	AQU	PSC	TAU	GEM	LEO	VIR	SCO	SAG
19	CAN	LEO	VIR	SCO	SCO	CAP	AQU	ARI	TAU	CAN	LEO	VIR	SCO	SAG
20	CAN	LEO	LIB	SCO	SAG	CAP	PSC	ARI	GEM	CAN	VIR	LIB	SCO	SAG
21	LEO	VIR	LIB	SAG	SAG	AQU	PSC	TAU	GEM	LEO	VIR	LIB	SAG	CAP
22	LEO	VIR	SCO	SAG	SAG	AQU	ARI	TAU	CAN	LEO	LIB	SCO	SAG	CAP
23	LEO	LIB	SCO	CAP	CAP	PSC	ARI	GEM	CAN	LEO	LIB	SCO	CAP	AQU
24	VIR	LIB	SCO	CAP	CAP	PSC	ARI	GEM	CAN	VIR	LIB	SCO	CAP	AQU
25	VIR	LIB	SAG	AQU	AQU	ARI	TAU	CAN	LEO	VIR	SCO	SAG	CAP	PSC
26	LIB	SCO	SAG	AQU	AQU	ARI	TAU	CAN	LEO	LIB	SCO	SAG	AQU	PSC
27	LIB	SCO	CAP	PSC	PSC	TAU	GEM	CAN	VIR	LIB	SAG	CAP	AQU	ARI
28	SCO	SAG	CAP	PSC	PSC	TAU	GEM	LEO	VIR	LIB	SAG	CAP	PSC	ARI
29	SCO	SAG	AQU	—	ARI	GEM	CAN	LEO	VIR	SCO	SAG	AQU	PSC	TAU
30	SCO	CAP	AQU	—	ARI	GEM	CAN	VIR	LIB	SCO	CAP	AQU	ARI	TAU
31	—	CAP	PSC	—	TAU	—	LEO	—	LIB	SAG	—	PSC	—	GEM

Outdoor Planting Table

■ The best time to plant flowers and vegetables that bear crops *above ground* is during the *light* of the Moon; that is, from the day the Moon is new to the day it is full. Flowering bulbs and vegetables that bear crops *below ground* should be planted during the *dark* of the Moon; that is, from the day after it is full to the day before it is new again. The Moon Favorable columns at right give these days, which are based on the Moon's phases for 2006 and the safe periods for planting in areas that receive frost. Consult **page 40** for dates of frosts and lengths of growing seasons. See the **Left-Hand Calendar Pages, 96–122,** for the exact days of the new and full Moons.

■ **Aboveground crops are marked ***

■ **(E) means early (L) means late**

■ **Map shades correspond to shades of date columns.**

* **Barley**	
* **Beans**	**(E)**
	(L)
Beets	**(E)**
	(L)
* **Broccoli plants**	**(E)**
	(L)
* **Brussels sprouts**	
* **Cabbage plants**	
Carrots	**(E)**
	(L)
* **Cauliflower plants**	**(E)**
	(L)
* **Celery plants**	**(E)**
	(L)
* **Collards**	**(E)**
	(L)
* **Corn, sweet**	**(E)**
	(L)
* **Cucumbers**	
* **Eggplant plants**	
* **Endive**	**(E)**
	(L)
* **Flowers**	
* **Kale**	**(E)**
	(L)
Leek plants	
* **Lettuce**	
* **Muskmelons**	
Onion sets	
* **Parsley**	
Parsnips	
* **Peas**	**(E)**
	(L)
* **Pepper plants**	
Potatoes	
* **Pumpkins**	
Radishes	**(E)**
	(L)
* **Spinach**	**(E)**
	(L)
* **Squashes**	
Sweet potatoes	
* **Swiss chard**	
* **Tomato plants**	
Turnips	**(E)**
	(L)
* **Watermelons**	
* **Wheat, spring**	
* **Wheat, winter**	

Planting Dates	Moon Favorable	Planting Dates	Moon Favorable	Planting Dates	Moon Favorable	Planting Dates	Moon Favorable
2/15-3/7	2/27-3/7	3/15-4/7	3/29-4/7	5/15-6/21	5/27-6/11	8/1-30	6/1-11, 6/25-30
3/15-4/7	3/29-4/7	4/15-30	4/27-30	5/7-6/21	5/7-13, 5/27-6/11	5/30-6/15	5/30-6/11
8/7-31	8/7-9, 8/23-31	7/1-21	7/1-10	6/15-7/15	6/25-7/10	–	–
2/7-28	2/13-26	3/15-4/3	3/15-28	5/1-15	5/14-15	5/25-6/10	5/25-26
9/1-30	9/8-21	8/15-31	8/15-22	7/15-8/15	7/15-24, 8/10-15	6/15-7/8	6/15-24
2/15-3/15	2/27-3/14	3/7-31	3/7-14, 3/29-31	5/15-31	5/27-31	6/1-25	6/1-11, 6/25
9/7-30	9/7, 9/22-30	8/1-20	8/1-9	6/15-7/7	6/25-7/7	–	–
2/11-3/20	2/11-12, 2/27-3/14	3/7-4/15	3/7-14, 3/29-4/13	5/15-31	5/27-31	6/1-25	6/1-11, 6/25
2/11-3/20	2/11-12, 2/27-3/14	3/7-4/15	3/7-14, 3/29-4/13	5/15-31	5/27-31	6/1-25	6/1-11, 6/25
2/15-3/7	2/15-26	3/7-31	3/15-28	5/15-31	5/15-26	5/25-6/10	5/25-26
8/1-9/7	8/10-22	7/7-31	7/11-24	6/15-7/21	6/15-24, 7/11-21	6/15-7/8	6/15-24
2/15-3/7	2/27-3/7	3/15-4/7	3/29-4/7	5/15-31	5/27-31	6/1-25	6/1-11, 6/25
8/7-31	8/7-9, 8/23-31	7/1-8/7	7/1-10, 7/25-8/7	6/15-7/21	6/25-7/10	6/1-30	6/1-11, 6/25-30
2/15-28	2/27-28	3/7-31	3/7-14, 3/29-31	5/15-6/30	5/27-6/11, 6/25-30	6/1-30	6/1-11, 6/25-30
9/15-30	9/22-30	8/15-9/7	8/23-9/7	7/15-8/15	7/25-8/9	–	–
2/11-3/20	2/11-12, 2/27-3/14	3/7-4/7	3/7-14, 3/29-4/7	5/15-31	5/27-31	6/1-25	6/1-11, 6/25
9/7-30	9/7, 9/22-30	8/15-31	8/23-31	7/1-8/7	7/1-10, 7/25-8/7	–	–
3/15-31	3/29-31	4/1-17	4/1-13	5/10-6/15	5/10-13, 5/27-6/11	5/30-6/20	5/30-6/11
8/7-31	8/7-9, 8/23-31	7/7-31	7/7-10	6/15-30	6/25-30	–	–
3/7-4/15	3/7-14, 3/29-4/13	4/7-5/15	4/7-13, 4/27-5/13	5/7-6/20	5/7-13, 5/27-6/11	5/30-6/15	5/30-6/11
3/7-4/15	3/7-14, 3/29-4/13	4/7-5/15	4/7-13, 4/27-5/13	6/1-30	6/1-11, 6/25-30	6/15-30	6/25-30
2/15-3/20	2/27-3/14	4/7-5/15	4/7-13, 4/27-5/13	5/15-31	5/27-31	6/1-25	6/1-11, 6/25
8/15-9/7	8/23-9/7	7/15-8/15	7/25-8/9	6/7-30	6/7-11, 6/25-30	–	–
3/15-4/7	3/29-4/7	4/15-30	4/27-30	5/7-6/21	5/7-13, 5/27-6/11	6/1-30	6/1-11, 6/25-30
2/11-3/20	2/11-12, 2/27-3/14	3/7-4/7	3/7-14, 3/29-4/7	5/15-31	5/27-31	6/1-15	6/1-11
9/7-30	9/7, 9/22-30	8/15-31	8/23-31	7/1-8/7	7/1-10, 7/25-8/7	6/25-7/15	6/25-7/10
2/15-4/15	2/15-26, 3/15-28, 4/14-15	3/7-4/7	3/15-28	5/15-31	5/15-26	6/1-25	6/12-24
2/15-3/7	2/27-3/7	3/1-31	3/1-14, 3/29-31	5/15-6/30	5/27-6/11, 6/25-30	6/1-30	6/1-11, 6/25-30
3/15-4/7	3/29-4/7	4/15-5/7	4/27-5/7	5/15-6/30	5/27-6/11, 6/25-30	6/1-30	6/1-11, 6/25-30
2/1-28	2/13-26	3/1-31	3/15-28	5/15-6/7	5/15-26	6/1-25	6/12-24
2/20-3/15	2/27-3/14	3/1-31	3/1-14, 3/29-31	5/15-31	5/27-31	6/1-15	6/1-11
1/15-2/4	1/15-28	3/7-31	3/15-28	4/1-30	4/14-26	5/10-31	5/14-26
1/15-2/7	1/29-2/7	3/7-31	3/7-14, 3/29-31	4/15-5/7	4/27-5/7	5/15-31	5/27-31
9/15-30	9/22-30	8/7-31	8/7-9, 8/23-31	7/15-31	7/25-31	7/10-25	7/10, 7/25
3/1-20	3/1-14	4/1-30	4/1-13, 4/27-30	5/15-6/30	5/27-6/11, 6/25-30	6/1-30	6/1-11, 6/25-30
2/10-28	2/13-26	4/1-30	4/14-26	5/1-31	5/14-26	6/1-25	6/12-24
3/7-20	3/7-14	4/23-5/15	4/27-5/13	5/15-31	5/27-31	6/1-30	6/1-11, 6/25-30
1/21-3/1	1/21-28, 2/13-26	3/7-31	3/15-28	4/15-30	4/15-26	5/15-6/5	5/15-26
10/1-21	10/7-21	9/7-30	9/8-21	8/15-31	8/15-22	7/10-31	7/11-24
2/7-3/15	2/7-12, 2/27-3/14	3/15-4/20	3/29-4/13	5/15-31	5/27-31	6/1-25	6/1-11, 6/25
10/1-21	10/1-6	8/1-9/15	8/1-9, 8/23-9/7	7/17-9/7	7/25-8/9, 8/23-9/7	7/20-8/5	7/25-8/5
3/15-4/15	3/29-4/13	4/15-30	4/27-30	5/15-6/15	5/27-6/11	6/1-30	6/1-11, 6/25-30
3/23-4/6	3/23-28	4/21-5/9	4/21-26	5/15-6/15	5/15-26, 6/12-15	6/1-25	6/12-24
2/7-3/15	2/7-12, 2/27-3/14	3/15-4/15	3/29-4/13	5/1-31	5/1-13, 5/27-31	5/15-31	5/27-31
3/7-20	3/7-14	4/7-30	4/7-13, 4/27-30	5/15-31	5/27-31	6/1-15	6/1-11
1/20-2/15	1/20-28, 2/13-15	3/15-31	3/15-28	4/7-30	4/14-26	5/10-31	5/14-26
9/1-10/15	9/8-21, 10/7-15	8/1-20	8/10-20	7/1-8/15	7/11-24, 8/10-15	–	–
3/15-4/7	3/29-4/7	4/15-5/7	4/27-5/7	5/15-6/30	5/27-6/11, 6/25-30	6/1-30	6/1-11, 6/25-30
2/15-28	2/27-28	3/1-20	3/1-14	4/7-30	4/7-13, 4/27-30	5/15-6/10	5/27-6/10
10/15-12/7	10/22-11/5, 11/20-12/4	9/15-10/20	9/22-10/6	8/11-9/15	8/23-9/7	8/5-30	8/5-9, 8/23-30

Tide Corrections

■ Many factors affect the times and heights of the tides: the coastal configuration, the time of the Moon's southing (crossing the meridian), and the Moon's phase. The High Tide column on the **Left-Hand Calendar Pages, 96–122,** lists the times of high tide at Commonwealth Pier in Boston Harbor. The heights of some of these tides, reckoned from Mean Lower Low Water, are given on the **Right-Hand Calendar Pages, 97–123.** Use this table to calculate the approximate times and heights of high tide at the places shown. Apply the time difference to the times of high tide at Boston **(pages 96–122)** and the height difference to the heights at Boston **(pages 97–123).**

E X A M P L E :

■ The conversion of the times and heights of the tides at Boston to those at Cape Fear, North Carolina, is given below:

High tide at Boston	11:45 A.M.
Correction for Cape Fear	−3 55 hrs.
High tide at Cape Fear	7:50 A.M.
Tide height at Boston	11.6 ft.
Correction for Cape Fear	−5.0 ft.
Tide height at Cape Fear	6.6 ft.

Estimations derived from this table are *not* meant to be used for navigation. *The Old Farmer's Almanac* accepts no responsibility for errors or any consequences ensuing from the use of this table.

Coastal Site	Difference: Time (h. m.)	Height (ft.)
Canada		
Alberton, PE	*−5 45	−7.5
Charlottetown, PE	*−0 45	−3.5
Halifax, NS.	−3 23	−4.5
North Sydney, NS	−3 15	−6.5
Saint John, NB	+0 30	+15.0
St. John's, NL	−4 00	−6.5
Yarmouth, NS	−0 40	+3.0
Maine		
Bar Harbor	−0 34	+0.9
Belfast	−0 20	+0.4
Boothbay Harbor	−0 18	−0.8
Chebeague Island	−0 16	−0.6
Eastport	−0 28	+8.4
Kennebunkport	+0 04	−1.0
Machias	−0 28	+2.8
Monhegan Island	−0 25	−0.8
Old Orchard	0 00	−0.8
Portland	−0 12	−0.6
Rockland	−0 28	+0.1
Stonington	−0 30	+0.1
York	−0 09	−1.0
New Hampshire		
Hampton	+0 02	−1.3
Portsmouth	+0 11	−1.5
Rye Beach	−0 09	−0.9
Massachusetts		
Annisquam	−0 02	−1.1
Beverly Farms.	0 00	−0.5
Boston	0 00	0.0

Coastal Site	Difference: Time (h. m.)	Height (ft.)
Cape Cod Canal		
East Entrance	−0 01	−0.8
West Entrance	−2 16	−5.9
Chatham Outer Coast . .	+0 30	−2.8
Inside	+1 54	**0.4
Cohasset	+0 02	−0.07
Cotuit Highlands.	+1 15	**0.3
Dennis Port	+1 01	**0.4
Duxbury–Gurnet Point . .	+0 02	−0.3
Fall River	−3 03	−5.0
Gloucester	−0 03	−0.8
Hingham	+0 07	0.0
Hull	+0 03	−0.2
Hyannis Port	+1 01	**0.3
Magnolia–Manchester . .	−0 02	−0.7
Marblehead	−0 02	−0.4
Marion	−3 22	−5.4
Monument Beach	−3 08	−5.4
Nahant	−0 01	−0.5
Nantasket	+0 04	−0.1
Nantucket	+0 56	**0.3
Nauset Beach	+0 30	**0.6
New Bedford.	−3 24	−5.7
Newburyport.	+0 19	−1.8
Oak Bluffs	+0 30	**0.2
Onset–R.R. Bridge	−2 16	−5.9
Plymouth	+0 05	0.0
Provincetown	+0 14	−0.4
Revere Beach	−0 01	−0.3
Rockport	−0 08	−1.0
Salem	0 00	−0.5

Coastal Site	Difference: Time (h. m.)	Height (ft.)
Scituate	−0 05	−0.7
Wareham	−3 09	−5.3
Wellfleet	+0 12	+0.5
West Falmouth	−3 10	−5.4
Westport Harbor	−3 22	−6.4
Woods Hole		
Little Harbor	−2 50	**0.2
Oceanographic Institute	−3 07	**0.2
Rhode Island		
Bristol	−3 24	−5.3
Narragansett Pier	−3 42	−6.2
Newport.	−3 34	−5.9
Point Judith	−3 41	−6.3
Providence	−3 20	−4.8
Sakonnet	−3 44	−5.6
Watch Hill	−2 50	−6.8
Connecticut		
Bridgeport.	+0 01	−2.6
Madison.	−0 22	−2.3
New Haven	−0 11	−3.2
New London	−1 54	−6.7
Norwalk.	+0 01	−2.2
Old Lyme		
Highway Bridge.	−0 30	−6.2
Stamford	+0 01	−2.2
Stonington.	−2 27	−6.6
New York		
Coney Island	−3 33	−4.9
Fire Island Light	−2 43	**0.1
Long Beach.	−3 11	−5.7
Montauk Harbor	−2 19	−7.4
New York City–Battery. .	−2 43	−5.0
Oyster Bay	+0 04	−1.8
Port Chester	−0 09	−2.2
Port Washington	−0 01	−2.1
Sag Harbor	−0 55	−6.8
Southampton		
Shinnecock Inlet	−4 20	**0.2
Willets Point	0 00	−2.3
New Jersey		
Asbury Park	−4 04	−5.3
Atlantic City	−3 56	−5.5
Bay Head–Sea Girt . . .	−4 04	−5.3
Beach Haven.	−1 43	**0.24
Cape May	−3 28	−5.3
Ocean City	−3 06	−5.9
Sandy Hook.	−3 30	−5.0
Seaside Park	−4 03	−5.4
Pennsylvania		
Philadelphia	+2 40	−3.5
Delaware		
Cape Henlopen	−2 48	−5.3

Coastal Site	Difference: Time (h. m.)	Height (ft.)
Rehoboth Beach	−3 37	−5.7
Wilmington.	+1 56	−3.8
Maryland		
Annapolis	+6 23	−8.5
Baltimore	+7 59	−8.3
Cambridge.	+5 05	−7.8
Havre de Grace	+11 21	−7.7
Point No Point.	+2 28	−8.1
Prince Frederick		
Plum Point	+4 25	−8.5
Virginia		
Cape Charles.	−2 20	−7.0
Hampton Roads	−2 02	−6.9
Norfolk	−2 06	−6.6
Virginia Beach	−4 00	−6.0
Yorktown.	−2 13	−7.0
North Carolina		
Cape Fear	−3 55	−5.0
Cape Lookout	−4 28	−5.7
Currituck.	−4 10	−5.8
Hatteras		
Inlet.	−4 03	−7.4
Kitty Hawk.	−4 14	−6.2
Ocean	−4 26	−6.0
South Carolina		
Charleston.	−3 22	−4.3
Georgetown.	−1 48	**0.36
Hilton Head.	−3 22	−2.9
Myrtle Beach	−3 49	−4.4
St. Helena		
Harbor Entrance.	−3 15	−3.4
Georgia		
Jekyll Island	−3 46	−2.9
St. Simon's Island.	−2 50	−2.9
Savannah Beach		
River Entrance	−3 14	−5.5
Tybee Light	−3 22	−2.7
Florida		
Cape Canaveral.	−3 59	−6.0
Daytona Beach	−3 28	−5.3
Fort Lauderdale	−2 50	−7.2
Fort Pierce Inlet	−3 32	−6.9
Jacksonville		
Railroad Bridge	−6 55	**0.1
Miami Harbor Entrance	−3 18	−7.0
St. Augustine.	−2 55	−4.9

*Varies widely; accurate within only 1½ hours. Consult local tide tables for precise times and heights.

**Where the difference in the Height column is so marked, height at Boston should be multiplied by this ratio.

Tidal Glossary

Apogean Tide: A monthly tide of decreased range that occurs when the Moon is at apogee (farthest from Earth).

Diurnal Tide: A tide with one high water and one low water in a tidal day of approximately 24 hours.

Mean Lower Low Water: The arithmetic mean of the lesser of a daily pair of low waters, observed over a specific 19-year cycle called the National Tidal Datum Epoch.

Neap Tide: A tide of decreased range that occurs twice a month, when the Moon is in quadrature (during its first and last quarters, when the Sun and the Moon are at right angles to each other relative to Earth).

Perigean Tide: A monthly tide of increased range that occurs when the Moon is at perigee (closest to Earth).

Semidiurnal Tide: A tide with one high water and one low water every half day. East Coast tides, for example, are semidiurnal, with two highs and two lows during a tidal day of approximately 24 hours.

Spring Tide: A tide of increased range that occurs at times of syzygy each month. Named not for the season of spring but from the German *springen* ("to leap up"), a spring tide also brings a lower low water.

Syzygy: The nearly straight-line configuration that occurs twice a month, when the Sun and the Moon are in conjunction (on the same side of Earth at the new Moon) and when they are in opposition (on opposite sides of Earth at the full Moon). In both cases, the gravitational effects of the Sun and the Moon reinforce each other, and tidal range is increased.

Vanishing Tide: A mixed tide of considerable inequality in the two highs and two lows, so that the lower high (or higher low) may become indistinct or appear to vanish.

Time Corrections

■ Times for Sun and Moon rise and set, bright star transits, and planetary observations are given for Boston on **pages 96-122, 79,** and **80-81,** respectively. Use the Key Letter shown to the right of each time on those pages with this table to find the number of minutes (adjusted for location and time zone) that you must add to or subtract from Boston time to get the correct time for your city. (Because of complex calculations for different locales, times may not be precise to the minute.) If your city is not listed, use the figures for the city closest to you in latitude and longitude. Boston's latitude is 42° 22' and its longitude is 71° 03'. Canadian cities are at the end of the table. For information on the use of Key Letters and this table, see **How to Use This Almanac, page 92.**

TIME ZONES: Codes represent *standard time.* Atlantic is −1, Eastern is 0, Central is 1, Mountain is 2, Pacific is 3, Alaska is 4, and Hawaii-Aleutian is 5.

State	City	North Latitude °	'	West Longitude °	'	Time Zone Code	A (min.)	B (min.)	C (min.)	D (min.)	E (min.)
AK	Anchorage	61	10	149	59	4	−46	+27	+71	+122	+171
AK	Cordova	60	33	145	45	4	−55	+13	+55	+103	+149
AK	Fairbanks	64	48	147	51	4	−127	+ 2	+61	+131	+205
AK	Juneau	58	18	134	25	4	−76	−23	+10	+49	+86
AK	Ketchikan	55	21	131	39	4	−62	−25	0	+29	+56
AK	Kodiak	57	47	152	24	4	0	+49	+82	+120	+154
AL	Birmingham	33	31	86	49	1	+30	+15	+ 3	−10	−20
AL	Decatur	34	36	86	59	1	+27	+14	+ 4	− 7	−17
AL	Mobile	30	42	88	3	1	+42	+23	+ 8	− 8	−22
AL	Montgomery	32	23	86	19	1	+31	+14	+ 1	−13	−25
AR	Fort Smith	35	23	94	25	1	+55	+43	+33	+22	+14
AR	Little Rock	34	45	92	17	1	+48	+35	+25	+13	+ 4
AR	Texarkana	33	26	94	3	1	+59	+44	+32	+18	+ 8
AZ	Flagstaff	35	12	111	39	2	+64	+52	+42	+31	+22
AZ	Phoenix	33	27	112	4	2	+71	+56	+44	+30	+20
AZ	Tucson	32	13	110	58	2	+70	+53	+40	+24	+12
AZ	Yuma	32	43	114	37	2	+83	+67	+54	+40	+28
CA	Bakersfield	35	23	119	1	3	+33	+21	+12	+ 1	− 7
CA	Barstow	34	54	117	1	3	+27	+14	+ 4	− 7	−16
CA	Fresno	36	44	119	47	3	+32	+22	+15	+ 6	0
CA	Los Angeles–Pasadena–Santa Monica	34	3	118	14	3	+34	+20	+ 9	− 3	−13
CA	Palm Springs	33	49	116	32	3	+28	+13	+ 1	−12	−22
CA	Redding	40	35	122	24	3	+31	+27	+25	+22	+19
CA	Sacramento	38	35	121	30	3	+34	+27	+21	+15	+10
CA	San Diego	32	43	117	9	3	+33	+17	+ 4	− 9	−21
CA	San Francisco–Oakland–San Jose	37	47	122	25	3	+40	+31	+25	+18	+12
CO	Craig	40	31	107	33	2	+32	+28	+25	+22	+20
CO	Denver–Boulder	39	44	104	59	2	+24	+19	+15	+11	+ 7
CO	Grand Junction	39	4	108	33	2	+40	+34	+29	+24	+20
CO	Pueblo	38	16	104	37	2	+27	+20	+14	+ 7	+ 2
CO	Trinidad	37	10	104	31	2	+30	+21	+13	+ 5	0
CT	Bridgeport	41	11	73	11	0	+12	+10	+ 8	+ 6	+ 4
CT	Hartford–New Britain	41	46	72	41	0	+ 8	+ 7	+ 6	+ 5	+ 4
CT	New Haven	41	18	72	56	0	+11	+ 8	+ 7	+ 5	+ 4
CT	New London	41	22	72	6	0	+ 7	+ 5	+ 4	+ 2	+ 1
CT	Norwalk–Stamford	41	7	73	22	0	+13	+10	+ 9	+ 7	+ 5
CT	Waterbury–Meriden	41	33	73	3	0	+10	+ 9	+ 7	+ 6	+ 5
DC	Washington	38	54	77	1	0	+35	+28	+23	+18	+13
DE	Wilmington	39	45	75	33	0	+26	+21	+18	+13	+10

State	City	North Latitude °	'	West Longitude °	'	Time Zone Code	A (min.)	B (min.)	C (min.)	D (min.)	E (min.)
FL	Fort Myers	26	38	81	52	0	+87	+63	+44	+21	+ 4
FL	Jacksonville	30	20	81	40	0	+77	+58	+43	+25	+11
FL	Miami	25	47	80	12	0	+88	+57	+37	+14	− 3
FL	Orlando	28	32	81	22	0	+80	+59	+42	+22	+ 6
FL	Pensacola	30	25	87	13	1	+39	+20	+ 5	−12	−26
FL	St. Petersburg	27	46	82	39	0	+87	+65	+47	+26	+10
FL	Tallahassee	30	27	84	17	0	+87	+68	+53	+35	+22
FL	Tampa	27	57	82	27	0	+86	+64	+46	+25	+ 9
FL	West Palm Beach	26	43	80	3	0	+79	+55	+36	+14	− 2
GA	Atlanta	33	45	84	24	0	+79	+65	+53	+40	+30
GA	Augusta	33	28	81	58	0	+70	+55	+44	+30	+19
GA	Macon	32	50	83	38	0	+79	+63	+50	+36	+24
GA	Savannah	32	5	81	6	0	+70	+54	+40	+25	+13
HI	Hilo	19	44	155	5	5	+94	+62	+37	+ 7	−15
HI	Honolulu	21	18	157	52	5	+102	+72	+48	+19	− 1
HI	Lanai City	20	50	156	55	5	+99	+69	+44	+15	− 6
HI	Lihue	21	59	159	23	5	+107	+77	+54	+26	+ 5
IA	Davenport	41	32	90	35	1	+20	+19	+17	+16	+15
IA	Des Moines	41	35	93	37	1	+32	+31	+30	+28	+27
IA	Dubuque	42	30	90	41	1	+17	+18	+18	+18	+18
IA	Waterloo	42	30	92	20	1	+24	+24	+24	+25	+25
ID	Boise	43	37	116	12	2	+55	+58	+60	+62	+64
ID	Lewiston	46	25	117	1	3	−12	− 3	+ 2	+10	+17
ID	Pocatello	42	52	112	27	2	+43	+44	+45	+46	+46
IL	Cairo	37	0	89	11	1	+29	+20	+12	+ 4	− 2
IL	Chicago–Oak Park	41	52	87	38	1	+ 7	+ 6	+ 6	+ 5	+ 4
IL	Danville	40	8	87	37	1	+13	+ 9	+ 6	+ 2	0
IL	Decatur	39	51	88	57	1	+19	+15	+11	+ 7	+ 4
IL	Peoria	40	42	89	36	1	+19	+16	+14	+11	+ 9
IL	Springfield	39	48	89	39	1	+22	+18	+14	+10	+ 6
IN	Fort Wayne	41	4	85	9	0	+60	+58	+56	+54	+52
IN	Gary	41	36	87	20	1	+ 7	+ 6	+ 4	+ 3	+ 2
IN	Indianapolis	39	46	86	10	0	+69	+64	+60	+56	+52
IN	Muncie	40	12	85	23	0	+64	+60	+57	+53	+50
IN	South Bend	41	41	86	15	0	+62	+61	+60	+59	+58
IN	Terre Haute	39	28	87	24	0	+74	+69	+65	+60	+56
KS	Fort Scott	37	50	94	42	1	+49	+41	+34	+27	+21
KS	Liberal	37	3	100	55	1	+76	+66	+59	+51	+44
KS	Oakley	39	8	100	51	1	+69	+63	+59	+53	+49
KS	Salina	38	50	97	37	1	+57	+51	+46	+40	+35
KS	Topeka	39	3	95	40	1	+49	+43	+38	+32	+28
KS	Wichita	37	42	97	20	1	+60	+51	+45	+37	+31
KY	Lexington–Frankfort	38	3	84	30	0	+67	+59	+53	+46	+41
KY	Louisville	38	15	85	46	0	+72	+64	+58	+52	+46
LA	Alexandria	31	18	92	27	1	+58	+40	+26	+ 9	− 3
LA	Baton Rouge	30	27	91	11	1	+55	+36	+21	+ 3	−10
LA	Lake Charles	30	14	93	13	1	+64	+44	+29	+11	− 2
LA	Monroe	32	30	92	7	1	+53	+37	+24	+ 9	− 1
LA	New Orleans	29	57	90	4	1	+52	+32	+16	− 1	−15
LA	Shreveport	32	31	93	45	1	+60	+44	+31	+16	+ 4
MA	Brockton	42	5	71	1	0	0	0	0	0	− 1
MA	Fall River–New Bedford	41	42	71	9	0	+ 2	+ 1	0	0	− 1
MA	Lawrence–Lowell	42	42	71	10	0	0	0	0	0	+ 1
MA	Pittsfield	42	27	73	15	0	+ 8	+ 8	+ 8	+ 8	+ 8
MA	Springfield–Holyoke	42	6	72	36	0	+ 6	+ 6	+ 6	+ 5	+ 5
MA	Worcester	42	16	71	48	0	+ 3	+ 2	+ 2	+ 2	+ 2
MD	Baltimore	39	17	76	37	0	+32	+26	+22	+17	+13

State	City	North Latitude °	'	West Longitude °	'	Time Zone Code	A (min.)	B (min.)	C (min.)	D (min.)	E (min.)
MD	Hagerstown	39	39	77	43	0	+35	+30	+26	+22	+18
MD	Salisbury	38	22	75	36	0	+31	+23	+18	+11	+ 6
ME	Augusta	44	19	69	46	0	−12	− 8	− 5	− 1	0
ME	Bangor	44	48	68	46	0	−18	−13	− 9	− 5	− 1
ME	Eastport	44	54	67	0	0	−26	−20	−16	−11	− 8
ME	Ellsworth	44	33	68	25	0	−18	−14	−10	− 6	− 3
ME	Portland	43	40	70	15	0	− 8	− 5	− 3	− 1	0
ME	Presque Isle	46	41	68	1	0	−29	−19	−12	− 4	+ 2
MI	Cheboygan	45	39	84	29	0	+40	+47	+53	+59	+64
MI	Detroit–Dearborn	42	20	83	3	0	+47	+47	+47	+47	+47
MI	Flint	43	1	83	41	0	+47	+49	+50	+51	+52
MI	Ironwood	46	27	90	9	1	0	+ 9	+15	+23	+29
MI	Jackson	42	15	84	24	0	+53	+53	+53	+52	+52
MI	Kalamazoo	42	17	85	35	0	+58	+57	+57	+57	+57
MI	Lansing	42	44	84	33	0	+52	+53	+53	+54	+54
MI	St. Joseph	42	5	86	26	0	+61	+61	+60	+60	+59
MI	Traverse City	44	46	85	38	0	+49	+54	+57	+62	+65
MN	Albert Lea	43	39	93	22	1	+24	+26	+28	+31	+33
MN	Bemidji	47	28	94	53	1	+14	+26	+34	+44	+52
MN	Duluth	46	47	92	6	1	+ 6	+16	+23	+31	+38
MN	Minneapolis–St. Paul	44	59	93	16	1	+18	+24	+28	+33	+37
MN	Ortonville	45	19	96	27	1	+30	+36	+40	+46	+51
MO	Jefferson City	38	34	92	10	1	+36	+29	+24	+18	+13
MO	Joplin	37	6	94	30	1	+50	+41	+33	+25	+18
MO	Kansas City	39	1	94	20	1	+44	+37	+33	+27	+23
MO	Poplar Bluff	36	46	90	24	1	+35	+25	+17	+ 8	+ 1
MO	St. Joseph	39	46	94	50	1	+43	+38	+35	+30	+27
MO	St. Louis	38	37	90	12	1	+28	+21	+16	+10	+ 5
MO	Springfield	37	13	93	18	1	+45	+36	+29	+20	+14
MS	Biloxi	30	24	88	53	1	+46	+27	+11	− 5	−19
MS	Jackson	32	18	90	11	1	+46	+30	+17	+ 1	−10
MS	Meridian	32	22	88	42	1	+40	+24	+11	− 4	−15
MS	Tupelo	34	16	88	34	1	+35	+21	+10	− 2	−11
MT	Billings	45	47	108	30	2	+16	+23	+29	+35	+40
MT	Butte	46	1	112	32	2	+31	+39	+45	+52	+57
MT	Glasgow	48	12	106	38	2	− 1	+11	+21	+32	+42
MT	Great Falls	47	30	111	17	2	+20	+31	+39	+49	+58
MT	Helena	46	36	112	2	2	+27	+36	+43	+51	+57
MT	Miles City	46	25	105	51	2	+ 3	+11	+18	+26	+32
NC	Asheville	35	36	82	33	0	+67	+55	+46	+35	+27
NC	Charlotte	35	14	80	51	0	+61	+49	+39	+28	+19
NC	Durham	36	0	78	55	0	+51	+40	+31	+21	+13
NC	Greensboro	36	4	79	47	0	+54	+43	+35	+25	+17
NC	Raleigh	35	47	78	38	0	+51	+39	+30	+20	+12
NC	Wilmington	34	14	77	55	0	+52	+38	+27	+15	+ 5
ND	Bismarck	46	48	100	47	1	+41	+50	+58	+66	+73
ND	Fargo	46	53	96	47	1	+24	+34	+42	+50	+57
ND	Grand Forks	47	55	97	3	1	+21	+33	+43	+53	+62
ND	Minot	48	14	101	18	1	+36	+50	+59	+71	+81
ND	Williston	48	9	103	37	1	+46	+59	+69	+80	+90
NE	Grand Island	40	55	98	21	1	+53	+51	+49	+46	+44
NE	Lincoln	40	49	96	41	1	+47	+44	+42	+39	+37
NE	North Platte	41	8	100	46	1	+62	+60	+58	+56	+54
NE	Omaha	41	16	95	56	1	+43	+40	+39	+37	+36
NH	Berlin	44	28	71	11	0	− 7	− 3	0	+ 3	+ 7
NH	Keene	42	56	72	17	0	+ 2	+ 3	+ 4	+ 5	+ 6
NH	Manchester–Concord	42	59	71	28	0	0	0	+ 1	+ 2	+ 3

State	City	North Latitude °	'	West Longitude °	'	Time Zone Code	A (min.)	B (min.)	C (min.)	D (min.)	E (min.)
NH	Portsmouth............	43	5	70	45	0	– 4	– 2	– 1	0	0
NJ	Atlantic City..........	39	22	74	26	0	+23	+17	+13	+ 8	+ 4
NJ	Camden	39	57	75	7	0	+24	+19	+16	+12	+ 9
NJ	Cape May............	38	56	74	56	0	+26	+20	+15	+ 9	+ 5
NJ	Newark–East Orange...	40	44	74	10	0	+17	+14	+12	+ 9	+ 7
NJ	Paterson	40	55	74	10	0	+17	+14	+12	+ 9	+ 7
NJ	Trenton.............	40	13	74	46	0	+21	+17	+14	+11	+ 8
NM	Albuquerque	35	5	106	39	2	+45	+32	+22	+11	+ 2
NM	Gallup...............	35	32	108	45	2	+52	+40	+31	+20	+11
NM	Las Cruces	32	19	106	47	2	+53	+36	+23	+ 8	– 3
NM	Roswell..............	33	24	104	32	2	+41	+26	+14	0	–10
NM	Santa Fe.............	35	41	105	56	2	+40	+28	+19	+ 9	0
NV	Carson City–Reno	39	10	119	46	3	+25	+19	+14	+ 9	+ 5
NV	Elko	40	50	115	46	3	+ 3	0	– 1	– 3	– 5
NV	Las Vegas	36	10	115	9	3	+16	+ 4	– 3	–13	–20
NY	Albany	42	39	73	45	0	+ 9	+10	+10	+11	+11
NY	Binghamton	42	6	75	55	0	+20	+19	+19	+18	+18
NY	Buffalo	42	53	78	52	0	+29	+30	+30	+31	+32
NY	New York	40	45	74	0	0	+17	+14	+11	+ 9	+ 6
NY	Ogdensburg	44	42	75	30	0	+ 8	+13	+17	+21	+25
NY	Syracuse.............	43	3	76	9	0	+17	+19	+20	+21	+22
OH	Akron	41	5	81	31	0	+46	+43	+41	+39	+37
OH	Canton	40	48	81	23	0	+46	+43	+41	+38	+36
OH	Cincinnati–Hamilton...	39	6	84	31	0	+64	+58	+53	+48	+44
OH	Cleveland–Lakewood ..	41	30	81	42	0	+45	+43	+42	+40	+39
OH	Columbus............	39	57	83	1	0	+55	+51	+47	+43	+40
OH	Dayton	39	45	84	10	0	+61	+56	+52	+48	+44
OH	Toledo..............	41	39	83	33	0	+52	+50	+49	+48	+47
OH	Youngstown..........	41	6	80	39	0	+42	+40	+38	+36	+34
OK	Oklahoma City.......	35	28	97	31	1	+67	+55	+46	+35	+26
OK	Tulsa................	36	9	95	60	1	+59	+48	+40	+30	+22
OR	Eugene	44	3	123	6	3	+21	+24	+27	+30	+33
OR	Pendleton	45	40	118	47	3	– 1	+ 4	+10	+16	+21
OR	Portland	45	31	122	41	3	+14	+20	+25	+31	+36
OR	Salem	44	57	123	1	3	+17	+23	+27	+31	+35
PA	Allentown–Bethlehem ..	40	36	75	28	0	+23	+20	+17	+14	+12
PA	Erie.................	42	7	80	5	0	+36	+36	+35	+35	+35
PA	Harrisburg	40	16	76	53	0	+30	+26	+23	+19	+16
PA	Lancaster	40	2	76	18	0	+28	+24	+20	+17	+13
PA	Philadelphia–Chester...	39	57	75	9	0	+24	+19	+16	+12	+ 9
PA	Pittsburgh–McKeesport	40	26	80	0	0	+42	+38	+35	+32	+29
PA	Reading	40	20	75	56	0	+26	+22	+19	+16	+13
PA	Scranton–Wilkes-Barre..	41	25	75	40	0	+21	+19	+18	+16	+15
PA	York	39	58	76	43	0	+30	+26	+22	+18	+15
RI	Providence	41	50	71	25	0	+ 3	+ 2	+ 1	0	0
SC	Charleston	32	47	79	56	0	+64	+48	+36	+21	+10
SC	Columbia	34	0	81	2	0	+65	+51	+40	+27	+17
SC	Spartanburg	34	56	81	57	0	+66	+53	+43	+32	+23
SD	Aberdeen	45	28	98	29	1	+37	+44	+49	+54	+59
SD	Pierre	44	22	100	21	1	+49	+53	+56	+60	+63
SD	Rapid City	44	5	103	14	2	+ 2	+ 5	+ 8	+11	+13
SD	Sioux Falls...........	43	33	96	44	1	+38	+40	+42	+44	+46
TN	Chattanooga..........	35	3	85	19	1	+79	+67	+57	+45	+36
TN	Knoxville	35	58	83	55	0	+71	+60	+51	+41	+33
TN	Memphis.............	35	9	90	3	1	+38	+26	+16	+ 5	– 3
TN	Nashville	36	10	86	47	1	+22	+11	+ 3	– 6	–14
TX	Amarillo.............	35	12	101	50	1	+85	+73	+63	+52	+43

State/ Province City	North Latitude ° '	West Longitude ° '	Time Zone Code	Key Letters A (min.)	B (min.)	C (min.)	D (min.)	E (min.)
TX Austin	30 16	97 45	1	+82	+62	+47	+29	+15
TX Beaumont	30 5	94 6	1	+67	+48	+32	+14	0
TX Brownsville	25 54	97 30	1	+91	+66	+46	+23	+ 5
TX Corpus Christi	27 48	97 24	1	+86	+64	+46	+25	+ 9
TX Dallas–Fort Worth	32 47	96 48	1	+71	+55	+43	+28	+17
TX El Paso	31 45	106 29	2	+53	+35	+22	6	– 6
TX Galveston	29 18	94 48	1	+72	+52	+35	+16	+ 1
TX Houston	29 45	95 22	1	+73	+53	+37	+19	+ 5
TX McAllen	26 12	98 14	1	+93	+69	+49	+26	+ 9
TX San Antonio	29 25	98 30	1	+87	+66	+50	+31	+16
UT Kanab	37 3	112 32	2	+62	+53	+46	+37	+30
UT Moab	38 35	109 33	2	+46	+39	+33	+27	+22
UT Ogden	41 13	111 58	2	+47	+45	+43	+41	+40
UT Salt Lake City	40 45	111 53	2	+48	+45	+43	+40	+38
UT Vernal	40 27	109 32	2	+40	+36	+33	+30	+28
VA Charlottesville	38 2	78 30	0	+43	+35	+29	+22	+17
VA Danville	36 36	79 23	0	+51	+41	+33	+24	+17
VA Norfolk	36 51	76 17	0	+38	+28	+21	+12	+ 5
VA Richmond	37 32	77 26	0	+41	+32	+25	+17	+11
VA Roanoke	37 16	79 57	0	+51	+42	+35	+27	+21
VA Winchester	39 11	78 10	0	+38	+33	+28	+23	+19
VT Brattleboro	42 51	72 34	0	+ 4	+ 5	+ 5	+ 6	+ 7
VT Burlington	44 29	73 13	0	0	+ 4	+ 8	+12	+15
VT Rutland	43 37	72 58	0	+ 2	+ 5	+ 7	+ 9	+11
VT St. Johnsbury	44 25	72 1	0	– 4	0	+ 3	+ 7	+10
WA Bellingham	48 45	122 29	3	0	+13	+24	+37	+47
WA Seattle–Tacoma– Olympia	47 37	122 20	3	+ 3	+15	+24	+34	+42
WA Spokane	47 40	117 24	3	–16	– 4	+ 4	+14	+23
WA Walla Walla	46 4	118 20	3	– 5	+ 2	+ 8	+15	+21
WI Eau Claire	44 49	91 30	1	+12	+17	+21	+25	+29
WI Green Bay	44 31	88 0	1	0	+ 3	+ 7	+11	+14
WI La Crosse	43 48	91 15	1	+15	+18	+20	+22	+25
WI Madison	43 4	89 23	1	+10	+11	+12	+14	+15
WI Milwaukee	43 2	87 54	1	+ 4	+ 6	+ 7	+ 8	+ 9
WI Oshkosh	44 1	88 33	1	+ 3	+ 6	+ 9	+12	+15
WI Wausau	44 58	89 38	1	+ 4	+ 9	+13	+18	+22
WV Charleston	38 21	81 38	0	+55	+48	+42	+35	+30
WV Parkersburg	39 16	81 34	0	+52	+46	+42	+36	+32
WY Casper	42 51	106 19	2	+19	+19	+20	+21	+22
WY Cheyenne	41 8	104 49	2	+19	+16	+14	+12	+11
WY Sheridan	44 48	106 58	2	+14	+19	+23	+27	+31
CANADA								
AB Calgary	51 5	114 5	2	+13	+35	+50	+68	+84
AB Edmonton	53 34	113 25	2	– 3	+26	+47	+72	+93
BC Vancouver	49 13	123 6	3	0	+15	+26	+40	+52
MB Winnipeg	49 53	97 10	1	+12	+30	+43	+58	+71
NB Saint John	45 16	66 3	–1	+28	+34	+39	+44	+49
NS Halifax	44 38	63 35	–1	+21	+26	+29	+33	+37
NS Sydney	46 10	60 10	–1	+ 1	+ 9	+15	+23	+28
ON Ottawa	45 25	75 43	0	+ 6	+13	+18	+23	+28
ON Peterborough	44 18	78 19	0	+21	+25	+28	+32	+35
ON Thunder Bay	48 27	89 12	0	+47	+61	+71	+83	+93
ON Toronto	43 39	79 23	0	+28	+30	+32	+35	+37
QC Montreal	45 28	73 39	0	– 1	+ 4	+ 9	+15	+20
SK Saskatoon	52 10	106 40	1	+37	+63	+80	+101	+119

Mind-Manglers

Answers appear on page 251.

WHICH IS LARGER . . .

1. A bushel or a peck?
2. A league or a mile?
3. A foot or a fathom?
4. A yard or a perch?
5. A rod or a furlong?
6. A chain or a pole?
7. A span or a foot?
8. A barrel or a bushel?
9. A section or a township?
10. An acre or a section?
11. A gill or a gallon?
12. A carat or an ounce?
13. A gram or a pound?
14. A ream or a quire?
15. A bale or a bundle?

–F. Jacus, Hillsborough, New Jersey

A PERFECT SQUARE

Place the numbers 1 through 9 in three rows in such a way that adding them together up or down, across, or from corner to corner always makes 15.

COUNT 'EM

1. When a cattle rancher counts his herd by twos, threes, fours, fives, or sixes, he always has one left over. When he counts it by sevens, he has none remaining. What is the smallest number of cattle his herd could have?

2. If you divide this number by two, you get a remainder of one; by four, a remainder of three; by five, a remainder of four; and by six, a remainder of five. What is the number?

SPORTS CHALLENGE

Match each term on the left with the correct sport on the right.

1.	Dink	A.	Billiards
2.	Sling	B.	Curling
3.	Catching a crab	C.	Golf
4.	Riposte	D.	Tennis
5.	Trackstand	E.	Rowing
6.	Jerk	F.	Bowling
7.	Swisher	G.	Fencing
8.	Turkey	H.	Rugby
9.	Stutz	I.	Skiing
10.	Gimme	J.	Bike racing
11.	Maul	K.	Basketball
12.	Cradling	L.	Weight lifting
13.	Kiss	M.	Gymnastics
14.	Wedeln	N.	Badminton
15.	Hog	O.	Lacrosse

Classified Advertising

HEALTH & BEAUTY (cont.)

DETOX FOOT PATCHES. On your feet all day? A must! Sample one! Call 888-452-4968. Web site: www.mysticwondersinc.com

JUST LIKE GRAMMA'S RELIABLE OLD SALVE! New Wonder Balm, absolute must! Price/information: 888-452-4968. www.mysticwondersinc.com

CHRONIC AND SEVERE PAIN SUFFERERS Info: SASE $3 m/o, PO Box 35703, Houston TX 77235. www.scarterusa.originallimu.com

HERBS

MORE THAN 200 LIVE HERB, VEGETABLE, and perennial plants. Easy online ordering! Free plant offer. www.alwayssummerherbs.com

HOME PRODUCTS

LESS/NO DETERGENT using Earth Friendly Laundry Ball. Brochure, FREE sample of Wonder Balm. 888-452-4968. www.mysticwondersinc.com

INVENTORS/INVENTIONS/PATENTS

AMERICA'S LEADING INVENTION COMPANY helps to submit ideas/inventions to industry. Patent services. 1-888-439-IDEA.

MAINE RESORTS

ATLANTIC EYRIE LODGE, Bar Harbor, Maine. Acadia National Park. 55 Oceanview rooms. Call 800-HabaVue. On-Line Reservations available. info@AtlanticEyrieLodge.com Fax: 207-288-8500. www.AtlanticEyrieLodge.com

INTIMATE OCEANFRONT HOTEL townhomes and house. The Bayview, 111 Eden Street, Bar Harbor, Maine. Call 800-356-3585 or visit us and book online at www.thebayviewbarharbor.com

BAR HARBOR AND ACADIA National Park. 150 oceanview rooms. Atlantic-Oakes-by-the-Sea. Open year-round. 800-33-MAINE (62463) or reserve online. Indoor Pool and Outdoor Pool. Exercise Room and Tennis Courts. WI-FI available. www.barharbor.com

NURSERY STOCK

TREE/SHRUB SEEDLINGS direct from grower. Plants for landscaping, wildlife food and cover, timber, and Christmas tree production. Free color catalog. Carino Nurseries, PO Box 538AL, Indiana PA 15701. 800-223-7075. www.carinonurseries.com

OF INTEREST TO ALL

VISUALIZE DESIRED RESULTS: Create a successful future. Request instructions. Farrar's, Box 210526, Normandy MO 63121.

JEHOVAH'S WITNESSES, friends, family, discover facts society's hiding. Free, confidential. Box 454, Metaline Falls WA 99153. Visit our Web site: www.macgregorministries.org

PERSONALS

ASIAN BRIDES! WORLDWIDE! Friendship, romance, lifemates! Color photos/details: P.I.C., PO Box 4601-FA, Thousand Oaks CA 91362. 805-492-8040. Web site: www.pacisl.com

MEET LATIN WOMEN seeking marriage. All ages. Free brochures and Singles Vacations DVD. TLC, 713-896-9993 or www.tlcworldwide.com

IT'S FREE! Ladies talk to local guys. It's new, fun, and exciting! Call 800-485-4047. 18+.

DIAL-A-MATE LIVE TALK and voice personals. 10,000 singles call every day! Try it free! Call 800-234-5558. 18+.

POULTRY

GOSLINGS, DUCKLINGS, GUINEAS, chicks, turkeys, bantams, quails, pheasants. Books and equipment. 1-717-365-3694. Hoffman Hatchery, PO Box 129P, Gratz PA 17030. Visit our Web site: www.hoffmanhatchery.com

REAL ESTATE

LET THE GOVERNMENT PAY for your new or existing home. 100+ programs. Visit our Web site: www.usgovernmentinformation.com Free information: 707-448-3210. (8KE1)

CLAIM GOVERNMENT LAND. 320 acres/person now available. www.usgovernmentinformation.com Free recorded message: 707-448-1887. (4KE1)

SEEDS & PLANTS

THE ORIGINAL "Grow Your Own" seed company. Tobacco, medicinal plants, tropicals, and more. Free catalog. E.O.N.S., Dept./FA, PO Box 4604, Hallandale FL 33008. Phone: 954-455-0229. www.eonseed.com

SEPTIC SUPPLIES

SEPTIC SYSTEM PREVENTATIVE maintenance: 8 cents per day. Natural, nonchemical. Free information package. 800-599-9980. www.pro-agdirect.com

SPIRITUAL ADVICE

CHRISTINA specializes in reuniting lovers, helps with all problems. Guaranteed immediate results. Free reading. 423-614-0902.

FREE SPIRITUAL CATALOG—Luck, Money, and Love can be yours. Huge Spiritual Catalog with more than 1,000 items to Set You Free! Church Goods Co., PO Box 718, Glenview IL 60025.

MISS LISA, astrology reader and advisor. Extraordinary powers. Call for help with all problems. 912-283-3206.

READINGS BY ANGELA. Reunites lovers. Solves all problems. 100% guaranteed. One FREE reading. 940-612-4757.

REMOVES EVIL SPELLS, court cases. Where others fail, I guarantee results in 24 hours. Mrs. Jackson, 334-281-1116.

FLORIDA'S BEST SPIRITUAL PSYCHIC reader. Advice on all matters of life, love, marriage, business, health. Guaranteed results. Call now, 813-503-1860.

WORLD-RENOWNED READER. Are you unhappy? Unlucky? Health, love, business. Removes bad luck. Free reading. 903-742-6201.

FREE LOVE ADVICE. Free 5-minute accurate psychic. Specialty: love, romance, relationships. 800-560-9144. 18+. www.romance.asknow.com

$1.95 PSYCHIC READING. 10-minute reading for $1.95. Get answers: love, money, career, resolve problems. 800-561-7488. 18+. www.truereading.com

READINGS BY NORA. Specializing in reuniting lovers, helps in all problems. Free reading. 817-461-2683.

SPIRITUAL HEALERS

REV. NOAH GIBSON, NEW ORLEANS, LA. Powerful and gifted healer. Free spiritual reading. 504-272-4437.

REVEREND GINGER—Indian healer—works miracles, guaranteed in hours. Specializing in reuniting the separated. Call 504-463-3358.

SISTER SHIRLEY. Spiritual Healer. Helps solve all problems. Love. Money. Marriage. Nature. Bad luck. Sickness. 912-844-0427.

REVEREND DOCTOR MILLER. Do you have bad luck? Are you sick? Need help? Reverend Miller reunites lovers. Stops divorce. Removes unnatural illness and curses. Guaranteed results. 912-876-4895.

SISTER ANGIE, specializing in healing, removing evil influences, roots, and reuniting loved ones. 912-278-6223.

SPIRITUALISTS

MRS. ROBERTS, INDIAN SPIRITUALIST healer, removes bad luck, evil curses, sickness, pain. Reunites lovers, marriages. Spiritual cleaning available. Why suffer? Will come to you. 770-994-1466. 6940 Old National Hwy., College Park GA 30349.

MRS. RAINBOW. Helps in all problems. Reunites lovers in 24 hours! 626-339-8606.

GINGER, SOUL MATE SPECIALIST and love spells. Psychic & Advisor. Helps in all problems in life. 213-840-2790.

FREE SAMPLE READING! Mrs. Ruth, southern-born spiritualist, removes evil, bad luck. Helps with all problems. 334-616-6363.

SISTER LENA SPIRITUALIST. Solves all problems. Love, money, marriage, bad luck, evil influences. Guaranteed results. Call for help! 813-503-1860.

SECRET'S OUT! Other healers seek Mrs. Powers's help. You can too! Really powerful help guaranteed! 678-277-9389.

SISTER PEGGY. Are you in pain or lost? Don't know where to go for help? Remove evil and bad luck. I will help you get your life back! Call now! Help right away. 215-551-7531.

AMAZING SPIRITUAL HEALER, Mrs. Wanda. Solves personal problems, love, money, health, bad luck, nature. Results guaranteed. 910-671-9034.

TRAVEL/RESORTS/VACATION

ALL-INCLUSIVE PACKAGES TO HAWAII, Mexico, Caribbean. Great Prices. Cruises. Call Great Connections Travel, 888-574-0311 or 520-886-7340.

TREES & SHRUBS

CATALOG FREE! Tree seedlings. Wholesale prices. Flickinger's Nursery, Box 245, Sagamore PA 16250. 800-368-7381.

ANTIQUE APPLE TREES. 100+ varieties! Catalog $3.00. Urban Homestead, 818-B Cumberland St., Bristol VA 24201.

WANTED TO BUY

CASH FOR 78-RPM RECORDS! Send $2 (refundable) for illustrated booklet identifying collectible labels, numbers, with actual prices I pay. Docks, Box 691035(FA), San Antonio TX 78269-1035.

The Old Farmer's Almanac classified rates (15-word min.): $20.50 per word. Payment required with order: MC, Visa, AmEx, and Discover/NOVUS accepted. For ad rates, Web classifieds, or ad information, contact Bernie Gallagher at OFAads@aol.com or 203-263-7171, or fax 203-263-7174. Write to: Gallagher Group, PO Box 959, Woodbury, CT 06798. *The 2007 Old Farmer's Almanac* closing date is 05/10/06.

Index to Advertisers

ANSWERS TO

Mind-Manglers

from page 242

WHICH IS LARGER? 1. bushel; 2. league; 3. fathom; 4. perch; 5. furlong; 6. chain; 7. foot; 8. barrel; 9. township; 10. section; 11. gallon; 12. ounce; 13. pound; 14. ream; 15. bale

A PERFECT SQUARE

6, 7, 2

1, 5, 9

8, 3, 4

COUNT 'EM

1. 301   2. 59

SPORTS CHALLENGE 1. D; 2. N; 3. E; 4. G; 5. J; 6. L; 7. K; 8. F; 9. M; 10. C; 11. H; 12. O; 13. A; 14. I; 15. B

MANGLE OUR MINDS

Got a mind-bending math or word puzzle that will challenge even the nimblest number crunchers? Send it to us! We may use it in the Almanac. E-mail your puzzle to (subject: Mind-Manglers) almanac@yankeepub.com or send via regular mail to The Old Farmer's Almanac, P.O. Box 520, Dublin, NH 03444. Include the solution clearly stated. All submittals become the property of Yankee Publishing Inc., which reserves the rights to the material. □□

Amusement

Anecdotes & Pleasantries

A sampling from the hundreds of letters, clippings, and e-mails sent to us by Almanac
readers from all over the United States and Canada during the past year.

A Special Ted Williams Anecdote

It's absolutely the truth, too.

Courtesy of S.E.R., Worcester, Massachusetts

■ It so happened that in December 1995, State Senator Stephen Lynch of Massachusetts
was asked to be on the platform with other dignitaries for the opening of the

Ted Williams Tunnel, connecting downtown Boston with Logan Airport. As he settled himself, Lynch found that, much to his delight and surprise, he was sitting next to the great Ted Williams himself.

After a few nervous moments, he finally got up the courage to ask Ted a question that he and many other baseball fans had been dying to ask: What did Ted think of the "ridiculously high" salaries now often being paid to "only so-so ballplayers"?

Ted thought for a moment and then answered, "I suppose if they can get that kind of money from the boys upstairs, good for them."

A bit surprised by Ted's answer, Senator Lynch then asked him how much he thought he would be getting for a salary if he were still playing. "I'd say about three million," Ted replied.

"Only three million?" Lynch asked, shocked. "Last of the .400 hitters, greatest batter in the history of baseball, and all you think you'd get today would be three million?"

Ted turned to look directly at the young senator and, with a smile, said, "Well, you gotta realize . . . I'm 77 years old."

Flash! The Flea Is Now Only the World's *Second-Best* Jumper!

Every champion has to realize that he or she will eventually get beaten.

Courtesy of E. B., Toronto, Ontario (as per an article by Alicia Chang for the Associated Press)

■ In an American scientific experiment back in 1910, a flea jumped nearly eight inches into the air and performed a long jump of 13 inches. As a result, the flea, relative to its size, has always been assumed to be the world's best jumper.

But wait. Recently, after an extensive study that utilized a high-speed camera, researchers at the University of Cambridge, England (who, apparently, had a fair amount of time on their hands), have come up with a superior jumper. It's known as the spittle bug (or froghopper). This tiny, green insect is found throughout the world but is prevalent along the Pacific coast and in eastern sections of the United States and Canada. According to

researchers, a spittle bug can leap more than two feet into the air, That's more than three times as high as a flea can jump and is equal to a man jumping clear over the Gateway Arch in St. Louis or the CN Tower in Toronto.

Incidentally, while feeding—sucking the juice from alfalfa and clover—the spittle bug cleverly covers itself in bubbles of white, foamy saliva in order to protect itself from the sun, birds, and so on. So, hey, this little guy isn't only the world's new champion jumper, he's pretty smart, too.

We've Heard of "Diet Change," but This Is Carrying Things Too Far

Courtesy of C.J.S., Atlanta, Georgia (as per an article by Jeff Donn for the Associated Press)

■ A few years ago, French doctors who X-rayed and then operated on a man who had complained of pain, loss of appetite, and constipation were amazed to discover 350 coins—about 12 pounds total, in both French currency and euros—and jewelry in his stomach. The patient, who was 62 years old, suffered from a rare condition called pica. The name comes from the Latin word for magpie, a bird believed to eat just about anything. Those afflicted have a compulsion to eat things not normally consumed as food, such as ash, dirt, chalk, soap, burned matches, even toothbrushes, and, in one case, forks. The gentleman, who died from complications soon thereafter, had consumed the coins and jewelry over about ten years.

Speaking of Which, Have You Tried the 1952 Utensil Diet?

Courtesy of M. J., Hot Springs, South Dakota

■ Do the words "low-carb" and "fat-free" have you wishing for simpler times and less complicated meal preparations? Instead of avoiding certain foods, eliminate the utensils. "Cut down on your silverware, and

you'll cut down on your weight," promised *Woman's Day* magazine in 1952. Try the "knife, fork, and spoon" diet concept, adapted for these pages:

Breakfast: Eat a fairly substantial breakfast but set your place without a knife, so you can't spread butter or jam on your toast.

continued

Lunch: Have only soup or sandwich, easily eaten without a fork, and you won't be able to indulge in macaroni, sausages, or chocolate cake.

Dinner: Dine on an apple, grapes, or crackers and cheese for dessert and take your tea or coffee without cream and sugar; no spoon needed.

You're Never Too Old to Score

Courtesy of V.M.P., Tulsa, Oklahoma

■ The oldest woman to score a hole in one in golf was Erna Ross. She was 95 years and 257 days old when she accomplished the feat at the Everglades Club, Palm Beach, Florida, on April 23, 1986.

■ The oldest man was Harold Stilson from Boca Raton, Florida. He did it at the age of 101 at the Deerfield Country Club, Deerfield Beach, Florida, on May 16, 2001.

One Simple Way to Become Smarter

Courtesy of Reuters

■ Researchers have recently discovered that chewing gum can improve your memory by 35 percent. When volunteers at the University of Northumbria, Newcastle Upon Tyne, in England were shown a series of words, gum chewers remembered the most words right away and 25 minutes later. The explanation may be that gum chewing increases blood flow to the brain and stimulates insulin production—both good for the part of the brain that involves memory.

So, What Are You Afraid of?

Courtesy of R.L.T., Chicago, Illinois, who credits Corporate Transition Solutions Inc.

■ A fire? A tornado? Well, what about simply falling down a flight of stairs? Here's a brief summary of the most common everyday hazards we face and the number of hospital visits each caused, as reported by the U.S. Consumer Product Safety Commission a few years ago:

■ Stairs: 1,088,000
■ Nails, screws, tacks, and bolts: 180,000
■ Ramps and landings: 13,000

At the bottom of the list were these . . .

■ Pillows: 5,000
■ Crayons and chalk: 3,500
■ Electric Christmas decorations: 3,300
■ Vending machines: 2,900
■ And, finally, hammocks—which sent about 2,500 people to the hospital

Pillows?

Country Fare

Courtesy of S. R., Worcester, Massachusetts

■ Into a general store came a lanky young man, complaining that the ham that he had purchased there was not good.

"Why, that ham's all right," insisted the storekeeper.

"No, it ain't," said the young man. "That ham is spoiled."

"Why, how could that ham be spoiled," continued the storekeeper, "when it was cured only last week?"

"Well, mister, that ham may have been cured last week, but it's got a relapse now and that's the truth!"

Quite a Pickup Line

Courtesy of J. B., Seattle, Washington

■ I've been told that this is an absolutely true story. (But who knows?) It concerns a woman who went into her local newspaper office to write the obituary for her recently deceased husband. The editor informed her that the fee for a submitted obituary was one dollar per word, aside from the name and address. She paused, reflected, and then said, "Well, then, let it read, 'Billy Bob died.'"

"Sorry, ma'am," replied the editor, "but I'm afraid there's a seven-word minimum on all submitted obituaries."

Somewhat flustered, the woman thought for a minute and then instructed the editor to write, "Billy Bob died. 1983 pickup for sale."

Rudolph Is a Girl?

Courtesy of M. C., Jaffrey Center, New Hampshire

■ According to the Alaska Department of Fish and Game, although both male and female reindeer grow antlers each summer, male reindeer shed theirs from late November to mid-December. Female reindeer retain their antlers until after they give birth in the spring. So, because, as we all know, all of Santa's reindeer have antlers, then all have to be girls, including Rudolph . . . er, Rudolphine?

Share Your Anecdotes & Pleasantries

Send your contribution for the 2007 edition of *The Old Farmer's Almanac* by January 31, 2006, to "A & P," The Old Farmer's Almanac, P.O. Box 520, Dublin, NH 03444; or e-mail it to almanac@yankeepub.com (subject: A & P).

A Reference Compendium

compiled by Mare-Anne Jarvela

R
E
F
E
R
E
N
C
E

A Table Foretelling the Weather Through All the Lunations of Each Year, or Forever

T his table is the result of many years of actual observation and shows what sort of weather will probably follow the Moon's entrance into any of its quarters. For example, the table shows that the week following January 22, 2006, will be cold and windy, because the Moon enters the last quarter that day at 10:14 A.M. EST. (See the **Left-Hand Calendar Pages, 96–122,** for 2006 Moon phases.)

EDITOR'S NOTE: *Although the data in this table is taken into consideration in the yearlong process of compiling the annual long-range weather forecasts for* The Old Farmer's Almanac, *we rely far more on our projections of solar activity.*

Time of Change	Summer	Winter
Midnight to 2 A.M.	Fair	Hard frost, unless wind is south or west
2 A.M. to 4 A.M.	Cold, with frequent showers	Snow and stormy
4 A.M. to 6 A.M.	Rain	Rain
6 A.M. to 8 A.M.	Wind and rain	Stormy
8 A.M. to 10 A.M.	Changeable	Cold rain if wind is west; snow, if east
10 A.M. to noon	Frequent showers	Cold with high winds
Noon to 2 P.M.	Very rainy	Snow or rain
2 P.M. to 4 P.M.	Changeable	Fair and mild
4 P.M. to 6 P.M.	Fair	Fair
6 P.M. to 10 P.M.	Fair if wind is northwest; rain if wind is south or southwest	Fair and frosty if wind is north or northeast; rain or snow if wind is south or southwest
10 P.M. to midnight	Fair	Fair and frosty

This table was created about 170 years ago by Dr. Herschell for the Boston Courier; *it first appeared in* The Old Farmer's Almanac *in 1834.*

Safe Ice Thickness*

Ice Thickness	Permissible Load	Ice Thickness	Permissible Load
3 inches	Single person on foot	12 inches	Heavy truck (8-ton gross)
4 inches	Group in single file	15 inches	10 tons
7½ inches	Passenger car (2-ton gross)	20 inches	25 tons
8 inches	Light truck (2½-ton gross)	30 inches	70 tons
10 inches	Medium truck (3½-ton gross)	36 inches	110 tons

*Solid, clear, blue/black pond and lake ice

■ Slush ice has only half the strength of blue ice.
■ The strength value of river ice is 15 percent less.

Winter Weather Terms

Winter Storm Outlook
■ Issued prior to a winter storm watch. An outlook is issued when forecasters believe that storm conditions are possible, usually 48 to 60 hours before the beginning of a storm.

Winter Storm Watch
■ Indicates the possibility of a winter storm and is issued to provide 12 to 36 hours' notice. A watch is announced when the specific timing, location, and path of a storm are undetermined. Be alert to changing weather conditions, and avoid unnecessary travel.

Winter Storm Warning
■ Indicates that a severe winter storm has started or is about to begin. A warning is issued when more than six inches of snow, a significant ice accumulation, a dangerous windchill, or a combination of the three is expected. Anticipated snow accumulation during a winter storm is six or more inches in 24 hours. You should stay indoors during the storm.

Heavy Snow Warning
■ Issued when snow accumulations are expected to approach or exceed six inches in 12 hours but will not be accompanied by significant wind. The warning could also be issued if eight or more inches of snow accumulation is expected in a 24-hour period. During a heavy snow warning, freezing rain and sleet are not expected.

Blizzard Warning
■ Indicates that sustained winds or frequent gusts of 35 miles per hour or greater will occur in combination with considerable falling and/or blowing snow for at least three hours. Visibility will often be reduced to less than one-quarter mile.

Whiteout
■ Caused by falling and/or blowing snow that reduces visibility to zero miles—typically only a few feet. Whiteouts are most frequent during blizzards and can occur rapidly, often blinding motorists and creating chain-reaction crashes involving multiple vehicles.

Northeaster
■ Usually produces heavy snow and rain and creates tremendous waves in Atlantic coastal regions, often causing beach erosion and structural damage. Wind gusts associated with these storms can exceed hurricane force in intensity. A northeaster gets its name from the strong, continuous, northeasterly ocean winds that blow in over coastal areas ahead of the storm.

Sleet
■ Frozen or partially frozen rain in the form of ice pellets that hit the ground so fast that they bounce and do not stick to it. However, the pellets can accumulate like snow and cause hazardous conditions for pedestrians and motorists.

Freezing Rain
■ Liquid precipitation that turns to ice on contact with a frozen surface to form a smooth ice coating called a glaze.

Ice Storm Warning
■ Issued when freezing rain results in ice accumulations measuring one-half-inch thick or more. This can cause trees and utility lines to fall down, causing power outages.

Windchill Advisory
■ Issued when windchill temperatures are expected to be between –20° and –34°F.

Windchill Warning
■ Issued when windchill temperatures are expected to be below –34°F.

R
E
F
E
R
E
N
C
E

Windchill

As wind speed increases, the air temperature against your body falls. The combination of cold temperature and high wind can create a cooling effect so severe that exposed flesh can freeze. (Inanimate objects, such as cars, do not experience windchill.)

To gauge wind speed: At 10 miles per hour, you can feel wind on your face; at 20, small branches move, and dust or snow is raised; at 30, large branches move and wires whistle; at 40, whole trees bend.

TEMPERATURE (°F)

Calm	35	30	25	20	15	10	5	0	−5	−10	−15	−20	−25	−30	−35
5	31	25	19	13	7	1	−5	−11	−16	−22	−28	−34	−40	−46	−52
10	27	21	15	9	3	−4	−10	−16	−22	−28	−35	−41	−47	−53	−59
15	25	19	13	6	0	−7	−13	−19	−26	−32	−39	−45	−51	−58	−64
20	24	17	11	4	−2	−9	−15	−22	−29	−35	−42	−48	−55	−61	−68
25	23	16	9	3	−4	−11	−17	−24	−31	−37	−44	−51	−58	−64	−71
30	22	15	8	1	−5	−12	−19	−26	−33	−39	−46	−53	−60	−67	−73
35	21	14	7	0	−7	−14	−21	−27	−34	−41	−48	−55	−62	−69	−76
40	20	13	6	−1	−8	−15	−22	−29	−36	−43	−50	−57	−64	−71	−78
45	19	12	5	−2	−9	−16	−23	−30	−37	−44	−51	−58	−65	−72	−79
50	19	12	4	−3	−10	−17	−24	−31	−38	−45	−52	−60	−67	−74	−81
55	18	11	4	−3	−11	−18	−25	−32	−39	−46	−54	−61	−68	−75	−82
60	17	10	3	−4	−11	−19	−26	−33	−40	−48	−55	−62	−69	−76	−84

WIND SPEED (mph)

Frostbite occurs in 30 minutes or less.

EXAMPLE: When the temperature is 15°F and the wind speed is 30 miles per hour, the windchill, or how cold it feels, is −5°F. For a Celsius version of the Windchill table, visit **Almanac.com/weathercenter.** –*courtesy National Weather Service*

Is It Raining, Drizzling, or Misting?

	NUMBER OF DROPS (per sq. ft. per sec.)	DIAMETER OF DROPS (mm)	INTENSITY (in. per hr.)
Cloudburst	113	2.85	4.0
Excessive rain	76	2.4	1.6
Heavy rain	46	2.05	0.6
Moderate rain	46	1.6	0.15
Light rain	26	1.24	0.04
Drizzle	14	0.96	0.01
Mist	2,510	0.1	0.002
Fog	6,264,000	0.01	0.005

REFERENCE

Saffir-Simpson Hurricane Scale

This scale assigns a rating from 1 to 5 based on a hurricane's intensity. It is used to give an estimate of the potential property damage and flooding expected along the coast from a hurricane landfall. Wind speed is the determining factor in the scale, as storm surge values are highly dependent on the slope of the continental shelf in the landfall region. Wind speeds are measured using a 1-minute average.

CATEGORY ONE. Average wind: 74–95 mph. No real damage to building structures. Damage primarily to unanchored mobile homes, shrubbery, and trees. Also, some coastal road flooding and minor pier damage.

CATEGORY TWO. Average wind: 96–110 mph. Some roofing material, door, and window damage to buildings. Considerable damage to vegetation, mobile homes, and piers. Coastal and low-lying escape routes flood 2 to 4 hours before arrival of center. Small craft in unprotected anchorages break moorings.

CATEGORY THREE. Average wind: 111–130 mph. Some structural damage to small residences and utility buildings; minor amount of curtainwall failures. Mobile homes destroyed. Flooding near coast destroys smaller structures; larger structures damaged by floating debris.

CATEGORY FOUR. Average wind: 131–155 mph. More extensive curtainwall failures with some complete roof failure on small residences. Major beach erosion. Major damage to lower floors near the shore.

CATEGORY FIVE. Average wind: 156+ mph. Complete roof failure on many residences and industrial buildings. Some complete building failures; small buildings blown over or away. Major damage to lower floors located less than 15 feet above sea level (ASL) and within 500 yards of the shoreline.

Atlantic Tropical (and Subtropical) Storm Names for 2006

Alberto	Gordon	Michael	Tony
Beryl	Helene	Nadine	Valerie
Chris	Isaac	Oscar	William
Debby	Joyce	Patty	
Ernesto	Kirk	Rafael	
Florence	Leslie	Sandy	

Eastern North-Pacific Tropical (and Subtropical) Storm Names for 2006

Aletta	Gilma	Miriam	Tara
Bud	Hector	Norman	Vicente
Carlotta	Ileana	Olivia	Willa
Daniel	John	Paul	Xavier
Emilia	Kristy	Rosa	Yolanda
Fabio	Lane	Sergio	Zeke

Retired Atlantic Hurricane Names

These storms have been some of the most destructive and costly; as a result, their names have been retired from the six-year rotating list of names.

NAME	YEAR RETIRED	NAME	YEAR RETIRED	NAME	YEAR RETIRED
Frederic	1979	Diana	1990	Floyd	1999
Allen	1980	Klaus	1990	Keith	2000
Alicia	1983	Bob	1991	Lili	2002
Elena	1985	Andrew	1992	Fabian	2003
Gloria	1985	Opal	1995	Isabel	2003
Gilbert	1988	Roxanne	1995	Charley	2004
Joan	1988	Fran	1996	Frances	2004
Hugo	1989	Mitch	1998	Ivan	2004

Heat Index °F (°C)

	RELATIVE HUMIDITY (%)								
TEMPERATURE °F (°C)	40	45	50	55	60	65	70	75	80
100 (38)	109 (43)	114 (46)	118 (48)	124 (51)	129 (54)	136 (58)			
98 (37)	105 (41)	109 (43)	113 (45)	117 (47)	123 (51)	128 (53)	134 (57)		
96 (36)	101 (38)	104 (40)	108 (42)	112 (44)	116 (47)	121 (49)	126 (52)	132 (56)	
94 (34)	97 (36)	100 (38)	103 (39)	106 (41)	110 (43)	114 (46)	119 (48)	124 (51)	129 (54)
92 (33)	94 (34)	96 (36)	99 (37)	101 (38)	105 (41)	108 (42)	112 (44)	116 (47)	121 (49)
90 (32)	91 (33)	93 (34)	95 (35)	97 (36)	100 (38)	103 (39)	106 (41)	109 (43)	113 (45)
88 (31)	88 (31)	89 (32)	91 (33)	93 (34)	95 (35)	98 (37)	100 (38)	103 (39)	106 (41)
86 (30)	85 (29)	87 (31)	88 (31)	89 (32)	91 (33)	93 (34)	95 (35)	97 (36)	100 (38)
84 (29)	83 (28)	84 (29)	85 (29)	86 (30)	88 (31)	89 (32)	90 (32)	92 (33)	94 (34)
82 (28)	81 (27)	82 (28)	83 (28)	84 (29)	84 (29)	85 (29)	86 (30)	88 (31)	89 (32)
80 (27)	80 (27)	80 (27)	81 (27)	81 (27)	82 (28)	82 (28)	83 (28)	84 (29)	84 (29)

EXAMPLE: When the temperature is 88°F (31°C) and the relative humidity is 60 percent, the heat index, or how hot it feels, is 95°F (35°C).

The UV Index for Measuring Ultraviolet Radiation Risk

The U.S. National Weather Service daily forecasts of ultraviolet levels use these numbers for various exposure levels:

UV Index Number	Exposure Level	Time to Burn	Actions to Take
0, 1, 2	Minimal	60 minutes	Apply SPF 15 sunscreen
3, 4	Low	45 minutes	Apply SPF 15 sunscreen; wear a hat
5, 6	Moderate	30 minutes	Apply SPF 15 sunscreen; wear a hat
7, 8, 9	High	15–25 minutes	Apply SPF 15 to 30 sunscreen; wear a hat and sunglasses
10 or higher	Very high	10 minutes	Apply SPF 30 sunscreen; wear a hat, sunglasses, and protective clothing

"Time to Burn" and "Actions to Take" apply to people with fair skin that sometimes tans but usually burns. People with lighter skin need to be more cautious. People with darker skin may be able to tolerate more exposure.

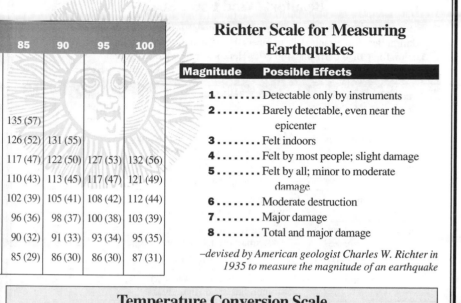

Richter Scale for Measuring Earthquakes

85	90	95	100
135 (57)			
126 (52)	131 (55)		
117 (47)	122 (50)	127 (53)	132 (56)
110 (43)	113 (45)	117 (47)	121 (49)
102 (39)	105 (41)	108 (42)	112 (44)
96 (36)	98 (37)	100 (38)	103 (39)
90 (32)	91 (33)	93 (34)	95 (35)
85 (29)	86 (30)	86 (30)	87 (31)

Magnitude	Possible Effects
1	Detectable only by instruments
2	Barely detectable, even near the epicenter
3	Felt indoors
4	Felt by most people; slight damage
5	Felt by all; minor to moderate damage
6	Moderate destruction
7	Major damage
8	Total and major damage

–devised by American geologist Charles W. Richter in 1935 to measure the magnitude of an earthquake

Temperature Conversion Scale

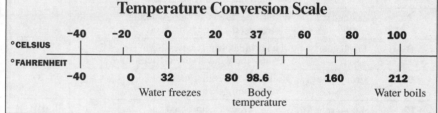

The Volcanic Explosivity Index (VEI) for Measuring Volcanic Eruptions

VEI	Description	Plume Height	Volume	Classification	Frequency
0	Nonexplosive	<100 m	1,000 m³	Hawaiian	Daily
1	Gentle	100–1,000 m	10,000 m³	Hawaiian/Strombolian	Daily
2	Explosive	1–5 km	1,000,000 m³	Strombolian/Vulcanian	Weekly
3	Severe	3–15 km	10,000,000 m³	Vulcanian	Yearly
4	Cataclysmic	10–25 km	100,000,000 m³	Vulcanian/Plinian	10 years
5	Paroxysmal	>25 km	1 km³	Plinian	100 years
6	Colossal	>25 km	10 km³	Plinian/Ultra-Plinian	100 years
7	Supercolossal	>25 km	100 km³	Ultra-Plinian	1,000 years
8	Megacolossal	>25 km	1,000 km³	Ultra-Plinian	10,000 years

REFERENCE

Beaufort Wind Force Scale

"Used Mostly at Sea but of Help to All Who Are Interested in the Weather"

Admiral Beaufort arranged the numbers 0 to 12 to indicate the strength of the wind from calm, force 0, to hurricane, force 12. Here's a scale adapted to land.

Beaufort Force	Description	When You See or Feel This Effect	Wind (mph)	(km/h)
0	Calm	Smoke goes straight up	less than 1	less than 2
1	Light air	Wind direction is shown by smoke drift but not by wind vane	1–3	2–5
2	Light breeze	Wind is felt on the face; leaves rustle; wind vanes move	4–7	6–11
3	Gentle breeze	Leaves and small twigs move steadily; wind extends small flags straight out	8–12	12–19
4	Moderate breeze	Wind raises dust and loose paper; small branches move	13–18	20–29
5	Fresh breeze	Small trees sway; waves form on lakes	19–24	30–39
6	Strong breeze	Large branches move; wires whistle; umbrellas are difficult to use	25–31	40–50
7	Moderate gale	Whole trees are in motion; walking against the wind is difficult	32–38	51–61
8	Fresh gale	Twigs break from trees; walking against the wind is very difficult	39–46	62–74
9	Strong gale	Buildings suffer minimal damage; roof shingles are removed	47–54	75–87
10	Whole gale	Trees are uprooted	55–63	88–101
11	Violent storm	Widespread damage	64–72	102–116
12	Hurricane	Widespread destruction	73+	117+

Fujita Scale (or F Scale) for Measuring Tornadoes

■ This is a system developed by Dr. Theodore Fujita to classify tornadoes based on wind damage. All tornadoes, and most other severe local windstorms, are assigned a single number from this scale according to the most intense damage caused by the storm.

F0 (weak)	40–72 mph, light damage
F1 (weak)	73–112 mph, moderate damage
F2 (strong)	113–157 mph, considerable damage
F3 (strong)	158–206 mph, severe damage
F4 (violent)	207–260 mph, devastating damage
F5 (violent)	261–318 mph (rare), incredible damage

Torro Hailstorm Intensity Scale

INTENSITY	DESCRIPTION OF DAMAGE
H0	True hail of pea size causes no damage
H1	Leaves and flower petals are punctured and torn
H2	Leaves are stripped from trees and plants
H3	Panes of glass are broken; auto bodies are dented
H4	Some house windows are broken; small tree branches are broken off; birds are killed
H5	Many windows are smashed; small animals are injured; large tree branches are broken off
H6	Shingle roofs are breached; metal roofs are scored; wooden window frames are broken away
H7	Roofs are shattered to expose rafters; cars are seriously damaged
H8	Shingle and tiled roofs are destroyed; small tree trunks are split; people are seriously injured
H9	Concrete roofs are broken; large tree trunks are split and knocked down; people are at risk of fatal injuries
H10	Brick houses are damaged; people are at risk of fatal injuries

Cloud Definitions

—Weatherstock

High Clouds
(bases start at an average of about 20,000 feet)

CIRRUS: Thin, featherlike, crystal clouds.

CIRROCUMULUS: Thin clouds that appear as small "cotton patches."

CIRROSTRATUS: Thin white clouds that resemble veils.

Middle Clouds
(bases start at about 6,500 feet)

ALTOCUMULUS: Gray or white layer or patches of solid clouds with rounded shapes.

ALTOSTRATUS: Grayish or bluish layer of clouds that can obscure the Sun.

Low Clouds
(bases start at anywhere up to 6,500 feet)

STRATUS: Thin, gray, sheetlike clouds with low bases; may bring drizzle and snow.

STRATOCUMULUS: Rounded cloud masses that form on top of a layer.

NIMBOSTRATUS: Dark, gray, shapeless cloud layers containing rain, snow, and ice pellets.

Clouds With Vertical Development
(clouds that form at almost any altitude and can reach to more than 39,000 feet)

CUMULUS: Fair-weather clouds with flat bases and dome-shape tops.

CUMULONIMBUS: Large, dark, vertical clouds with bulging tops that bring showers, thunder, and lightning.

REFERENCE

PHASES OF THE MOON

New

WAXING

First Quarter

Full

WANING

Last Quarter

New

Origin of Full-Moon Names

Historically, the Native Americans who lived in the area that is now the northern and eastern United States kept track of the seasons by giving a distinctive name to each recurring full Moon. This name was applied to the entire month in which it occurred. These names, and some variations, were used by the Algonquin tribes from New England to Lake Superior.

Name	Month	Variations
Full Wolf Moon	January	Full Old Moon
Full Snow Moon	February	Full Hunger Moon
Full Worm Moon	March	Full Crow Moon Full Crust Moon Full Sugar Moon Full Sap Moon
Full Pink Moon	April	Full Sprouting Grass Moon Full Egg Moon Full Fish Moon
Full Flower Moon	May	Full Corn Planting Moon Full Milk Moon
Full Strawberry Moon	June	Full Rose Moon Full Hot Moon
Full Buck Moon	July	Full Thunder Moon Full Hay Moon
Full Sturgeon Moon	August	Full Red Moon Full Green Corn Moon
Full Harvest Moon*	September	Full Corn Moon Full Barley Moon
Full Hunter's Moon	October	Full Travel Moon Full Dying Grass Moon
Full Beaver Moon	November	Full Frost Moon
Full Cold Moon	December	Full Long Nights Moon

The Harvest Moon is always the full Moon closest to the autumnal equinox. If the Harvest Moon occurs in October, the September full Moon is usually called the Corn Moon.

REFERENCE

Love calendar lore? Find more at Almanac.com.

When Will the Moon Rise Today?

A lunar puzzle involves the timing of moonrise. If you enjoy the out-of-doors and the wonders of nature, you may wish to commit to memory the following gem:

🌑 ☆ **The new Moon always rises at sunrise**

🌒 **And the first quarter at noon.**

🌓 ☆ **The full Moon always rises at sunset**

🌗 ☆ **And the last quarter at midnight.**

■ Moonrise occurs about 50 minutes later each day.

■ The new Moon is invisible because its illuminated side faces away from Earth, which occurs when the Moon lines up between Earth and the Sun.

■ One or two days after the date of the new Moon, you can see a thin crescent setting just after sunset in the western sky as the lunar cycle continues. (See pages 96–122 for exact moonrise times.)

Origin of Month Names

January Named for the Roman god Janus, protector of gates and doorways. Janus is depicted with two faces, one looking into the past, the other into the future.

February From the Latin word *februa,* "to cleanse." The Roman Februalia was a month of purification and atonement.

March Named for the Roman god of war, Mars. This was the time of year to resume military campaigns that had been interrupted by winter.

April From the Latin word *aperio,* "to open (bud)," because plants begin to grow in this month.

May Named for the Roman goddess Maia, who oversaw the growth of plants. Also from the Latin word *maiores,* "elders," who were celebrated during this month.

June Named for the Roman goddess Juno, patroness of marriage and the well-being of women. Also from the Latin word *juvenis,* "young people."

July Named to honor Roman dictator Julius Caesar (100 B.C.–44 B.C.). In 46 B.C., Julius Caesar made one of his greatest contributions to history: With the help of Sosigenes, he developed the Julian calendar, the precursor to the Gregorian calendar we use today.

August Named to honor the first Roman emperor (and grandnephew of Julius Caesar), Augustus Caesar (63 B.C.–A.D. 14).

September From the Latin word *septem,* "seven," because this had been the seventh month of the early Roman calendar.

October From the Latin word *octo,* "eight," because this had been the eighth month of the early Roman calendar.

November From the Latin word *novem,* "nine," because this had been the ninth month of the early Roman calendar.

December From the Latin word *decem,* "ten," because this had been the tenth month of the early Roman calendar.

R E F E R E N C E

Origin of Day Names

The days of the week were named by the Romans with the Latin words for the Sun, the Moon, and the five known planets. These names have survived in European languages, but English names also reflect an Anglo-Saxon influence.

English	Latin	French	Italian	Spanish	Saxon
SUNDAY	Solis (Sun)	dimanche	domenica	domingo	Sun
MONDAY	Lunae (Moon)	lundi	lunedì	lunes	Moon
TUESDAY	Martis (Mars)	mardi	martedì	martes	Tiw (the Anglo-Saxon god of war, the equivalent of the Norse Tyr or the Roman Mars)
WEDNESDAY	Mercurii (Mercury)	mercredi	mercoledì	miércoles	Woden (the Anglo-Saxon equivalent of the Norse Odin or the Roman Mercury)
THURSDAY	Jovis (Jupiter)	jeudi	giovedì	jucves	Thor (the Norse god of thunder, the equivalent of the Roman Jupiter)
FRIDAY	Veneris (Venus)	vendredi	venerdì	viernes	Frigg (the Norse god of love and fertility, the equivalent of the Roman Venus)
SATURDAY	Saturni (Saturn)	samedi	sabato	sábado	Saterne (Saturn, the Roman god of agriculture)

Best Planetary Encounters of the 21st Century

Me = Mercury   V = Venus   Mn = Moon   Ma = Mars   J = Jupiter   S = Saturn

In all of these cases, face west between twilight and 10 P.M. to see the conjunction.

DATE	OBJECTS	DATE	OBJECTS	DATE	OBJECTS
June 30, 2007	V, S	March 7, 2047	V, J	November 15, 2080	Ma, J, S
December 1, 2008	V, Mn, J	May 13, 2066	V, Ma		
February 20, 2015	V, Mn, Ma	July 1, 2066	V, S	November 17, 2080	Mn, Ma, J, S
		March 14, 2071	V, J		
June 30–July 1, 2015	V, J	June 21, 2074	V, J	December 24, 2080	V, J
July 18, 2015	V, Mn, J	June 27, 2074	V, Mn, J	March 6, 2082	V, J
December 20, 2020	J, S	June 28, 2076	Ma, J	April 28, 2085	Mn, Ma, J
March 1, 2023	V, J	October 31, 2076	Mn, Ma, S	June 13, 2085	Me, V, J
December 1–2, 2033	Ma, J	February 27, 2079	V, Ma	May 15, 2098	V, Ma
February 23, 2047	V, Ma	November 7, 2080	Ma, J, S	June 29, 2098	V, J

R E F E R E N C E

How to Find the Day of the Week for Any Given Date

To compute the day of the week for any given date as far back as the mid–18th century, proceed as follows:

■ Add the last two digits of the year to one-quarter of the last two digits (discard any remainder), the day of the month, and the month key from the key box below. Divide the sum by 7; the remainder is the day of the week (1 is Sunday, 2 is Monday, and so on). If there is no remainder, the day is Saturday. If you're searching for a weekday prior to 1900, add 2 to the sum before dividing; prior to 1800, add 4. The formula doesn't work for days prior to 1753. From 2000 to 2099, subtract 1 from the sum before dividing.

Example:
The Dayton Flood was on March 25, 1913.

Last two digits of year:	13
One-quarter of these two digits:	3
Given day of month:	25
Key number for March:	4
Sum:	45

45 ÷ 7 = 6, with a remainder of 3. The flood took place on Tuesday, the third day of the week.

KEY	
January.	1
leap year.	0
February.	4
leap year	3
March	4
April	0
May	2
June	5
July	0
August	3
September.	6
October.	1
November.	4
December	6

Easter Dates (2006–2010)

■ Christian churches that follow the Gregorian calendar celebrate Easter on the first Sunday after the full Moon that occurs on or just after the vernal equinox.

YEAR	EASTER
2006.	April 16
2007.	April 8
2008.	March 23
2009.	April 12
2010.	April 4

■ Eastern Orthodox churches follow the Julian calendar.

YEAR	EASTER
2006.	April 23
2007.	April 8
2008.	April 27
2009.	April 19
2010.	April 4

Triskaidekaphobia Trivia

Here are a few facts about Friday the 13th:

■ In the 14 possible configurations for the annual calendar (see any perpetual calendar), the occurrence of Friday the 13th is this:

6 of 14 years have one Friday the 13th.
6 of 14 years have two Fridays the 13th.
2 of 14 years have three Fridays the 13th.

■ There is no year without one Friday the 13th, and no year with more than three.

■ There are two Fridays the 13th in 2006. The next year to have three Fridays the 13th is 2009.

■ The reason we say "Fridays the 13th" is that no one can pronounce "Friday the 13ths."

REFERENCE

The Animal Signs of the Chinese Zodiac

The animal designations of the Chinese zodiac follow a 12-year cycle and are always used in the same sequence. The Chinese year of 354 days begins three to seven weeks into the western 365-day year, so the animal designation changes at that time, rather than on January 1. See page 95 for the exact date of the start of the Chinese New Year.

RAT
Ambitious and sincere, you can be generous with your money. Compatible with the dragon and the monkey. Your opposite is the horse.

1900	1936	1984
1912	1948	1996
1924	1960	2008
	1972	

DRAGON
Robust and passionate, your life is filled with complexity. Compatible with the monkey and the rat. Your opposite is the dog.

1904	1940	1988
1916	1952	2000
1928	1964	2012
	1976	

MONKEY
Persuasive, skillful, and intelligent, you strive to excel. Compatible with the dragon and the rat. Your opposite is the tiger.

1908	1944	1992
1920	1956	2004
1932	1968	2016
	1980	

OX OR BUFFALO
A leader, you are bright, patient, and cheerful. Compatible with the snake and the rooster. Your opposite is the sheep.

1901	1937	1985
1913	1949	1997
1925	1961	2009
	1973	

SNAKE
Strong-willed and intense, you display great wisdom. Compatible with the rooster and the ox. Your opposite is the pig.

1905	1941	1989
1917	1953	2001
1929	1965	2013
	1977	

ROOSTER OR COCK
Seeking wisdom and truth, you have a pioneering spirit. Compatible with the snake and the ox. Your opposite is the rabbit.

1909	1945	1993
1921	1957	2005
1933	1969	2017
	1981	

TIGER
Forthright and sensitive, you possess great courage. Compatible with the horse and the dog. Your opposite is the monkey.

1902	1938	1986
1914	1950	1998
1926	1962	2010
	1974	

HORSE
Physically attractive and popular, you like the company of others. Compatible with the tiger and the dog. Your opposite is the rat.

1906	1942	1990
1918	1954	2002
1930	1966	2014
	1978	

DOG
Generous and loyal, you have the ability to work well with others. Compatible with the horse and the tiger. Your opposite is the dragon.

1910	1946	1994
1922	1958	2006
1934	1970	2018
	1982	

RABBIT OR HARE
Talented and affectionate, you are a seeker of tranquility. Compatible with the sheep and the pig. Your opposite is the rooster.

1903	1939	1987
1915	1951	1999
1927	1963	2011
	1975	

SHEEP OR GOAT
Aesthetic and stylish, you enjoy being a private person. Compatible with the pig and the rabbit. Your opposite is the ox.

1907	1943	1991
1919	1955	2003
1931	1967	2015
	1979	

PIG OR BOAR
Gallant and noble, your friends will remain at your side. Compatible with the rabbit and the sheep. Your opposite is the snake.

1911	1947	1995
1923	1959	2007
1935	1971	2019
	1983	

REFERENCE

Sowing Vegetable Seeds

Sow or plant in cool weather	Beets, broccoli, brussels sprouts, cabbage, lettuce, onions, parsley, peas, radishes, spinach, Swiss chard, turnips
Sow or plant in warm weather	Beans, carrots, corn, cucumbers, eggplant, melons, okra, peppers, squash, tomatoes
Sow or plant for one crop per season	Corn, eggplant, leeks, melons, peppers, potatoes, spinach (New Zealand), squash, tomatoes
Resow for additional crops	Beans, beets, cabbage, carrots, kohlrabi, lettuce, radishes, rutabagas, spinach, turnips

A Beginner's Vegetable Garden

A good size for a beginner's vegetable garden is 10x16 feet. It should have crops that are easy to grow. A plot this size, planted as suggested below, can feed a family of four for one summer, with a little extra for canning and freezing (or giving away).

Make 11 rows, 10 feet long, with 6 inches between them. Ideally, the rows should run north and south to take full advantage of the sunlight. Plant the following:

ROW	
1	Zucchini (4 plants)
2	Tomatoes (5 plants, staked)
3	Peppers (6 plants)
4	Cabbage

ROW	
5	Bush beans
6	Lettuce
7	Beets
8	Carrots
9	Chard
10	Radishes
11	Marigolds (to discourage rabbits!)

Traditional Planting Times

■ Plant **corn** when elm leaves are the size of a squirrel's ear, when oak leaves are the size of a mouse's ear, when apple blossoms begin to fall, or when the dogwoods are in full bloom.

■ Plant **lettuce, spinach, peas,** and other cool-weather vegetables when the lilacs show their first leaves or when daffodils begin to bloom.

■ Plant **tomatoes, early corn,** and **peppers** when dogwoods are in peak bloom or when daylilies start to bloom.

■ Plant **cucumbers** and **squashes** when lilac flowers fade.

■ Plant **perennials** when maple leaves begin to unfurl.

■ Plant **morning glories** when maple trees have full-size leaves.

■ Plant **pansies, snapdragons,** and other hardy annuals after the aspen and chokecherry trees leaf out.

■ Plant **beets** and **carrots** when dandelions are blooming.

Growing Vegetables

Vegetable	Start Seeds Indoors (weeks before last spring frost)	Start Seeds Outdoors (weeks before or after last spring frost)	Minimum Soil Temperature to Germinate (°F)	Cold Hardiness
Beans		Anytime after	48–50	Tender
Beets		4 before to 4 after	39–41	Half-hardy
Broccoli	6–8	4 before	55–75	Hardy
Brussels sprouts	6–8		55–75	Hardy
Cabbage	6–8	Anytime after	38–40	Hardy
Carrots		4–6 before	39–41	Half-hardy
Cauliflower	6–8	4 before	65–75	Half-hardy
Celery	6–8		60–70	Tender
Corn		2 after	46–50	Tender
Cucumbers	3–4	1–2 after	65–70	Very tender
Lettuce	4–6	2–3 after	40–75	Half-hardy
Melons	3–4	2 after	55–60	Very tender
Onion sets		4 before	34–36	Hardy
Parsnips		2–4 before	55–70	Hardy
Peas		4–6 before	34–36	Hardy
Peppers	8–10		70–80	Very tender
Potato tubers		2–4 before	55–70	Half-hardy
Pumpkins	3–4	1 after	55–60	Tender
Radishes		4–6 before	39–41	Hardy
Spinach		4–6 before	55–65	Hardy
Squash, summer	3–4	1 after	55–60	Very tender
Squash, winter	3–4	1 after	55–60	Tender
Tomatoes	6–8		50–55	Tender

R
E
F
E
R
E
N
C
E

When to Fertilize	When to Water
After heavy bloom and set of pods	Regularly, from start of pod to set
At time of planting	Only during drought conditions
Three weeks after transplanting	Only during drought conditions
Three weeks after transplanting	At transplanting
Three weeks after transplanting	Two to three weeks before harvest
Preferably in the fall for the following spring	Only during drought conditions
Three weeks after transplanting	Once, three weeks before harvest
At time of transplanting	Once a week
When eight to ten inches tall, and again when first silk appears	When tassels appear and cobs start to swell
One week after bloom, and again three weeks later	Frequently, especially when fruits form
Two to three weeks after transplanting	Once a week
One week after bloom, and again three weeks later	Once a week
When bulbs begin to swell, and again when plants are one foot tall	Only during drought conditions
One year before planting	Only during drought conditions
After heavy bloom and set of pods	Regularly, from start of pod to set
After first fruit-set	Once a week
At bloom time or time of second hilling	Regularly, when tubers start to form
Just before vines start to run, when plants are about one foot tall	Only during drought conditions
Before spring planting	Once a week
When plants are one-third grown	Once a week
Just before vines start to run, when plants are about one foot tall	Only during drought conditions
Just before vines start to run, when plants are about one foot tall	Only during drought conditions
Two weeks before, and after first picking	Twice a week

Vegetable Gardening in Containers

Lack of yard space is no excuse for not gardening, because many vegetables can be readily grown in containers. In addition to providing five hours or more of full sun, you must give attention to choosing the proper container, using a good soil mix, observing planting and spacing requirements, fertilizing, watering, and selecting appropriate varieties. Here are some suggestions:

Vegetable	Type of Container	Recommended Varieties
Beans, snap	5-gallon window box	Bush 'Blue Lake', Bush 'Romano', 'Tender Crop'
Broccoli	1 plant/5-gallon pot 3 plants/15-gallon tub	'DeCicco', 'Green Comet'
Carrots	5-gallon window box at least 12 inches deep	'Danvers Half Long', 'Short 'n Sweet', 'Tiny Sweet'
Cucumbers	1 plant/1-gallon pot	'Patio Pik', 'Pot Luck', 'Spacemaster'
Eggplant	5-gallon pot	'Black Beauty', 'Ichiban', 'Slim Jim'
Lettuce	5-gallon window box	'Ruby', 'Salad Bowl'
Onions	5-gallon window box	'White Sweet Spanish', 'Yellow Sweet Spanish'
Peppers	1 plant/2-gallon pot 5 plants/15-gallon tub	'Cayenne', 'Long Red', 'Sweet Banana', 'Wonder', 'Yolo'
Radishes	5-gallon window box	'Cherry Belle', 'Icicle'
Tomatoes	Bushel basket	'Early Girl', 'Patio', 'Small Fry', 'Sweet 100', 'Tiny Tim'

TIPS

■ Clay pots are usually more attractive than plastic ones, but plastic pots retain moisture better. To get the best of both, slip a plastic pot into a slightly larger clay pot.

■ Avoid small containers. They often can't store enough water to get through hot days.

■ Add about one inch of coarse gravel in the bottom of the container to improve drainage.

■ Vegetables that can be easily transplanted are best suited for containers. Transplants can be purchased from local nurseries or started at home.

■ Feed container plants at least twice a month with liquid fertilizer, following the instructions on the label.

■ An occasional application of fish emulsion or compost will add trace elements to container soil.

■ Place containers where they will receive maximum sunlight and good ventilation. Watch for and control insect pests.

Fertilizer Formulas

Fertilizers are labeled to show the percentages by weight of nitrogen (N), phosphorus (P), and potassium (K). Nitrogen is needed for leaf growth. Phosphorus is associated with root growth and fruit production. Potassium helps the plant fight off diseases. A 100-pound bag of 10-5-10 contains 10 pounds of nitrogen, 5 pounds of phosphorus, and 10 pounds of potassium. The rest is filler.

Manure Guide

PRIMARY NUTRIENTS (pounds per ton)

Type of Manure	Water Content	Nitrogen	Phosphorus	Potassium
Cow, horse	60%–80%	12–14	5–9	9–12
Sheep, pig, goat	65%–75%	10–21	7	13–19
Chicken:				
Wet, sticky, and caked	75%	30	20	10
Moist, crumbly to sticky	50%	40	40	20
Crumbly	30%	60	55	30
Dry	15%	90	70	40
Ashed	None	None	135	100

TYPE OF GARDEN	BEST TYPE OF MANURE	BEST TIME TO APPLY
Flowers	Cow, horse	Early spring
Vegetables	Chicken, cow, horse	Fall, spring
Potatoes or root crops	Cow, horse	Fall
Acid-loving plants (blueberries, azaleas, mountain laurels, rhododendrons)	Cow, horse	Early fall or not at all

Soil Fixes

If you have . . .

CLAY SOIL: Add coarse sand (not beach sand) and compost.

SILT SOIL: Add coarse sand (not beach sand) or gravel and compost, or well-rotted horse manure mixed with fresh straw.

SANDY SOIL: Add humus or aged manure, or sawdust with some extra nitrogen. Heavy, clay-rich soil can also be added.

Soil Amendments

To improve soil, add . . .

BARK, GROUND: Made from various tree barks; improves soil structure.

COMPOST: Excellent conditioner.

LEAF MOLD: Decomposed leaves; adds nutrients and structure to soil.

LIME: Raises the pH of acidic soil; helps loosen clay soil.

MANURE: Best if composted; a good conditioner.

SAND: Improves drainage in clay soil.

TOPSOIL: Usually used with another amendment; replaces existing soil.

pH Preferences of Trees, Shrubs, Vegetables, and Flowers

An accurate soil test will tell you where your pH currently stands and will specify the amount of lime or sulfur that is needed to bring it up or down to the appropriate level. A pH of 6.5 is just about right for most home gardens, since most plants thrive in the 6.0 to 7.0 (slightly acidic to neutral) range. Some plants (blueberries, azaleas) prefer more strongly acidic soil, while a few (ferns, asparagus) do best in soil that is neutral to slightly alkaline. Acidic (sour) soil is counteracted by applying finely ground limestone, and alkaline (sweet) soil is treated with gypsum (calcium sulfate) or ground sulfur.

Common Name	Optimum pH Range	Common Name	Optimum pH Range	Common Name	Optimum pH Range
TREES AND SHRUBS		Spruce	5.0–6.0	Canna	6.0–8.0
Apple	5.0–6.5	Walnut, black	6.0–8.0	Carnation	6.0–7.0
Ash	6.0–7.5	Willow	6.0–8.0	Chrysanthemum	6.0–7.5
Azalea	4.5–6.0			Clematis	5.5–7.0
Basswood	6.0–7.5	**VEGETABLES**		Coleus	6.0–7.0
Beautybush	6.0–7.5	Asparagus	6.0–8.0	Coneflower, purple	5.0–7.5
Birch	5.0–6.5	Bean, pole	6.0–7.5	Cosmos	5.0–8.0
Blackberry	5.0–6.0	Beet	6.0–7.5	Crocus	6.0–8.0
Blueberry	4.0–6.0	Broccoli	6.0–7.0	Daffodil	6.0–6.5
Boxwood	6.0–7.5	Brussels sprout	6.0–7.5	Dahlia	6.0–7.5
Cherry, sour	6.0–7.0	Carrot	5.5–7.0	Daisy, Shasta	6.0–8.0
Chestnut	5.0–6.5	Cauliflower	5.5–7.5	Daylily	6.0–8.0
Crab apple	6.0–7.5	Celery	5.8–7.0	Delphinium	6.0–7.5
Dogwood	5.0–7.0	Chive	6.0–7.0	Foxglove	6.0–7.5
Elder, box	6.0–8.0	Cucumber	5.5–7.0	Geranium	6.0–8.0
Fir, balsam	5.0–6.0	Garlic	5.5–8.0	Gladiolus	5.0–7.0
Fir, Douglas	6.0–7.0	Kale	6.0–7.5	Hibiscus	6.0–8.0
Hemlock	5.0–6.0	Lettuce	6.0–7.0	Hollyhock	6.0–8.0
Hydrangea, blue-flowered	4.0–5.0	Pea, sweet	6.0–7.5	Hyacinth	6.5–7.5
		Pepper, sweet	5.5–7.0	Iris, blue flag	5.0–7.5
Hydrangea, pink-flowered	6.0–7.0	Potato	4.8–6.5	Lily-of-the-valley	4.5–6.0
		Pumpkin	5.5–7.5	Lupine	5.0–6.5
Juniper	5.0–6.0	Radish	6.0–7.0	Marigold	5.5–7.5
Laurel, mountain	4.5–6.0	Spinach	6.0–7.5	Morning glory	6.0–7.5
Lemon	6.0–7.5	Squash, crookneck	6.0–7.5	Narcissus, trumpet	5.5–6.5
Lilac	6.0–7.5	Squash, Hubbard	5.5–7.0	Nasturtium	5.5–7.5
Maple, sugar	6.0–7.5	Tomato	5.5–7.5	Pansy	5.5–6.5
Oak, white	5.0–6.5			Peony	6.0–7.5
Orange	6.0–7.5	**FLOWERS**		Petunia	6.0–7.5
Peach	6.0–7.0	Alyssum	6.0–7.5	Phlox, summer	6.0–8.0
Pear	6.0–7.5	Aster, New England	6.0–8.0	Poppy, oriental	6.0–7.5
Pecan	6.4–8.0	Baby's breath	6.0–7.0	Rose, hybrid tea	5.5–7.0
Pine, red	5.0–6.0	Bachelor's button	6.0–7.5	Rose, rugosa	6.0–7.0
Pine, white	4.5–6.0	Bee balm	6.0–7.5	Snapdragon	5.5–7.0
Plum	6.0–8.0	Begonia	5.5–7.0	Sunflower	6.0–7.5
Raspberry, red	5.5–7.0	Black-eyed Susan	5.5–7.0	Tulip	6.0–7.0
Rhododendron	4.5–6.0	Bleeding heart	6.0–7.5	Zinnia	5.5–7.0

REFERENCE

Lawn-Growing Tips

■ Test your soil: The pH balance should be 7.0 or more; 6.2 to 6.7 puts your lawn at risk for fungal diseases. If the pH is too low, correct it with liming, best done in the fall.

The best time to apply fertilizer is just before it rains.

If you put lime and fertilizer on your lawn, spread half of it as you walk north to south, the other half as you walk east to west to cut down on missed areas.

Any feeding of lawns in the fall should be done with a low-nitrogen, slow-acting fertilizer.

In areas of your lawn where tree roots compete with the grass, apply some extra fertilizer to benefit both.

Moss and sorrel in lawns usually means poor soil, poor aeration or drainage, or excessive acidity.

Control weeds by promoting healthy lawn growth with natural fertilizers in spring and early fall.

Raise the level of your lawnmower blades during the hot summer days. Taller grass resists drought better than short.

You can reduce mowing time by redesigning your lawn, reducing sharp corners and adding sweeping curves.

During a drought, let the grass grow longer between mowings, and reduce fertilizer.

Water your lawn early in the morning or in the evening.

Herbs to Plant in Lawns

Choose plants that suit your soil and your climate. All these can withstand mowing and considerable foot traffic.

Ajuga or bugleweed *(Ajuga reptans)*

Corsican mint *(Mentha requienii)*

Dwarf cinquefoil *(Potentilla tabernaemontani)*

English pennyroyal *(Mentha pulegium)*

Green Irish moss *(Sagina subulata)*

Pearly everlasting *(Anaphalis margaritacea)*

Roman chamomile *(Chamaemelum nobile)*

Rupturewort *(Herniaria glabra)*

Speedwell *(Veronica officinalis)*

Stonecrop *(Sedum ternatum)*

Sweet violets *(Viola odorata* or *V. tricolor)*

Thyme *(Thymus serpyllum)*

White clover *(Trifolium repens)*

Wild strawberries *(Fragaria virginiana)*

Wintergreen or partridgeberry *(Mitchella repens)*

A Gardener's Worst Phobias

Name of Fear	Object Feared
Alliumphobia	Garlic
Anthophobia	Flowers
Apiphobia	Bees
Arachnophobia	Spiders
Batonophobia	Plants
Bufonophobia	Toads
Dendrophobia	Trees
Entomophobia	Insects
Lachanophobia	Vegetables
Melissophobia	Bees
Mottephobia	Moths
Myrmecophobia	Ants
Ornithophobia	Birds
Ranidaphobia	Frogs
Rupophobia	Dirt
Scoleciphobia	Worms
Spheksophobia	Wasps

R E F E R E N C E

Growing Herbs

Herb	Propagation Method	Start Seeds Indoors (weeks before last spring frost)	Start Seeds Outdoors (weeks before or after last spring frost)	Minimum Soil Temperature to Germinate (°F)	Height (inches)
Basil	Seeds, transplants	6–8	Anytime after	70	12–24
Borage	Seeds, division, cuttings	Not recommended	Anytime after	70	12–36
Chervil	Seeds	Not recommended	3–4 before	55	12–24
Chives	Seeds, division	8–10	3–4 before	60–70	12–18
Cilantro/ coriander	Seeds	Not recommended	Anytime after	60	12–36
Dill	Seeds	Not recommended	4–5 before	60–70	36–48
Fennel	Seeds	4–6	Anytime after	60–70	48–80
Lavender, English	Seeds, cuttings	8–12	1–2 before	70–75	18–36
Lavender, French	Transplants	Not recommended	Not recommended	—	18–36
Lemon balm	Seeds, division, cuttings	6–10	2–3 before	70	12–24
Lovage	Seeds, division	6–8	2–3 before	70	36–72
Oregano	Seeds, division, cuttings	6–10	Anytime after	70	12–24
Parsley	Seeds	10–12	3–4 before	70	18–24
Rosemary	Seeds, division, cuttings	8–10	Anytime after	70	48–72
Sage	Seeds, division, cuttings	6–10	1–2 before	60–70	12–48
Sorrel	Seeds, division	6–10	2–3 after	60–70	20–48
Spearmint	Division, cuttings	Not recommended	Not recommended	—	12–24
Summer savory	Seeds	4–6	Anytime after	60–70	4–15
Sweet cicely	Seeds, division	6–8	2–3 after	60–70	36–72
Tarragon, French	Cuttings, transplants	Not recommended	Not recommended	—	24–36
Thyme, common	Seeds, division, cuttings	6–10	2–3 before	70	2–12

Spread (inches)	Blooming Season	Uses	Soil	Light*	Growth Type
12	Midsummer	Culinary	Rich, moist	○	Annual
12	Early to midsummer	Culinary	Rich, well-drained, dry	○	Annual, biennial
8	Early to midsummer	Culinary	Rich, moist	◑	Annual, biennial
18	Early summer	Culinary	Rich, moist	○	Perennial
4	Midsummer	Culinary	Light	○◑	Annual
12	Early summer	Culinary	Rich	○	Annual
18	Mid- to late summer	Culinary	Rich	○	Annual
24	Early to late summer	Ornamental, medicinal	Moderately fertile, well-drained	○	Perennial
24	Early to late summer	Ornamental, medicinal	Moderately fertile, well-drained	○	Tender perennial
18	Midsummer to early fall	Culinary, ornamental	Rich, well-drained	○◑	Perennial
36	Early to late summer	Culinary	Fertile, sandy	○◑	Perennial
18	Mid- to late summer	Culinary	Poor	○	Tender perennial
6–8	Mid- to late summer	Culinary	Medium-rich	◑	Biennial
48	Early summer	Culinary	Not too acid	○	Tender perennial
30	Early to late summer	Culinary, ornamental	Well-drained	○	Perennial
12–14	Late spring to early summer	Culinary, medicinal	Rich, organic	○	Perennial
18	Early to midsummer	Culinary, medicinal, ornamental	Rich, moist	◑	Perennial
6	Early summer	Culinary	Medium rich	○	Annual
36	Late spring	Culinary	Moderately fertile, well-drained	○◑	Perennial
12	Late summer	Culinary, medicinal	Well-drained	○◑	Perennial
7–12	Early to midsummer	Culinary	Fertile, well-drained	○◑	Perennial

*○ = full sun   ◑ = partial shade

R
E
F
E
R
E
N
C
E

Flowers and Herbs That Attract Butterflies

Allium. . . . . *Allium*	Mallow . . . . *Malva*
Aster . . . . *Aster*	Mealycup sage . . . . . . *Salvia farinacea*
Bee balm. . . . . *Monarda*	Milkweed . . . . *Asclepias*
Butterfly bush . . . . *Buddleia*	Mint . . . . *Mentha*
Catmint . . . . *Nepeta*	Oregano. . . . . *Origanum vulgare*
Clove pink. . . . . *Dianthus*	Pansy. . . . . *Viola*
Cornflower . . . . *Centaurea*	Parsley. . . . . *Petroselinum*
Creeping thyme . . . . . *Thymus serpyllum*	*crispum*
Daylily . . . . *Hemerocallis*	Phlox . . . . *Phlox*
Dill. . . . . *Anethum graveolens*	Privet. . . . . *Ligustrum*
False indigo . . . . *Baptisia*	Purple coneflower. . *Echinacea purpurea*
Fleabane . . . . *Erigeron*	Purple loosestrife. . . . . *Lythrum*
Floss flower . . . . *Ageratum*	Rock cress. . . . . *Arabis*
Globe thistle . . . . *Echinops*	Sea holly . . . . *Eryngium*
Goldenrod . . . . *Solidago*	Shasta daisy . . . . *Chrysanthemum*
Helen's flower . . . . *Helenium*	Snapdragon . . . . *Antirrhinum*
Hollyhock. . . . . *Alcea*	Stonecrop . . . . *Sedum*
Honeysuckle . . . . *Lonicera*	Sweet alyssum . . . . *Lobularia*
Lavender. . . . . *Lavendula*	Sweet marjoram. . . *Origanum majorana*
Lilac . . . . *Syringa*	Sweet rocket . . . . *Hesperis*
Lupine. . . . . *Lupinus*	Tickseed . . . . *Coreopsis*
Lychnis . . . . *Lychnis*	Zinnia . . . . *Zinnia*

Flowers* That Attract Hummingbirds

Beard tongue . . . . *Penstemon*	Trumpet honeysuckle . . . . *Lonicera*
Bee balm. . . . . *Monarda*	*sempervirens*
Butterfly bush . . . . *Buddleia*	Verbena . . . . *Verbena*
Catmint. . . . . *Nepeta*	Weigela. . . . . *Weigela*
Clove pink. . . . . *Dianthus*	
Columbine . . . . *Aquilegia*	**✻ Note: Choose varieties in red and orange shades.**
Coral bells . . . . *Heuchera*	
Daylily . . . . *Hemerocallis*	
Desert candle . . . . *Yucca*	
Flag iris . . . . *Iris*	
Flowering tobacco. . . . . *Nicotiana alata*	
Foxglove . . . . *Digitalis*	
Larkspur . . . . *Delphinium*	
Lily . . . . *Lilium*	
Lupine. . . . . *Lupinus*	
Petunia. . . . . *Petunia*	
Pincushion flower . . . . *Scabiosa*	
Red-hot poker . . . . *Kniphofia*	
Scarlet sage . . . . *Salvia splendens*	
Soapwort . . . . *Saponaria*	
Summer phlox . . . . . . *Phlox paniculata*	

Plant Resources

Bulbs

American Daffodil Society
4126 Winfield Rd., Columbus, OH 43220
www.daffodilusa.org

American Dahlia Society
1 Rock Falls Ct., Rockville, MD 20854
www.dahlia.org

American Iris Society
www.irises.org

International Bulb Society (IBS)
P.O. Box 336, Sanger, CA 93657
www.bulbsociety.org

Netherlands Flower Bulb Information Center
30 Midwood St., Brooklyn, NY 11225
718-693-5400 • www.bulb.com

Ferns

American Fern Society
326 West St. NW, Vienna, VA 22180
http://amerfernsoc.org

The Hardy Fern Foundation
P.O. Box 166, Medina, WA 98036
www.hardyferns.org

Flowers

American Peony Society
www.americanpeonysociety.org

American Rhododendron Society
P.O. Box 525, Niagra Falls, NY 14304
416-424-1942 • www.rhododendron.org

American Rose Society
P.O. Box 30,000, Shreveport, LA 71119
318-938-5402 • www.ars.org

Hardy Plant Society
Mid-Atlantic Group
1380 Warner Rd., Meadowbrook, PA 19046

International Waterlily and Water Gardening Society
6828 26th St. W., Bradenton, FL 34207
941-756-0880 • www.iwgs.org

Lady Bird Johnson Wildflower Center
4801 La Crosse Ave., Austin, TX 78739
512-292-4200 • www.wildflower.org

Perennial Plant Association
3383 Schirtzinger Rd., Hilliard, OH 43026
614-771-8431 • www.perennialplant.org

Fruits

California Rare Fruit Growers
The Fullerton Arboretum-CSUF
P.O. Box 6850, Fullerton, CA 92834
www.crfg.org

Home Orchard Society
P.O. Box 230192, Tigard, OR 97281
www.homeorchardsociety.org

North American Fruit Explorers
1716 Apples Rd., Chapin, IL 62628
www.nafex.org

Herbs

American Herb Association
P.O. Box 1673, Nevada City, CA 95959
530-265-9552 • www.ahaherb.com

The Flower and Herb Exchange
3094 North Winn Rd., Decorah, IA 52101
563-382-5990 • www.seedsavers.org

Herb Research Foundation
4140 15th St., Boulder, CO 80304
303-449-2265 • www.herbs.org

Herb Society of America
9019 Kirtland Chardon Rd.,
Kirtland, OH 44094
440-256-0514 • www.herbsociety.org

REFERENCE

Cooperative Extension Services

Contact your local state cooperative extension Web site to get help with tricky insect problems, best varieties to plant in your area, or general maintenance of your garden.

Alabama
www.aces.edu

Alaska
www.uaf.edu/coop-ext

Arizona
www.ag.arizona.edu/
extension

Arkansas
www.uaex.edu

California
www.ucanr.org

Colorado
www.ext.colostate.edu

Connecticut
www.canr.uconn.edu/ces

Delaware
http://ag.udel.edu/
extension

Florida
www.ifas.ufl.edu/
extension/ces.htm

Georgia
http://extension.caes.uga.edu

Hawaii
www2.ctahr.hawaii.edu/
extout/extout.asp

Idaho
www.uidaho.edu/ag/
extension

Illinois
www.extension.uiuc.edu/
welcome.html

Indiana
www.ces.purdue.edu

Iowa
www.extension.iastate.edu

Kansas
www.oznet.ksu.edu

Kentucky
www.ca.uky.edu

Louisiana
www.lsuagcenter.com/nav/
extension/extension.asp

Maine
www.umext.maine.edu

Maryland
www.agnr.umd.edu/mce/
index.cfm

Massachusetts
www.umassextension.org

Michigan
www.msue.msu.edu/msue

Minnesota
www.extension.umn.edu

Mississippi
www.msucares.com

Missouri
www.extension.missouri
.edu

Montana
http://extn.msu.montana.edu

Nebraska
www.extension.unl.edu

Nevada
www.unce.unr.edu

New Hampshire
www.ceinfo.unh.edu

New Jersey
www.rce.rutgers.edu

New Mexico
www.cahe.nmsu.edu/ces

New York
www.cce.cornell.edu

North Carolina
www.ces.ncsu.edu

North Dakota
www.ext.nodak.edu

Ohio
http://extension.osu.edu

Oklahoma
www.dasnr.okstate.edu/oces

Oregon
http://extension.oregonstate
.edu/index.php

Pennsylvania
www.extension.psu.edu

Rhode Island
www.edc.uri.edu

South Carolina
www.clemson.edu/
extension

South Dakota
http://sdces.sdstate.edu

Tennessee
www.utextension.utk.edu

Texas
http://texasextension.tamu
.edu

Utah
www.extension.usu.edu

Vermont
www.uvm.edu/~uvmext

Virginia
www.ext.vt.edu

Washington
http://ext.wsu.edu

West Virginia
www.wvu.edu/~exten

Wisconsin
www.uwex.edu/ces

Wyoming
http://uwadmnweb.uwyo
.edu/uwces

REFERENCE

Makeshift Measurers

When you don't have a measuring stick or tape, use what is at hand. To this list, add other items that you always (or nearly always) have handy.

Credit card . . . . 3⅜" x 2⅛"
Business card (standard). . . . . 3½" x 2"
Floor tile . . . . 12" square
Dollar bill . . . . 6⅛" x 2⅝"
Quarter (diameter) . . . . 1"
Penny (diameter) . . . . ¾"
Sheet of paper. . . . . 8½" x 11"
　　　　　　(legal size: 8½" x 14")

Your foot/shoe: _____
Your outstretched arms, fingertip
　to fingertip: _____
Your shoelace: _____
Your necktie: _____
Your belt: _____

If you don't have a scale or a measuring spoon handy, try these for size:
A piece of meat the size of your hand or a deck of cards – 3 to 4 ounces.
A piece of meat or cheese the size of a golf ball = about 1 ounce.
From the tip of your smallest finger to the first joint = about 1 teaspoon.
The tip of your thumb = about 1 tablespoon.

The idea of using available materials to measure is not new.
1 foot = the length of a person's foot.
1 yard = the distance from a person's nose to the fingertip of an outstretched arm.
1 acre = the amount of land an ox can plow in a day.

Hand Thermometer for Outdoor Cooking

■ Hold your palm close to where the food will be cooking: over the coals or in front of a reflector oven. Count "one-and-one, two-and-two," and so on (each pair is roughly equivalent to one second), for as many seconds as you can hold your hand still.

Seconds Counted	Heat	Temperature
6–8	Slow	250°–350°F
4–5	Moderate	350°–400°F
2–3	Hot	400°–450°F
1 or less	Very hot	450°–500°F

Miscellaneous Length Measures

ASTRONOMICAL UNIT (A.U.): 93,000,000 miles; the average distance from Earth to the Sun

BOLT: 40 yards; used for measuring cloth

CHAIN: 66 feet; one mile is equal to 80 chains; used in surveying

CUBIT: 18 inches; derived from distance between elbow and tip of middle finger

HAND: 4 inches; derived from the width of the hand

LEAGUE: usually estimated at 3 miles

LIGHT-YEAR: 5,880,000,000,000 miles; the distance light travels in a vacuum in a year at the rate of 186,281.7 miles per second

PICA: about ⅙ inch; used in printing for measuring column width, etc.

SPAN: 9 inches; derived from the distance between the end of the thumb and the end of the little finger when both are outstretched

Body Mass Index (BMI) Formula

Here's an easy formula to figure your Body Mass Index (BMI), thought to be a fairly accurate indicator of relative body size. **W** is your weight in pounds and **H** is your height in inches.

$$BMI = \left(\frac{W}{H^2}\right) \times 703$$

■ If the result is 18.5 to 24.9, you are within a healthy weight range.

■ If it's below 18.5, you are too thin.

■ From 25 to 29.9, you are overweight and at increased risk for health problems.

■ At 30 and above, you are considered obese and at a dramatically increased risk for serious health problems.

There are exceptions to the above, including children, expectant mothers, and the elderly. Very muscular people with a high BMI generally have nothing to worry about, and extreme skinniness is generally a symptom of some other health problem, not the cause.

Tape-Measure Method

■ Here's another way to see if you are dangerously overweight. Measure your waistline. A waist measurement of more than 35 inches in women and more than 40 inches in men, regardless of height, suggests a serious risk of weight-related health problems.

Calorie-Burning Comparisons

If you hustle through your chores to get to the fitness center, relax. You're getting a great workout already. The left-hand column lists "chore" exercises, the middle column shows the number of calories burned per minute per pound of body weight, and the right-hand column lists comparable "recreational" exercises. For example, a 150-pound person forking straw bales burns 9.45 calories per minute, the same workout he or she would get playing basketball.

Chore	Calories	Recreational
Chopping with an ax, fast	**0.135**	Skiing, cross-country, uphill
Climbing hills, with 44-pound load	**0.066**	Swimming, crawl, fast
Digging trenches	**0.065**	Skiing, cross-country, steady walk
Forking straw bales	**0.063**	Basketball
Chopping down trees	**0.060**	Football
Climbing hills, with 9-pound load	**0.058**	Swimming, crawl, slow
Sawing by hand	**0.055**	Skiing, cross-country, moderate
Mowing lawns	**0.051**	Horseback riding, trotting
Scrubbing floors	**0.049**	Tennis
Shoveling coal	**0.049**	Aerobic dance, medium
Hoeing	**0.041**	Weight training, circuit training
Stacking firewood	**0.040**	Weight lifting, free weights
Shoveling grain	**0.038**	Golf
Painting houses	**0.035**	Walking, normal pace, asphalt road
Weeding	**0.033**	Table tennis
Shopping for food	**0.028**	Cycling, 5.5 mph
Mopping floors	**0.028**	Fishing
Washing windows	**0.026**	Croquet
Raking	**0.025**	Dancing, ballroom
Driving a tractor	**0.016**	Drawing, standing position

Tile and Vinyl Flooring

Make a scale drawing of your room with all measurements clearly marked, and take it with you when you shop for tile flooring. Ask the salespeople to help you calculate your needs if you have rooms that feature bay windows, unusual jogs or turns, or if you plan to use special floor patterns or tiles with designs.

Ceramic Tile

■ Ceramic tiles for floors and walls come in a range of sizes, from 1x1-inch mosaics up to 12x12-inch (or larger) squares. The most popular size is the 4¼-inch-square tile, but there is a trend toward larger tiles (8x8s, 10x10s, 12x12s). Installing these larger tiles can be a challenge because the underlayment must be absolutely even and level.

■ Small, one-inch mosaic tiles are usually joined together in 12x12-inch or 12x24-inch sheets to make them easier to install. You can have a custom pattern made, or you can mix different-color tiles to create your own mosaic borders, patterns, and pictures.

Sheet Vinyl

■ Sheet vinyl typically comes in 6- and 12-foot widths. If your floor requires two or more pieces, your estimate must include enough overlap to allow you to match the pattern.

Vinyl Tile

■ Vinyl tiles generally come in 9- and 12-inch squares. To find the number of 12-inch tiles you need, just multiply the length of the room (in feet) by the width (rounding fractions up to the next foot) to get the number of tiles you need. Add 5 percent extra for cutting and waste. Measure any obstructions on the floor that you will be tiling around (such as appliances and cabinets), and subtract

that square footage from the total. To calculate the number of 9-inch tiles, divide the room's length (in inches) by 9, then divide the room's width by 9. Multiply those two numbers together to get the number of tiles you need, and then add 5 percent extra for cutting and waste.

Wallpaper

Before choosing your wallpaper, keep in mind that wallpaper with little or no pattern to match at the seams and the ceiling will be the easiest to apply, thus resulting in the least amount of wasted wallpaper. If you choose a patterned wallpaper, a small repeating pattern will result in less waste than a large repeating pattern. And a pattern that is aligned horizontally (matching on each column of paper) will waste less than one that drops or alternates its pattern (matching on every other column).

To determine the amount of wall space you're covering:

■ Measure the length of each wall, add these figures together, and multiply by the height of the walls to get the area (square footage) of the room's walls.

■ Calculate the square footage of each door, window, and other opening in the room. Add these figures together and subtract the total from the area of the room's walls.

■ Take that figure and multiply by 1.15, to account for a waste rate of about 15 percent in your wallpaper project. You'll end up with a target amount to purchase when you shop.

■ Wallpaper is sold in single, double, and triple rolls. Coverage can vary, so be sure to refer to the roll's label for the proper square footage. (The average coverage for a double roll, for example, is 56 square feet.) After choosing a paper, divide the coverage figure (from the label) into the total square footage of the walls of the room you're papering. Round the answer up to the nearest whole number. This is the number of rolls you need to buy.

■ Save leftover wallpaper rolls, carefully wrapped to keep clean.

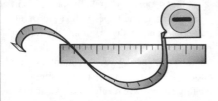

HOW MUCH DO YOU NEED?

Interior Paint

Estimate your room size and paint needs before you go to the store. Running out of a custom color halfway through the job could mean disaster. For the sake of the following exercise, assume that you have a 10x15-foot room with an 8-foot ceiling. The room has two doors and two windows.

For Walls

■ Measure the total distance (perimeter) around the room:

(10 ft. + 15 ft.) x 2 = 50 ft.

■ Multiply the perimeter by the ceiling height to get the total wall area:

50 ft. x 8 ft. = 400 sq. ft.

■ Doors are usually 21 square feet (there are two in this exercise):

21 sq. ft. x 2 = 42 sq. ft.

■ Windows average 15 square feet (there are two in this exercise):

15 sq. ft. x 2 = 30 sq. ft.

■ Take the total wall area and subtract the area for the doors and windows to get the wall surface to be painted:

> **400 sq. ft. (wall area)**
> **– 42 sq. ft. (doors)**
> **– 30 sq. ft. (windows)**
> **328 sq. ft.**

■ As a rule of thumb, one gallon of quality paint will usually cover 400 square feet. One quart will cover 100 square feet. Because you need to cover 328 square feet in this example, one gallon will be adequate to give one coat of paint to the walls. (Coverage will be affected by the porosity and texture of the surface. In addition, bright colors may require a minimum of two coats.)

For Ceilings

■ Using the rule of thumb for coverage above, you can calculate the quantity of paint needed for the ceiling by multiplying the width by the length:

10 ft. x 15 ft. = 150 sq. ft.

This ceiling will require approximately two quarts of paint. (A flat finish is recommended to minimize surface imperfections.)

For Doors, Windows, and Trim

■ The area for the doors and windows has been calculated above. (The windowpane area that does not get painted should allow for enough paint for any trim around doors and windows.) Determine the baseboard trim by taking the perimeter of the room, less 3 feet per door (3 ft. x 2 = 6 ft.), and multiplying this by the average trim width of your baseboard, which in this example is 6 inches (or 0.5 feet).

50 ft. (perimeter) – 6 ft. = 44 ft.
44 ft. x 0.5 ft. = 22 sq. ft.

■ Add the area for doors, windows, and baseboard trim.

> **42 sq. ft. (doors)**
> **+30 sq. ft. (windows)**
> **+22 sq. ft. (baseboard trim)**
> **94 sq. ft.**

One quart will be sufficient to cover the doors, windows, and trim in this example.

–courtesy M.A.B. Paints

HOW MUCH DO YOU NEED?
Lumber and Nails

The amount of lumber and nails you need will depend on your project, but these guidelines will help you determine quantities of each.

Lumber Width and Thickness (in inches)

Nominal Size	Actual Size DRY OR SEASONED	Nominal Size	Actual Size DRY OR SEASONED
1 x 3	$\frac{3}{4}$ x $2\frac{1}{2}$	2 x 3	$1\frac{1}{2}$ x $2\frac{1}{2}$
1 x 4	$\frac{3}{4}$ x $3\frac{1}{2}$	2 x 4	$1\frac{1}{2}$ x $3\frac{1}{2}$
1 x 6	$\frac{3}{4}$ x $5\frac{1}{2}$	2 x 6	$1\frac{1}{2}$ x $5\frac{1}{2}$
1 x 8	$\frac{3}{4}$ x $7\frac{1}{4}$	2 x 8	$1\frac{1}{2}$ x $7\frac{1}{4}$
1 x 10	$\frac{3}{4}$ x $9\frac{1}{4}$	2 x 10	$1\frac{1}{2}$ x $9\frac{1}{4}$
1 x 12	$\frac{3}{4}$ x $11\frac{1}{4}$	2 x 12	$1\frac{1}{2}$ x $11\frac{1}{4}$

Nail Sizes

The nail on the left is a 5d (five-penny) finish nail; on the right, 20d common. The numerals below the nail sizes indicate the approximate number of nails per pound.

Lumber Measure in Board Feet

Size in inches	12 ft.	14 ft.	16 ft.	18 ft.	20 ft.
1 x 4	4	$4\frac{2}{3}$	$5\frac{1}{3}$	6	$6\frac{2}{3}$
1 x 6	6	7	8	9	10
1 x 8	8	$9\frac{1}{3}$	$10\frac{2}{3}$	12	$13\frac{1}{3}$
1 x 10	10	$11\frac{2}{3}$	$13\frac{1}{3}$	15	$16\frac{2}{3}$
1 x 12	12	14	16	18	20
2 x 3	6	7	8	9	10
2 x 4	8	$9\frac{1}{3}$	$10\frac{2}{3}$	12	$13\frac{1}{3}$
2 x 6	12	14	16	18	20
2 x 8	16	$18\frac{2}{3}$	$21\frac{1}{3}$	24	$26\frac{2}{3}$
2 x 10	20	$23\frac{1}{3}$	$26\frac{2}{3}$	30	$33\frac{1}{3}$
2 x 12	24	28	32	36	40
4 x 4	16	$18\frac{2}{3}$	$21\frac{1}{3}$	24	$26\frac{2}{3}$
6 x 6	36	42	48	54	60
8 x 8	64	$74\frac{2}{3}$	$85\frac{1}{3}$	96	$106\frac{2}{3}$
10 x 10	100	$116\frac{2}{3}$	$133\frac{1}{3}$	150	$166\frac{2}{3}$
12 x 12	144	168	192	216	240

2d
875
3d
550
4d
300
5d
250
6d
175
7d
150
8d
100
9d
90
10d
70
12d
60
16d
45
20d
30

R E F E R E N C E

The Golden Rule

(It's true in all faiths.)

Brahmanism:
This is the sum of duty: Do naught unto others which would cause you pain if done to you.
Mahabharata 5:1517

Buddhism:
Hurt not others in ways that you yourself would find hurtful.
Udana-Varga 5:18

Christianity:
All things whatsoever ye would that men should do to you, do ye even so to them; for this is the law and the prophets.
Matthew 7:12

Confucianism:
Surely it is the maxim of loving-kindness: Do not unto others what you would not have them do unto you. *Analects 15:23*

Islam:
No one of you is a believer until he desires for his brother that which he desires for himself.
Sunnah

Judaism:
What is hateful to you, do not to your fellowman. That is the entire Law; all the rest is commentary. *Talmud, Shabbat 31a*

Taoism:
Regard your neighbor's gain as your own gain and your neighbor's loss as your own loss.
T'ai Shang Kan Ying P'ien

Zoroastrianism:
That nature alone is good which refrains from doing unto another whatsoever is not good for itself.
Dadistan-i-dinik 94:5

—courtesy Elizabeth Pool

Famous Last Words

■ **Waiting, are they? Waiting, are they? Well—let 'em wait.**
(In response to an attending doctor who attempted to comfort him by saying, "General, I fear the angels are waiting for you.")
—Ethan Allen, American Revolutionary general, d. February 12, 1789

■ **A dying man can do nothing easy.**
—Benjamin Franklin, American statesman, d. April 17, 1790

■ **Now I shall go to sleep. Good night.**
—Lord George Byron, British writer, d. April 19, 1824

■ **Is it the Fourth?**
—Thomas Jefferson, 3rd U.S. president, d. July 4, 1826

■ **Thomas Jefferson—still survives . . .**
(Actually, Jefferson had died earlier that same day.)
—John Adams, 2nd U.S. president, d. July 4, 1826

■ **Friends, applaud. The comedy is finished.**
—Ludwig van Beethoven, German-Austrian composer, d. March 26, 1827

■ **Moose . . . Indian . . .**
—Henry David Thoreau, American writer, d. May 6, 1862

■ **Go on, get out—last words are for fools who haven't said enough.**
(To his housekeeper, who urged him to tell her his last words so she could write them down for posterity.)
—Karl Marx, German political philosopher, d. March 14, 1883

■ **Is it not meningitis?**
—Louisa M. Alcott, American writer, d. March 6, 1888

■ **How were the receipts today at Madison Square Garden?**
—P. T. Barnum, American entrepreneur, d. April 7, 1891

■ **Turn up the lights, I don't want to go home in the dark.**
—O. Henry (William Sidney Porter), American writer, d. June 4, 1910

■ **Get my swan costume ready.**
—Anna Pavlova, Russian ballerina, d. January 23, 1931

■ **I should never have switched from Scotch to martinis.**
—Humphrey Bogart, American actor, d. January 14, 1957

■ **Is everybody happy? I want everybody to be happy. I know I'm happy.**
—Ethel Barrymore, American actress, d. June 18, 1959

■ **I'm bored with it all.**
(Before slipping into a coma. He died nine days later.)
—Winston Churchill, British statesman, d. January 24, 1965